THE LETTERS OF
MICHELANGELO

Volume One

1496 – 1534

Michelangelo

Giuliano Bugiardini
Casa Buonarroti, Florence

THE LETTERS OF
MICHELANGELO

Translated from the original Tuscan
Edited & Annotated

in Two Volumes

by

E. H. RAMSDEN

Volume One
1496–1534

STANFORD UNIVERSITY PRESS
1963

Stanford University Press
Stanford, California
1963

© E. H. Ramsden 1963

Designed by Margot Eates

Printed in Great Britain by W. & J. Mackay & Company Ltd, Chatham

Process and line blocks by The Bryant Engraving Company Ltd (Wace Group)
Basingwerk Parchment and Matt Art Papers by Grosvenor, Chater & Company Ltd
Bound in the United States of America

Contents of Volume I

Continued overleaf

Contents of Volume I

The Bibliography, with the list of abbreviations used in note references, and the Cross Index to Milanesi's Italian Edition of The Letters, refer to both Volumes, and therefore appear at the end of Volume II.

List of Plates

List of Plates

List of Plates

Acknowledgments

O nce the 'three main troubles about acknowledgments' have been pointed out, as was so disobligingly done some time ago in a fourth leader in *The Times*, the task of expressing one's patent indebtedness to others is apt to appear more difficult than it should, not because it is performed perfunctorily, which it is not, but because of a consciousness of the cynic's suspicion that it might be.

However, not wishing, in Michelangelo's words, 'to appear more ignorant and ungrateful than need be', I will endeavour to render honour where honour is due as gracefully as I can under the aforesaid inhibiting circumstances. It would be pleasant and in keeping with one's sense of obligation to make in each case a return in kind, after the manner of a more polished age – a length of silk for a doublet perhaps, or something of like nature – but, alas, the rewards of scholarship are incommensurate with its labours and one emerges, like Cellini at the casting of the *Perseus*, grateful enough for the earthenware replacements of the pewter that had to be sacrificed, and here, to the Trustees of the Gulbenkian Foundation of Lisbon, who kindly made me a grant for the completion of the work, let me say at once and for the first time publicly, 'For this relief much thanks'.

Next I would pay tribute to my Publishers, Peter Owen of Peter Owen Limited, and Leon Seltzer of the Stanford University Press, for their confidence, long patience and consideration during what must have seemed to them an interminable delay before I was able to deliver the completed manuscript – a delay that would have been even longer had it not been for the invaluable assistance of Mr. Arthur Wheen and his Staff in the Library of the Victoria and Albert Museum, and of the Staff in the Reading Room, in the Department of Manuscripts and in the Department of Prints and Drawings at the British Museum. I am similarly indebted also to the Prefect of the Vatican Library, to the Prefect of the Vatican Archives, the Most Reverend Monsignor Martino Giusti and to the Director of the State Archives in Rome, Professor Leopoldo Sandri, for their courteous and prompt answers to my somewhat importunate requests for information.

But chiefly I must place on record the extent to which I have been harried throughout by my Devil's Advocate, Margot Eates, who has uncomplainingly devoted seven years to the furtherance of a task, which, though not primarily her own, has nevertheless entailed an ever increasing sacrifice of all normal leisure. In addition, having studied the economic aspects of Michelangelo's career in connection with her own forthcoming publication of his *Ricordi*, she has contributed the five Appendixes dealing with monetary matters, besides preparing the Genealogical Tables and the short note on the Italian Hours. In comparison with having provided me with a scapegoat, should any fault be found with the Index, the fact that she typed out the entire work not less than four times may seem a minor achievement. She would, incidentally, be the last to wish me to omit to mention that in designing the typography her intention has been to provide a layout especially for scholars, which has, I venture to say, been admirably interpreted by our long-suffering Printers, W. & J. Mackay and Company Limited of Chatham, in which connection I should like to add a special word of thanks to Mr. Antony Mackay Miller for his patient co-operation.

As to the blocks, which were made by the Bryant Engraving Company, a subsidiary of the Wace Group, our gratitude to the Chairman, Mr. E. G. P. Wace, for his personal interest in every stage of their making, is in proportion to what we believe to be the excellence of the results.

The drawing for the brass for the cover was executed by Rita Ling, sculptor, to whom I am also indebted for certain information related to sculptural technique. I would add that her enthusiasm for the work as a whole has been a great source of encouragement.

The same is true of Richard Smart who, as soon as he heard of the project, generously placed certain books from his art library at my disposal 'for the duration' – a gesture from a bibliophile which I cannot too much appreciate. And as if this were not enough, he has read the whole work in galley and in page proof – an onerous undertaking in view of the complex checking and counter-checking that this has involved. His critical comments have also been of great assistance – some difference of opinion as to the use of some commas, notwithstanding.

I am similarly grateful to Miss Elfreda Powell who has also double-checked me on the proofs and has been tireless in her efforts to achieve consistency where previously no consistency was to be found.

It must be obvious to all but the meanest intelligence that a work on the scale of *The Letters* could not have been produced without the assistance of various specialists in a number of different fields, to whom I am the more beholden seeing that their own preoccupations were never at any time less urgent than my own. Thus, Ronald Lightbown, Assistant Keeper in the Library at the Victoria and Albert Museum, did everything possible to assist the progress of the work, not only by suggesting the most likely sources for the elucidation of some of the problems that have arisen, but also by being at great pains to help in the interpretation of obscure passages in the letters themselves – services for which it is difficult to express one's appreciation at all adequately. To Bernard Hamilton, Lecturer in Medieval History in the University of Nottingham, I am under an equivalent obligation, firstly for the translation of the Latin text of the brief of Paul III, which is given *in extenso* in Appendix 44, and of one or two other documents of which I have made use; and secondly for much patience in helping to decipher Lionardo Buonarroti's endorsements of his uncle's letters – a pastime that is apt to be conducive to the use of words 'not to be found in the Mass' and certainly not to be heard in the Manuscript Room of the British Museum. The fact that no such words were heard is surely a tribute enough in itself, without my saying anything more. As for the handwriting of Michelangelo's father, Lodovico Buonarroti, as exemplified in his endorsement of Letter 149, this could not have been deciphered at all without the expert assistance of Roy Strong, Assistant Keeper of the National Portrait Gallery, for whose co-operation I am also grateful.

To the Reverend Professor Malachi Martin, S.J., who kindly undertook certain researches for me in Rome I am particularly indebted, partly because they were in a field entirely different from his own, and partly because they were undertaken as a pleasure and not, in Michelangelo's words, as a *noia assai*, which they must have been. With the name of Father Martin I should like to couple that of Dr. Redig de Campos.

During the initial stages of the work I was enthusiastically supported by the Contessa Nina degli Alberti Polonsky. More recently Violet Oldak and Arthur Warner have always been prompt to help in the translation of difficult German texts – generally, as it befell, at the greatest possible inconvenience to themselves – which renders me the more sensible of the obligation under which I labour.

To those who have read thus far it must now be plain that the first stage of the 'three main troubles about acknowledgments', namely that 'there are almost always more people to thank than there are ways of saying "Thank you" ', has long been passed. But although it is better to be brief than tedious, I cannot on that account omit the names of many others who have done me kindnesses in one way or another and to that extent have contributed to such success as this publication of Michelangelo's letters may have. Perhaps, however, I may be pardoned for thanking them in groups.

It has not always been easy to obtain the necessary books and photographs; and without the ready help of many friends, or friends of friends, I should indeed have been in difficulties. Those I should like to mention are: Miss June Arlidge, Monsieur Frédéric Chartier, Miss Jean Hamilton, Signor Franco Giusti, Col. A. B. de Quincey, Mr. P. B. Spark, Miss Geraldine Talbot, Mrs. Jane Talbot, Mr. Keith Wallis, and Mr. Ken Wilson.

In a number of other connections I received both help and support from friends and strangers alike, including Professor Bernard Ashmole, F.B.A.; Miss Jean Barrie, of the Victoria and Albert Museum Library; Dr. A. Beglé and the Staff of the Istituto Italiano di Cultura, London; Madame Nanie Bridgman of the Bibliothèque Nationale; Mr. R. F. Dell, of the East Sussex Records Office; Dr. A. R. Eates; Dr. F. Ghisi; Signora Gabriella Giusti; Mr. Thomas Hancock, F.R.I.B.A.; Mr. Martin Holmes, F.S.A., of the London Museum; Dr. J. P. C. Kent, of the Department of Coins and Medals of the British Museum; The Lord Methuen and his Archivist at Corsham Court, Miss Wade; Dr. E. Morpurgo; Dr. W. O'Dea of the Science Museum, London; The Marchesa Iris Origo; Mrs. Jean Phillips; The Commendatore Giovanni Poggi, of the Casa Buonarroti, Florence; Dr. F. N. L. Poynter, Chief Librarian of the Wellcome Historical Medical Library; Sir Herbert Read; Mr. Graham Reynolds of the Victoria and Albert Museum; Professor and Mrs. Raymond de Roover; Dr. F. A. B. Ward of the Science Museum, London; and Mr. Berthold Wolpe.

And here 'With many thousand thanks' (and an inverted quotation) 'I take my leave'.

Chelsea, 1963   E.H.R.

Preface

The Letters

Of the countless letters written by Michelangelo during a long and arduous career some four hundred and ninety have survived and are known to us in the original autographs, in authenticated copies, or in published versions of letters that are no longer extant. Those contained in the first category are by far the most numerous, and except for a few to be found elsewhere – mainly in the Florentine State collections, in the Vatican Codex and in the Casa Vasari – are preserved in two principal archives, the Casa Buonarroti in Florence and the British Museum in London. The manuscripts in the former were acquired by the city, together with the house and the rest of its contents, by bequest in 1858, on the death of Cosimo Buonarroti, Michelangelo's last collateral descendant of the elder branch; those in the latter by the Museum by right of purchase in 1859 from Michelangelo Buonarroti, nephew of the aforesaid Cosimo.

Although selected letters have been quoted, either in whole or in part, by most of Michelangelo's biographers during the past four hundred years, it was not until 1875, when, in commemoration of the quatercentenary of Michelangelo's birth, the Florentine archivist, Gaetano Milanesi, published the text of all, save two of them, that the letters became generally available. Besides assembling the material from the various archives, a service of inestimable value for which all Michelangelo scholars continue to acknowledge their indebtedness, he facilitated their study still further by modernizing the spelling and by supplying the words and letters omitted in the abbreviated forms of the period, while in all other respects providing a faithful transcription of the originals. It is true that few difficulties are presented either by Michelangelo's unusually fair italic hand, or by the shortenings he used, but it would be idle to pretend that the present translation would ever have been undertaken without the use of Milanesi's text, despite the fact that recourse to the autographs in London has nevertheless been constant.

It will be noted that Milanesi's numbering of the letters and mine do not correspond: partly because, whereas he arranged them chronologically in groups, I have arranged them chronologically, regardless of these groups; and partly because he misdated a number of them, in many cases owing to the fact that his copyist in London sometimes failed to provide him with the correct details of the endorsements, upon which much of the accurate dating depends. The extensive researches undertaken since his time have, in addition, enabled us to correct numerous other misdatings. The number which Milanesi assigned to each letter, together with the appropriate information as to the archival source, the place where the letter was written and its known or (if bracketed) its assumed date, has therefore been given in the hanging shoulder note to each letter. The grounds on which any date, or any part of a date, has been altered or emended are set forth in a special section – The Dating and Sequence of the Letters – which is intended rather for the specialist than for the general reader who need not consult it unless he feels disposed to do so.

As the presentation of the letters in an unbroken sequence would have proved wearisome, I have adopted the method of so dividing them that each section coincides with a specific period in Michelangelo's artistic career; with a natural break in it, such as that constituted by the siege of Florence; or failing this, with the pontificates of the several Popes whom he served. Although this method has made for an unavoidable discrepancy in the number of letters in each section, it seemed better than any other, since no perfect solution of the problem presented itself. It may possibly do so – after we have gone to press.

The Critical Apparatus

If, as a correspondent, Michelangelo had had no end in view other than that of making it imperative for the scholar to investigate every conceivable aspect of Renaissance life, he could scarcely have succeeded better. So that although Milanesi provided a certain number of footnotes, some of them invaluable, they are in fact wholly inadequate and have had to be replaced by a more comprehensive system of annotation, in which certain of Milanesi's notes have been incorporated. Yet even so much in the letters would remain incomprehensible without further elucidation, and some forty appendixes have therefore been added. Thus the footnotes to the letters are designed to meet the immediate requirements of readers, some of whom may need all of the notes, all of whom may need some of the notes; the appendixes to supply further relevant information, to correct persistent misconceptions, or to clarify the position (in so far as this has been possible) in regard to certain outstanding problems. And in this connection I should like to make full acknowledgment of the extent to which I am beholden to my predecessors in the field of Michelangelo studies, and notably to Aurelio Gotti, to Karl Frey and to Ernst Steinmann, without whose stupendous researches in the past, my own contribution, such as it is, could not have been made.

As the Appendixes are in the nature of expositions rather than commentaries and are fully explanatory, it has been possible to obviate a tiresome use of further footnotes by incorporating the necessary references in the text. This was not, however, an acceptable solution in the case of the Introduction, which is purely discursive, being designed as a study of the life in terms of the relationships and of the character in terms of the destiny. The notes to which the superior numbers here refer have therefore been set at the end of the text, as they relate to sources only and need not be perused save by those who may wish to verify them – a task perhaps even more penitential than having to supply them.

The Translation

The publication of private letters that were never intended for publication would savour too much of temerity were it not that such publication has for so long been accepted as the price which fame pays to fortune, that it has come to be regarded rather as a form of homage than as an act of intrusion. Publication of the original text is one thing, however; its translation is another, since while the former speaks for itself, the latter requires an interpreter – and there's the rub.

A translation of the letters of Michelangelo is not therefore a task lightly to be undertaken, nor one to be approached save in a spirit of profound respect for a master before whom, as Eugène Guillaume remarked, *il faut toujours s'incliner*. Indeed, to suppose otherwise would merely be to betray a somewhat 'parvenu conviction'. I have therefore endeavoured throughout the work, both in the translation and in the critical apparatus, to preserve a scrupulous regard for truth, for there is, in my opinion, no sin more unpardonable in a writer than to attempt to foist his own tawdry ideas upon the great.

Unlike many Renaissance letters, those of Michelangelo were not stylistic exercises, but intimate communications addressed to his family and to his friends, often written in a hurry and sometimes under physical and mental stress. My first concern has therefore been to retain the character of the originals. I have made no attempt to smooth out such roughnesses of style as may from time to time occur, nor, except in the interests of intelligibility, to correct in, English, constructions that are in any case awkward in the Italian, since to do so would be to belie Michelangelo's mood and sequence of thought at the time that he was writing. Similarly, I have adhered to the form whereby he was in the habit of making abrupt transitions from one subject to another by the use of phrases such as – 'Concerning my marbles', 'As to Giovansimone', 'As regards the house' – without trying to vary it by the introduction of some more felicitous rendering, which would have been easy enough, had a translation of the letters into polished English prose been my intention, but this was not the object I had in view. The simple and direct way in which Michelangelo wrote lends itself naturally, however, to translation into English of a vigorous but less fluent style, many of the rather old-fashioned phrases he used being closely akin to our own. Again, I have not thought that any purpose would be served by striving for a complete consistency, particularly not in the translation of phrases, such as *in ogni modo*, which is amenable to slightly different renderings in different contexts, all of them equally permissible. To satisfy the requirements of each individual letter has therefore been my overriding concern throughout.

In order to make the letters as readable as possible I have not tried to follow Michelangelo's somewhat arbitrary use of paragraphs, since more would have been lost than gained thereby, nor, unlike Robert Carden, who translated about two hundred of the letters, have I retained the use of the second person singular, since, being no longer current, it would have lent a false and archaic flavour to the letters, which was as much to be avoided as any lapse into the neoteric infelicities of our own day. I have therefore tried to follow a middle course (by which I would not be thought to refer to the 'mean' of the new 'unauthorized' version), being, as I am, in agreement with the views of the late Ronald Knox that, failing 'a timeless English, the translator must do his best by using speech that comes natural to him, fortified a little by those good old English words which are out of favour, but not obsolete'. A frequent use of many of these old turns of phrase has proved the more necessary, inasmuch as many of the sentiments expressed in the letters are now outmoded. For this reason I have thought it not inappropriate to preserve a certain period flavour, particularly in the salutations, and to acknowledge, at least in passing, the graces of a less barbarian age.

In conclusion perhaps I should say something about the three main difficulties I have encountered in the translation. The first is inherent in the disparity between the resources of the respective tongues; that is to say, between the poverty of Italian (as of other Romance languages) and the richness of English. For whereas in the former one word has to suffice for a number of slightly different meanings, depending upon the context; in the latter a different word must be used in each case; so that there is always a tendency for the one to be too specific and the other too general. The second difficulty has been that of finding in the cruder modes of address in English an equivalent for the more courteous style used in Italian, especially where the polite form of the third person singular is employed. For the elegance of *Vostra Signoria* we have no substitute and I have therefore had to make use sometimes of one device and sometimes of another in order to convey the varying degrees of formality required by any given letter. The third difficulty has been that of rendering the effect of expressions that are, in fact, either untranslatable or would be ineffective if preserved in English. In such cases, which are comparatively few, I have accordingly sought rather for implicit than for explicit approximations, being guided by the consideration, 'What, in like case, would we say in English?' Finally, there has been the problem of the translation of the word *pazienza* which carries a whole world of meaning in itself and for which, except on rare occasions, our word 'patience' will not suffice. As it cannot invariably be translated in the same way, I have adopted different expedients in different contexts, but even so I am not sure that I remain satisfied with the solutions I have found. But that would perhaps be expecting too much, since in any event at the end of it all I feel rather like the actor who, at the close of his career, is reputed to have made this entry in his diary – 'Have played Hamlet for the last time; am beginning to understand the part.'

THE INTRODUCTION

The Introduction

If on the morning of June 25th 1496 it had been announced in Rome that the day would be marked by no event comparable in importance with that of the arrival of an unknown Florentine sculptor, the announcement would have been received not with astonishment, but with incredulity. Certainly, the Pope, at ease in the Belvedere,[1]* would not have believed that the name of the newcomer who, on the following Sunday, waited upon the Cardinal di San Giorgio in 'his new house' would ring down the centuries, while his own would be virtually forgotten, save by historians and by the few who, in an appropriate context, might murmur doubtfully and without enthusiasm, 'Alexander VI – the Borgia Pope?' Thus it is, however, that the whirligig of time brings in his revenges; for eminence and the trappings of power are no earnest of immortality, nor the burdens of a lesser inheritance an impediment to glory, since greatness is all.

But what in these days of misapplied superlatives do we mean by greatness? To think of it in terms of the ancient prerogative, *noblesse oblige*, is to postulate an unnecessary condition and thereby to obscure its deeper meaning. To say that, like beauty, it too belongs to 'the order of transcendentals' and is therefore easier to recognize than to describe is to beg the question. But while here, as in all things, there is a 'suchness' or quintessential element which cannot be defined, like the informing spirit in man which remains elusive, some consideration of those qualities which make for greatness yet lies within our scope.

Contrary to what might be supposed, it is as much by the profoundness of their humanity as by the loftiness of their genius that the supremely great are to be distinguished from their fellows. For it is not pre-eminently the saint or the superman, if such exist, who ultimately command our applause, but rather the type of the tragic character *par excellence*; that is to say, the man who, though cast in an heroic mould, is not untouched by human frailty. This is because our constitution is such that we are moved less by the miraculous than by deeds accessible to our understanding, albeit beyond our performance. And particularly is this true where the deeds in question do not presuppose gifts of an exceptional or unprecedented kind, but a capacity for moral action which, theoretically at least, is within the compass of all men capable of conceiving it.

For those able to contemplate life with some measure of detachment, like the poet who 'sees life steadily and sees it whole', it is not difficult to perceive that there are many

* *The superior numbers used throughout the Introduction refer to sources only and are not otherwise relevant to the text. The references are listed on pp. lv–lvii.*

ways in which it may be regarded. To some it is merely a haphazard affair, made up of disconnected events of little importance; to some it is a battle to be fought and a victory to be won; to others it is rather 'a walk to be taken for the sake of the view'; or to others, yet again, a tragi-comedy to be played out for the sake of the dénouement. In some respects the last analogy is the most apposite, for life also is a potential unity, having a beginning, a middle and an end and may likewise be deemed to subserve a moral purpose. But just as only a work of a high dramatic order can be classified as tragedy, so only lives lived on a commensurate scale can be described as great.

If, therefore, life has meaning in proportion to its form, then, like a work of art, in order to satisfy the conception of greatness, it, too, must fulfil the requirement of being 'serious, complete and of a certain magnitude'.[2] It must be 'serious' in the sense that there is in it an implicit acknowledgment that man's primary obligation is the living of an uncorrupt life in the sight of God; it must be 'complete' in the sense that there is a full realization of its potentialities; it must be 'of a certain magnitude' in the sense that there is in it an inherent virtue not wholly different in kind from that exemplified by other men, but surpassing in grace, in quality and in distinction that which is ordinarily achieved. But if there is no true greatness without virtue, and this is axiomatic, similarly there is no true virtue without humility, since the uniquely gifted among men, though not unaware of their superior endowments, are characterized rather by a consciousness of imperfection than by any tendency to presume. For the finer a man's perceptions, the more certainly must he stand in awe before the Godhead – 'the very fountain of Beauty itself'.

Understandably and not entirely without reason, such lives provide, at once an inspiration and a challenge to the world of their own time and to that of posterity. To some minds they appear divine and worthy of emulation; to others inhuman and beyond endurance, so that it is almost as if the one no less than the other, though in a different spirit, were to say with Themistocles, 'the trophies of Miltiades will not suffer me to sleep'. The tribute in either case is the same, however, since it is the noble, and not the ignoble, whom envious tongues seek to decry. Yet even so, the effect of conflicting opinions cannot but be to obscure the truth, and progressively so, through succeeding generations. It is therefore incumbent upon the historian to preserve a middle course between what may well be regarded as excessive adulation, on the one hand, and excessive denigration on the other, inasmuch as the assessments of history depend for their validity not only upon the nature of the evidence available, but, in no less a degree, upon the nature of the insight with which that evidence is interpreted. Furthermore, without imagination, understanding and respect there can be no proper evaluation and nothing to compensate for one of the anomalies – and indeed one of the weaknesses – of criticism, namely, that as often as not the lesser find themselves in the invidious position of assessing the merits of the greater.

As touching Michelangelo, there is no name in the whole history of art more exalted than his; no master upon whom more extravagant praises were lavished in his own lifetime; no artist whose disposition has been less understood by posterity. Perhaps, as it were, in an attempt to redress the balance of nature, since his genius was not to be gainsaid, historians, biographers and critics alike have frequently sought to distinguish between the man and his achievement and to extol the one at the expense of the other. Indeed, from a perusal of some of the general commentaries, one is left with the impression of a mannerless, irascible, intractable boor, a man without charm, caring little for his obligations, melancholy, morose and savage withal.

To deny these imputations is not to infer that Michelangelo was faultless; like everyone else he had his failings, of which he was, perhaps, more conscious than most. For though he might defend himself and his fellows against those who maintained, 'among a thousand lies', that 'eminent painters are eccentric and that their conversation is harsh and intolerable', he was at pains to show that in striving to preserve the conditions necessary for their work 'they are only human all the time',[3] however the hostile and the ignorant might choose to interpret their reserve.

These observations, which were recorded with obvious fidelity by Francisco d'Ollanda in the pages of his so-called Portuguese Dialogues, are important for two reasons. Not only do they show the kind of charges that were brought against him, but they also amplify certain passages which occur both in Michelangelo's own letters and in those of his correspondents. But while there were many among his contemporaries who sought to belittle him on one pretext or another, and sometimes perhaps for no more sufficient reason than that they grew tired of hearing him forever called 'divine', they are less to be blamed than those of his later critics, who, though in a better position to take every aspect of the matter into account owing to their greater historical detachment, have nevertheless failed to do so. For while all writers have not been equally imperceptive, there are few who have considered the shortcomings of Michelangelo's character, such as they were, in relation to the circumstances of his life; and fewer still who have realized to the full the tragic implication of his destiny.

Seldom, or more probably never, in the annals of history can an artist have been so much the victim of his own genius. A life of more continuous servitude, toil, anxiety and frustration would be difficult to conceive, for, as Michelangelo himself remarked to his friend, Giorgio Vasari, a few years before his death, 'they who become the asses of princes early in life bear a burden even beyond the grave'.[4] And therein, in fact, lay the beginning and the end of the whole tragedy. It is thus in terms of this burden and against the background of the tumults and uncertainties of the period in which he lived that Michelangelo must be judged. The exercise of an informed historical imagination is therefore fundamental if any approximation either to justice or to truth is to be achieved.

What he suffered personally in the way of misrepresentation by those who looked upon him with jealous eyes, though naturally more acute, was in some respects less appalling than the slurs that have since been cast upon him. To some inquisitors nothing is sacrosanct; and when one considers the kind of scrutiny to which he has been subjected during the centuries, one can but reflect that when he spoke of burdens to be borne even beyond the grave, he spoke more truly than he knew. For if, being, above all, a man of honour and having a proper regard for his personal reputation, he cried out against the calumniators of his own generation, what would he have said of those who, having nothing better to do than to malign the great, have not hesitated to do so, nor scrupled to fabricate 'a Michelangelo of their own',[5] a figure lacking in all verisimilitude and bearing no resemblance to anyone but themselves?

Much that has been written about him may therefore be entirely disregarded, but just because the unscrupulous have presumed to confound fact with fiction and to invent when they did not know, it becomes the more imperative in the interests of truth to accept even the conclusions of the acknowledged authorities with reservation, unless they are correctly drawn from premises that can be shown to be valid. In other words, no categorical statements can be made about him that are not based on original sources, whether on Michelangelo's own writings or on the testimony of his contemporaries. Everything else remains a matter of speculation, which is perhaps not altogether unavoidable, especially where a controversial figure like Michelangelo is concerned; besides which some allowance must always be made for the fact that however dispassionate a critic may contrive to be, he is bound to betray his bias in one way or another, if only because biography, like a work of art, cannot but be 'a part of nature seen through a temperament'.

For this reason some among his principal biographers have necessarily understood him better than others, for while none has denied him an essential nobility of spirit, and all have alleged certain things against him, each has, as it were, presented the case in accordance with the terms of his chosen brief.

Although more sensible than most of the peculiar irony of Michelangelo's fate, Romain Rolland[6] was obsessed by the conviction that he had no-one to blame for it but himself. *On parle quelquefois de la fatalité qui s'acharna contre lui*, he wrote. *Cette fatalité fut lui-même.* It was not his masters, Rolland contended, who were responsible for the frustration he continually encountered, but he himself, by reason of his innate timidity, his inability to refuse anything that was asked of him, his perpetual indecision; in effect, a want of compatibility between his temperament and his endowments – endowments to which, as a character, he was in fact unequal. Not only was he *faible*, according to Rolland, he was *faible de toute façon*, and that notwithstanding the compelling power of his genius. In contrast to Beethoven, 'who was gay by nature', Michelangelo, as Rolland saw him, was joyless to a point of melancholy that effectually isolated him from his fellows. For all his converse with the great of the earth, his violence, his pride and his suspicion were inimical to any intimate or lasting friendship, to which, indeed, his restlessness of spirit and his creative energy constituted a further barrier. *Il fut seul. Il haït: il fut haï. Il aima: il ne fut pas aimé. On l'admirait et on le craignait.* Such, then, contrary to his own volition, was the void Michelangelo created around him. Yet despite this insistence upon *ses faiblesses, son humeur sauvage*, Rolland was by no means unmindful of his virtues. His goodness, his kindness, his generosity, he acknowledged as being beyond question, just as in the greatness of his stature he recognized the very personification of the High Renaissance, the incarnation of the Italian genius and the glory of the century to which he belonged.

If an advocate for the defence were needed to refute the foregoing charges of pusillanimity, none more ardent, though not, on that account, necessarily more persuasive, could be found than Henry Thode[7] – an advocate in whose eyes Michelangelo could do no wrong. Such faults as he felt bound to admit he excused as being but the inevitable consequences of 'the struggle between a high courage and an oppressive fate'. Throughout his life this man whose goodness, greatness, compassion and purity of heart we can only venerate and glorify, was constantly beset by toils, turmoils and troubles of every kind. Hurt and disappointed, hampered and frustrated, as he was, a prey to 'gnawing anxiety and overwhelming despair', should he be blamed for those violent outbursts of temper (or, more expressively, *Heftigheit*, a term which cannot be adequately rendered in English), in which he gave vent to the bitterness and exasperation by which he was consumed? Or should he be met with sympathy for 'the sufferings of his genius'? Far from being shocked by these outbursts, those who have penetrated to the heart of his unique personality must surely bow in wonder, as it were before a storm, which they recognize to be but a 'necessary phenomenon of mighty nature'. Powerfully though he might justify him in regard to these exhibitions of *terribilità*, Thode was not, however, under any misapprehension as to their effects, since, as he said, 'there can be no doubt that his passionate temperament had a fatal influence on his career'. It caused endless interruptions to his work, it exposed him to much misunderstanding and needlessly increased the number of his enemies, for all of which Michelangelo himself must take the blame. Apart from this turbulence of spirit, which proved, after all, more harmful to himself than to anyone else, the only other weakness of his nature which Thode could find was that frankly irreconcilable opposition between his courage, on the one hand, and his instinct for self-preservation on the other. Beyond this, it was essentially as a colossus that Thode conceived him, a man who knew the gamut of human emotions from the heights of rapture to the depths of despair and 'who carried a whole world within himself'. Such, however, was the harshness of the contrast between the world of his imagination and that of his experience, and such the profoundness of 'his unsatisfied yearning to be loved' that as he grew older the melancholy to which he was prone became intensified, until at last he came to long for release from the fetters of a world in which 'he sought in vain for his equals'. At the same time, had it not been for the very strength of his passions, and for this capacity for suffering, a capacity commensurate only with his genius, would Michelangelo have been the sublime artist and the illustrious man that he was?

Broadly speaking, the views expressed by Rolland and by Thode may be said to represent the two extremes of opinion, towards one or other of which the majority of writers have tended, while almost invariably maintaining the same common ground that exists between them.

Thus, Hermann Grimm,[8] who held melancholy to be the leading feature of Michelangelo's character, a melancholy perhaps increased by his disfigurement, saw him as a man solitary and austere, bitter, gloomy, ironical and of a violent will; passionate and proud, sensitive and suspicious, yet at the same time gentle, tolerant and kind; unwilling, for all the outspokenness, of his opinions, to give unnecessary offence and impartial in his praise of others.

John Harford,[9] on the other hand, described his natural disposition as being 'fiery and impetuous, especially when touched upon the point of honour'. But in so saying, he did not discount the melancholy strain, though he refrained from giving it undue prominence. 'His irreproachable morals,' he writes, 'united to his philosophical turn of mind and his devotion to art disposed him to contemplation and solitude and very naturally imparted a certain tinge of melancholy to his looks and temperament. Hence, he acquired the reputation of being haughty and singular, yet his heart was inclined to friendship and he enjoyed the intimacy of many of the best writers and most distinguished men of his day.' In short, Harford envisaged him as an altogether more urbane personality, one whose 'somewhat stern and lofty independence was blended with the kindest consideration for the feelings and interests of his friends and dependants. Magnanimous and singleminded, he was throughout much of his life in conflict with the vices and intrigues of the age in which he lived.'

Similarly, Raymond Duppa,[10] who regarded him as a man 'in all essential points entitled to honour and esteem', spoke of him in these words, 'He was impetuous when he felt the slightest attack upon his integrity and hasty in his decisions, which gave him an air of irascibility; but he was not morose in his disposition nor cynical in his habits. To all who were in need of assistance from his fortune or his talents, he exercised a princely liberality; and to those of honourable worth, however low their station, he was kind and benevolent . . . nor ever refused his aid.'

A more detailed analysis of the character has, of course, become possible since the time of Grimm, Harford and Duppa, who wrote before the invaluable material bequeathed to Florence in 1858 by Cosimo Buonarroti, Michelangelo's last collateral descendant, was made available to scholars.

John Addington Symonds,[11] whose bias was in any case different, was at an advantage in this respect and did not fail to profit by his opportunities. Having enumerated the supposed frailties of Michelangelo's nature, namely 'a passionate violence of temper . . . extreme suspiciousness and irritability; solitary habits, amounting to misanthropy . . . eccentricity and melancholy bordering on madness', he goes on to remark that 'his biographers, Condivi and Vasari, thought these charges worthy of serious refutation, which proves they were current'. Speaking for himself he nevertheless came to the conclusion that 'there remained a good deal in the popular conception which could not be dismissed, and which has recently been corroborated by the publication of his correspondence'. 'The opinion that Michelangelo was a man of peculiar and in some respects not altogether healthy nervous temperament', he continues, 'will force itself upon all those who have fairly weighed the evidence of the letters in connection with the events of his life.' At the same time, he refuted the extreme conclusions reached by Parlagreco in his psychological study of Michelangelo's nature, contenting himself with the observation that he 'suffered from constitutional depression', a form of melancholy that 'might be ascribed to that *morbus eruditorum* of which Burton speaks'. There is, moreover, as he goes on to show, 'nothing in those paroxysms of crossness on which so much stress has been laid . . . to justify the hypothesis of more than a hyper-sensitive nervous temperament' without which 'how could an artist of Michelangelo's calibre and intensity perform his life's work?' This, in the main, is the substance of Symonds's thesis, which he develops at length, but in too great detail, notwithstanding its interest and importance, for further consideration here.

From the foregoing epitomes it will be clearly seen that Michelangelo's principal biographers have, on the whole, differed less over the qualities to be ascribed to him than over the emphasis to be placed upon them. By exaggerating any one characteristic the impression of the entire personality can easily be falsified and thrown out of balance and it is this which has constantly been done. Occasional moods have been stressed and treated as if they were habitual; reactions which would excite no comment if viewed in proper perspective have been given undue prominence and it has frequently been forgotten that the role of the artist as hero is not one that is played either consciously or unconsciously by the man himself. To transform a career as intrinsically dramatic as Michelangelo's into a melodrama, besides being unnecessary, is to deprive it of its essential dignity and to diminish rather than to heighten the significance of a life which requires neither apology nor embellishment, a life of great tribulation, sublime in its striving to accept and to obey the Will of God.

The story of Michelangelo's first visit to Rome in 1496, at the age of twenty-one, and the circumstances of his departure from Florence in the company of a gentleman in the suite of Raffaello Riario, the Cardinal di San Giorgio, is related in some detail by Condivi,[12] who had it from Michelangelo himself many years afterwards. From his account of the *Sleeping Cupid*, which had been sold to the Cardinal as an antique, it is clear that even at that time Michelangelo's potential genius as a sculptor had already been recognized, notwithstanding the fact that the dealer, Baldassare del Milanesi, who had cheated both Michelangelo and the Cardinal had been made (some thought mistakenly) to take back the *Cupid* and to repay the two hundred ducats he had received for it. But to repudiate it as an antique was not to impugn the intrinsic merits of the carving itself which, when it subsequently passed into the Mantuan Collection in 1502 was described by Isabella d'Este as being 'without a peer among the works of modern times'.[13]

From Michelangelo's own account of his arrival in Rome and of what ensued, as given in his letter to Lorenzo di Piero Francesco de' Medici,[14] which he wrote shortly afterwards, we are left with the impression of a young man as simple and direct as he was honest and unassuming, but there is nothing to confirm this impression, apart from one or two of his letters to members of his own family written at about the same time. Though obviously confident that he could acquit himself tolerably well in any commission he undertook, he made no claims, but quietly informed the Cardinal that although he could do nothing as fine as the figures he saw about him, the Cardinal 'should see what he could do'. By the end of the century, however, with the uncovering of the *Madonna della Febbre*, which he executed for Jean Bilhères de Lagraulas (otherwise known as Giovanni della Groslaye), Cardinal di San Dionisio, the whole of Rome knew beyond a peradventure exactly what he could do. Of his own reactions at this time we know nothing, beyond the fact that, having heard the work attributed by certain strangers to *il Gobbo nostro*, that is to say, to Cristoforo Solari of Milan, he forthwith concealed himself in the chapel and during the night carved his own name across the baldric, thus completing the only work he ever signed.[15]

It was thus as a master of renown that he returned to Florence shortly afterwards, there to be recognized as famous among the sculptors of his day. For the next four years he remained in his native city, being engaged first on the *David* and afterwards on the cartoon for *The Battle of Cascina*, for which reason there is an interval in the family correspondence. But more valuable than any information about his personal life that might have emerged from a continuance of the letters is the evidence of the esteem in which he was held by his fellow citizens. This is afforded by a communication addressed by Piero Soderini, the Gonfalonier for life, to the Cardinal di Volterra in November 1506, after Michelangelo had been compelled, much against his will, to leave Florence and to enter the service of the Pope.

Early in 1505, when the *Cascina* cartoon was only half finished, what were probably the happiest years of Michelangelo's life were brought abruptly to an end. On the advice of his architect, Giuliano da Sangallo, Pope Julius II summoned Michelangelo to Rome and there entrusted him with the commission for his Tomb.[16] Although in referring to the proposed monument Michelangelo claimed that it would be 'the mirror of all Italy', there is nothing in the tone of his reference to suggest that this was expressive of anything more than his own enthusiasm for a project of which, in his heart of hearts, he knew himself to be capable. An account of what later befell is given in his letter to Giuliano da Sangallo of August 1506 and in another to the Cardinal Farnese,[17] written many years later. Here let it suffice to say that it was in a turmoil of outraged pride and passionate indignation that he threw himself on his horse and rode post to Florence, having been refused admittance to the audience chamber by order of the Pope, only a year after he had undertaken the commission.

Much has been made of this flight from Rome, as of his previous flight from Florence when the Medici fell into disfavour in 1494, on the ground that it affords proof of his congenital timidity. But it is questionable whether it affords proof of anything of the kind. For historians who live remote from scenes of political violence and who go in no fear of the assassin's knife themselves, it is no doubt easy to assume a boldness which they are prompt to deny to others, who had perhaps more cause to be afraid. It may be allowed, however, that Michelangelo was by nature impulsive and being, in all probability, more sensitive than most, it was only to be expected that he would react sharply and sometimes, at moments of stress, with what afterwards proved to have been undue alarm.

On the first occasion, when he left Florence shortly before the expulsion of Piero de' Medici, it was a time of wild civic agitation and unrest and of wilder rumours and prognostications, which the fervours of the 'meddlesome friar' did nothing to abate. It was only natural, therefore, as Grimm has convincingly shown,[18] that a youth in Michelangelo's position should have become apprehensive. He had, after all, been a member of the Medici household ever since Lorenzo the Magnificent had assigned him a place at his table; and although Piero the Unfortunate might boast that he had two remarkable men in his establishment,[19] one of whom was Michelangelo, he would have been powerless to avert the consequences of his own unpopularity, had these been visited upon them, and no-one knew whether they would be or not. It may therefore be accounted prudent rather than perfidious on Michelangelo's part that he should not have waited to see, particularly when he had neither obligations nor responsibilities to detain him and when no purpose would have been served had he remained. It is true that at a later date he was accused by his brothers of 'running after friars and fictions',[20] a jibe which may hark back to this period, but one which he stoutly rebutted. Be this as it may, he certainly possessed clearer historical foresight than they and being a man politically wise in his generation, always remained averse to meddling with public affairs, in which, as he knew, far more was to be lost than gained. This attitude he was always careful to maintain himself and to commend to his family, in whose discretion, political or otherwise, he had little confidence.

On the occasion of the second flight, though he had, as he confessed to Sangallo, some fear of assassination, it was not this that had precipitated his flight, but rather his mortification at the insult that had been put upon him. This is confirmed both by the arrogance of the message he returned by the Pope's horsemen, when he was overtaken at Poggibonsi, and by what he himself said to Julius when he finally made his submission in Bologna at the end of November or the beginning of December 1506.

The interest of this episode lies primarily in its betrayal of the Pope's real attitude towards Michelangelo, for whom he had previously shown too high a regard not to excite the jealousy and animosity of other artists. Now, though undeniably displeased over an act of defiance that had lasted some six or seven months, Julius was, in fact, far more anxious to placate than to punish him, as is shown by the readiness with which he vented his indignation upon someone else the instant the opportunity occurred. 'You should have sought us', exclaimed the Pope wrathfully, as soon as Michelangelo appeared, 'but you have waited for us to seek you.' Undaunted, Michelangelo knelt down and in a clear voice besought his pardon, pleading in mitigation of his fault that he had not erred deliberately, but only *because he could not bear to be turned away as he had been*. On hearing this, Julius made no reply, but remained with his head lowered, as if perplexed. Whereupon a prelate, who had been deputed to intercede for Michelangelo, interposed saying, 'Your Holiness, mark not his fault, for he has erred through ignorance. Except for their art, all painters are like this.' In a fury the Pope turned upon him. 'You have vilified him,' he said, 'when We have said nothing. It is you who are ignorant and despicable, not he. Get out of my sight; you have mistaken your office.' And, as he made no move to go, the luckless bishop was hustled unceremoniously from the chamber. As soon as he had gone, Julius motioned Michelangelo to approach and having pardoned him, ordered him not to leave Bologna until he had received a commission.[21]

In thus trying issues with the Pope in a way in which, as Piero Soderini had pointed out to him, a King of France would not have done, Michelangelo could scarcely have done himself a better service. For if there was a lesson to be learnt from the incident it was a lesson to be learnt not by himself, but by the Pope. Henceforth, though he might press him hard and frequently did, Julius was always careful not to go too far for fear of what he might do, so that, in one sense, Michelangelo had gained the upper hand. In some measure he had, of course, had it all along, in so far as Julius 'who loved him in his heart and had a more jealous care for him than for anyone else about him' had been sufficiently anxious to regain his services to enter into negotiations even with the Signoria in order to obtain them. And it was only when he had been informed by Soderini that the Signoria was not prepared to go to war over him that Michelangelo had consented to return, and even then only when he was sent with the status of an ambassador 'because violence was not offered to public persons without being offered to those who had sent them'. Soderini had, however, been justified when he assured him that he had nothing to fear from the Pope, who was kind and only desired to recall him because he wished him well.[22] Impulsive, sensitive and proud, Michelangelo had, in effect, triumphed.

Piero Soderini was a man of the world, yet even so, it seems likely that his assurances were based less upon what he surmised to be the Pope's probable intention than upon his own experience of the kind of reaction Michelangelo habitually evoked in people at all favourably disposed towards him. He certainly knew him well and possessed, as it happened, a deeper insight into his character than almost anyone else. In the letter of recommendation to his brother, Francesco Soderini, the Cardinal di Volterra, which Michelangelo took with him when he left for Bologna, he was therefore at pains to emphasize a feature of his temperament which, though fundamental, has commonly been too little regarded when not actually overlooked, namely, his need of encouragement and, above all, of affection, to which he was always prompt to respond. On November 27th 1506 Piero Soderini accordingly addressed himself to the Cardinal in these words:

> The bearer of this will be Michelangelo, the sculptor, whom we are sending in order to gratify His Holiness, Our Lord. We assure Your Eminence that he is a gallant young man and in his profession without an equal in Italy, perhaps in the whole world. His nature is such that with encouragement and kindness he will accomplish anything; show him courtesy and affection and he will accomplish things that will astonish the beholder. We would inform Your Eminence that he has begun an historical composition for the Republic that will be much admired, and likewise xii apostles, each 4½ *braccia* in height, that will prove a prodigious work. We commend him whole-heartedly to Your Eminence.[23]

At no period of his career could any artist, however celebrated, have asked for higher commendation than this, much less could he have done so virtually at the outset. Nevertheless the commission for the bronze statue of Julius II, which resulted, caused him far less pleasure than pain, being, as it was, a source of anxiety and hardship while it was in progress and of disappointment and disillusionment afterwards. The four and half ducats with which he was left in hand[24] on its completion can hardly have seemed an adequate compensation for the labours involved in working with insufficient help, in a medium to which he was unaccustomed, while living in conditions which, as he informed his brother, Buonarroto, would have appalled him. Even the feeling of triumph at having cast the figure and the sense of elation when it was set up must have been short-lived, the meanness of his reward being equalled only by the briefness of the time for which the outcome of his labours endured.[25]

There were two motives by which Michelangelo was actuated, in the main, during the fifteen months that he was occupied with the statue of Julius II in Bologna and during the ensuing four years while he was engaged on the painting of the Sistine vault in Rome. The first concerned his own reputation; the second the welfare of his family. Being a creative genius of the first rank, it was only to be expected that, above all else, he should covet honour, and seeing that he did so, he was certainly prepared to work for it. From Bologna he wrote to Buonarroto in October 1507 saying, 'I am well and will soon have finished. I am expecting to be greatly honoured', though he hastened to add, with characteristic humility, 'all by the grace of God'. Then a few weeks later he wrote again, this time in more detail. 'I do nothing but work day and night and have endured and am enduring such fatigue that if I had to do the work over again I do not believe I should survive, because it has been a tremendous undertaking, and had it been in anyone else's hands it would have been a disaster. But I think someone's prayers must have helped me and kept me well, because the whole of Bologna was of the opinion that I should never finish it.'[26] Towards the end of the painting of the Sistine vault he wrote in a similar vein. ' I work harder than anyone who has ever lived. I'm not well and am worn out with this stupendous labour and yet I'm patient in order to achieve the desired end.'[27] But this time, after his disappointment over the bronze figure, he was less sanguine and only once spoke of expectations greater than that he would be paid in full on the completion of the work. Yet here again he was to be deceived and foiled of his object, at least as far as the material rewards were concerned. 'I have finished the chapel I have been painting; the Pope is very well satisfied. But other things have not turned out for me as I'd hoped',[28] was all that he said on the completion of his labours. This is the only mention of the vault after it had been uncovered, but of the tremendous renown which it brought him, and to which he cannot have been indifferent, his letters betray nothing.

The second object he had in view, which was that of providing for his family, he endeavoured to do partly from his own immediate payments and partly from the income to be derived from capital investments in land. How early in his career he became convinced that it was incumbent upon him to provide for them cannot be determined with certainty, but it would appear to have been at the turn of the century. In February 1500 his father, Lodovico, had written to him while he was still in Rome, complaining bitterly about the state of penury in which he found himself and lamenting that Michelangelo himself was also in want. 'I have five sons', he wrote, 'and not one of them could give me a cup of cold water.'[29] Towards the end of the same year he wrote again, this time expressing concern at the conditions of hardship in which Michelangelo was living, according to the report he had received from Buonarroto, who had recently returned from a visit to Rome. In this letter, which is full of solicitude for Michelangelo's well-being, Lodovico urged him to take care of himself, not to go to extremes of privation in his way of living and to return to Florence as soon as possible. He also referred with gratitude to Michelangelo's care for his brothers and to his desire to invest money for them in a shop, a desire of which this is the first mention.[30] The generosity of this gesture is the more marked inasmuch as it was made at a time when Michelangelo himself was possessed only of the most slender resources. But the mention of it at this juncture could scarcely have proved more unfortunate, because it was so long before he was able to fulfil his intention that the brothers finally came to regard it as a right of which they were too long deprived. Throughout his stay in Bologna and subsequently while in Rome he repeatedly encouraged them with assurances of what he hoped to do for them, and once even went so far as to say that he thought of nothing else day or night.[31] But each time he was baulked and it was only in July 1513 that he was at last able to send them enough to enable them to set up a business of their own.[32] How well or ill advised he was in taking this step, which he did in answer to Buonarroto's importunity, is debatable, because four months later, before the partnership was finally arranged, he received an anonymous letter from a friend in Florence, addressed to him 'as to a son', warning him that it would be wiser to invest the money for his father and his brothers either in property or in the *Monte*, from which they could draw the income without being able to touch the capital. The writer ventured to counsel him to this effect because he said that it had come to his ears that one of the brothers had intimated that once the money was in their hands the investment would be lost to Michelangelo for good and all.[33] That Buonarroto was not the brother in question we may be sure, for despite one serious quarrel, the details of which are lost to us,[34] and jibes of a typical brotherly kind on both sides, he and Michelangelo were clearly fond of each other. Of the four brothers, Buonarroto, who seems always to have done what was asked of him, was easily Michelangelo's favourite. Even after he had made a failure of the shop,[35] as he seems to have done a year or so before his death of plague in the summer of 1528, Michelangelo's willingness to help him never abated[36] and he cared for him to the last.

Giovansimone, the black sheep of the family, whose abilities Michelangelo was never tempted to over-estimate, presents something of an enigma. At best he might be described as temperamental; at worst as wanting. He was obviously a cause of anxiety to the family, who appear, generally, to have been disposed to humour him, except when his behaviour became more than usually insufferable, as on the occasion when Michelangelo sent him the letter of admonishment he deserved, for having gone so far as to threaten his father and to set light to the farm buildings. From the tone of this letter,[37] and even more so from that of the three he wrote him from Bologna,[38] we are left with the impression, if not of a simpleton, at least of a ne'er-do-well, who was neither mentally nor physically robust. Michelangelo never had any illusions about his behaviour and was well aware that he and the others had gone round Florence complaining about him, in spite of all that he had tried to do for them and was still prepared to do, because, as he said in a letter written shortly after Lodovico's death, 'I care more about fulfilling my obligations than about the things you say.'[39] In later years Giovansimone seems to have settled down to an uneventful life of little interest, but except for an occasional letter about some business matter, Michelangelo never carried on a correspondence with him, any more than he did with his youngest brother Sigismondo, who, as a personality, emerges even less than Giovansimone. He is known to have been in the service of the Republic at Modigliana[40] during the troubles of 1527, but for the most part he spent his life 'trudging after oxen' at Settignano, to Michelangelo's extreme annoyance.[41] But to him, likewise, Michelangelo was disposed to do a kindness when the opportunity occurred, as a touchingly grateful letter of 1531 attests.[42]

In view of the sacrifices Michelangelo was continually prepared to make and continually made in order to raise his family from 'the state of misery'[43] in which they were living when he resolved to help them, the truth of Michelangelo's constant asseverations that all the labours he had undertaken and all the hardships he had endured had been for the sake of his father in the first place, and of his brothers, in the second, cannot for a moment be doubted. 'But this,' as he once wrote, with some bitterness, 'you have never either recognized or believed – May God forgive us all'.[44] The main trouble with Lodovico lay, however, in his inability to reconcile himself to the change in the family fortunes that had taken place after the failure of his father's bank many years before, so that he would persist in trying to live like a gentleman 'without a trade', a role impossible to sustain on the meagre proceeds of his farm lands. He had therefore at last been constrained to apply for a minor appointment in the Customs.[45] All this gave him a grudge against life and he became, in consequence, querulous, self-pitying and gullible to the point of believing any tale that was put about, not excepting calumnies even where Michelangelo himself was concerned, the son to whom he owed everything and of whom, in his own peculiar fashion, he was genuinely fond. Because he was a weak man and because 'to be weak is miserable, doing or suffering', Lodovico presented in many respects a pathetic figure. Only a weak man and a foolish one would have thought of drawing upon Michelangelo's account without permission, as he did in 1510, prior to taking up his appointment as *podestà* at San Casciano; only a pitiable one would have been reduced to a state of such abject contrition when Michelangelo unexpectedly returned to Florence and discovered his indiscretion.[46] Needless to say, Michelangelo not only forgave him, but with his accustomed generosity made it easy for him to repay what he had borrowed, and then only asked for it in part.[47]

But it was Lodovico's credulity as much as his foolishness that led to the many misunderstandings that arose. Though sometimes nettled and sometimes hurt, Michelangelo was always ready to make allowances and, when the occasion demanded it, was even prepared in a spirit of moving humility to plead with the old man as if he himself had been at fault.[48] But at last even he lost patience, and in a furious letter[49] to his father, in which he no longer addressed him as *Carissimo* or *Reverendissimo padre* but simply as *Lodovico*, he gave vent to the suppressed emotion engendered by years of ingratitude in a torrent of sarcasm and contempt. It is a pity that this is Michelangelo's last surviving letter to him, because it might be supposed on the strength of it that the estrangement was permanent, which was not so. A number of Lodovico's letters to his son are still extant and happily the last one, dated January 15th 1531,[50] written at Settignano shortly after his return from Pisa, not long after the siege had been raised, and shortly before his death, which took place in the first half of the same year,[51] is indicative of his real feeling for Michelangelo, just as Michelangelo's *capitolo*[52] – *Ancor che 'l cor già mi premessa tante*, written after his father's death – is indicative of his own sentiments. The relevant paragraph of Lodovico's letter is as follows:

> May God be thanked for His grace in having inspired you to be so charitable towards me, that I remain alive without having to beg or borrow, and if in truth I have been saved from hunger, it is thanks to God and then to you, who have shown me such kindness. May God reward you in this world and in the next.

He then asks Michelangelo of his great charity to take care of Buonarroto's children, 'because they are of our flesh and his' and concludes with the words, 'I can say no more. May God be with you always.'

※

From Michelangelo's remark to Buonarroto made in a letter written during the early stages of the work on the Sistine vault, 'I have no friends of any sort and want none',[53] it might be concluded that Jonathan Richardson was justified when he said that 'if not Melancholy', Michelangelo was 'very sombrous',[54] but in actuality the comment is as far from the truth as the original remark is misleading. No doubt it represented what Michelangelo felt at the time, but being preoccupied by the enormous difficulties of the task on which he was engaged – particularly as painting was not his profession[55] – while living in a state verging upon privation and enduring great physical fatigue, the time was not propitious and his profound need of friendship no less than his commensurate gift for it were alike obscured to him.

During the three and a half years following the completion of the vault conditions were different. The easy-going Medici Pope, Leo X, had succeeded Julius II in March 1513 and under a new contract for the Tomb negotiated with the della Rovere heirs, Michelangelo was able to enjoy a period comparatively free from anxiety. Although he worked, as always, prodigiously hard, he was at least employed upon the art of his own choice besides being in a position to employ such assistance as he needed. He was thus at liberty to make friends if he felt so inclined and proof is not wanting that he did so and that he was an immense favourite in an intimate Florentine circle. One of his friends, Giovanni Gellesi da Prato, who was living in Rome, clearly missed him when, in 1515, he went on a short visit to Florence and thence to Carrara. 'Dearest Michelangelo,' he wrote, 'since your departure I am left like an orphan in this vast Babylonia, so dear to me was your company. . . . If you were to reply it would not only be a satisfaction to me, which I greatly desire, but to all your friends who would, as you know, derive from it as much solace as I.' He went on to refer to a supper party to which Domenico Buoninsegni had been invited in Michelangelo's stead, but intimated that amid these pleasures his thoughts would be elsewhere.[56]

Further proof of the high regard in which he was held at this period is provided by the letter of introduction[57] which Donna Argentina Malaspina, wife of the exiled Piero Soderini, sent to her brother Lorenzo, Marquis of Fosdenone, a year later when Michelangelo went to Carrara. In it she asks her brother to do everything he can for him, as he 'is much loved by my husband and is a gentleman of such excellent breeding and of such a quality that we do not believe there is a man like him in Europe today'. She assured him, furthermore, that if he were to invite Michelangelo to stay for a few days, he would greatly enjoy his conversation, 'as he is well versed in architecture, artillery and fortifications'. In conclusion, she begged him, should Michelangelo fall ill, to look after him as if he were a member of their own family, since thereby he could do herself and her husband no greater favour. Similarly, in another letter written at about the same time, Soderini himself expressed his willingness to do Michelangelo any service, *per l'amore delle virtù vostre e bontà*.[58]

Michelangelo's departure for Carrara on this occasion was a cause of great consternation to another Florentine friend of his, Lionardo, the saddler, whose fears lest the work on the Tomb might, on this account, be delayed or abandoned proved to be better founded than he knew and better than Michelangelo himself could have anticipated. For the rest of the pontificate of Leo X Michelangelo found himself involved not only with the disastrous project for the façade of San Lorenzo in Florence, but, what was worse, with the opening up of the quarries at Pietra Santa and, when the contract for the façade was cancelled, with the continuation of the work already in progress at the New Sacristy.[59]

The reason most commonly advanced for what Michelangelo believed to be Leo's desire to 'keep him occupied'[60] at a distance from Rome, is characteristically set forth by Duppa, who remarks that, 'As the patronage of the Great may sometimes depend upon the docility of the person on whom it is bestowed, it has been supposed that the independent spirit of Michelangelo was ill-calculated to conciliate the accomplished spirit of Leo X. However this may be, no evidence appears that he ever refused submission to his will or opposed his authority with disrespect; but without seeking for other causes, it is easy to conceive that Michelangelo was not likely to have the favour of a prince in whose mind there was no point of resemblance to his own.'[61] In this vindication of Michelangelo (whose potential churlishness is nevertheless assumed) Duppa regretfully differs from Leo's biographer, William Roscoe,[62] 'who apologizes for Michelangelo's perverseness of temper'. It is possible, of course, that Leo may have been influenced to some extent in this matter by Raphael, his chosen artist, to whom he was much attached, who probably had no more desire than his compatriot, Bramante, had had, to encourage Michelangelo's presence at court. Sebastiano Luciani, Michelangelo's most intimate friend outside the Florentine circle, was indubitably of this opinion, as may be seen from a letter of his to Michelangelo written a few months after Raphael's death, when the decoration of certain rooms at the Vatican was under consideration. Being anxious to see at least some part of the work allocated to himself and to Michelangelo (though it seems that the latter had no wish for the commission) he wrote, saying that he had approached the Pope with this end in view 'in order to show the malignant that there are other demi-gods beside Raphael and his pupils', a supposition about which he says that he understands from the letters of Lionardo, the saddler, that 'you are more incensed than I am'.[63]

It would not appear, however, that Leo, who was extremely sentimental, harboured any personal animosity against Michelangelo. On the contrary, Sebastiano assures him in another letter that 'if you were to come to Rome you could obtain anything you wanted, not castles, but a city, because I know in what esteem the Pope holds you. When he speaks of you, it is, as it were, of a brother and almost with tears in his eyes. He told me that you were brought up together and he made it clear that he knows and likes you, but you frighten everyone, even Popes.'[64]

This letter apparently upset Michelangelo, who thought Sebastiano was accusing him of being unapproachable, an accusation which Sebastiano hastened to repudiate in his letter of November 9th 1520, when he wrote saying, 'As to your *terribilità*, which you gainsay – I for my part do not consider you unapproachable (*terribile*). You might be surprised if I had not written to you openly about this, because you do not appear to me to be unapproachable except in art – that is to say you are the greatest master that has ever existed. That is my opinion; if I'm wrong, so much the worse for me.'[65] It will be observed that the term *terribilità* was the word Michelangelo had apparently used in his reply to Sebastiano's previous letter; it was not the word Sebastiano had originally used; though some ten years later he, too, could not refrain from saying to Michelangelo, whom he loved only 'this side idolatry' – 'You are always the same; you are too great'.[66]

But if Leo X found Michelangelo unapproachable, his cousin, Cardinal Giulio de' Medici, who succeeded to the papal throne in 1523, certainly did not. He had known him for a number of years and had always liked him; indeed, it may fairly be said that some of his happiest hours during a troubled pontificate were spent either in Michelangelo's company or in that of those who had been in touch with him in Florence. Whenever he granted an audience to any of Michelangelo's correspondents he always enquired after him and often asked to see his letters, which he would frequently read several times and would sometimes pocket. Lionardo the saddler, who had recently returned from Florence, tells of one such audience in his letter to Michelangelo of March 10th 1526.[67] He says that the Pope had received him with the greatest eagerness and kindness imaginable and had asked him in detail about the progress of the work on the Library and the New Sacristy and about the method of blocking out the figures for the Tombs.[68] He had also enquired as to why Michelangelo was not getting on with the work and how it was that one of the figures had been broken, to which Lionardo replied that this was not the case, but that it had been put about by those who were envious of Michelangelo's standing with His Holiness, adding that on occasion, in order to get rid of the chatterboxes who wanted to have a look, Michelangelo himself had said some such thing and had even given it out that he was behindhand. At this the Pope laughed so heartily that it was afterwards said that he could not have enjoyed the conversation more. 'Thus,' says Lionardo, 'laughing with pleasure, he kept me for an hour with his hand on my shoulder, and would not let me go.'

Nor was Clement's interest in the progress of the work at San Lorenzo limited to the kind of information that Lionardo was able to give him; he required also the fullest details about the designs proposed and about the technical aspects of their realization, details about which he showed himself to be not only knowledgeable, but adroit in ways one would scarcely have expected. He did not hesitate to question Michelangelo's measurements, to make stipulations about the quality of the plaster to be used, and to enter sound objections of a purely practical kind. For instance in regard to the siting of certain windows in the roof, which Michelangelo had suggested, he remarked dryly that they would be both novel and beautiful, but that a couple of *frati* would be required to do nothing else but keep them free from dust.[69]

During this period Michelangelo was being pressed to the uttermost, but while continually making new demands upon him Clement was not altogether unmindful of the fact that there was a limit even to Michelangelo's capacity for work which, in this instance, was exceeded only by his own passionate desire to see the project completed. He was therefore insistent that Michelangelo should engage as many additional *scarpellini* as he needed and accordingly sent word begging him to remember that 'one man cannot do everything and we pontiffs do not live long'[70] – the latter sentiment being one that he had already expressed a few months previously in a note addressed to Michelangelo himself, written and signed with his own hand.[71] On the second occasion the Pope had said to Fattucci, 'write him a nice letter and tell him I shall always approve of what he does'. From all this it will be seen, as a case in point, how unfounded was Pastor's contention that 'the Pope bore with truly astonishing patience the rudeness and ill-temper of the irascible artist',[72] since it is obvious that he had no occasion to bear with anything of the kind.

Normally, the necessary correspondence between the Pope in Rome and Michelangelo in Florence during this period was carried on by the go-betweens appointed for the purpose. The business arrangements were in the hands of the banker, Jacopo Salviati (Leo X's brother-in-law), in Rome and of his agent in the Salviati bank in Florence, Giovanni Spina; while in his friend, Giovan Francesco Fattucci, a chaplain of Santa Maria del Fiore, who was then in Rome, Michelangelo had a personal representative who was appointed to act for him, not only in matters concerning San Lorenzo, but also in the negotiations over the Tomb of Julius II, in which Salviati and Spina were also involved.

Apart from their mutual interest in the affairs for which they were responsible, these three men had another bond in common, namely their affection and respect for Michelangelo both as an artist and as a man. In 1524, for example, when Michelangelo had written to express his thanks for the arrangement that had been made for the provision of a monthly salary, Salviati, addressing him as *Michelangelo mio amantissimo*, had assured him that his thanks were superfluous, because his virtues merited far more than he had yet received and had urged him to speak his mind freely whenever he desired anything of the Pope, who was both anxious and disposed to content him. 'So give your mind wholly to the work,' he had concluded, 'and leave the worry to me.'[73] And that this was no mere gesture on Salviati's part is borne out by the endless trouble he was always prepared to take on Michelangelo's behalf, whether it concerned the furtherance of his business or professional interests or the restoration of his shattered morale, when taunts and insults were heaped upon him by those who, being jealous of his prestige, sought only to hinder and impede him. In the closing passage of one such letter, in which he had endeavoured in the most tactful way possible to soothe Michelangelo's ruffled feelings, he finally contented himself with the words, 'As to myself I will say nothing because I am certain that up till now you have never realized my attitude towards you nor how dear to me is everything that concerns your honour and advancement.'[74]

Michelangelo's life at this period was still being made a burden by the base intrigues of his old enemies Domenico Buoninsegni and Bernardo Niccolini, who, though they were no longer in control of the marble supplies or of any other aspect of the work at San Lorenzo, continued, for reasons discussed elsewhere,[75] to make things as difficult for him as possible. It was therefore with a sense both of relief and pleasure that Michelangelo now needed to deal only with Giovanni Spina, a man of very different calibre and one in whom Clement himself recognized that he had 'a good instrument'. But Spina's respect and liking for Michelangelo were not greater than Michelangelo's for him.[76] Distraught as he was during these years by the conflicting claims of the Pope in respect of San Lorenzo and of the della Rovere heirs in respect of the Tomb of Julius II, he was not easy to deal with; being unable to continue with the one or to give his mind wholly to the other, he had certain scruples about accepting his salary while at the same time he complained about the poverty with which he was having to contend, and although Spina once lost his temper with him over this,[77] and not without reason, his courtesy, his kindness and his consideration were unfailing and Michelangelo had much cause to be grateful to him. And it is perhaps no mean tribute to the charm of Spina's character that it should be in virtue of his solicitude that he should ultimately be remembered. Thus, one evening he sent Michelangelo a note saying that he had been able to make certain arrangements about which Michelangelo had been anxious. He then continued, 'I had meant to come and see you tomorrow morning to tell you all about it. Afterwards I thought I would send this note round to you this evening; I should like you to sleep tonight with a quiet mind. Let me know if there is anything I can do and I will always do everything in my power to solace you. To you do I commend me. May God keep you. From my house, September 14th 1524.'[78]

Giovan Francesco Fattucci, Michelangelo's principal go-between in Rome, was likewise devoted to his service. The two men, who knew each other intimately, were deeply attached. Both lived on into old age and although in later years, when Fattucci had returned to Florence and Michelangelo was resident in Rome, they rarely corresponded, they always remained friends. The date of Fattucci's death has not been established, but Michelangelo was still asking after him in 1553, although his last extant letter was written three years earlier. The interest of their main correspondence, which was carried on from the end of 1523 to the end of 1526, and is concerned for the most part with the progress of the work at San Lorenzo and the negotiations for a third contract for the Tomb of Julius II, lies in the frankness of their communication. When, at times, Fattucci was driven into a state of exasperation by what appeared to be Michelangelo's fantastic perversity over certain matters, and by his phenomenal ability to misinterpret what was said to him,[79] he never hesitated to say so, criticisms which Michelangelo, despite his tendency to flare up, seems to have taken in good part. Another feature of their correspondence at this period is its revelation of Michelangelo's disregard of his own interests when he thought that for his own good Fattucci should return home,[80] and of the kindly way in which, in the midst of his many preoccupations, he found time during her son's absence from Florence, to visit the old mother whom Fattucci so dearly loved.[81] But it is above all in his letter of February 8th 1526 that Fattucci's genuine compassion, as well as his profound affection for Michelangelo is shown. The passage in question was written in reply to a suggestion that Michelangelo should offer him a salary for all the work he was doing for him in Rome. 'Now as to my affairs,' he began, 'I do not know who has put this *giribizo* into your head about my asking a salary of you, as if I were but a hireling. I have never thought, nor ever shall, but of doing everything in my power for you and yours. The salary I want from you is this – that as long as I live I may always place myself and everything that I have at your service. I never wanted any return from anyone and I never made friends in order to profit by them, but in order to serve. In the meantime banish this notion from your mind, because all I want from you is your affection.'[82]

A few months after this letter was written the correspondence was brought to a close and the work with which it was principally concerned to a standstill, owing to the impending conflict between Clement VII and Charles V, which ultimately brought such deadly havoc in its train. In the spring of 1527 Rome was sacked and until December of the same year when he escaped to Orvieto, the Pope remained a prisoner in his own Castel Sant' Angelo.[83]

Perhaps the most profound comment on this appalling disaster was that made in a letter addressed to Vittoria Colonna by Baldassare Castiglione, who wrote from Valladolid on August 25th 1527 – 'I have not ventured to write to Your Ladyship for a long time, not wishing to recall what I could not say and you could not hear without intense pain. Now that such overwhelming calamities have made us all one in misery, I feel that we may be allowed to forget, and perhaps ought to forget, the past; to open our eyes, or at least to emerge from our human ignorance as far as our frailty allows and to recognize that we know nothing. . . .'[84]

If, being at a distance, Castiglione, Nuncio to Charles V, was thus overcome by the horrors of which he had only heard, how much more deeply must Clement himself have been affected. Yet in spite of all that he had witnessed, he seems to have emerged without having learned a single salutary lesson. Neither humbled nor enlightened by his experiences, he survived with but one over-mastering desire – to punish Florence for her perfidy in casting out the Medici during the time of his tribulation, to which end he was even ready to make common cause with the Emperor by whom he had been so bitterly wronged. A more laudable desire, and one that was second only to this lust for vengeance, was his longing for Michelangelo to continue his work on the Tombs at

San Lorenzo. Thus, in March 1528, while he himself was still living in conditions of acute privation at Orvieto, prior to his return to Rome, he authorized the payment of five hundred ducats to enable Michelangelo to proceed.[85] But for the time being the two principal ends he had in view were to prove mutually exclusive; since it was only after the capitulation of Florence in August 1530[86] that Michelangelo was again at liberty to return to his art and by this time he was capable of doing so only to the detriment of his health. Like everyone else he had suffered severely as a result of the siege and over and above this he was consumed with anxiety about the shortly expiring contract for the Tomb of Julius. His condition at last appeared to be so grave that his assistant, Antonio Mini, Mini's uncle, Giovanbattista Mini, and the painter Giuliano Bugiardini, all of whom were closely in touch with him, took counsel together and, thinking that the Pope would wish to be informed of the situation, decided to write to Bartolomeo Valori, his commissary-general in Florence. The letter, which was written by Mini's uncle on behalf of the three of them, is dated September 29th 1531.[87] In it he says that Michelangelo, accompanied by Antonio and by Bugiardini, had recently spent two evenings with him; that he had found Michelangelo very drawn and emaciated, and that he and the others had come to the conclusion that he would not live very long unless a remedy were found for his ills. He worked too hard, ate little and poorly and slept less, and a short while before had been suffering from a flux, headaches and giddiness, added to which he was depressed. As he had a strong constitution, matters could be put right if the Pope were to order him not to work in the New Sacristy, which was cold and damp, but elsewhere during the winter, and were to arrange the matter of the Tomb with the Duke of Urbino. As a result of this letter and in order to protect him from the many demands made upon him, Clement, by a brief dated November 21st,[88] forbade him on pain of excommunication to undertake any work whatsoever save that in connection with the Medici Tombs and commanded him to take better care of his health, which the Pope had so much at heart.

To suppose that Michelangelo was melancholy by nature, on the ground that he was often depressed and sometimes distraught, would be to betray a fundamental misunderstanding of his character, since contrary to what has always been believed, his capacity for laughter was at least as great as his capacity for tears. Had it been otherwise, as an artist he might still have had the world at his feet, but as a man he would never have been loved by his friends with a devotion that must be almost unprecedented. Men may bow before the great, but *terribilità* is not an endearing characteristic, nor are the habitually gloomy and morose the idols of their fellows. To evoke the love and the respect of all sorts and conditions of men certainly argues the possession of exceptional qualities, but, perhaps more importantly still, it presupposes the gift of the common touch – an ability to look upon the world not only with compassion and understanding but also with humour and in lightness of heart when the mood befits, and in this ability Michelangelo was never lacking.

Unexpectedly, it may be thought, Michelangelo was always an incorrigible tease and at times might even have been described as 'a fellow of infinite jest, of most excellent fancy'. This quizzical attitude of mind, combined with that natural ease of manner which springs from an innate courtesy, served to commend him to people in all walks of life and not least to those in high place and accustomed to an altogether more conventional, but less attractive mode of approach. 'Whenever Buonarroti comes to see me', said Clement VII, 'I am always seated and I ask him to sit down, because he certainly will, without leave or licence.'[89] But Clement did not esteem him any the less on this score, since he 'respected this man like one sacred and used to converse with him familiarly on subjects both grave and gay as he would have done with his equals'.[90] After all not everyone had had the courage to write to him asking for 'a bull giving licence to rob';[91] not everyone would have had the good sense to treat his proposal for a colossus as a joke, which it was not meant to be;[92] not everyone would have had the wit to allude to Giovanbattista Figiovanni (that 'lying prior' of San Lorenzo, as Fattucci called him) as 'a huckster in the market place' or to refer obliquely to his insolence in having described the design for the Laurentian Library as 'a dovecot'. All these are allusions which Clement cannot fail to have enjoyed, despite some momentary annoyance at Michelangelo's rejection of the idea. For just as Figiovanni did himself no good in the eyes of the Pope by seeking to belittle Michelangelo, since it only confirmed him in his view that Figiovanni was 'a beast', so Michelangelo did himself no harm by categorically refusing, by means of a skilful subterfuge, to have anything to do with an impossible and unworthy project, since Clement seems only to have been the more desirous that he should be master in his own sphere as he, the Pope, was in his.[93]

These letters, like an earlier one to Cardinal Dovizi[94] recommending the services of Sebastiano Luciani, which had been the talk of the entire Vatican, reveal however something else besides the sardonic nature of Michelangelo's wit, and that is the soundness of his judgment of character. In each case he had the precise measure of his correspondent and knew exactly how far he could go with impunity, nor was a single quip miscalculated.

Happily, among the many troubled letters that have survived, there are two belonging to this period which show him as he really was with his friends, when momentarily released from his burdensome preoccupations. One is the letter to Fattucci about Guidotto's dog, which is a piece of sheer nonsense; the other is the one to Sebastiano about the dinner party given by Cuio Dini, which he had so much enjoyed.[95]

But it is not only in his own letters that the light-hearted side of Michelangelo's nature and his love of badinage is proclaimed. He liked to be amused and would keep company with almost anyone who could divert him and make him laugh. Jacopo l'Indaco was one such, 'a charming gossip who always detested work' with whom at one time Michelangelo often took his meals, as he 'was fond of chatting with him and took delight in the pranks he frequently played', though he eventually grew tired of it 'as generally happens in such friendships which consist in frequent gossiping without rhyme or reason', as Vasari remarked, adding sententiously, 'for one could not call it conversation'.[96] Michelangelo was also vastly entertained by the doings of Topolino, who naïvely 'imagined himself to be a good sculptor, though he was a very poor one', but this did not prevent Michelangelo from taking an interest in his work, though he sometimes nearly died of laughter in the process.[97] Similarly, he liked the society of Domenico Menighella, a poor painter, but a very amusing man, who sometimes came to Michelangelo for drawings. Whereupon 'Michelangelo, who could scarcely be persuaded to work for kings, would put aside everything to make simple designs suited to his friend's style and requirements'. These drawings Menighella used to copy and would then go about the country selling them to the peasants. Afterwards he used to cause Michelangelo endless amusement by telling him of his adventures, and how he once added a splendid cope to a figure of St. Francis to please a patron.[98] Bugiardini who was much in Michelangelo's company at one time, especially after the siege, was also a simple fellow, but obviously likeable. On one occasion he was in great difficulty over a composition on which he was working and begged Michelangelo to help him. 'Taking compassion on him, Michelangelo picked up a piece of charcoal and sketched in a row of naked figures, foreshortened in various attitudes',[99] as he was desired. Bugiardini thanked him and after some further difficulty, ultimately completed the work 'in such a way' as Vasari observes, 'that no-one could have supposed that Michelangelo had ever looked at it'. On another occasion Bugiardini did a *Night*, based on Michelangelo's figure in the New Sacristy, but not being satisfied with the owl only, added a 'lantern, a candle, a night-cap, pillows and bats and other things suggestive of darkness', which caused Michelangelo almost to choke with laughter when he saw it.

Very shortly after Bugiardini, Giovanbattista Mini and his nephew Antonio had conferred together over Michelangelo's health, Antonio Mini was obliged, for personal and family reasons, to leave Michelangelo's service, which must have meant a sad parting for both of them, after all that they had been through together both before and during the siege. He had been with Michelangelo for about seven years, having been engaged at the end of 1523.[100] As a pupil Mini was not apt, it being rather a case of 'Draw, Antonio, draw, Antonio – draw and don't waste time',[101] but as a personal assistant or factotum he was admirable. He went everywhere with Michelangelo, did everything for him and was constantly employed on domestic errands of all kinds, particularly after Buonarroto's death, as we learn from the *Ricordi*, in which his name frequently occurs. This was exactly the kind of help and support Michelangelo had always needed, and from the outset of his career to its close he never ceased to require someone to serve him in this capacity; but in this respect he sometimes fared better and sometimes worse with the assistants whom he employed. Piero d'Argenta, who was with him until 1509, always remained extremely attached to him and they were still in communication many years later,[102] but two of his successors, Silvio Falcone and Piero Urbano, were less satisfactory and both were eventually dismissed from his service. In what way Falcone had erred we do not know, except that he had disobeyed Michelangelo's orders – an act of folly he never ceased to regret. He wrote several times begging to be taken back, averring that if this were possible he would consider himself 'the first of men' and in a letter, written not less than fifteen years after his dismissal, he said with great earnestness, 'When I remember the love you bore me while I was in your service, I do not know how I could repay it; and now I tell you that only through having been in your service, wherever I may now happen to be, honour and courtesy are paid me, and this is wholly due to your excellent renown and not to any merit of my own.' But alas for Piero Urbano, who paid no heed to Falcone's warning not to follow his bad example nor to behave as he had done.[103] Instead he was guilty of a gross betrayal of Michelangelo's confidence and that in spite of all the interest and care that had been lavished upon him.[104] In Rome, where he was sent in 1521 to complete *The Risen Christ*, which he practically spoilt, he behaved outrageously;[105] in Florence, when he was left in charge he caused ructions with the family and made so much mischief that Michelangelo at length had no alternative but to discharge him, after giving him a sound beating at the workshop.[106] With a character like Urbano's, Michelangelo's fatherly kindness and consideration were misplaced, but with a character like Mini's the case was entirely different. On Mini's departure for France in November 1531 Michelangelo, in order to assist him to make his fortune and to provide doweries for his two sisters, gave him a number of presents, which included nothing less than the cartoon and the painting of *Leda and the Swan*, besides two chests of models and other designs. But things went wrong and Mini was not only disappointed of his hopes, but tricked into the bargain.[107] Giuliano Buonaccorsi, with whom he had temporarily deposited the picture, refused to release it to him on his return from Paris, averring that the work he had in his possession had not been brought to him by Mini and did not belong to him. This unlooked-for calamity caused Mini so much distress that he became ill and through sheer misery and frustration he died shortly afterwards, not only having lost the dearest of his possessions, but having parted from the master whom he 'loved more than anything in the world'.[108]

There is an undated letter of Michelangelo's in the Buonarroti Archives which may have been written shortly after his return to Florence in July 1533,[109] following a sojourn in Rome of nearly a year, during which time he had engaged Francesco d'Amadore, always known as Urbino, in Antonio Mini's place. In the letter in question he deals with a certain proposal that had been made to him of taking another lad into his service, the son of a foreigner, who had had the temerity to urge it upon him by saying that if Michelangelo were but to see the boy, 'he would chase him not only into the house, but into bed'. In view of the gossip that was current in Florence about the supposed nature of Michelangelo's association with young men, to which he himself refers in another letter,[110] it cannot be believed that this innuendo was not deliberately calculated. On Michelangelo's own showing, however, the suspicions of his contemporaries were unfounded. The contempt with which he dismissed the insolent insinuations of the boy's father, though sufficient to show that they were baseless, constitutes a less convincing proof to the sceptical than the fact that he should have referred to the incident at all, seeing that he could easily have passed it over. In the second letter referred to above he was not concerned with trying to disabuse the mind of a third person about his relationship with Febo di Poggio by saying to him 'You are quite wrong in supposing that my interest in the young man is a sexual interest, because it is nothing of the kind': he was simply saying to the young man himself, '*You* know that there is no truth in the things people say, because *you yourself have proof to the contrary*'.

Since, on the evidence of these letters and having regard to the character of the man himself, there is no ground for supposing that Michelangelo was a paederast, what was the foundation of his friendship with Gherardo Perini, Andrea Quaratesi, Febo di Poggio and perhaps others also, whose names have not come down to us? Nothing more nor less, it would seem, than the mutual attraction existing between a profoundly affectionate older man, who had no children of his own, and young people no less susceptible than their elders to the charms of the magnetic personality of a man who liked and understood them. Gherardo Perini's letters to him were certainly very affectionate, but not more so than countless others he was always receiving from people of all ages and professions. Although Gherardo was well acquainted with Fattucci, Piloto, and others of the Florentine circle, to whom he was accustomed to send greetings, he was living for the most part in Pesaro during the period to which his letters to Michelangelo belong. In them there is nothing to suggest anything but a normal relationship and a special regard for Michelangelo to whom, in one of his three letters, he signed himself 'Yours as a son'.[111]

Not only from his own letters to Michelangelo, 'which are full of tokens of a childish affection' but from another in which he is mentioned, Andrea Quaratesi appears to have been similarly attached to him. Andrea, whose likeness has survived for us in one of Michelangelo's rare portrait drawings,[112] belonged to a noted Florentine family and was Michelangelo's junior by thirty-seven years. He seems to have been a delicate youth and on one occasion, when he had been prevented from supping with Michelangelo owing to an attack of fever, he apologized saying, 'But I shall see to it that I come to supper this evening, if I have to come on all fours'.[113] And when in December 1532 he was again ill while Michelangelo was in Rome, and Giovanni Norchiati, a canon of San Lorenzo, went to see him on Michelangelo's behalf, he sent Michelangelo a thousand greetings, saying that he longed for his return, which was, Norchiati assured him, 'not his desire only, but that of all your friends and acquaintances'.[114] Only in the case of Febo di Poggio, therefore, does Michelangelo seem to have wasted his affection upon a youth unworthy of his regard, and one who was not ashamed to take advantage of his generosity.[115]

To say that these friendships testify to what may be described as the paternal aspect of Michelangelo's nature (the term avuncular now having only a pompous or ludicrous connotation) is not to say that he took no pleasure in the physical beauty of his young friends, if they were so endowed, since a fine eye was, after all, one of his principal assets as an artist. But there is no reason, on this account, to confound a heightened perception of man as 'the beauty of the world! the paragon of animals' with 'the lust of the flesh and the lust of the eyes' in a perverted sense. It may be observed, moreover, that despite his preoccupation with the human figure in his art, Michelangelo's eye for form was not confined to it, if Condivi may be believed when he says that 'he loved not only human beauty, but beauty universally, every beautiful thing – a beautiful horse, a beautiful dog, a beautiful landscape, a beautiful plant, a beautiful mountain, a beautiful forest and every place and thing beautiful and rare'.[116] What Condivi does not remark upon, however, is the charm of Michelangelo's observation of commonplace things and of the simple occupations of everyday life. This interest in domestic detail is illustrated in the Sistine vault, notably in the spandrels and lunettes, many of which are handled with an extraordinary tenderness – a tenderness of which his love of his young friends may be said to be, in some sort, an extension.

In Michelangelo's own day there was, as we know, a certain amount of gossip and speculation about his private affairs, and there has been ever since. Thus, some 'talk' or malicious rumour must have reached Rome in December 1521, when Lionardo the saddler, whom we may conjecture to have been an older man, wrote to him in guarded terms that are difficult to interpret. At the conclusion of a letter dated the 24th he advised Michelangelo 'to abandon practices harmful to the body and the mind, in order that they may not hurt the soul'. Most unfortunately Michelangelo's reply to this exhortation has not been preserved, but on January 4th 1522 Lionardo acknowledged it, saying, among a number of other things, 'One piece of news among the others you give me surpasses all the rest, and that is that you are cured of a malady from which few men recover, but I am not surprised, on the other hand, because few are like you. Persevere.' Then on January 22nd he wrote again to the same effect – 'I am delighted you are free of a malady dangerous to soul and body'.[117]

Cryptic references of this sort are, of course, designed to baffle the curious and there is little doubt that they succeed in doing so. It therefore seems almost an intrusion in this instance to try to penetrate further or to attempt explanations as to their meaning, which can, at best, never be other than tentative. But as it has not been vouchsafed that the rest should be silence, some further consideration must be given to the problems which they pose. According to Giovanni Papini, the malady – *malattia* – in question was the *mal francese*,[118] but to begin with we cannot be sure that *malattia* was here used in a specifically physical sense, since it can be given a more general connotation, as in the announcement, *Popolo, e non è il Frate la tua malattia*.[119] Supposing, however, that the word was here used in the normal way and not obliquely, there still seems no reason why Papini should connect this illness with Michelangelo's indisposition of 1520;

alternatively, if there are grounds for so doing, they should have been stated. Because of Lionardo's allusion to the soul, Papini infers that the 'illness' from which Michelangelo was suffering was the result of sin, in which case it could be, he says, none other than the *morbus gallicus* – a possible inference perhaps, but still only an inference, on the basis of which Papini does not hesitate at a later stage to assert categorically, 'as we have seen, when over forty years of age, Michelangelo had a venereal disease'.[120] But Papini cannot have it both ways. If he is right in identifying the *malattia* with the *mal francese*, then in the context of the early sixteenth century he is wrong both in describing it as a 'venereal disease' and in supposing that it was morally reprehensible, since at this period, only some twenty-five years after it had first made its appearance in Florence, it was regarded as a pestilence and spread as such. One of the earliest mentions of it is in the *Diario* of Luca Landacci, in which, on May 28th 1496, he made this entry: 'A certain complaint began to be prevalent here, which is called French boils and looks like small-pox; it went on increasing and no cure could be found for it.' And indeed, it spread so rapidly in the insanitary conditions of Renaissance Italy that on December 5th of the same year Landucci, who was an apothecary by trade and therefore in a better position to know than most, made a further entry to this effect: 'At this time the complaint of French boils had spread all through Florence and the surrounding country and also to every city in Italy and it lasted a long time.'[121] The *mal francese* having therefore no specific connection in the eyes of Michelangelo's contemporaries with 'the soft embraces of love', the notion of sin in relation to it must be ruled out. It must be emphasized, furthermore, that in his poem *Siphilis sive Morbus Gallicus*, which was published in 1530, the Veronese physician, Girolamo Fracastoro, treats of it purely and simply as a contagious disease, like any other, without the least suspicion or suggestion that it might have been venereal in origin. Had it been otherwise he could not have dedicated the work to Cardinal Bembo, which was rendered possible because 'no moral stigma attached to it in those days'.[122]

Apart from the above arguments against the assumption that Michelangelo had been suffering from the *morbus gallicus*, it is open to doubt whether the passages in Lionardo's letters are capable of having this construction put upon them. In view of Lionardo's obvious relief at receiving Michelangelo's assurances that his fears and suspicions were groundless, something more serious than an illness seems to be indicated, in which case not fornication, but a homosexual relationship might be implied. But to say this is *not* necessarily to go to the length of imputing 'the unmentionable vice', against which the sternest measures had from time to time been taken in Florence, where, for all that it was held in abhorrence, it had long been rife. What prompted Lionardo to caution Michelangelo when and as he did we shall, in all likelihood, never know, but one thing at least we may deduce from these hopelessly inadequate premises, and that is that whatever the practices to which Michelangelo had been addicted, he had been cured of them by January 1522, and for all we know, long before that. The only suggestion of a relationship in which something more intimate may perhaps have been involved is afforded by the five more or less impassioned poems[123] addressed to him by Giovanni da Pistoia (who may probably be identified with Giovanni di Benedetto, later Secretary of the Florentine Academy) to whom Michelangelo addressed the sardonic sonnet, *I'ho già fatto un gozzo in questo stento*[124] which he wrote during the time he was working on the Sistine vault. About this friendship we know nothing else, except that the two men afterwards quarrelled, judging by Giovanni's fifth sonnet, *Chosi intervien, quando un perfetto amore*, but as to when this parting took place we cannot even hazard a guess.

From an examination of the foregoing arguments we are led inevitably to a consideration of the cognate problem of Michelangelo's sexual orientation. This has long been a subject of interest, curiosity and debate, as if it were really within either the province or the capacity of the mediocre to propose a norm for the genius. Nevertheless, however little people may or may not know about Michelangelo, of two things are they infallibly certain; namely, that he had improper relations with young men, on the one hand, and a late love affair with Vittoria Colonna, on the other. To this the pertinent information that he died at Amboise is sometimes added. From the time of Carlo Parlogreco onwards, he has also been subjected to a certain amount of psychological and pseudo-psychological investigation, while in addition, writers on kindred subjects have tended whenever possible, to introduce his name in order to lend a cachet to their theses.

In Havelock Ellis's submission, 'there can be no doubt that Michelangelo was an invert', and that 'this abnormality provides the key to the whole of his art'.[125] In using the term 'invert', Ellis does so, not in accordance with Krafft-Ebing's definition, *anima muliebris in corpore virili inclusa*, but in accordance with his own. Hence, by sexual inversion he means 'a deviation of the sexual instinct towards a person of the same sex, owing to a congenital abnormality'.[126] In other words, sexual inversion as here used means a homosexual, as opposed to a heterosexual, focus of the emotions. But while describing Michelangelo as being indifferent to women though extremely sensible to the beauty of men, Ellis is firm in his insistence on the fact that we are not, on that account, warranted in supposing that he had physical relations with men. As we have already seen, little if anything can be said about this, and then only with the strictest reservation.

Is Ellis right, however, in reaffirming what has so often been said before – that Michelangelo was indifferent to women? On the strength of his poetry alone it is surely obvious that this was not so. What could be more normal in sentiment and observation, for instance, than the sonnet *Quanto si gode, lieta e ben contesta*,[127] which he wrote in Bologna, on the back of a letter from Buonarroto dated December 24th 1507, presumably during a moment of leisure when nearing the end of his labours on the colossal bronze of Julius II? Although Michelangelo was thirty-three when he wrote it, this poem is characterized by a sensuous charm that is eminently youthful, which may be said to afford some ground for thinking that, like many whose creative energies are otherwise absorbed, Michelangelo's development in this direction was typically late. There is, however, no ground for supposing, as some have done, that the lady addressed was his mistress. It would seem, on the contrary, more probable that he did not even know her name, but that his artist's eye had been caught by her beauty and his poet's imagination by the seductiveness of her person.

His early Madonnas, in their singular serenity and purity of heart, provide another case in point. Though evidently the product of a contemplative vision untroubled by desire, they certainly do not spring from an attitude of indifference. Like the domestic scenes, mentioned above, which he portrayed with rare pleasure and understanding, they reveal anything but an insensitivity to the charms of women. His perceptible love of children, who figure prominently in his work up to the end of his third Roman period, would suggest, moreover, a temperament, in some respects, peculiarly adapted to the incidental pleasures of married life.

Finally, there is the *Leda*; in so far as the quality of the original may be assessed in the versions that have come down to us. If the question were asked in relation to it, 'Could it have been painted by anyone without personal experience of a normal kind?', no categorical answer could be given, more especially not in the case of an artist of unusual imaginative powers. But if the question were differently put and it were asked – 'Could it have been painted by such an artist, if he were wholly inverted in the sense described?', then the answer would probably be in the negative. At the same time, it is important to observe that, notwithstanding its patent eroticism, the picture can be contemplated without embarrassment and is so entirely devoid of any suspicion of prurience that perhaps only a Victorian could have supposed it to be unsuitable for public exhibition,[128] or a *Piagnone* have thought of destroying it.

Taking the *Leda* and the *Aurora* as his touchstones, Papini, who discredits the notion that Michelangelo was ever a paederast, is emphatic in the assertion of his normality, and, on the assumption that both works presuppose the direct experience of a heterosexual relationship, hastens to repudiate another supposition, namely that Michelangelo was impotent.[129]

To justify this ultimate intrusion, some more definitive argument is required to support any conclusion that may be reached, one way or the other, since for a number of reasons the possibility cannot be discounted. But as the problem can be better discussed in a different connection, it will here suffice to remark upon a feature of his work which, analogously considered, may perhaps have a personal explanation, of which, in terms of his art, even Michelangelo himself may have been unaware. Can it be that in the art of a man of whom, as Pierre Langéard has rightly said, *la nudité chez Michelange est austère*,[130] there is no psychological explanation for what may well be regarded as the placing of an undue emphasis upon the pudenda? If there is, then the possibility that this overemphasis is, in some way, compensatory cannot be overlooked. It may be that in the mature perfection of his male figures Michelangelo sought subconsciously for a counterbalance to some defect or partial defect, either physical or psychosomatic, within himself. On any other hypothesis it is difficult to account for the frankness of a statement and the frequency of its repetition which even his contemporaries regarded as excessive.[131] For although Aretino's invective commands no respect, it must be allowed that in the case of the *David* the Florentines themselves deemed the addition of a codpiece desirable.[132] Had Michelangelo been an artist of a different type, with obvious sensual or erotic leanings, the question as to the cause of this particular idiosyncrasy would not arise; but seeing that of all artists he is one of the most asexual, it cannot be avoided. For it is precisely in its asexual aspect that the secret of much of his art resides, in regard to which let us hear the conclusion of the whole matter, as it is epitomized in Langéard's words – *Les figures plastiques les plus belles, les héros littéraires les plus admirés sont à l'image de l'artiste peu ou prou intersexuels.*[133] The more complex problem of his personal bias is, however, less easily resolved.

It was not until the beginning of 1531, about five months after Florence had capitulated,[134] that Michelangelo began to renew communications with his friends in Rome. In a short letter, dated February 24th,[135] written in response to a call he had received from Domenico Menighella, made at Michelangelo's request, Sebastiano Luciani spoke feelingly of the acute anxiety he had experienced on Michelangelo's account during the siege and of his own continuing bewilderment at the disasters that had overtaken them in Rome, which he described as being beyond anything they could have conceived. Indeed, such was the traumatic effect of all that they had witnessed, that he confessed that after four years he still did not seem to be the Bastiano he had been before the sack and was still unable to collect himself. Before very long, however, he had begun to concern himself with Michelangelo's affairs and from April onwards he acted as his go-between in the newly reopened negotiations with the Duke of Urbino over the Tomb of Julius, which had been interrupted first by the sack and then by the siege.

Some time after October 3rd and before November 21st Sebastiano was appointed *Piombatore* in succession to Fra Mariano Fetti, a dignity with which he was immensely pleased, though the thought of becoming a *frate* caused him as much amusement as he knew it would cause Michelangelo, to whom he wrote, declaring that he was 'the finest *fratazo* in Rome'.[136] To the implied honour of this appointment he adverted in his next letter, that of December 5th, in which, while dealing at length with the progress of the negotiations, he expressed his conviction that once the matter had been settled, the Pope would surely seek to content him, for, as he said, 'It would seem to me fitting, if His Holiness has made Cavalieri a knight and me a *Frate*, that he should, much more fitttingly, make you a duke or a king.' But all that Michelangelo coveted was peace of mind, which depended, in turn, upon an honourable settlement of the Julius affair. To this end Sebastiano fought manfully; being prepared, it seems, to undertake anything in defence of Michelangelo's reputation, if we may judge from his letter of April 6th 1532, in which he revealed his attitude with perhaps only a touch of hyperbole – 'Do not marvel if I seem to you to have taken up the sword in your cause, for God knows I would hazard my own life, my poor son's and all that I have for your sake.'[137]

Thus, by March 1532 Sebastiano was able to advise him that the terms of the new contract were virtually agreed and that with his presence and the Pope's favour everything would be completed to his satisfaction. At an earlier stage of the proceedings Michelangelo had been apprehensive about his reception in Rome, owing no doubt to the part he had played in the defence of Florence during the siege when, certain tales having been repeated to the Pope, who had shrugged his shoulders, saying, 'Michelangelo is wrong; I never did him any harm.' But Sebastiano assured him that his fears were groundless and that everyone was looking forward with great pleasure to his arrival and were all anxious to please him. If, in exemplification of his name, the Pope's clemency towards him may be taken as a tribute to Michelangelo's virtues, much more must it be recognized as evidence of his own magnanimity, a consciousness of which, on Michelangelo's part, must necessarily have increased the emotional strain of his first audience – an occasion which both men must have found profoundly moving; Michelangelo being faced by a Pope aged almost beyond recognition, though not wholly broken, by the appalling tragedy through which he had passed; Clement by a man whom he still loved and honoured in spite of what, from his personal point of view (Michelangelo's obligations as a Florentine apart) must have seemed an almost unpardonable defection. In like manner, passionately though his friends desired to see him and he them, their meeting after the ordeals which they had all undergone, he in Florence and they in Rome, cannot have been otherwise than poignant, the visible marks of the years being, no doubt, out of proportion to the actual time that had elapsed, besides which how many an empty glass must have been turned down.

During this brief visit of under three weeks Michelangelo stayed at the Belvedere as the guest of his friend Benvenuto della Volpaia, the clockmaker, who had there been appointed to the keepership. Earlier in the year, when Michelangelo's visit had first been mooted, Benvenuto had been assiduous over the arrangements for his reception,[138] informing him, among a number of other things, that as soon as he knew he was expected, he would be on the look out from the vantage point of Bramante's winding staircase, where Michelangelo would be able to see him as he approached, and there is no reason to suppose that he was less attentive when the time came. Michelangelo evidently enjoyed his visit and on his return to Florence at the beginning of May wrote appreciatively to Benvenuto in acknowledgment of the hospitality accorded him. He received in reply a letter in which Benvenuto protested that such formalities were unnecessary between them and that even if he were to receive no letters for a thousand years the friendship would remain unimpaired, such were his feelings towards him.[139] Unhappily, however, much less than a thousand years remained to him as he died suddenly a month later through over-exertion in the intense heat of the summer of that year. In Sebastiano del Piombo's temporary absence from Rome the news of his death was conveyed to Michelangelo by Pierantonio Cecchini,[140] a member of Cardinal Ridolfi's household, who, with typical Renaissance courtesy, refrained from offering his condolences, knowing, as he said, how close their friendship had been.

On the occasion of this first visit Michelangelo had been unable to stay in his own house, because of the disrepair into which it had fallen, partly owing to his long absence, and partly owing to the devastation that had been wrought by the German and Spanish hordes throughout the city during the sack. In a postscript to his letter of February 24th Sebastiano had informed him of its lamentable condition, since little more than the walls remained standing, and of what was worse – namely that all the worked marbles for the architectural frame of the Tomb had fallen or been cast down. In August 1532, however, when, with the Pope's permission, Michelangelo returned to Rome for a prolonged stay, he decided to take up residence in the Macel de' Corvi, some preliminary repairs having presumably been carried out in the meantime. Knowing the conditions, both Sebastiano and another friend, Bartolomeo Angiolini, were much concerned about the arrangements and were careful to provide at least the minimum furnishings, as we know from Sebastiano's letter of August 13th[141] and Angiolini's of the 16th.[142] In the latter Angiolini concludes with an expression of his desire to serve him in other ways, and from a brief note of September 1532, relating to a monetary transaction, it would appear that at that date he was already acting as his man of business, which he continued to do when Michelangelo returned to settle permanently in Rome two years later. It is certain, in any case, that when in July 1533 Michelangelo reluctantly returned to Florence to continue the work on the Medici Tombs, it was Angiolini who took over the superintendence of his property, the house and garden which he visited frequently, in order that he might keep him informed about everything – the arrangements about the wine, the ripening of the figs, the maturing of the grapes, the well-being of the cock – *messer gallo triomfano* – the hens, and the cats who lamented his absence, happily without serious loss of appetite – all of which were evidently matters of interest.

During the four months of Michelangelo's penultimate sojourn in Florence, Angiolini wrote to him constantly and always in the most affectionate terms, addressing him in one letter, written shortly after he left Rome, as *Honr^do & sopra tutti li altri da me amato michelagniolo Car^smo*, since, like so many of Michelangelo's friends who knew him well and really cared for him, Angiolini loved him devotedly – sometimes, in his case, it might seem, almost too well for his own tranquility. For some reason that is not given, but is referred to several times, he felt himself to be incalculably in Michelangelo's debt, as witness one passage in particular, which occurs in his letter of August 2nd, where he wrote, 'When I consider how enormous are my obligations to you, I do not think that if I lived a thousand years I could ever repay you for the least part of them. I therefore pray God that He may repay you for me in such a way that you cannot gainsay it.'

Although neither of them could have realized the possibility at the time, Angiolini's prayer may perhaps have been already answered, since from their correspondence it would appear that it was he who had introduced Michelangelo to Tommaso de' Cavalieri,[143] with whom he formed the deepest and most enduring friendship of his life. Cavalieri was the only one among the many friends of this period who outlived him and was the one whom he 'loved far more than all the rest'.[144] This was why he had been so reluctant to leave Rome; this was why he was so restless and unhappy in Florence. It is true that the new ducal régime by which the old republican order had been supplanted was anathema to him and that he had, in consequence, some fear for his life, but this was not the prime cause of his discontent. Hence, when he took leave of Florence for the last time a year later the pain inseparable from such a departure was mitigated: not because he was not anxious on political grounds to be gone, but for the all-sufficient reason that, wherever he might be, his heart was already in Rome.[145]

References to which the superior numbers in the text of the Introduction relate

1. *Sanuto, I, 224.*
2. *Aristotle, Poetics, VI.*
3. *d'Ollanda, trans. Holroyde, pp. 236 et seq.*
4. *Vasari, VIII, p. 310.*
5. *No. 227.*
6. *Rolland, pp. 25 et passim.*
7. *Thode, I, pp. 229 et passim.*
8. *Grimm, I, pp. 256 et passim.*
9. *Harford, II, pp. 211 et seq.*
10. *Duppa, pp. 257 et seq.*
11. *Symonds, II, pp. 360 et seq.*
12. *Condivi, XVIII.*
13. *Venturi, A., Arch. Stor. dell'Arte, 1888, p. 4.*
14. *No. 1.*
15. *Vasari, VII, p. 152.*
16. *Appendixes 11 & 28.*
17. *Nos. 8, 227.*
18. *Grimm, I, pp. 131 et seq.*
19. *Condivi, XII.*
20. *No. 107.*
21. *Condivi, XXXII.*
22. *Ibid., XXXIX et seq. & Appendix 9.*
23. *Gaye, II, p. 91.*
24. *No. 157.*
25. *No. 40, n.1.*
26. *Nos. 35, 37.*
27. *No. 77.*
28. *No. 83 & Appendix 9.*
29. *Steinmann, Sixt. II, p. 787*
30. *Frey, Briefe, p. 1.*
31. *No. 76.*
32. *No. 92.*
33. *Frey, Briefe, p. 20.*
34. *No. 258.*
35. *Wittkower & Steinmann, p. 445, & Wolfe, p. 69.*
36. *No. 182.*
37. *No. 49.*
38. *Nos. 22, 23, 24.*
39. *No. 185.*
40. *Gotti, II, p. 19.*
41. *No. 272.*

42. Frey, *Briefe*, p. 309.

43. No. 363.

44. No. 82.

45. Condivi, VIII, IX.

46. Frey, *Briefe*, pp. 16–18.

47. No. 60.

48. No. 149.

49. No. 154.

50. Repertorium Kunst., XXIX, 1906, p. 398.

51. Appendix 22.

52. Guasti, p. 297.

53. No. 51.

54. Hale, p. 77.

55. No. 45.

56. Frey, *Briefe*, p. 23.

57. Ibid., p. 28.

58. Ibid., p. 30.

59. Appendixes 14, 13, 16.

60. No. 227.

61. Duppa, pp. 93 et seq.

62. Roscoe, IV, p. 226.

63. Milanesi, Corr., p. 16.

64. Ibid., p. 20.

65. Ibid., p. 24.

66. Ibid., p. 44.

67. Frey, *Briefe*, pp. 276 et seq.

68. Appendix 16.

69. Frey, *Briefe*, pp. 161, 286, 268.

70. Ibid., p. 279.

71. Ibid., p. 271.

72. Pastor, X, p. 361.

73. Frey, *Briefe*, p. 208.

74. Ibid., p. 264.

75. Appendix 14.

76. No. 164.

77. Frey, *Briefe*, p. 265.

78. Ibid., p. 235.

79. Ibid., p. 218.

80. No. 173.

81. Frey, *Briefe*, p. 237 & No. 173.

82. Ibid., p. 273.

83. Appendix 19.

84. Serassi, I, p. 171.

85. Frey, *Briefe*, p. 294.

86. Appendix 21.

87. Gaye, II, pp. 228 et seq.

88. Steinmann, Sixt. II, p. 742.

89. Holroyde, p. 237 n.

90. Condivi, XLVI.

91. No. 125.

92. No. 176 & Frey, *Briefe*, p. 271.

93. Frey, *Briefe*, pp. 293, 277.

94. No. 145 & Appendix 15.

95. Nos. 171, 170.

96. Vasari, III, p. 681.

97. Ibid., VII, p. 283.

98. Ibid., VII, p. 282.

99. Ibid., VI, p. 207 et seq.

100. Frey, *Briefe*, p. 197.

101. Wilde, p. 62 (31 recto & Plate LIII).

102. Frey, *Briefe*, pp. 304 et seq.

103. Symonds, II, pp. 341 et seq. & Frey, *Briefe*, pp. 84 et seq. (Note: Symonds refers to two Silvios, but they were almost certainly one and the same.)

104. Milanesi, p. 578 & Nos. 142, 143 etc.

105. Milanesi, Corr. pp. 28 et seq.

106. No. 149.

107. Tolnay, III, pp. 190 et seq.

108. Frey, *Briefe*, p. 318.

109. No. 195 & Appendix 24.

110. No. 198.

111. Frey, Dicht., pp. 504 et seq.

112. Plate XXVI.

113. Wilde, p. 97.

114. Frey, *Briefe*, p. 324.

115. Symonds, II, p. 403 & Appendix 25.

116. *Condivi, LXV.*

117. *Frey, Briefe, pp. 185, 186, 188.*

118. *Papini, p. 498.*

119. *Landucci, p. 165.*

120. *Papini, p. 512.*

121. *Landucci, pp. 132, 141.*

122. *Fracastoro, p. 179.*

123. *Frey, Dicht., pp. 260 et seq. & Papini, p. 192.*

124. *Guasti, p. 158.*

125. *Ellis, pp. 40 et seq.*

126. *Ibid., p. 13.*

127. *Guasti, p. 178.*

128. *Gould, p. 98.*

129. *Papini, pp. 511 et seq.*

130. *Langéard, p. 164.*

131. *Pastor, XII, pp. 658 et seq.*

132. *Gaye, II, pp. 332 et seq.*

133. *Langéard, p. 177.*

134. *Appendix 19.*

135. *Milanesi, Corr., p. 36.*

136. *Ibid., p. 44. (Note: This undated letter was written some time between October 3rd and November 21st 1531. It is to this letter that the postscript on p. 68 belongs. It therefore precedes Sebastiano del Piombo's next letter, dated December 5th 1531, on p. 74.)*

137. *Ibid., p. 96.*

138. *Gotti, II, p. 75. (Note: The date 1531 is O.S. cf. Milanesi, Corr., p. 80.)*

139. *Frey, Briefe, p. 325.*

140. *Ibid., p. 327.*

141. *Milanesi, Corr., p. 102.*

142. *Symonds, II, pp. 390 et seq.*

143. *Appendix 23.*

144. *Vasari, VII, p. 271.*

145. *Draft 6.*

Chronology : 1475-1534

This chronology is designed as a framework to the letters, in order that Michelangelo's main movements and the work on which he was principally engaged during successive periods may be co-ordinated with his correspondence. The works executed under contract, or to which specific dates may be assigned, are indicated in larger type; those that were executed pari passu or to which no specific dates may be assigned, are indicated in smaller type. The relative type sizes have, therefore, no relevance to the question of artistic merit.

For exhaustive chronologies the reader is referred to A. Venturi, IX, Pt. I, pp. 627–714, or to H. Thode, I, pp. 343–484.

1475	CAPRESE AND FLORENCE
	Michelangelo born at Caprese in the Casentino where his father, Lodovico, was Podestà – *Monday, March 6th.*
	Lodovico and his family returned to Florence on the termination of his office – *April 1st.*
	Michelangelo put to nurse at Settignano.
1481	Death of Michelangelo's mother Francesca, aged about 26.
1485	Marriage of Lodovico to Lucrezia Ubaldini, his second wife.
	Michelangelo attended the school of Francesco da Urbino from about this time.
1488	Michelangelo apprenticed to Domenico and David Ghirlandaio – *April 1st.*
1489	Entered the sculpture school in the Medici Garden under Bertoldo di Giovanni, a pupil of Donatello.
1490	Received into the household of Lorenzo the Magnificent.
1492	Death of Lorenzo the Magnificent – *April 8th.*
	Michelangelo returned to his father's house but subsequently went back to live in the Casa de' Medici.
	Studied anatomy in rooms provided by the Prior of S. Spirito.
1494	FLORENCE, BOLOGNA, VENICE, BOLOGNA
	Flight to Bologna and Venice – *October.* Returned to

MADONNA OF THE STAIRS
BATTLE OF THE CENTAURS
HERCULES
WOODEN CRUCIFIX FOR S. SPIRITO

		Bologna. Lived in the house of Gianfrancesco Aldovrandi.
S. PETRONIO AND AN ANGEL FOR THE ARK OF S. DOMENICO, BOLOGNA		Expulsion of Piero de' Medici, 'the Unfortunate', from Florence – *November 9th*. Rise to power of Savonarola.
	1495	BOLOGNA, FLORENCE
		Michelangelo returned to Florence.
S. JOHN SLEEPING CUPID	*1496*	FLORENCE, ROME
		Arrived in Rome – *June 25th*.
	1497	ROME, CARRARA
BACCHUS		Death of Michelangelo's stepmother, Lucrezia – *July*.
		Commissioned to execute the *Pietà* – the *Madonna della Febbre*. Went to quarry the marble required in Carrara – *November*.
	1498	CARRARA, ROME
		In Cararra at least until April.
MADONNA DELLA FEBBRE		Execution of Savonarola in Florence – *May 22nd*.
		Michelangelo in Rome. Formal contract for the Pietà – *August 27th*.
	1499	ROME
		Pietà probably completed by the end of the year.
	1500	ROME
		No records exist of the work on which Michelangelo was engaged in this year.
	1501	ROME, FLORENCE
		Michelangelo in Florence. Contract for the 15 figures for the Piccolomini Chapel in Siena – *May 22nd*. *[See below]*
		Contract for the *David* – *August 16th*.
DAVID DONI TONDO	*1502*	FLORENCE
		Contract for the bronze *David* – *August 12th*. *[Completed by Benedetto da Rovezzano in 1508]*

Chronology : 1475-1534

1503   FLORENCE

Contract for figures of the 12 Apostles for S. Maria del Fiore – *April 24th.* [*Contract not fulfilled*]

Election of Pius III (Francesco Piccolomini) – *September 22nd.*

Death of Pius III – *October 19th.*

Election of Julius II (Giuliano della Rovere) – *November 1st.*

DAVID
DONI TONDO

1504   FLORENCE

Completion of the *David* – *April.*

New agreement for the figures for the Piccolomini Chapel – *October 11th.* [*Contract not fulfilled*]

Commission to execute the fresco, *The Battle of Cascina,* for the Sala del Consiglio – *October.*

1505   FLORENCE, ROME, CARRARA

Summoned to Rome by Julius II. Commissioned to execute his Tomb – *March.*

THE BATTLE OF CASCINA
(cartoon)
BRUGES MADONNA
PITTI AND TADDEI TONDI

Went to Carrara to quarry the marbles required – *April.*

Returned to Rome – *December.*

1506   ROME, FLORENCE, BOLOGNA

Fled from Rome to Florence – *April 17th.*

CASCINA CARTOON COMPLETED

Left for Bologna to make his submission to the Pope – *November (28th).*

Commissioned to execute the bronze statue of Julius II – *December.*

1507   BOLOGNA

Remained in Bologna, being engaged on the bronze statue.

JULIUS II
(seated figure in bronze)

1508   BOLOGNA, FLORENCE, ROME

Completed the bronze statue – *February.*

Returned to Florence – *February.*

Emancipated by Lodovico from paternal control – *March 13th.*

Recalled to Rome by Julius II.

Commissioned to paint the vault of the Sistine Chapel. Initial payment – *May 10th.*

1509 ROME

Engaged on the Sistine vault.

1510 ROME, FLORENCE, BOLOGNA

Completed the first half of the Sistine vault – *August.*

Went to Bologna via Florence to obtain payment from the Pope – *September.*

Returned to Rome – *October.*

In Florence en route for Bologna, to obtain a second payment – *December.*

PAINTING OF THE SISTINE VAULT

1511 FLORENCE, ROME

Returned to Rome to proceed with the second half of the Sistine vault – *January 7th.*

1512 ROME, FLORENCE

In Florence on a brief visit – *June.*

Returned to Rome – *July.*

Sack of Prato – *August 29th.* Return of the Medici to Florence – *September.*

Uncovering of the completed vault of the Sistine Chapel – *October 31st.*

Michelangelo prepared new designs for the Tomb of Julius II – *November.*

In Florence on a brief visit. Returned to Rome – *December.*

TOMB OF JULIUS II
(MOSES, THE CAPTIVES AND THE ARCHITECTURAL FRAME)

1513 ROME

Death of Julius II – *February 20th/21st.*

Election of Leo X (Giovanni de' Medici) – *March 11th.*

First Contract for the Tomb of Julius between Michelangelo and the della Rovere heirs – *May 6th.*

Chronology : 1475-1534

	1514	ROME, FLORENCE
		Contract for *The Risen Christ* – *June 14th.*
		In Florence on a brief visit – *August.*
	1515	ROME, FLORENCE, CARRARA
		In Florence on a brief visit – *April.*
		In Carrara to obtain marbles for the Tomb – *September.*
TOMB OF JULIUS II (MOSES, THE CAPTIVES AND THE ARCHITECTURAL FRAME)	1516	ROME, FLORENCE, CARRARA
		Second Contract for the Tomb of Julius II. Left Rome for Florence – *July 8th.*
		In Florence – *August.*
		Left for Carrara – *September.*
		Left Carrara for Rome in connection with a design for the proposed façade of S. Lorenzo in Florence – *December 5th.*
	1517	CARRARA, FLORENCE
		Returned to Carrara – *January 9th.*
		Engaged at the quarries.
		Returned to Florence to prepare a model of the façade – *August.* Remained there for the rest of the year.
	1518	ROME, CARRARA, FLORENCE, PIETRA SANTA
		In Rome – *January.*
FAÇADE OF S. LORENZO TOMB OF JULIUS II		Contract for the façade of S. Lorenzo – *January 19th.* Returned to Carrara.
		Returned to Florence en route for Pietra Santa, where he opened up the new marble quarries during the course of the year – *February.*
		Purchased the site for a workshop in the Via Mozza in Florence – *November 24th.*
	1519	PIETRA SANTA, ROME, FLORENCE, CARRARA
		In Rome on a brief visit – *July.*
		Returned to Pietra Santa – *August.*

lxii

FAÇADE OF S. LORENZO
TOMB OF JULIUS II

NEW SACRISTY, S. LORENZO
THE MEDICI TOMBS
LAURENTIAN LIBRARY
TOMB OF JULIUS II

Visited Carrara to see his apprentice Pietro Urbano who was ill – *August/September*.

Returned to Florence – *September 12th*.

1520   FLORENCE

Cancellation of the Contract for the façade of S. Lorenzo – *March 10th*.

Engaged on designs of the New Sacristy of S. Lorenzo – *November*.

1521   FLORENCE, CARRARA

Sent Pietro Urbano to Rome to complete *The Risen Christ* – *March*.

Went to Carrara to order marbles for the New Sacristy. Returned to Florence – *April*.

Dismissed Pietro Urbano from his service – *September/ October*.

Death of Leo X – *December 1st*.

1522   FLORENCE

Continued work on the New Sacristy.

Election of Adrian VI (Adrian Dedel of Utrecht) – *January 9th*.

Entry of Adrian VI into Rome – *August 29th*.

1523   FLORENCE, ROME

Death of Adrian VI – *September 14th*.

Election of Clement VII (Giulio de' Medici) – *November 19th*.

Michelangelo in Rome on a brief visit of congratulation to Clement VII – *December*.

Engagement of Antonio Mini by Piero Gondi in Michelangelo's absence – *December 12th*.

1524   FLORENCE

Michelangelo occupied on models for the Medici Tombs, designs for interior details of the New Sacristy and on designs and preliminary work for the Laurentian Library.

Accepted a monthly salary of 50 ducats from the Pope –
January.

1525	FLORENCE

Appointed Giovan Francesco Fattucci as his attorney in
the negotiations for a new Contract for the Tomb of
Julius II – *June 14th.*

1526   FLORENCE

Prepared designs for the ciborium and doorway of the
New Sacristy – *February.*

Progressed with work on the Library – *April.*

Progressed with work on the Tombs and the interior of
the New Sacristy – *June.*

Requested to curtail expenses owing to political events –
November 4th.

Negotiations over the Tomb of Julius II brought to a
standstill – *November 4th.*

NEW SACRISTY, S. LORENZO
THE MEDICI TOMBS
LAURENTIAN LIBRARY
TOMB OF JULIUS II

1527   FLORENCE

Sack of Rome – *May 6th.*

Expulsion of the Medici from Florence – *May 17th.*

Brief of Michelangelo's appointment to superintend the
fortifications at Bologna – *November 29th. [No action was
taken in respect of this.]*

Clement VII escaped to Orvieto – *December 9th.*

1528   FLORENCE

Death of Michelangelo's brother Buonarroto – *July 2nd.*

Michelangelo engaged on preparations for the anticipated
siege of Florence – *October.*

1529   FLORENCE, PISA, LEGHORN, FERRARA

Elected a member of the *Nove della Milizia* – *January 10th.*

Appointed *governatore generale* of the Tuscan fortifications –
April 29th – and thereafter inspected fortifications at Pisa
and Leghorn – *April, May, June.*

FLORENTINE FORTIFICATIONS
LEDA AND THE SWAN

WORK AT S. LORENZO SUSPENDED

Left for Ferrara to study the fortifications there – *July 28th.*

Returned to Florence from Ferrara – *September (9th).*

FLORENTINE FORTIFICATIONS
LEDA AND THE SWAN

WORK AT S. LORENZO SUSPENDED

Fled to Venice – *September 21st.*

Declared a rebel by the *Balìa* – *September 30th.*

Florence invested by the Papal forces – *October 10th.*

Michelangelo left Venice for Ferrara – *November 9th.*

Returned to Florence – *November (20th).*

1530 FLORENCE

Florence capitulated – *August 12th.*

1531 FLORENCE

Death of Michelangelo's father, Lodovico.

Completion of *The Dawn* and *The Night* for the Medici Tombs – *September.*

Brief forbidding Michelangelo to work for anyone save the Pope – *November 21st.* Antonio Mini left Michelangelo's service.

1532 FLORENCE, ROME

Michelangelo left for Rome – *April (6th).*

Third Contract for the Tomb of Julius II – *April 29th.* Michelangelo left for Florence.

Alessandro de' Medici proclaimed Duke of Florence – *May 1st.*

Michelangelo returned to Rome – *August (end).*

MEDICI TOMBS
LAURENTIAN LIBRARY
TOMB OF JULIUS II

1533 In Florence on a brief visit – *March.* Subsequently returned to Rome, perhaps after refusing to ride out with Duke Alessandro to determine the site for the new citadel, on which work was begun on May 29th.

Returned to Florence – *July 10th.*

Met Clement VII at San Miniato del Tedesco – *September 22nd.*

Returned to Rome – *November.*

1534 ROME, FLORENCE, ROME

Returned to Florence for the last time – *(May/June).*

Returned to live permanently in Rome – *September 23rd.*

Death of Clement VII – *September 25th.*

I

LETTERS
1 - 5

From Rome
1496 - 1499

1. The Courtyard of Cardinal Riario's Palace   *Palazzo della Cancellaria, Rome*

I. From Rome : 1496-1499

¶ [To Lorenzo di Pier Francesco de' Medici in Florence]

1

Christ. On the 2nd day of July 1496.[1]

State Archives
Florence
Mil. cccxlii
From Rome
July 2nd
1496

Magnificent Lorenzo, etc.[2] — This is only to let you know that we arrived safely last Saturday and at once went to call upon the Cardinal di San Giorgio,[3] to whom I presented your letter. He seemed pleased to see me and immediately desired me to go and look at certain figures;[4] this took me all day, so I could not deliver your other letters that day. Then on Sunday, having gone to his new house, the Cardinal sent for me. I waited upon him, and he asked me what I thought of the things I had seen. In reply to this I told him what I thought; and I certainly think he has many beautiful things. Then the Cardinal asked me whether I had courage enough to attempt some work of art of my own. I replied that I could not do anything as fine, but that he should see what I could do. We have bought a piece of marble for a life-sized figure and on Monday I shall begin work.

Then last Monday I presented your other letters to Pagolo Rucellai,[5] who placed the money at my disposal, and to the Cavalcanti[6] likewise. Then I gave Baldassare[7] his letter and asked him for the cupid, saying that I would return the money. He replied very sharply that he would sooner smash it into a hundred pieces; that he had bought the cupid and it was his; that he had letters showing that the buyer was satisfied and that he had no expectation of having it to return. He complained bitterly about you, saying that you had maligned him. Some of our Florentines sought to arrange matters between us, but they effected nothing. Now I count upon acting through the Cardinal, for thus I am advised by Baldassare Balducci.[8] You shall be informed as to what ensues. That's all this time. I commend me to you. May God keep you from harm.

MICHELANGELO IN ROME

1. *This letter was written on Michelangelo's first visit to Rome at the age of twenty-one. The extant copy is not in his hand (see Tolnay, I, p. 56). It is addressed to 'Sandro Botticelli in Florence', and may therefore be a copy made for the painter who, like Michelangelo, had enjoyed the patronage of Lorenzo the Magnificent.*

2. *Lorenzo di Pier Francesco belonged to the younger branch of the Medici family (see Appendix 2) Michelangelo had executed a little St. John for him.*

3. *Raffaello Riario, Cardinal di San Giorgio (1450–1521), was Michelangelo's first patron in Rome, whither he went in the company of one of the Cardinal's gentlemen.*

4. *The Cardinal had a collection of antique sculpture in the Palazzo Riario – his new house – now known as the Palazzo della Cancellaria.*

5. *Paolo di Pandolfo Rucellai (1464–1509). He was a Florentine banker and only temporarily resident in Rome (Passerini, Ruc., p. 153).*

6. *The Cavalcanti were merchant bankers in Rome, one of many houses which later transacted business on Michelangelo's behalf.*

7. *Baldassare del Milanese, a dealer, had sold Michelangelo's 'Sleeping Cupid' as an antique. The deception was discovered, and Michelangelo was anxious to obtain its return (Condivi, XVIII). It was acquired by Isabella d'Este in 1502 and eventually passed from the Mantuan collection into that of Charles I. In all probability it perished in the fire at Whitehall Palace in 1698.*

8. *Baldassare Balducci, a Florentine merchant employed in the bank of Jacopo Gallo. He was a friend and patron of Michelangelo's.*

2

¶ DOMINO LODOVICO BUONARROTI IN FLORENCE

*Buonarroti
Archives
Mil. i
From Rome
July 1st
1497*

In the Name of God. On the first day of July 1497.

Most revered and dear father — Do not be surprised at my not returning, because I've not yet been able to settle up my affairs with the Cardinal and I do not want to leave without first receiving satisfaction and being remunerated for my pains. With these grand masters one has to go slowly, because they cannot be coerced. But in any event I expect to be rid of everything this coming week.

I must inform you that Fra Lionardo[1] returned here – to Rome – and said that he had been obliged to flee from Viterbo and that he had had his habit taken away and wished to go home. So I gave him a gold ducat[2] which he asked of me for the journey, but I expect you know about this, as he must have arrived there by now.

I don't think I have anything else to tell you, as I'm unsettled and do not yet know how things will go, but I hope to be with you soon. I'm well and hope you are too. Commend me to my friends.

MICHELANGELO SCULPTOR IN ROME

1. *Lionardo was Michelangelo's elder brother (see Appendix 1). He was a follower of Savonarola and*

had become a Dominican friar in 1491. He is known to have been in the convent of San Marco in Florence in 1510.

2. *For this and all other coinage values see Appendix 3.*

3

¶ DOMINO LODOVICO BUONARROTI IN FLORENCE

In the name of God. On the 19th day of August 1497.

*Buonarroti
Archives
Mil. ii
From Rome
August 19th
1497*

Dearest father, etc. — This is to let you know that Buonarroto[1] arrived here on Friday. As soon as I knew of it I went to the inn to see him and he explained to me by word of mouth how things are going with you. He tells me that the haberdasher, Consiglio,[2] is giving you a lot of trouble, that he won't come to any agreement and that he wants to have you arrested.[3] I advise you to see to it that you do come to an agreement and pay him a few ducats on account; send and let me know what you agree to give him and I'll send it to you, if you haven't got it. Although I have very little money, as I've told you, I'll contrive to borrow it, so that you do not have to withdraw it from the Funds,[4] as Buonarroto said. Don't be surprised that I have at times written to you so tetchily, for at times I'm very troubled by reason of the many things that befall those who live away from home.

I undertook to do a figure for Piero de' Medici[5] and bought the marble; and then never began it, because he hasn't done as he promised me. So I'm working on my own and doing a figure for my own pleasure. I bought a piece of marble for five ducats, but it wasn't a good piece and the money was thrown away; then I bought another piece for another five ducats, and this I'm working for my own pleasure. So you must realize that I, too, have expenses and troubles. However, what you ask of me I'll send you, even if I should have to sell myself as a slave.

Buonarroto arrived safely and is lodging at the inn. He's got a room where he's comfortable and will lack for nothing as long as he likes to stay. I have nowhere convenient to have him with me, as I lodge with others, but it suffices that I'll not let him lack for anything. I'm well and hope you are too.

MICHELANGELO IN ROME

1. *Michelangelo's favourite brother (see Appendix 1), who visited him shortly after the death of their stepmother in July.*

2. *Lodovico Buonarroti was in debt to his brother-in-law, Consiglio d'Antonio Cisti, for at least ninety gold florins – hence the dispute. The debt does not appear to have been liquidated until 1502.*

3. *i.e. for debt.*

4. *i.e. 'il Monte', the Florentine Public Debt. For this and other financial and banking transactions see Appendix 4.*

5. *Piero de' Medici, the eldest son of Lorenzo the Magnificent (see Appendix 2). He was at this time resident in Rome, having been banished from Florence in 1494.*

4

*Buonarroti
Archives
Mil. xlvii
From Rome
(October 1497)*

¶ BUONARROTO DI LODOVICO BUONARROTI IN FLORENCE

For your information, Buonarroto, I've paid two ducats to Baldassare[1] here, so that he may make them payable to you there through Francesco Strozzi.[2] So when you get the letter[3] go and see him and he will pay them to you. Try to apply yourself, as I told you to. Explain to Lodovico both what I told you and what I advise. That's all. God be with you.

MICHELANGELO IN ROME

1. *Baldassare Balducci.*

2. *Probably Francesco di Vanni Strozzi (d. c.1528), a member of the famous family of merchant bankers. He had held office as a Prior in 1492 (Litta, IV, tav. xii).*

3. *i.e. the bill of exchange. See Appendix 4.*

5

*British Museum
Mil. viii
From Rome
(August 1499)*

¶ TO LODOVICO DI BUONARROTA SIMONI IN FLORENCE

Most revered father — I recently had a letter from a nun who says she is an aunt of ours. She commends herself to me and says she is very poor and in the utmost need and asks alms of me. For this purpose I am sending you five broad ducats, so that for the love of God you may give her four and a half, and with the remaining half please ask Buonarroto to buy me, either from Francesco Granacci[1] or from some other painter, an ounce of varnish, or as much as he can get for the said money, providing that it is of the best quality to be had in Florence. If there is no really good varnish available, tell him to leave it. The said nun, our aunt, belongs, I believe, to the Monastery of San Giuliano. Please will you find out whether it is true that she is in such a state of want, since she writes to me through a channel I do not like. I therefore have my doubts as to

6

whether it may not be some other nun, trying to take us in. If therefore you find that it is not true, keep the money for yourself. It will be paid to you by Bonifazio Fazi.[2]

I have nothing else to tell you at the moment, because I am not yet decided about anything of which I can inform you. I will tell you more when I have the leisure.

YOUR MICHELANGELO SCULPTOR IN ROME

1. *Francesco Granacci (1469–1543), a friend of Michelangelo's from the time they were fellow students in the 'bottega' of Domenico Ghirlandajo (1449–1494).*

2. *Bonifazio Fazi (or Fazzi) was Michelangelo's banker in Florence at this period.*

II

LETTERS
6 – 8

From Rome and Florence
1506

2. *The Madonna and Child* *Michelangelo*
Notre Dame, Bruges

II. From Rome and Florence : 1506

British Museum
Mil. iii
From Rome
January 31st
1506

Most revered father — I learn from a letter of yours that the *Spedalingo*[2] has not returned to Florence and consequently that you have not been able to settle up about the farm as you desired.[3] I, too, am much worried about this, as I supposed you would have taken it by now. I'm wondering whether the *Spedalingo* did not go away on purpose, in order not to have to relinquish the income from it, but to retain both the money and the farm. Keep me informed, for if this were so, I would take my money out of his hands and keep it elsewhere.

As to my affairs here, all would be well if my marbles were to come, but as far as this goes I seem to be most unfortunate, for since I arrived[4] here there have not been two days of fine weather. A barge, which had the greatest luck not to come to grief owing to the bad weather, managed to put in with some of them a few days ago; and then, when I had unloaded them, the river suddenly overflowed its banks and submerged them, so that as yet I haven't been able to begin anything; however, I'm making promises to the Pope[5] and keeping him in a state of agreeable expectation so that he may not be angry with me, in the hope that the weather may clear up so that I can soon begin work – God willing.

Please will you take all those drawings – that is, all those sheets I put into that bag I mentioned to you – and make a small parcel of them and send it to me by carrier. But see that they are carefully packed, so that they don't get wet, and take care when you pack them that not even the smallest of the sheets goes astray, and give the parcel into the charge of the carrier, because some of them are very important, and write and tell me by whom you are sending them and what I must pay him.

As to Michele,[6] I wrote to him telling him to put that chest of mine in a safe place under cover and then to come here to Rome immediately, and on no account to fail to do this. I don't know what he has done. Please will you put him in mind of this. Also would you please put yourself to a little trouble over the following two things: that is, in having that chest of mine put under cover in a safe place; the other is that marble of Our Lady;[7] I want you to have it moved into the house, likewise, and not to let anyone see it. I am not sending you the money for these two things, because I think they're small items. But should you have to borrow it, please do so, because when my marbles arrive I shall soon be sending you money for this and for yourself.

I wrote asking you to find out from Bonifazio[8] to whom in Lucca he had made payable the fifty ducats that I'm paying to Matteo Cucherello[9] at Carrara, and to add the agent's name in the unsealed letter I sent you, and to send it on to Carrara to the said Matteo, so that he may know to whom he has to go in Lucca for the said money. I assume you have done this. Please will you write and tell me also to whom Bonifazio made them payable in Lucca, so that I may know the name and can write to Matteo in Carrara and tell him to whom he has to go in Lucca for the said money. That's all. Don't send me anything except what I ask for – my clothes and shirts you and Giovan Simone[10] can have. Pray God my affairs may go well; and see, in any case, that up to a thousand ducats are invested for me in land, as we agreed.

On the thirty-first day of January 1506.

YOUR MICHELANGELO IN ROME

Lodovico, please will you send on this letter for Piero d'Argiento,[11] which is among those I'm sending you, and please will you see that he gets it. I think he would get it all right through the Ingesuati,[12] because he often goes there to see the brothers. I leave it to you.

1. *Lodovico had been appointed to an office in the Customs through the patronage of Lorenzo the Magnificent.*

2. *Leonardo Buonafè (1450–1545), the Head of the Hospital of Santa Maria Nuova. He held the office of Spedalingo from 1500–1527. For the banking facilities afforded by certain hospitals at this period see Appendix 5.*

3. *The property in question was the farm at Pazzolatica which was purchased on January 27th 1506. It is included in Michelangelo's Property Return made in 1534. See Appendix 6. The transaction had therefore already been completed when he wrote this letter, but he was under the impression that Lodovico had not obtained possession of the property for which he had evidently put down the money.*

4. *From April until the end of November 1505, when he returned to Rome, Michelangelo had been in Carrara quarrying marble for the Tomb of Julius II and was now awaiting its arrival.*

5. *Julius II (Giuliano della Rovere), whose pontificate lasted from 1503–1513, had summoned Michelangelo to Rome in 1505 and commissioned him to execute his Tomb.*

6. *Michele di Piero di Pippo, called Battaglino da Settignano. He was a scarpellino, i.e. stone-mason, employed to do the initial blocking out of figures under a sculptor's instructions.*

7. *Probably the Bruges Madonna which was shipped to Flanders in August of the same year (Gotti, II, p. 51).*

8. *Bonifazio Fazi.*

9. *Matteo Cucherello da Carrara and Guido d'Antonio di Biagio had entered into an agreement with Michelangelo on December 10th 1505 for further deliveries of marble (Milanesi, p. 631).*

10. *Giovan Simone, Michelangelo's brother, next in age to Buonarroto. See Appendix 1.*

11. *Piero Paesano d'Argenta, an assistant or 'garsone' employed by Michelangelo from January 1498 to June 1509.*

12. *The Frati Ingesuati, a religious community which specialized in the making of stained-glass windows and in the supplying of fine azure. See Vasari, VI, p. 631.*

¶ TO BUONARROTO DI LODOVICO BUONARROTI, FLORENCE

7

Buonarroti Archives Mil. lxxvii From Rome (February/ March 1506)

Buonarroto — I learn from a letter of yours how things are going at home. I am very sorry about it, and still more so, seeing the need you are in, and particularly Lodovico, who, you write me, is in need of getting himself something to put on his back.

A few days ago I wrote and told Lodovico that I have four hundred broad ducats worth of marble here and that I owe a hundred and forty broad ducats on it, and that I haven't a *quattrino*. I'm telling you the same thing, so that you may see that for the time being I cannot help you, as I have to pay off this debt and I'm still obliged to live and besides this to pay the rent. So that I have burdens enough. But I hope to be rid of them soon and to be able to help you.

You wrote asking me to look for an opening for you. I should not know either what to find or what to look for. I will send for you as soon as I can and you can stay in Rome until you find some opening to suit yourself. That's all. I will enclose a letter for Granaccio. Please give it to him and remind him to do me the service I ask of him.

MICHELANGELO SCULPTOR IN ROME

¶ TO MAESTRO GIULIANO DA SANGALLO, FLORENTINE, ARCHITECT TO THE POPE IN ROME

8

Buonarroti Archives Mil. cccxliii From Florence May 2nd 1506

Giuliano[1] — I learn from your letter that the Pope took my departure amiss, but that His Holiness is ready to place the money at my disposal and to do all that we were agreed upon, and that I am to return and to have no anxieties about anything.

As to my departure, the truth is that at table on Holy Saturday I heard the Pope say to a jeweller and to the Master of Ceremonies,[2] to whom he was talking, that he did not wish to spend one *baiocco* more either on small stones or on large ones. At this I was much taken aback; however, before leaving I asked him for some part of what I needed to continue the work. His Holiness told me to return on Monday, and I returned on Monday, and on Tuesday and on Wednesday and on Thursday, as he was aware. Finally, on

3. *Giuliano da Sangallo*

Piero di Cosimo
Mauritzhuis, The Hague

Friday morning I was turned out, in other words, I was sent packing, and the fellow who turned me away said that he knew who I was, but that such were his orders. At this, having heard on the said Saturday the said words, and seeing their effect, I was overwhelmed with despair. But this was not the one and only reason for my departure; there was something else besides, which I do not want to write about – it is enough that I had cause to think that if I remained in Rome, my own tomb would be sooner made than the Pope's. This, then, was the reason for my sudden departure.[3]

Now you write to me on behalf of the Pope. So will you read this letter to the Pope and inform His Holiness that I am more than ever ready to continue the work. But if it is indeed his wish to execute the Tomb,[4] he should not trouble himself as to where I do it, provided that at the end of five years, as we agreed, it shall be set up in St. Peter's, wherever he chooses, and that it shall be a work of art such as I have promised; for I am certain that if it is carried out, there will be nothing to equal it the world over.

Now, if His Holiness wishes to proceed, let him place the sum agreed at my disposal here in Florence, whence I will write to him. I have quantities of marble on order at Carrara, which I will have sent here, and similarly I will send for the supplies I have in Rome. Even if it were to mean a considerable loss to me, I should not mind, if I could do the work here. And I would forward the pieces one by one, as they are completed, by which arrangement His Holiness would derive as much pleasure from them as if I were working in Rome – nay, more, because he would see the finished things, without having any further bother about them. And for the said money and for the said work I will pledge myself as His Holiness directs and will give him here in Florence whatever security he shall demand. Be it what it may, Florence is my full and sufficient security. And I should add that there is no possibility of doing the said work for the same price in Rome, owing to the many facilities which exist here, but do not exist there; again I shall work better here and with greater zeal, as I shall not have so many things to think of. Meanwhile, my dearest Giuliano, I beg you to answer me as soon as possible. That's all. On the second day of May 1506.[5]

YOUR MICHELANGELO SCULPTOR IN FLORENCE

---

1. *Giuliano da Sangallo (1445–1517), with whom, as a fellow Florentine, the young Michelangelo was on very friendly terms. It was at his suggestion that Julius II had summoned Michelangelo to Rome.*

2. *Presumably Johannes Burchard of Strasburg, who died on May 26th 1506 and was succeeded by Paris de Grassis (1470–1528), who had held office as the second of the two Masters of Ceremonies since 1503.*

3. *See Volume II, No. 227.*

4. *See Appendixes 11 and 28.*

5. *For an interesting sequel to this letter see Gotti, II, p. 52.*

III

LETTERS
9 - 40

From Bologna
1506 - 1508

4. *The Façade of San Petronio*   *Bologna*

III. From Bologna : 1506-1508

British
Museum
Mil. xlviii
From Bologna
December 19th
1506

¶ To Buonarroto di Lodovico di Buonarrota Simoni in Florence

deliver to the shop of lorenzo strozzi, arte di lana,[1] in porta rossa

9

Buonarroto — I have received a letter of yours to-day, this nineteenth day of December, in which you refer Pietro Orlandini[2] to me, requiring me to do him the service he asks. For your information, he has written asking me to have the blade of a dagger made for him and to see that it is a fine piece of work. As things are I do not know how I can serve him both quickly and well; for one thing it is not my profession, and for another, I haven't time to attend to it. However, I'll do my best to see that he is served within a month.

As to your affairs and particularly those of Giovansimone, I understand entirely. I'm glad that he is betaking himself to your shop and wants to get on, because I want to help him like the rest of you; and if God helps me, as he has always done, I hope by Lent to have done what I have to do here,[3] when I'll come home and do what I've promised you whatever happens. As to the money you write to me about, which Giovansimone wants to invest in a shop, I think he ought to wait another four months and do it with a flash and a bang all at one go. I know you understand what I mean and that suffices. Tell him from me to try to get on, but if he really wants the money you write to me about, he would have to draw on what there is in Florence, because as yet I have nothing to send him from here, because I cannot count on even the small payment I'm getting for the work I'm doing, and anything might happen to shatter my world. In the meantime I urge you to be patient for the next few months, until I get home.

As regards Giovansimone's coming here – I do not advise him to as yet, because I'm living in a mean room for which I bought only one bed and there are four of us sleeping in it,[4] and I would not have the means to put him up properly. But if he wants to come nevertheless, let him wait until I've cast the figure I'm doing, when I'll send back Lapo[5] and Lodovico[6] who are helping me and will send him a horse, so that he may come, but not like a vagabond. That's all. Pray to God for me and that things may go well.

Michelangelo sculptor in Bologna

---

1. *The Arte di Lana, the Guild of Wool Merchants, was one of the principal guilds of Florence. Buonarroto was apprenticed to the wool trade in the shop of Lorenzo di Filippo Strozzi (1482–1549).*

2. *'Orlandini' should read 'Aldobrandini'. Michelangelo refers to him correctly in subsequent letters.*

3. *Following his flight from Rome in April 1506, Michelangelo had been obliged to make his submission to the Pope at the end of November of the same year. This he did at Bologna, whither Julius II had gone to take possession of the city as a domain of the Papacy, and to assert his rights as suzerain. He made his entry with great pomp on November 10th, the Bentivoglio having taken their departure shortly before. Having made his submission Michelangelo was required to undertake the execution of a colossal seated statue of the Pope in bronze.*

4. *This passage has commonly been quoted as affording evidence of Michelangelo's habitual way of life, whereas it does precisely the reverse, or he would not be at such pains to emphasize its discomforts. With the entire Papal Court and a supporting army quartered on the city, accommodation must have been almost unobtainable (Pastor, VI, pp. 266 et seq.). Cf. No. 39.*

5. *Lapo d'Antonio di Lapo (1465–1526), a Florentine sculptor, who from 1491 was among the 'maestri' working on the Duomo. He obtained leave to go to Bologna to assist Michelangelo on December 10th.*

6. *Lodovico di Guglielmo Lotti (b. 1458), had worked as a youth in Antonio del Pollaiuolo's workshop, but subsequently devoted himself to bronze casting (Milanesi, p. 8).*

10

British Museum Mil. xlix From Bologna January 22nd 1507

¶ To Buonarroto di Lodovico di Buonarrota Simoni in Florence
DELIVER TO THE SHOP OF LORENZO STROZZI, ARTE DI LANA, OPPOSITE THE PHARMACY DELLA PALLA, IN PORTA ROSSA

Buonarroto — I received a letter of yours a few days ago from which I learn that Lodovico has done a deal with Francesco[1] over Mona Zanobia's farm. As to Giovansimone, you again inform me that he is betaking himself to the shop where you work and that he has a desire to come here to Bologna. I haven't replied to you before, because I haven't had the time until to-day.

As to the farm mentioned above, you tell me that Lodovico has done a deal and will be informing me. For your information, if he has written to me about it, I never received the letter you speak of. So let him know of this so that he may not be alarmed at having no reply if he has written to me.

As to Giovansimone, I'll tell you my opinion so that you can tell him on my behalf. It is this, that it would not please me that he should come here before I have cast this figure I'm doing. I have a good reason for saying this – do not ask me why – let it suffice that as soon as I have cast it I will certainly arrange for him to come, when it will be less of a worry, because I shall be rid of the weight of expense I now have on my shoulders.

I expect to be ready about mid Lent to cast this figure of mine, so pray God it may go well for me, because if it goes well I hope to have the good fortune to be in favour with this Pope. And if I cast it by mid Lent and it goes well, I hope to be home during the Easter festival and will do what I have promised you without fail, if you will both try to get on.

Tell Pietro Aldobrandini[2] that I have ordered his blade from the best master of his craft here, who told me I should have it this coming week. As soon as I get it I'll send it to him, if I think it's a good piece of work; if not, I'll have it remade. Also tell him not to be surprised if I'm not doing him this service as quickly as I should, because I'm so short of time I cannot help it.

On the twenty-second day of January 1506.[3]

MICHELANGELO DI LODOVICO BUONARROTI SCULPTOR IN BOLOGNA

1. *Lodovico's brother. See Appendix 1.*

2. *Probably Pietro di Lorenzo Aldobrandini (b. 1471). He was approved under the Scrutiny of 1524 and thereby became eligible for civic offices (Litta IV, tav. iii).*

3. *N.S. 1507.*

¶ TO BUONARROTO DI LODOVICO SIMONI IN FLORENCE
DELIVER TO THE SHOP OF THE STROZZI, ARTE DI LANA, IN PORTA ROSSA

11

*Buonarroti
Archives
Mil. 1
From Bologna
February 1st
1507*

Buonarroto — I learn from a letter of yours how things are going with regard to that small farm. I'm extremely relieved and very pleased about it, provided that the thing is a really sound proposition.

As to Baroncello's affairs, I have made full enquiries, and from what I hear the matter is much more serious than you make out; and I, for my part, seeing that it is not just, could not ask for it.[1] We are all of us bound to help Baroncello, and this we will do, particularly in those things which lie in our power.

For your information, on Friday afternoon at two o'clock[2] Pope Julius came to the premises[3] where I'm working and stayed to watch me at work for about half an hour; then he gave me his blessing and went away. He was evidently pleased with what I am doing. For this I think we must thank God above all, and this I beg you to do and to pray for me.

I must also inform you how on Friday morning I dismissed Lapo and Lodovico, who have been assisting me here. Lapo I sent packing because he is a deceitful good-for-nothing fellow, who did not do what I wanted. Lodovico, however, is not so bad, and I would have kept him on for another two months. But Lapo, so that he might not be the only one in disgrace, influenced him in such a fashion that they have both gone off. I am telling you this, not because I take any account of them, for they are not worth three *quattrini* between them, but in order that Lodovico may not be alarmed about it, if they go talking to him. Tell him on no account to listen to them. And if you yourself want to know more about them, go to Messer Angelo, Herald to the Signoria,[4] because I have written and told him about the whole affair, and he, of his kindness, will explain it to you.

As to Giovansimone, I understand. I'm pleased that he is betaking himself to your masters' shop and that he is trying to get on. Encourage him to do this, because if this thing goes well, I hope to put you both in a good position, when you are trained. As to the business of the other land adjoining Mona Zanobia's, if Lodovico likes it, tell him to look into the matter and to let me know. I believe, or rather it is said here that the Pope will be leaving here round about Carnival.

On the first day of February 1506.[5]

MICHELANGELO DI LODOVICO DI BUONARROTA SIMONI SCULPTOR IN BOLOGNA

1. *The unspecified 'it' would appear to have been some favour to be asked on Baroncello's behalf, perhaps of the Pope. Baroncello Baroncelli was in correspondence with Michelangelo about a site in Florence, perhaps that in the Via Mozza, in May 1518 (Tolnay, I, p. 46).*

2. *For the Italian method of reckoning the hours of the day at this period see Appendix 7.*

3. *The Stanza del Pavaglione, behind the Cathedral (Podestà, p. 108). It may have been on this occasion that Michelangelo enquired of the Pope whether he should represent him with a book in his left hand – a question to which the warrior, Julius, replied, 'A book! Nay a sword, rather.' (Condivi, XXXII).*

4. *Angelo di Lorenzo Manfidi da Poppi. He became second Herald to the Signoria in 1500. On the death of the first Herald, Francesco Filareti, c. 1505/6, he succeeded him and held office until his death in 1527. Both Heralds had been present at the meeting held on January 25th 1504 to decide the site on which Michelangelo's 'David' was to be erected (Milanesi, pp. 9, 620 et seq.).*

5. *N.S. 1507.*

12

British Museum Mil. li From Bologna February 1st 1507

¶ TO BUONARROTO DI LODOVICO DI BUONARROTA SIMONI IN FLORENCE
DELIVER TO THE SHOP OF LORENZO STROZZI, IN PORTA ROSSA, ARTE DI LANA

Buonarroto — I learn from a letter of yours[1] what you have done in the matter of Mona Zanobia's farm; I am very pleased about this, provided that the thing is a sound proposition. I will attend to the rest of the business when the time comes.

As to Baroncello's affairs, I have made full enquiries and from what I'm told the matter is much more serious than you make out. However, I'm not in favour of asking it,[2] because if I did not get it, I should be dissatisfied, and if I did get it, it would mean

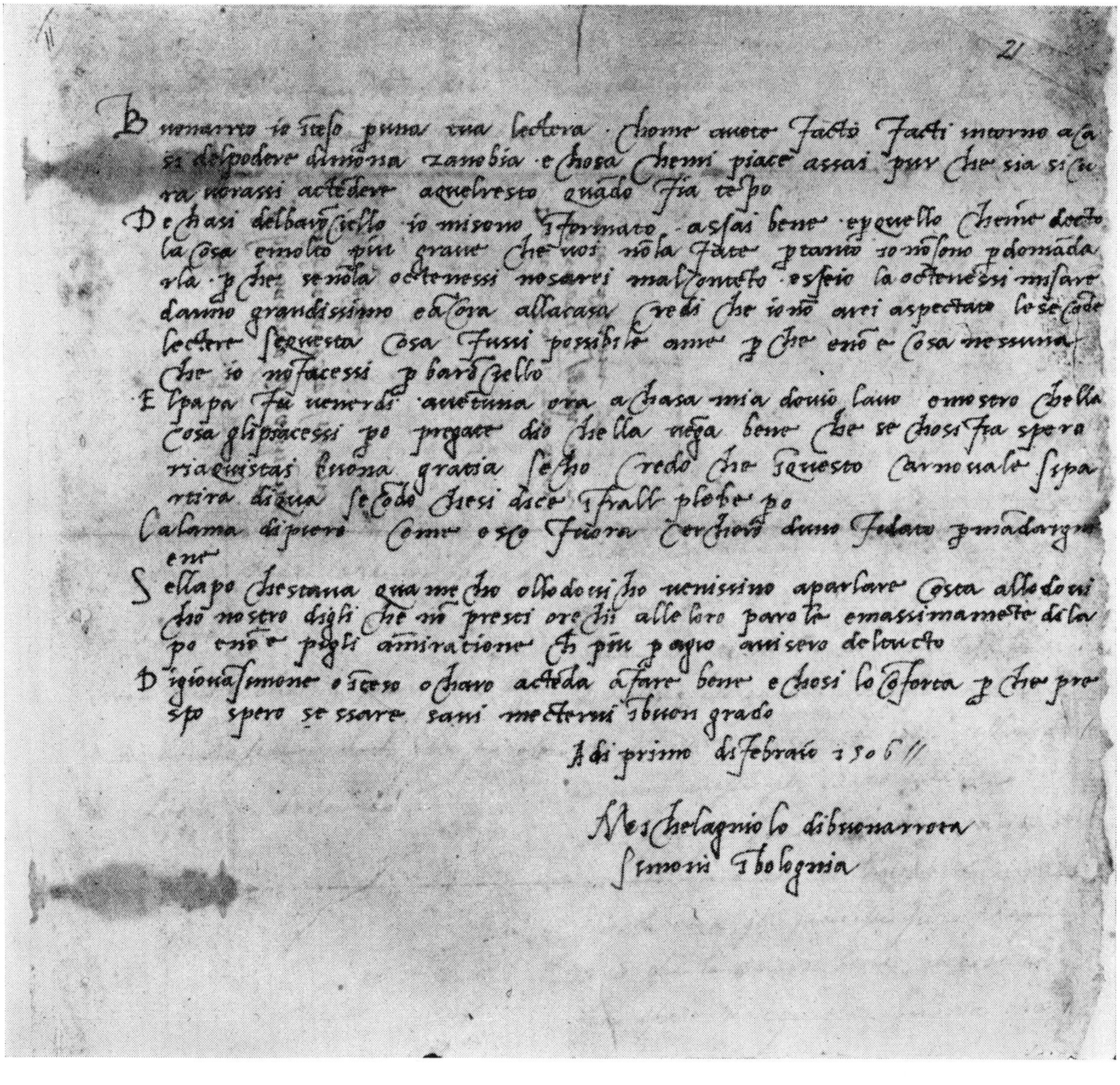

Buonarroto io o inteso p(er) una tua lectera chome avete facto facti intorno a ca-
si del podere di mona zanobia e chosa che mi piace assai pur che sia sicu-
ra vorassi actedere a quel resto quado fia tepo

De chasi del barriscello io mi sono informato assai bene e quello che mi e decto
la cosa e molto piu grave che voi non la fate p(er)tanto io non sono p(er) domada-
rla p(er)che se non la octenessi ne sarei mal contento e s'io la octenessi ne sare
danno grandissimo e ancora alla casa credi che io non arei aspectato le se conde
lectere se questa cosa fussi possibile a me p(er)che e non e cosa nessuna
che io non facessi p(er) bardicello

El papa fu venerdi a vetuna ora a chasa mia dov'io lavoro e mostro che lla
cosa gli piacessi p(er)o pregate Idio che lla vega bene che se chosi fia spero
riaquistar buona gratia se chio credo che se questo cardinale si spa
rtira di qua secondo che si dice fralle plebe p(er)o

La lama di piero come esco fuora cerchero dun fidato p(er) mandargne-
ne

Sellapo chestava qua me cho ollodovicho venissino a parlare cosca allodovi
cho nostro digli che non presti orechi alle loro parole e massimamente della
po e non e p(er) gli ammiratione ch(e) piu p(r)egio a(m)mi servo de louto

Digiovansimone o scrcto o charo actenda a fare bene e chosi lo conforta p(er)che pro-
spo spero se ssare sani mecterni i buon grado

Adi primo di febraio 1506

Michelagniolo di buonarrota
scultore i bologna

5. *Facsimile of Letter No. 12 (recto)* — *British Museum, London*

a great loss to me and to the family as well. Believe me, I should not have waited for the second letter, if this course were possible to me; because there is nothing I would not do for Baroncello.

On Friday[3] at two o'clock the Pope came to the premises where I'm working and showed his pleasure in the thing I'm doing; so pray God it may go well; for if it does, I hope to regain his favour. I believe he is leaving here during Carnival, according to rumours among the people, at least.

Piero's blade – when I go out, I will try to find someone trustworthy to send it by. If Lapo, who has been assisting me here, or Lodovico, go talking in Florence to our Lodovico, tell him not to listen to what they say, particularly not to Lapo, and not to be alarmed about it, as I will tell you all about it when I have the leisure. As to Giovansimone, I understand. I'm glad he's trying to get on; encourage him to do this, because I hope soon, when you are trained, to put you both in a good position.

On the first day of February 1506.[4]

MICHELANGELO DI BUONARROTA SIMONI IN BOLOGNA

1. *Owing to the uncertainty of delivery it was usual to send several letters dealing with the same topics, in the expectation that one at least would reach its destination. In this and the previous letter, both dated February 1st, we have a case in point. Note the somewhat abbreviated form of the second, the hurried and awkward phrasing of which, particularly in the last paragraph, has been deliberately retained in translation. Cf. No. 15.*

2. *For the unspecified 'it', see n. 1 to the previous letter.*

3. *January 29th.*

4. *N.S. 1507.*

13

British Museum Mil. iv From Bologna February 8th 1507

¶ TO LODOVICO DI LIONARDO DI BUONARROTA SIMONI IN FLORENCE
DELIVER TO THE SHOP OF LORENZO STROZZI, ARTE DI LANA, IN PORTA ROSSA

On the eighth day of February, 1506.[1]

Dearest[1] father — I have to-day received a letter of yours, from which I learn that you have been told a long story by Lapo and Lodovico. I value your reproof, since I deserve to be reproved as a miserable sinner, no less than others, and perhaps more so. But I would have you know that I have done no wrong in this matter, about which you reprove me, either to them, or to anyone else, unless it be that I did more for them than I need have done; and all those with whom I have ever had dealings know very well what I pay them and if anyone knows this, Lapo and Lodovico know it better than others; since in six weeks the one has received twenty-seven ducats and the other eighteen broad ducats, as well as expenses; so please do not let yourself be carried away. When they complained about me you should have asked them how long they were with me and what they had received, and then you could have asked them what they had to complain about. But their real grievance, and particularly that wretch Lapo's, was this – they had given everyone to understand that they were the ones doing this work, or at least jointly with me, and they had no notion, particularly Lapo, that they were not master, until I sent them packing; and by this alone did he perceive that he was in my service. And having already made much ado and begun to boast about the Pope's favours, he was amazed that I should send him packing like a cur. I regret the seven ducats he had of me, but when I return I shall certainly make him give them back; and if he had any conscience, he would also return the rest of what he had. But enough – I will not enlarge further, as I have written at length to Messer Angelo about the affair, to whom I beg you to go and, if you can, take Granaccio with you, and get him [i.e. *Messer Angelo*] to read you the letter which I have written to him and then you will realize what a crew they are. But please keep to yourself what I have written about Lodovico, because, if I do not find any others to come here to do the casting, I could see about having him back, since I didn't really dismiss him – only Lapo, who because he was too ashamed to return alone, led Lodovico astray as well, in order to raise his own spirits. The Herald will tell you all about it and how you must act in the matter. Have no further speech with Lapo, because it is too ignominious, since they are beneath us.

As to Giovansimone, I do not think he should come here, because the Pope is leaving during Carnival and is going, I believe, in the direction of Florence, and is not leaving a settled state of affairs behind him here, where there is some apprehension, according to rumours which it is better not to enquire into or to write about;[2] let it suffice, even if nothing should happen, and I do not think it will, that I do not want to have the responsibility of brothers on my shoulders. Don't be alarmed about this, and do not mention it to a soul, for needing men as I do, I should not be able to get anyone to come to me, and besides I still think that things will go well. I shall soon be home, and will do what I can to content Giovansimone and the others, please God. Tomorrow I will write again about certain moneys I am sending you, and what you must do with them. I agree about Piero – he will vouch for me there, for he is an honest man, as he has always been.

YOUR MICHELANGELO IN BOLOGNA

I will tell you one thing more in answer to Lapo's charge that I treated him badly. I only want to give you one instance; it is this. I bought seven hundred and twenty pounds of wax, but before I bought it I told Lapo to find out where it was to be had and to arrange the deal and I would give him the money to get it. Lapo went and returned, saying that it was not to be had for a *grosso* less than nine ducats and twenty *bolognini* per hundredweight, that is nine ducats and forty *soldi,* and that I should get it at once, as I had found a bargain. I told him to go and see whether he could get the forty *soldi* per hundredweight taken off and that then I would take it. He replied, 'It is not in the nature of these Bolognese to take a *quattrino* less than they ask.' At this point I became suspicious and let the matter drop. Then the same day, I drew Piero[3] aside and told him in private to go and see for how much per hundredweight he could obtain the wax. Piero went to the same merchant as Lapo and arranged the deal for eight and a half ducats, and I accepted it. Furthermore I sent Piero to get his commission, and he got this too. This is one of the ways in which I treated him badly. I am well aware that he thinks it strange that I should take any notice of his duplicity. Eight ducats a month and his expenses were not enough for him, but he must set about to deceive me and may have done so many times, for all I know, since I trusted him. Never have I seen a man with a more honest face, and thus, with his frank air, I think he must have taken in other people. So do not place any reliance on him and pretend not to see him.

1. *N.S. 1507. The opening 'Carissimo' was incorrectly transcribed as 'Reverendissimo' (British Museum, Add. MSS. 23.140. f. 3).*

2. *The Pope left Bologna on Monday, February 22nd, after a visit of three months, 'although the work of reorganizing the affairs of the city was by no means completed' (Pastor, VI, pp. 286 et seq.).*

3. *Piero d'Argenta (not, as usually stated, Pietro Urbano), who had been with Michelangelo in Rome in 1498. Although Piero left his service in June 1509, he always remained entirely devoted to him. They were still in correspondence over twenty years later (Poggi, Mich., pp. 113 et seq.).*

14

¶ To Buonarroto di Lodovico Buonarrota Simoni in Florence
DELIVER TO THE SHOP OF LORENZO STROZZI, ARTE DI LANA, IN PORTA ROSSA

*Buonarroti
Archives
Mil. lii
From Bologna
February 13th
1507*

Buonarroto — This is a covering note for two letters – one is to go to Piero Aldobrandini and the other to Rome to Giovanni Balducci.[1] See that you give the one to Bonifazio Fazi to forward, and give the other to the said Piero.

As to the behaviour of that wretched pair, I have not had time to write fully about their rascalities, so I beg you all – and see that you tell Lodovico – not to discuss the affair with anyone, because it is beneath us, and that suffices.

On the thirteenth day of February 1506.[2]

MICHELANGELO IN BOLOGNA

1. *Giovanni Balducci, his banker in Rome.*
2. *N.S. 1507.*

¶ To Buonarroto di Lodovico di Buonarrota Simoni in Florence
DELIVER TO THE SHOP OF LORENZO STROZZI, ARTE DI LANA, IN PORTA ROSSA

15

*Buonarroti
Archives
Mil. liii
From Bologna
February 24th
1507*

Buonarroto — I sent certain moneys home with certain instructions to Lodovico fifteen days ago and have never had a reply. I am astounded; therefore tell Lodovico to let me know whether he received them, and whether he has carried out my instructions about them. Tell him to let me know without fail, as I am worried about it and astounded at his lack of consideration; he is indeed a person to be entrusted with matters of importance another time! I should have thought he would have written a hundred letters, so that I might have had at least one of them. See that he lets me know without fail what he has done, and that he so consigns the letter that it reaches me.

As to Piero's dagger, I sent yesterday to see if it was ready, but he still has to gild it.[1] He has played me about for a month, but he really couldn't help it, because before the Papal Court departed he had to furnish all the courtiers with weapons and has had a great deal of business to attend to; which is why he has kept me waiting so long. Tell Piero to make no doubt that he shall have it without fail within a few days. The Pope departed on Monday morning at nine o'clock.[2] And if you want to know what orders he left about my thing, go to the Herald and he will explain to you. I have no time for writing.

On the twenty-fourth day of February.

MICHELANGELO IN BOLOGNA

1. *The engraved and gold-filled scroll or lattice decoration near the top of the blade, which is characteristic of early sixteenth-century Italian weapons, is presumably here referred to. Incidentally, there is nothing in the letters to support Tolnay's suggestion that Michelangelo designed the dagger (Tolnay, I, p. 223), but much to show that he did not.*

2. *According to the Venetian envoy, the Pope left Bologna not at nine, but at seven o'clock in the morning. Travelling via Imola, Forli, Urbino, etc., he reached Rome and made a ceremonial entry on Palm Sunday, March 28th (Sanuto, VI, 551, and VII, 43).*

¶ To Buonarroto di Lodovico Buonarroti in Florence
DELIVER TO THE SHOP OF LORENZO STROZZI, ARTE DI LANA, IN PORTA ROSSA

16

*Buonarroti
Archives
Mil. liv
From Bologna
March 6th
1507*

Buonarroto — I have not replied before to your letter, or to Piero Aldobrandini's, because I was unwilling to write until I had got the said Piero's dagger. It is two months since I ordered it from a blade-smith, who has the reputation of being the best master of his craft here, and although he has trifled with me all along, I did not want, after all, to have it made by someone else, nor to take one ready made. However, if the aforesaid Piero feels that I have trifled with him, he has every reason, but I couldn't help it.

I have now recovered, or rather got the said dagger, but only this morning and with great difficulty – so much so, that my Piero was for beating the smith over the head with it, having had to go back so many times. For your information, the bearer of this letter will be Chiaro di Bartolomeo, the gold-beater, who will have the dagger. Pay the carriage to the said Chiaro, whatever it comes to, and give the dagger to Piero. If he is not pleased with it, tell him to let me know and I'll have another one made for him. And tell him that after the Court arrived here every craft and craftsman rose in esteem and standing, so he must not be surprised that I have been so long in sending it to him, for I too have been trifled with; as this blade-smith alone had more business while the Court was here than the whole of Bologna ever had before. I've no time for writing. I wrote to Lodovico telling him that I have had his letters and that I have been duped, as he will have heard. On the sixth day of March 1506.[1]

MICHELANGELO DI LODOVICO BUONARROTI IN BOLOGNA

1. *N.S. 1507. Written on his thirty-second birthday.*

17 ¶ TO BUONARROTO DI LODOVICO DI BUONARROTA SIMONI IN FLORENCE
DELIVER TO THE SHOP OF LORENZO STROZZI, ARTE DI LANA, IN PORTA ROSSA

*Buonarroti
Archives
Mil. lv
From Bologna
March 26th
1507*

Buonarroto — A few days ago I had a letter of yours from which I learnt all about Piero Aldobrandini and his dagger. I assure you that, but for your sake, I should have left him to tittle-tattle as much as he liked. For your information, the blade, which I sent and which you have received, is made to his measurements, that is to say, to those of the said Piero; because he sent me a paper pattern of it in a letter and wrote me that I should have it made exactly to measure. This I did, so if he wanted a dagger, he should not have sent me the measurements of a rapier. But I want to say in this letter what I would rather not have said, which is this – do not associate with him, because he is not an associate for you – and that suffices. And if he comes to you for the aforesaid dagger, do not on any account let him have it. Be nice to him, and say I have given it to a friend of mine, and leave it at that. For your information, it has cost me nineteen *carlini* here, and thirteen *quattrini* for the duty.

My affairs here are going well, thank God, and I hope within a month to cast my figure. So pray God that the thing turns out well, so that I may soon come home, for I am prepared to do what I've promised you. Help and encourage Giovansimone, and tell him to write to me sometimes, and tell Lodovico that I am well and that before I cast my figure he shall certainly know of it. Commend me to Granaccio when you see him. That's all I have to tell you. Here the plague has broken out, and is of a deadly kind, because no-one who gets it recovers, although so far there are not many houses affected – perhaps forty, according to what I'm told. On the twenty-sixth day of March.

MICHELANGELO SCULPTOR IN BOLOGNA

If you've given Piero the dagger, do not say anything more to him about it; but if you have not given it to him, do not give it to him on any account.

¶ To Buonarroto di Lodovico di Buonarrota Simoni in Florence
   DELIVER TO THE SHOP OF LORENZO STROZZI, ARTE DI LANA, IN PORTA ROSSA, OR
   TO THE HERALD AT THE PALAZZO DE' SIGNORI IN FLORENCE

18

*British
Museum
Mil. lvi
From Bologna
March 29th
1507*

Buonarroto — This this[1] because I [*have written*] to Messer Angelo, which letter will be with this. Give it to him at once, because it is important. That's all I have to tell you. I informed you a few days ago about Riccione, the goldsmith. I assume you have had it. Things here are going well. Tell Lodovico that when the time comes to cast my figure I'll let him know.

On the twenty-ninth day of March 1506.[2]

MICHELANGELO SCULPTOR IN BOLOGNA

1. *Sic. This note with its repetitions, omissions and misdating was obviously written in a great hurry.*

2. *Misdated for 1507, the new year, according to the Style of the Incarnation, having begun on March 25th. In the following letter he remembers the turn of the year. For the facsimile of the recto and verso of this letter see Plate 6.*

¶ To Buonarroto di Lodovico di Buonarrota Simoni in Florence
   DELIVER TO THE SHOP OF LORENZO STROZZI, ARTE DI LANA, IN PORTA ROSSA

19

*Buonarroti
Archives
Mil. lvii
From Bologna
March 31st
1507*

Buonarroto — I have to-day received a letter of yours enclosing one from Lodovico. I am not answering Lodovico's because I haven't time, but you will know how I am from this and so can inform him, which will suffice.

For your information, I am well and my thing is also going well. Thank God. It is true that it has taken a month longer than I reckoned, so that I have not yet written to

Lodovico to tell him when I am casting it, or rather, when I want to cast it, because it isn't yet time. However, don't be alarmed about it, because I will let him know when it is time; I reckon a month to-day, or thereabouts.

As to the business of starting you off in a shop, or rather forming a company, I certainly want to do so, but you must have patience until I come home.

You tell me that Piero did not want the dagger. I am delighted that he didn't want it and that he wasn't pleased with it; perhaps because it was not its fate to be worn at his belt, and particularly because I hear that if he doesn't want it, someone else does – namely Filippo Strozzi.[1] Therefore, if you see that he likes it, go and make him a present of it, as from yourself, and do not say anything to him about the cost. For your information, I have not seen the blade, so, should it not be good enough, don't give it to him, so that you may not look a fool, since his requirements are different from Piero's. I will enclose with this a letter to be forwarded to Sangallo in Rome. Make arrangements to send it to him. I believe, if you give it to Baccio d'Agniolo,[2] he could send it safely. Commend me to him.

On the last day of March 1507.

MICHELANGELO BUONARROTI SCULPTOR IN BOLOGNA

1. *Filippo Strozzi (1489–1538), brother of Lorenzo Strozzi, in whose shop Buonarroto was apprenticed.*

2. *Baccio d'Agniolo Baglioni (1462–1543), architect and wood-carver (Vasari, V, p. 349).*

20

*British
Museum
Mil. lviii
From Bologna
April 14th
1507*

❡ TO BUONARROTO DI LODOVICO DI BUONARROTA SIMONI IN FLORENCE
DELIVER TO THE SHOP OF LORENZO STROZZI, ARTE DI LANA, IN PORTA ROSSA

Buonarroto — This is a covering note to a letter for Messer Angelo. See that you give it to him at once. I have no time to write more, nor to reply to Giovansimone. I'm well and my thing is going well, thank God. I'll write more fully when I have the leisure; and that suffices.

On the fourteenth day of April.

MICHELANGELO SCULPTOR IN BOLOGNA

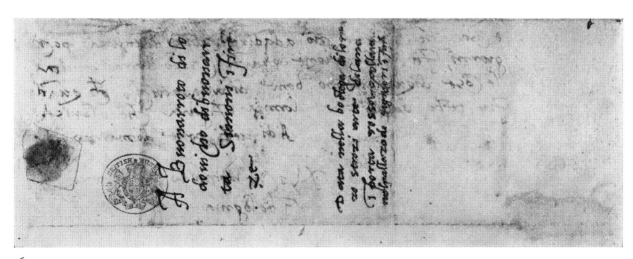

6. *Facsimile of Letter No. 18 (recto & verso)*   *British Museum, London*

21

*British
Museum
Mil. lix
From Bologna
April 20th
1507*

¶ To Buonarroto di Lodovico di Buonarrota Simoni in Florence
DELIVER TO THE SHOP OF LORENZO STROZZI, ARTE DI LANA, IN PORTA ROSSA IN FLORENCE

Buonarroto — I have to-day received a letter of yours, dated the seventeenth of April, from which I learn what a roundabout way my letters take to reach you. I cannot help it, because the arrangements for this are bad here. I note a number of things in your letter to which I'm not replying, because there's no need. I'm sorry you behaved so lousily[1] to Filippo Strozzi over such a small thing; but as it's done, it can't be undone.

I'm writing to Giovansimone about my affairs and he will let you know how I'm doing and you two can tell Lodovico.

Would you go to the Herald and tell him that never having had a reply from him regarding Messer Bernardino,[2] I assume that the said Maestro Bernardino is not for coming here on account of the plague. I have therefore taken on a Frenchman instead, who will serve me well. This I did because I couldn't wait any longer. See that he knows of this, that is Messer Angelo, and commend me to him and ask him to commend me to his lordship the Gonfalonier.[3] Commend me to Giovanni da Ricasoli[4] when you see him.

On the twentieth day of April.

MICHELANGELO IN BOLOGNA

1. *Not modern slang. 'Pidocchiosamente' from 'pidocchio', a louse. Perhaps he had sold the dagger to Strozzi instead of making him a present of it.*

2. *Bernardino d'Antonio del Ponte di Milano, Master of Ordnance to the Republic of Florence (1504–1512). He eventually obtained leave on May 7th 1507 to go to Bologna to help Michelangelo with the casting (Milanesi, p. 75).*

3. *Piero Soderini (1452–1522). He was appointed Gonfaloniere di Giustizia for life in 1502, but resigned his office on the return of the Medici in 1512.*

4. *Giovanni di Marco Ricasoli (1468–1519). He married Maria di Luca Pitti (Passerini, Ric., tav. iv).*

22

*Buonarroti
Archives
Mil. cxxiv
From Bologna
April 20th
1507*

¶ To Giovan Simone di Lodovico di Buonarrota Simoni in Florence

Giovan Simone — I have not answered a letter of yours which I received several days ago, as I haven't had time. Now I am writing to let you know that up to now my thing here goes well, so that I hope it will turn out well, please God. And if it does, that is, if I succeed in this thing, I will leave at once, or rather I will return home, and will do everything I have promised to do for you all, that is, to help you with what I have, in the way you wish and our father wishes. So keep up your spirits and apply yourself at the shop to the best of your ability, because I hope you will soon open a shop of your own, with your own money; and if you understand your trade and know what you are about, it will be a great advantage to you. So put your heart into it.

You write me that a friend of yours, who is a doctor, has told you that the plague is a dangerous disease and that one may die of it.[1] I'm glad to hear it, because there is a lot of it about here, and still these Bolognese don't realize that one may die of it. Therefore, it would be a good thing if he were to come here, as he might perhaps get them to learn from his own experience, which would be a great boon to them. That's all I have to tell you. I am fit and well and hope soon to be home. On the twentieth day of April.

I've no more paper.

MICHELANGELO IN BOLOGNA

---

1. *The terms of this letter are distinctly curious, having regard to the fact that it was addressed to a man of twenty-nine. The evidently sarcastic reference to the plague and the implication that the Bolognese were not taking proper precautions can perhaps be accounted for by Michelangelo's anxiety to discourage Giovansimone from visiting Bologna.*

¶ To Giovan Simone di Lodovico di Buonarrota Simoni in Florence
DELIVER TO THE SHOP OF LORENZO STROZZI, ARTE DI LANA, IN PORTA ROSSA

23

Giovan Simone — I replied to a letter of yours a few days ago. I assume you have had it and understand what I have in mind. But if you haven't had it, you will gather the same thing from this as from the other I wrote you.

I believe Buonarroto has explained to you what I have in mind and this is definite; as soon as I come home – please God – I am for setting you both up as you desire, either on your own or in a company, whichever we think the sounder method. Keep up your spirits and rest assured that I mean what I say. I have no time for writing, so will write more fully another time. I am well and have finished the wax of my figure. This coming week I shall begin to make the outer mould[1] and I think this will be completed in twenty or twenty-five days. Then I shall give the order for casting and if it turns out well, in a short time I shall be home.

On the twenty-eighth day of April.

MICHELANGELO IN BOLOGNA

Buonarroti Archives Mil. cxxv From Bologna April 28th 1507

---

1. *The third stage in the direct method of cire perdue bronze casting.*

24

*Buonarroti
Archives
Mil. cxxvi
From Bologna
May 2nd
1507*

⁋ To Giovan Simone di Lodovico di Buonarrota Simoni in Florence
DELIVER TO THE SHOP OF LORENZO STROZZI, ARTE DI LANA, IN PORTA ROSSA, FLORENCE

Giovan Simone — Several days ago I had a letter of yours which gave me great pleasure. Thereupon I wrote you two letters, but I suppose the luck I usually have with the others I have likewise had with these – that is to say, you haven't had them.

This is to let you know that before two months are out I shall be home, please God; and the promises I have made to Buonarroto and to you I am prepared to carry out. I am not writing to you in detail about what I have in mind, nor of the extent to which I desire to help you, because I don't want others to know about our affairs. But keep up your spirits, because there is something greater – or rather, better – in store for you than you think. That is all I can say to you about it.

For your information, everyone here is smothered in armour and for four days now the whole country has been under arms and in a great uproar, the Papal supporters in particular being threatened by the exiles, that is to say, by the Bentivogli,[1] who with a great following attempted to re-enter the city. But by his high courage and prudence, together with the excellent precautions he has taken, I believe his lordship the Legate[2] has once again rid the country of them, because at six o'clock this evening news came from their camp that they have turned back, with little honour to themselves. That's all. Pray God for me, and be light-hearted, as I shall soon be home.

On the second day of May.

MICHELANGELO IN BOLOGNA

1. *The sons of Giovanni Bentivoglio (1443–1508), the former lord of Bologna, had made a premature attempt to regain control of the city. Their attempt failed. As a reprisal the splendid palace they had built for themselves was razed to the ground. 'The work of spoliation began on . . . May 3rd', the day after this letter was written (Ady, Bent., p. 200). Cf. Sanuto, VII, 68.*

2. *The Papal Legate, Antonio Ferreri, Cardinal-Archbishop of Gubbio, who had been left in command of the city on the departure of the Pope. He was recalled to Rome in August 1507, because of his extortionate and irregular practices, and died in disgrace a year later.*

25

*British
Museum
Mil. lx
From Bologna
May 26th
1507*

⁋ To Buonarroto di Lodovico di Buonarrota Simoni in Florence
DELIVER TO THE SHOP OF LORENZO STROZZI, ARTE DI LANA, IN PORTA ROSSA IN FLORENCE

Buonarroto — I had a letter of yours through Maestro Bernardino, who has arrived here, from which I learn that you are all well, except Giovansimone, who has not yet recovered. I am very sorry about this and grieved not to be able to help him. But I hope soon to be home and to do what will please him and the rest of you. So help and encourage him and tell him to keep up his spirits. Also tell Lodovico that I expect to cast my figure without fail by the middle of next month. So if he wishes to have prayers said or something, to the end that it may turn out well, have it done then and tell him that I beg him to do so.

I have no time to write to you about anything else. Things are going well.

On the twenty-sixth day of May.

MICHELANGELO IN BOLOGNA

¶ TO BUONARROTO DI LODOVICO SIMONI IN FLORENCE

26

*British
Museum
Mil. lxi
From Bologna
June 20th
1507*

Buonarroto — I have not written to you for some days, as I did not want to write until I had cast my figure, having expected to cast it sooner than I succeeded in doing. For your information, it is not yet cast, but we shall cast it without fail this Saturday; and in a few days I think I shall be home, if it turns out well, as I anticipate.

That's all I have to tell you. I am fit and well, and I expect you all are too.

On the twentieth day of June.

MICHELANGELO IN BOLOGNA

¶ TO BUONARROTO DI LODOVICO DI BUONARROTA SIMONI IN FLORENCE
DELIVER TO THE SHOP OF LORENZO STROZZI, ARTE DI LANA, IN PORTA ROSSA

27

*Buonarroti
Archives
Mil. lxii
From Bologna
July 1st
1507*

Buonarroto — We have cast my figure, and it has turned out in such a way that I firmly believe I shall have to re-do it. I am not telling you all about it in detail, because I have other things to think about – let it suffice that the thing has turned out badly. I thank God for it, because I expect everything is for the best.[1] I shall know in a few days from now what I have to do and will let you know. Let Lodovico know about it and keep up your spirits. And if it turns out that I have to re-do it and that I cannot return home, I will make arrangements to do as I have promised you, whatever happens, in the best way I can.

On the first day of July.

MICHELANGELO IN BOLOGNA

1. *Cf. Luca Landucci on the burning of his house in 1507 – 'But I accept adversity like prosperity and thus give thanks to the Lord for the one as for the other' (Diario, p. 283).*

28

British
Museum
Mil. lxiii
From Bologna
July 6th
1507

❡ To Buonarroto di Lodovico di Buonarrota Simoni in Florence
DELIVER TO THE SHOP OF LORENZO STROZZI, ARTE DI LANA, IN PORTA ROSSA

Buonarroto — For your information, we have cast my figure, with which I have not been over-lucky, the reason being that Maestro Bernardino, either through ignorance or by accident, did not melt the stuff properly; it would take too long to tell you how it happened. It is enough that my figure has come out up to the waist; the rest of the stuff, that is half the metal, remained unmelted in the furnace, in such a way that I shall have to have the furnace taken down to extract it. This I am doing, and will have it remade again this week, and next week I shall do the recasting of the top and will finish filling the mould, and I think that, after a bad start, the thing will go very well, but not without a great deal of anxiety, exertion and expense. I could have believed that Maestro Bernardino could cast without fire, so great was my faith in him; nevertheless, it is not that he is not a good craftsman, nor that he did not put his heart into it. But he who tries may fail.[1] And he has indeed failed to my loss and to his own also, because he has so disgraced himself that he can no longer hold up his head in Bologna.

If you see Baccio d'Agniolo, read him this letter and ask him to let Sangallo know about it in Rome, and commend me to him and to Giovanni da Ricasoli and commend me to Granaccio. I expect, if the thing goes well, to be quit of it within two or three weeks and to return home. If it does not go well, I may perhaps have to re-do it. I will keep you informed about it all.

Let me know how Giovansimone is.

On the sixth day of July.

[Unsigned]

Enclosed with this will be a letter to be forwarded to Rome to Giuliano da Sangallo. Send it safely and as soon as you can. If he should be in Florence, give it to him.

1. *A variant of the old Tuscan proverb, 'He fails not who attempts not'.*

29

Buonarroti
Archives
Mil. lxiv
From Bologna
July 10th
1507

❡ To Buonarroto di Lodovico di Buonarrota Simoni in Florence
DELIVER TO THE SHOP OF LORENZO STROZZI, ARTE DI LANA, IN PORTA ROSSA

Buonarroto — I learn from a letter of yours that you are all fit and well. I'm very glad to hear it. After a bad start I think my thing here will go very well, although as yet I know nothing. We have recast the top part which went wrong, as I wrote you, and I have not yet been able to see how the thing has turned out, because the casing is so hot that it cannot yet be uncovered. Next week I shall know for certain and will inform you. Maestro Bernardino left here yesterday. If he should say anything to you, be nice to him – and leave it at that.

On the tenth day of July.

MICHELANGELO IN BOLOGNA

¶ TO BUONARROTO DI LODOVICO DI BUONARROTA SIMONI IN FLORENCE
DELIVER TO THE SHOP OF LORENZO STROZZI, ARTE DI LANA, IN PORTA ROSSA, FLORENCE

30

*Buonarroti
Archives
Mil. lxv
From Bologna
July 1507*

Buonarroto — My thing could have turned out better, or again much worse. At least it has come out whole, from what I can make out, although as yet I haven't uncovered it completely. I reckon it will take several months to clean it up,[1] as it has come out very dirty. One must thank God, nevertheless, because, as I say, it could have turned out worse. If Salvestro del Pollaiuolo[2] or the others should say anything to you, tell them I don't need anyone, as I don't want the responsibility of anyone on my shoulders, because I've spent so much that I scarcely have enough to live on myself, let alone to keep others. Next week I will let you know, as I shall have uncovered the whole figure.

MICHELANGELO IN BOLOGNA

1. *Raking out the core, sawing off the bronze rods at the points where the metal had been poured, repairing any inequalities, tooling and burnishing the surface.*

2. *Salvestro del Pollaiuolo (1472–1533), a nephew of Antonio and Piero del Pollaiuolo.*

¶ TO BUONARROTO DI LODOVICO DI BUONARROTA SIMONI IN FLORENCE
DELIVER TO THE SHOP OF LORENZO STROZZI, ARTE DI LANA, IN PORTA ROSSA

31

*Buonarroti
Archives
Mil. lxvi
From Bologna
August 2nd
1507*

Buonarroto — I did not write to you last week, as I wasn't able to. For your information, the further I uncovered my figure the better I found it had turned out, and I see that it is not as bad as I had expected, and considering what might have happened it seems to me I have come off well. So we must thank God. As far as I can see, the business of cleaning it up will certainly take six weeks. So that, since you have had to be patient so long, you must be patient a little longer. Help and encourage Giovansimone on my behalf, and let me know how he is, and the others also. Explain everything

37

to Lodovico. Commend me to my friends, that is, to Giovanni da Ricasoli, to Granaccio and to Messer Angelo.

On the second day of August 1507.

MICHELANGELO IN BOLOGNA

32

Buonarroti Archives Mil. lxvii From Bologna August 3rd 1507

¶ To Buonarroto di Lodovico di Buonarrota Simoni in Florence
DELIVER TO THE SHOP OF LORENZO STROZZI, ARTE DI LANA, IN PORTA ROSSA

Buonarroto — This is a covering letter for one to be forwarded to Rome to Giuliano da Sangallo. Please send it by the safest way, because it is very important. I am not writing to you about anything else, as only this morning I have sent you another letter, from which you will hear that the thing is going well.

On the third day of August.

MICHELANGELO IN BOLOGNA

33

Buonarroti Archives Mil. lxviii From Bologna August 10th 1507

¶ To Buonarroto di Lodovico di Buonarrota Simoni in Florence
DELIVER TO THE SHOP OF LORENZO STROZZI, ARTE DI LANA, IN PORTA ROSSA, FLORENCE

Buonarroto — I have to-day received a letter of yours from which I learn that you are all fit. I'm very pleased to hear it. I too am fit, and expecting my thing to go well. It is true there is a great deal of hard work to do; nevertheless, I can rest assured that I have no more risks to run, nor undue expenses to meet, as my only obligation is to hand over the finished work where it stands. I have replied to a letter of Sangallo's, and the letter will be enclosed with this. Give it to him. Would you go and see Messer Angelo, the Herald, and tell him that I have not yet answered him, as I have not been able to, and that the thing goes well; and commend me to him and to Tommaso, the Commissary.[1] You write me of the heat in Florence and of the high cost of everything; for your information, it has been the same in Bologna, for since I have been here it has only rained once and has been hotter than I ever believed it could be anywhere on earth. Wine here is dear, as it is with you, but as bad as can be, and everything else likewise, which makes for a miserable existence and I long to be quit of it.

On the tenth day of August.

MICHELANGELO IN BOLOGNA

38

1. *Tommaso di Balduccio di Rinaldo Balducci, one of the six Commissaries – Comandatori – who were included among the officials of the Republic and formed part of what was known as the 'Famiglia di Palazzo' (Milanesi, p. 84).*

¶ To Buonarroto di Lodovico di Buonarrota Simoni in Florence
DELIVER TO THE SHOP OF LORENZO STROZZI, ARTE DI LANA, IN PORTA ROSSA

34

Buonarroti Archives Mil. lxix From Bologna September 29th 1507

Buonarroto — I have not had any letters from you now for over a month. I do not know why. So please send me news, either you or Giovansimone, and let me know how you are getting on. I do not often write to you, as I haven't time, as there has been more and more to be done in connection with this undertaking of mine, so that if it were not for my great application, I should be here for another six months. However I expect to have finished by All Saints or very nearly, applying myself as I do, so that I can scarcely snatch the time to eat. Keep up your spirits and in the meantime have patience, because the thing goes well. Let me know how you are getting on. Make my apologies to Sangallo for not having written to him, and to the Herald when you see them. That's all.

On the twenty-ninth day of September.

MICHELANGELO IN BOLOGNA

¶ To Buonarroto di Lodovico di Buonarrota Simoni in Florence
DELIVER TO THE SHOP OF LORENZO STROZZI, ARTE DI LANA, IN PORTA ROSSA

35

British Museum Mil. lxx From Bologna October 16th 1507

Buonarroto — I have not had time to answer your last letter as I should have done; but for your information I am well, and will soon have finished and am expecting to be greatly honoured – all by the grace of God. As soon as I have finished I will return home and arrange everything about which you have written to me, in a way that will satisfy you and Lodovico and Giovansimone likewise. Please will you go and see the Herald and Tommaso, the Commissary. Tell them that I haven't time to write to them now, or rather to answer their most welcome letters; but next time, without fail, I will let them have news in answer to theirs. Also, please will you go and see Sangallo and tell him that I expect to be finished soon and find out how he is and say that next time I will write to him too, and tell him how the thing goes. That's all.

On the . . . day of October.

MICHELANGELO IN BOLOGNA

36

British Museum Mil. lxxi From Bologna October 19th 1507

¶ To Buonarroto di Lodovico di Buonarrota Simoni in Florence
DELIVER TO THE SHOP OF LORENZO STROZZI, ARTE DI LANA, IN PORTA ROSSA

Buonarroto — I have received a letter of yours, from which I learn how Sangallo is. I will not answer yours further, because there is no need. It suffices that I am safely into port with my work, so keep up your spirits. Several letters will be enclosed with this. Deliver them safely and quickly. I do not know what date we have reached, but yesterday was St. Luke's. Find out for yourself.

MICHELANGELO IN BOLOGNA

37

British Museum Mil. lxxii From Bologna November 10th 1507

¶ To Buonarroto di Lodovico di Buonarrota Simoni in Florence
DELIVER TO THE SHOP OF LORENZO STROZZI, ARTE DI LANA, IN PORTA ROSSA

Buonarroto — I am astonished that you write to me so seldom. I think, moreover, that you have more time to write to me than I to you. So let me know frequently how you are getting on.

I learn from your last that you have good reason to desire me to return soon. This statement has perplexed me for several days. Therefore, when you write to me, write and explain matters plainly and clearly, so that I may understand. And let that suffice.

For your information, my desire to return as soon as possible is much greater than your desire that I should, because I'm living here in the greatest discomfort and in a state of extreme fatigue; I do nothing but work day and night and have endured and am enduring such fatigue that if I had to do the work over again I do not believe I should survive, because it has been a tremendous undertaking and had it been in anyone else's hands it would have been a disaster.[1] But I think someone's prayers[2] must have helped me and kept me well, because the whole of Bologna was of the opinion that I should never finish it. No-one has believed, either before or since it was cast, that I could ever cast it. Let it suffice that I have brought it to a successful conclusion, but I shall not have finished it by the end of this month, as I had expected, but next month at any rate it will be finished and I will return. So keep up your spirits, all of you, because I will do as I have promised you whatever happens. Encourage Lodovico and Giovansimone on my behalf, and write and tell me how Giovansimone is getting on, and apply yourself to learning your trade and working at the shop, so that you may know what you are about when you need to; which will be before long. On the tenth day of November.

MICHELANGELO IN BOLOGNA

1. *The colossal seated statue of Julius II was between nine and ten feet in height. When he had met all the expenses involved, Michelangelo emerged, after the extraordinary labours of fourteen months, with four and a half ducats in hand to compensate him for his pains.*

2. *The reference is probably to Fra Lorenzo Viviani, who in a letter to Michelangelo in Florence, dated March 15th 1508, mentions prayers, fasts and vigils undertaken on his behalf (Tolnay, I, pp. 250 et seq.).*

¶ To Buonarroto di Lodovico di Buonarrota Simoni in Florence
DELIVER TO THE SHOP OF LORENZO STROZZI, ARTE DI LANA, IN PORTA ROSSA

British Museum Mil. lxxiii From Bologna December 21st 1507

38

Buonarroto — I am sending you a letter enclosed with this, which is very important and is to be forwarded to the Cardinal of Pavia[1] in Rome; so as soon as you have received it go to Sangallo and see whether he has the means to send it safely. And if Sangallo is not in Florence, or cannot send it, write a covering letter and send it to Giovanni Balducci and ask him on my behalf to send it to Pavia, that is to say, to the said Cardinal, and tell Giovanni that I shall be in Rome this Lent and commend me to him. Commend me also to Sangallo and tell him that I have his business in mind and that I shall soon be home. Send the said letter without fail, because I cannot leave here, unless I have a reply.

On the twenty-first day of December.

MICHELANGELO IN BOLOGNA

1. *Francesco Alidosi, Cardinal of Pavia, who had conducted the negotiations with the Signoria prior to Michelangelo's submission to Julius II in 1506 (Gaye, II, pp. 91, 93), was responsible for seeing that Michelangelo fulfilled his obligations. Alidosi became Legate of Bologna in succession to Cardinal Ferreri, but was murdered for his mishandling of affairs by Francesco Maria della Rovere, Duke of Urbino, the nephew of Julius II, on May 24th 1511.*

¶ To Buonarroto di Lodovico di Buonarrota Simoni in Florence
DELIVER TO THE SHOP OF LORENZO STROZZI, ARTE DI LANA, IN PORTA ROSSA

British Museum Mil. lxxiv From Bologna January 5th 1508

39

Buonarroto — I learn from your last that you have done me a good service over the letter to Pavia. I'm grateful, as I think it will arrive safely. I am very grieved that you haven't been well, as you write me; however, be patient and keep up your spirits, because I shall be home shortly and will arrange for you to do as you wish, either with Lorenzo Strozzi or on your own, whichever seems to you the sounder and more

41

profitable. I cannot tell you exactly when I shall be leaving here, as I do not yet know, but I think I shall leave at all events within a fortnight, or rather be ready to leave. To me it seems like a thousand years, for such is the way in which I'm living here that if you knew what it's like you would be appalled. That's all. Do not write to me again at Bologna, unless there is something important, because the arrangements for letters are bad. Encourage all the others on my behalf. I do not know what day we have got to, but I do know that tomorrow is Epiphany.

MICHELANGELO IN BOLOGNA

40

*Buonarroti
Archives
Mil. lxxv
From Bologna
February (13th)
1508*

¶ TO BUONARROTO DI LODOVICO DI BUONARROTA SIMONI IN FLORENCE
DELIVER TO THE SHOP OF LORENZO STROZZI, ARTE DI LANA, IN PORTA ROSSA

Buonarroto — I thought I would have been home a fortnight ago, because I expected that, as soon as my figure was finished, they would have put it in place. Now they dilly-dally with me and do nothing about it, and I have orders from the Pope not to leave until it is in place;[1] so that I seem to be held up. I will wait and see till the end of this week, and if they give no further instructions, I shall come away whatever happens, without paying any attention to my orders.

With this will be a letter to be forwarded to the Cardinal of Pavia, in which I am recounting the whole thing, so that he cannot complain. So write a covering note and direct it to Giuliano da Sangallo on my behalf, and ask him to deliver it with his own hand.

[Unsigned]

1. *The statue of Julius II was finally set up on the façade of San Petronio, above the great door, on the afternoon of February 21st, amid the applause of the people, such a concourse having assembled, according to a contemporary document in the Bolognese Archives, that the directors of the work were impeded. It is described in another MS. as 'a seated bronze portrait of Julius II . . . with the tiara on his head, his right hand in the attitude of benediction, and his left holding a key'. It did not, however, long remain in place. On December 30th 1511, when for a brief space the Bentivoglio returned to Bologna, it was cast down and smashed to pieces. From part of the bronze Duke Alfonzo d'Este of Ferrara subsequently made a cannon which was thereafter called the 'Giulia'. For the history of this work see Podestà, pp. 107 et seq. and Tolnay, I, pp. 219 et seq.*

IV

LETTERS
41 - 83

From Rome
1508 - 1512

7. *The Sistine Chapel*   *The Vatican, Rome*

IV. From Rome : 1508-1512

¶ To the Reverend Father in Christ, Frate Jacopo Jesuato in Florence

41

*Buonarroti
Archives
Mil. cccxliv
From Rome
May 13th
1508*

Frate Jacopo — As I have to have certain things painted here, or rather to paint them,[1] I have occasion to inform you of the fact, as I need a certain amount of fine quality azure,[2] and if you have some you could provide me with immediately, it would be a great convenience to me. So arrange to send to your brethren here as much of the fine quality as you have available and I promise to take it at the just price.[3] And before I collect the azure I'll have your money paid to you, either here or in Florence, whichever you prefer.

On the thirteenth day of May.[4]

YOUR MICHELANGELO SCULPTOR IN ROME

1. *This is the first mention of the painting of the vault of the Sistine Chapel. See Appendix 9.*

2. *The Monastery of San Giusto alle Mura e i Gesuati appears to have been the recognized source for the supply of azures. Cf. Benozzo Gozzoli to Piero de' Medici, September 23rd 1459 – 'I have obtained from the Jesuati two ounces of azure of the quality at three broad florins the ounce.' (Gaye, I, p. 193).*

3. *The notion of 'the just price' was an ethical concept of the Middle Ages developed by St. Thomas Aquinas. Michelangelo frequently uses the phrase which in certain contexts may be rendered by the term 'market price' or 'a reasonable price'.*

4. *The year is supplied from a covering letter from Granacci to Frate Jacopo, which is dated in full.*

¶ To Buonarroto di Lodovico Simoni in Florence

42

*British
Museum
Mil. lxxvi
From Rome
July 2nd
1508*

Buonarroto — The bearer of this letter will be a young Spaniard,[1] who is coming to Florence to study painting and has asked me to arrange for him to see the cartoon I began at the *Sala*.[2] So try in any case to arrange for him to have the keys, and if you can help him in any way, do so for my sake, because he is a nice lad.

Giovansimone is here and was ill last week, which was no small worry to me, beside the other worries I have. However, he is all right now. I think he will soon be returning to Florence,[3] if he does as I advise, because I don't think the air here agrees with him. Commend me to Tommaso, the Commissary, and to the Herald.

On the second day of July.

MICHELANGELO IN ROME

Commend me to Giovanni da Ricasoli.

1. *Probably Alonso Berruguete, who later copied the cartoon.*

2. *The Sala del Papa, in which the cartoon for 'The Battle of Cascina' was kept. The cartoon itself was actually completed, but the fresco was not begun, so that, by an elliptical usage, Michelangelo refers to the unfinished work. See Appendix 8.*

3. *Lodovico wrote to Michelangelo on July 21st saying that Giovansimone had arrived in Florence (Steinmann, Sixt. II, p. 701).*

43 ¶ TO BUONARROTO DI LODOVICO DI BUONARROTA SIMONI IN FLORENCE

British Museum Mil. lxxviii From Rome July 29th 1508

Buonarroto — I am sending you the renunciation of the inheritance from Francesco,[1] which I have executed through a notary, as Lodovico sent and asked me to do. So as soon as you get it give it to Lodovico, as he knows it will be in this letter. I must inform you that Piero Basso[2] fell ill and left here on Tuesday, whether I would or no. I was put out about it, because I am left alone and also because I'm afraid he may die on the way. But so much fear of the air here was put into his head, that I could never have kept him, though I believe, from what others tell me, that he would have recovered in four days, if he had stayed. So let me know if he has arrived there.

Enclosed with this will be a letter for a man called Giovanni Michi,[3] who wanted to work here with me previously and again writes to me that he wants to come. In this letter I have told him in reply what he will have to do, if he wants to come. So would you go to San Lorenzo, where he tells me he is working, and try to find him and give him the letter and try to get a definite answer, because I cannot remain alone, besides which, no-one trustworthy is to be found. Let me know at once.

I wrote asking you to confirm the purchase of that piece of land belonging to Niccolò della Buca, and to arrange settlement for a month hence. I assume you have so arranged it. As I have to send money to Florence about the middle of August for the purchase of azure, I will include the money for Niccolò. Explain to Lodovico. I have no time for writing.

I learnt that the Spaniard has not had permission to go to the *Sala*.[4] I was indeed

46

grateful! But beg them[5] on my behalf, when you see them, to treat others in the same way, and commend me to them.[6]

On the last day of July.[7]

MICHELANGELO IN ROME

A letter for Granaccio will also be enclosed with this. Give it to him, because it's important.

1. *Francesco Buonarroti, Michelangelo's uncle, who died on June 18th 1508. In order to avoid payment of his debts, Lodovico and his sons renounced the inheritance; Lodovico and his three sons in Florence by an instrument executed in Florence on July 26th, Michelangelo by an instrument executed in Rome on July 27th 1508 (Milanesi, p. 94).*

2. *Piero Basso, a scarpellino and father of Bernardino, mentioned in subsequent letters. For the cause of the bad air in Rome and its ill effects. See Lanciani, p. 69 et seq. and Vasari, passim.*

3. *Giovanni Michi received the letter on August 5th and left for Rome a few days later. He was still in Michelangelo's service in 1510 (Frey, Briefe, p. 8).*

4. *See previous letter and Appendix 8.*

5. *i.e. Messer Angelo the Herald and Tommaso Balducci the Commissary, who held the keys of the Sala del Papa.*

6. *The second 'ancora' in Milanesi's text is intrusive. The reference is evidently sarcastic.*

7. *Not in fact July 31st but July 29th, according to Buonarroto's endorsement on receipt of the letter.*

¶ TO BUONARROTO DI LODOVICO DI BUONARROTA SIMONI IN FLORENCE
DELIVER TO THE SHOP OF LORENZO STROZZI

44

*British
Museum
Mil. lxxix
From Rome
August 5th
1508*

Buonarroto — Eight days ago today I sent the renunciation; I assume you have had it. You tell me that you have written to me about Baccino. I do not know whom you mean and if you wrote I haven't had the letter. Lodovico wrote to me, perhaps a month ago, about Baccio di Mariotto;[1] I don't know whether you mean him. Let me know whom you do mean.

About the farmer Bastiano[2] I agree; if he were willing to work properly there would be no need to replace him. I do not want to suggest that the man is a rogue; it was through me, owing to the wonders he told me he would work at the farm, that Lodovico put him in there. Now he has forgotten it, the scamp, but I have not forgotten it. Tell him from me that if he doesn't discharge his obligations he'd better not wait till I get there, which might turn out to be pretty quickly.

I wrote and told you that Pier Basso fell ill and left here whether I would or no. Let me know whether he has arrived there yet. I've no time for writing. On the . . . day of August.

MICHELANGELO IN ROME

1. *Baccio di Mariotto is mentioned by Buonarroto in a letter also dated August 5th in which he encloses a letter for the said Baccio, who was therefore presumably in Rome, as he asks Michelangelo to deliver it, if he can. Buonarroto also informs Michelangelo of Pier Basso's safe arrival on August 3rd and says that he is full of his praises (Frey, Briefe, p. 8).*

2. *The word 'lavoratore' was applied to any man who worked the land, whether as a farm labourer or as a tenant farmer (Origo, p. 244). In this instance the latter is clearly implied. Lodovico had written to Michelangelo on July 21st complaining about Bastiano (Steinmann, Sixt., II, p. 701).*

45

British Museum Mil. x From Rome January 27th 1509

¶ TO LODOVICO DI BUONARROTA SIMONI IN FLORENCE

Dearest father — I have to-day received a letter of yours which, when I had grasped its meaning, disturbed me very much. I have no doubt that you are more alarmed and fearful than need be. I should be glad if you would let me know what you think she[1] can do to you, that is, the worst she can do, if she uses every means in her power. There is nothing else I can say to you. It upsets me to hear that you are in such a state of fear. I therefore urge you to make good preparation for your defence, by getting proper advice and then to think no more about it. For if she were to take away everything you have in the world, you would not lack the means to live and to be comfortable, if there were no-one else but me. So keep up your spirits. I am still in a great quandary, because it is now a year[2] since I had a *grosso* from this Pope and I do not ask for anything because my work does not seem to me to go ahead in a way to merit it. This is due to the difficulty of the work and also because it is not my profession.[3] In consequence, I lose my time fruitlessly. May God help me. If you are in need of money, go to the *Spedalingo* and get him to give you up to fifteen ducats and let me know what remains.

That painter, Jacopo,[4] whom I got to come here, left recently; and as he has been complaining about me here, I suppose he will also complain in Florence. Turn a deaf ear and leave it at that. For he was in the wrong a thousand times over and I have every cause to complain about him. Pretend not to notice him. Tell Buonarroto I'll reply to him another time.

On the twenty 7th day of January.

YOUR MICHELANGELO IN ROME

1. *Mona Cassandra di Cosimo Bartoli, the widow of Lodovico's brother, Francesco. She brought a lawsuit against her brother-in-law and nephews for the recovery of her dowery.*

2. *He had in fact received the first payment for the Sistine vault eight months previously, on May 10th 1508, when he was paid five hundred ducats on account, in accordance with the terms of a 'scritta' issued by Cardinal Alidosi of Pavia and countersigned by himself (Milanesi, p. 563).*

3. *Throughout his life Michelangelo regarded himself primarily as a sculptor.*

4. *Jacopo di Sandro, not Jacopo l'Indaco, as stated by Milanesi (Tolnay, II, pp. 224-5).*

¶ To Lodovico di Buonarrota Simoni in Florence

British Museum Mil. v From Rome June 1509

46

Most revered father — I learn from your last that it is said in Florence that I am dead. It is a matter of little importance, because I am still alive. So let them say what they like, and do not mention me to anyone, because there are some malicious people about. I'm bent upon working as hard as I can. I've had no money from the Pope for thirteen months now, but I expect to have some at all events within six weeks, as I made very good use of what I had. If he were not to give me any, I should have to borrow money to come home, because I haven't a *quattrino*. However, I can't be robbed. God grant things may go better.

I understand about Mona Cassandra. I do not know what to say about it. If I had the money, I would find out whether the case could be heard here[1] without loss to me, that is to say, loss of time, but I should have to appoint an attorney and as yet I have nothing to spend. Let me know when the time comes how the thing goes, and if you need money, go to Santa Maria Nuova to the *Spedalingo*, as I have already told you to. There is nothing more I can say. Here I'm living ill-content and not too well, faced with an enormous task, without anyone to manage for me and without money. However, I have good hope that God will help me. Commend me to Giovanni da Ricasoli and to Messer Angelo, the Herald.

YOUR MICHELANGELO IN ROME

1. *The most eminent legal authorities in Italy were the public notaries who practised at the seat of the Curia Romana. Litigants often preferred to have their suits heard in Rome, but when that was not possible they sometimes had the necessary documents drawn up by one of the notaries in question (Barraclough, p. 26).*

47

*British
Museum
Mil. vi
From Rome
(June) 1509*

¶ To Lodovico di Buonarrota Simoni in Florence

Most revered father — I assured you in my last letter that I was not dead, although I did not feel too well; now however, now however *[sic]* I have fully recovered, thank God.

I learn from your last how the case is going. I am very concerned, because I'm sure that with these notaries one is bound to be the loser whatever happens and to be cheated all round, because they're all thieves.[1] Nevertheless, I suppose she herself will be paying out money too. If you are unable to come to a reasonable agreement, I urge you to defend yourself as well as you can, and above all, whatever you do, do it without dismay, for there is no undertaking, however great, which, if undertaken without dismay, does not appear small.[2] In this affair we must not consider the expense. And when there is nothing left to spend God will help us.

As to having the case heard here, I will arrange it if it is possible, as I know that she would have to spend more here than there, and she might yet come and ask mercy of us. The truth is, I could not make a start unless I had some money from the Pope. Keep me informed; and if you can come to an agreement, don't hold out over trifles. But if she wants you to make an arrangement which seems to you unfair, don't do it, because we will find some means of defending ourselves whatever happens. Keep me informed and don't mind if I don't answer you, because very often I cannot.

YOUR MICHELANGELO IN ROME

1. *The notaries of the period were a byword for incompetence and dishonesty. See Origo, pp. 203-5.*

2. *Is this perhaps a reflection of Michelangelo's own attitude to the painting of the Sistine vault, which he did not want to undertake?*

48

*British
Museum
Mil. vii
From Rome
(June) 1509*

¶ To Lodovico di Buonarrota Simoni in Florence

Most revered father — I learn from your last how things are going at home and how Giovansimone is behaving. I have not had, these ten years, worse news than on the evening I read your letter, because I thought I had arranged things for them in such a way that they were looking forward to setting up a good shop with the help I have promised them, and with this expectation were applying themselves to becoming

50

proficient and to learning their trade, so as to be able to carry it on when the time came. Now I see that they are doing the contrary, and particularly Giovansimone, whence I realize that it is useless to help him. And if, on the day I received your letter, I had been able to, I would have mounted my horse and by this time have settled everything. But not being able to do this, I'm writing him the letter I think he deserves, and if from now on he does not mend his ways, or indeed if he takes so much as the value of a straw out of the house, or does anything else to displease you, I beg you to let me know, because I will try to get leave from the Pope and will come home and show him the error of his ways.

I want you to realize that all the toil and sweat I have continually endured has been no less for your sake than for mine and that what I have bought, I have bought so that it might be yours as long as you live; because had it not been for you, I should not have bought it. Therefore, if you would like to let the house and lease the farm, do entirely as you choose; and with that income and with what I will give you, you can live like a gentleman, and if the summer were not approaching, as it is,[1] I would tell you to do so now and to come and stay here with me. But it is not the season, for you would not long survive the summer here. I have thought of taking away the money he has for the shop, and giving it to Gismondo that he and Buonarroto together might do the best they can, and of your letting those houses and the farm at Pazolatica, and of your retiring, with that income and with the help I can give you in addition, to some place where you would be comfortable and could have someone to look after you, either in Florence or just outside, and leaving that ne'er-do-well to nurse his arse. Please think of your own interest and whatever course you pursue let it be of your own choosing, and in all that you do I'm willing to help you as far as I possibly can. Keep me informed.

As to Cassandra, I have taken advice about having the case heard here. I am told that I should spend three times as much here as I should there, which is certainly true, because what can be done for a *grosso* there, cannot be done for two *carlini*[2] here. Besides, I have no friend here on whom I could rely and I cannot attend to a thing like this myself. It seems to me that if you are prepared to attend to it, you should take the usual course, as reason dictates, and that you should defend yourself as well as you possibly can, and for the money you need I will not fail you as long as I have any. Also, be as little fearful as you can, because this is not a matter in which life is at stake. That's all. Keep me informed, as I said above.

YOUR MICHELANGELO IN ROME

---

1. *Milanesi assigned this letter to August, but in view of this statement it cannot be dated later than the end of June.*

2. *It was an acknowledged fact that wherever the Papal Court was in residence the cost of living was much higher than elsewhere in Italy.*

49

Buonarroti
Archives
Mil. cxxvii
From Rome
(June) 1509

¶ To Giovan Simone di Lodovico Buonarroti in Florence

Giovan Simone — It is said that if one treats a good man well, he becomes better, but a ne'er-do-well becomes worse. I have tried for some years now, by deeds and by kind words, to induce you to live virtuously and at peace with your father and with the rest of us; and yet you continually become worse. I do not say that you are a ne'er-do-well, but you behave in a way that no longer pleases me, either me, or the others. I could give you a long lecture on your behaviour, but it would be mere words to you, like the others I've given you. To be brief, I can tell you one thing for certain – that you possess nothing in this world; both your expenses and the roof over your head I provide for you, and have provided for some time now, for the love of God, believing you to be my brother like the others. Now I'm certain that you are not my brother, because if you were, you would not threaten my father. On the contrary, you are a brute, and as a brute I shall treat you. For your information, he who thinks fit to threaten or to strike his father is held to hazard his life. But enough – I tell you you possess nothing in this world. And if I hear the least little thing about you, I will ride post to Florence and show you the error of your ways and teach you to destroy your own belongings and to set fire to houses and farms you have earned for yourself.[1] You are not in the position you think. If I do come home, I will give you cause to weep scalding tears, and you will learn what grounds you have for your presumption.

I tell you once again that if you mean to behave and to honour and revere your father, I will help you like the others, and in a little while will arrange for you to set up a good shop. If you do not do so, I will come home and arrange your affairs in such a way that you will know what you are better than you have ever known it, and will realize what you do possess in this world, and will be aware of it wherever you go. What I lack in words, I will make up for in deeds.

Michelangelo in Rome

I cannot help but write you another couple of lines to this effect – for twelve years now I have gone about all over Italy, leading a miserable life; I have borne every kind of humiliation, suffered every kind of hardship, worn myself to the bone with every kind of labour, risked my very life in a thousand dangers, solely to help my family; and now, when I begin to raise it up a little, you alone must be the one to confound and destroy in one hour what I have accomplished during so many years and with such pains. By the Body of Christ, to prevent this I am ready to confound, if need be, ten thousand such as you. So behave yourself and do not provoke those who have enough else to bear.

1. *Milanesi's emendation '[non] à' guadagniati tu' would appear to be unnecessary.*

52

¶ To Lodovico di Buonarrota Simoni in Florence

*British
Museum
Mil. xxii
From Rome
September 15th
1509*

Dearest father — I have given Giovanni Balducci here in Rome three hundred and fifty broad ducats in gold,[1] made payable to you in Florence. So as soon as you get this go to Bonifazio Fazi and he will pay them over to you, that is to say, he will give you three hundred and fifty broad ducats in gold. When you have received them take them to the *Spedalingo* and get him to enter them as you remember he entered the others for me. You will have a few ducats over in small change, which I wrote[2] and told you to keep. If you have not taken them, take them for your own use; and if you need more, take what you need; for I will give you whatever you need, even if I spend everything. And if there is any need for me to write to the *Spedalingo*, let me know.

I learn from your last letter how the matter is going; I'm very concerned about it; I cannot do anything to help you further. But all the same don't alarm yourself and don't be in the least depressed about it, because to lose one's possessions is not to lose one's life.[3] I will do more than make up to you what you will lose; but I would remind you not to count upon it, because one can never be sure. However, do your best and thank God that if this trouble had to come it has come at a time when you can help yourself better than you could have done in the past. Make the most of life and let your possessions go rather than fret about them; because I would rather have you alive, though poor, than you dead and all the gold in the world. And if those chatterboxes and others there reproach you, let them talk, for they know nothing and are without compassion.

On the fifteenth day of September.

Your Michelangelo sculptor in Rome

When you take the money to the *Spedalingo* take Buonarroto with you, and for a very good reason do not either of you mention it to a soul, that is to say, neither you nor Buonarroto are to talk about my sending money, either on this occasion or on any other.

---

1. *This sum is part of the second payment made to him in respect of the Sistine vault. For this and all other payments see Appendix 9.*

2. *This is evidently one of several versions of the same letter. Cf. No. 12, n. 1.*

3. *This refers to the conclusion of the case, brought by Mona Cassandra for the recovery of her dowery which Lodovico evidently lost.*

51

*British
Museum
Mil. lxxx
From Rome
October 17th
1509*

⁋ To Buonarroto di Lodovico di Buonarrota Simoni in Florence

Buonarroto — I got the bread; it is good, but not good enough to trade in, because there would be little profit.[1] I gave the boy five *carlini* and he would hardly give it to me. I am informed by your last that Lorenzo[2] will be passing through Rome and that you want me to entertain him. I don't think you realize how I am living here. However, I must forgive you for that. I will do what I can. As to Gismondo, I learn that he is coming here to expedite his affairs. Tell him from me not to place any reliance on me, not because I do not love him as a brother, but because I cannot help him in any way. I am obliged to care for myself before others, and I cannot supply my own necessities. I am living here in a state of great anxiety and of the greatest physical fatigue; I have no friends of any sort and want none. I haven't even time enough to eat as I should. So you mustn't bother me with anything else, for I could not bear another thing.

As to the shop, I urge you to be diligent. I'm pleased that Giovansimone is beginning to do well. Try to increase your capital legitimately or at least to preserve what you've got, so that you may know how to manage more important things later on; because I hope when I return home that you will set up on your own, if you are men enough. Tell Lodovico that I have not answered him, because I haven't had time. And don't be surprised when I don't write.

Michelangelo sculptor in Rome

1. *The implications of this proposal are not clear, as Buonarroto was in the wool trade. In the autograph the word 'pane' = bread is perfectly clear and admits of no confusion with the word 'panno' = cloth.*

2. *Lorenzo Strozzi, who later acquired a reputation for epicureanism, and even sought to surpass in extravagance the great Sienese banker, Agostino Chigi – an aim not difficult but impossible of achievement. See Pastor, VIII, p. 121 and Lanciani, pp. 301 et seq.*

52

*British
Museum
Mil. lxxxi
From Rome
(July) 1510*

⁋ To Buonarroto di Lodovico Simoni in Florence

Buonarroto — I learn from your last that you are all well and that Lodovico has been offered another appointment.[1] I am pleased about all this and urge him to accept, if it is so arranged that he can afterwards return to his post in Florence. Here I'm working as usual and will have finished my painting by the end of next week, that is to say, the part I began, and when I have uncovered it,[2] I think I shall receive payment and will try to get leave to come home for a month. I do not know what will ensue, but I need it, because I'm not very well. I have no time to write more. I will let you know what ensues.

MICHELANGELO SCULPTOR IN ROME

1. *Lodovico held office as Podestà at San Casciano from September 22nd 1510 to March 22nd 1511.*

2. *It was not until his return from his campaign against the French in Italy that the Pope viewed the finished section of the vault for the first time. This, according to an entry in the Diary of Paris de Grassis, was when he heard Vespers in the Sistine Chapel on the vigil of the Feast of the Assumption, August 14th 1511 (Tolnay, II, p. 235).*

¶ TO LODOVICO DI BUONARROTA SIMONI IN FLORENCE

53

British Museum Mil. xx From Rome September 5th 1510

Dearest father — I had a letter of yours this morning, the 5th day of September, which distressed me and continues to distress me very much, learning as I do that Buonarroto is ill. I beg you, as soon as you get this, to let me know how he is, because if he's really ill I could ride post to Florence this coming week, although it might mean a great loss to me. This is because the five hundred ducats I've earned in accordance with the agreement are due to me, and as much again which the Pope has to give me to put the rest of the work in hand. But he has gone away[1] and has left me no instructions, so that I find myself without any money and do not know what I ought to do. I do not want him to be angry if I were to leave, and to lose my due, but to remain is hard. I've written him a letter and await a reply. However, if Buonarroto is in danger, let me know, because I'll leave everything. Make good provision that he may not lack for money to help him. Go to Santa Maria to the *Spedalingo*, and show him my letter, if he doesn't believe you, and get him to give you fifty or a hundred ducats, whichever you want, and have no scruples. Don't worry, for God has not created us in order to abandon us. Reply at once and let me know definitely whether I must come or not.

YOUR MICHELANGELO SCULPTOR IN ROME

1. *The Pope left Rome on August 17th 1510 to 'accompany his army in the campaign against Ferrara, the most advanced outpost of the French in Italy'. In the course of his progress he reached Bologna on September 22nd 1510, where he remained until January 2nd 1511, having been taken seriously ill in the previous October (Pastor, VI, pp. 332 et seq.). It was during this illness that he grew the beard with which he is depicted in the portrait by Raphael (Plate 8). Michelangelo, being in need of money, went twice to Bologna during this time, once in September and again at the end of the year.*

8. *Pope Julius II*

After Raphael
National Gallery, London

¶ To Lodovico di Buonarrota Simoni in Florence

54

*British
Museum
Mil. xxi
From Rome
September 7th
(1510)*

Father dearest — I was very distressed to learn from your last letter that Buonarroto is ill. So as soon as you get this, go to the *Spedalingo* and get him to give you fifty or a hundred ducats, if you need them, and see that he is well provided with everything necessary, and that he does not lack for money. I explained to you that here I am owed five hundred ducats by the Pope, and as much again, which he has to give me to put up the scaffolding and to continue the other half of my work. But he has gone away and has left me no instructions. I have written him a letter. I do not know what will ensue. I would have come home as soon as I had your last letter, but if I leave without permission, I'm afraid the Pope might be angry and I might lose what is due to me. Don't forget, if Buonarroto is still ill, let me know at once, because, if you think it necessary, I will ride post and will be home in two days; since men are worth more than money. Let me know at once, because I am very distressed.

On the 7th day of September.

YOUR MICHELANGELO SCULPTOR IN ROME

¶ To Buonarroto di Lodovico di Buonarrota Simoni in Florence

55

*British
Museum
Mil. lxxxii
From Rome
October 26th
1510*

Buonarroto — I yesterday received from the Papal Datary[1] five hundred gold ducats of the Camera, and have given four hundred and sixty three and a half of them to Giovanni Balducci here in Rome, so that he can pay me in Florence, or rather transfer to Bonifazio Fazi four hundred and fifty broad ducats in gold. I have made them payable to you. Therefore, as soon as you get this go to Bonifazio and he will pay them over to you, that is to say, he will give you four hundred and fifty broad ducats in gold. If he cannot pay them over to you for about ten days,[2] have patience. Then, at all events, he will have them paid to you. Take them to Santa Maria Nuova to the *Spedalingo* and have them put to my account like the rest, and take either Giovansimone or Gismondo with you, or both of them, and do not withdraw the money from the bank, if the *Spedalingo* is not in Florence. Then, when you have had them put to my account with the *Spedalingo*, let me know immediately exactly how much money I have there. And do not talk to anyone about matters of this kind. I will write to Lodovico next time. If you see Michelangelo Tanagli,[3] tell him from me that for two months now I have had so many worries and vexations that I have not been able to write to him at all, but that I will do my best to find him a cornelian or a good medal, thank him for the cheese and tell him that I will write to him next Saturday. On the twenty-sixth day of October 1510.

MICHELANGELO SCULPTOR IN ROME

1. *Lorenzo Pucci (1458–1531), a Florentine, afterwards Cardinal de' Santi Quattro Coronati.*

2. *The period of usance on a bill of exchange.*

3. *Michelangelo di Bernardino Tanagli (c.1470–c.1530), a Sienese sculptor. He worked on the tomb of Adrian VI to designs by Peruzzi. For an account of his character, see Cellini, II, xxx.*

56

British Museum Mil. lxxxiii From Rome November 23rd 1510

¶ TO BUONARROTO DI LODOVICO SIMONI IN FLORENCE

Buonarroto — Enclosed with this will be a letter for Messer Angelo. Give it to him at once. I think in a few days' time I shall have to go back to Bologna, because the Papal Datary, with whom I returned from Bologna, promised when he left here that as soon as he reached Bologna he would make provision for me to continue the work. It is a month since he left, and as yet I have heard nothing. I will wait until the end of next week; then, if there is no news, I think I will go to Bologna and will pass through Florence. And that's all. Let Lodovico know of this and tell him that I am well.

On the twenty-third . . . 1510.

MICHELANGELO SCULPTOR IN ROME

57

British Museum Mil. lxxxiv From Rome January 11th 1511

¶ TO BUONARROTO DI LODOVICO DI BUONARROTA SIMONI IN FLORENCE
DELIVER TO THE SHOP OF LORENZO STROZZI, ARTE DI LANA

Buonarroto — I arrived here safely on Tuesday evening, thank God. I have since received the money which was promised by letter when I was in Florence. In this will be enclosed a first bill of exchange[1] for two hundred and twenty-eight broad gold ducats from Lanfredino Lanfredini.[2] Try to get it accepted and paid at the same time, and when you get the money take it to the *Spedalingo* and have it entered to my account and see that the last amount I sent direct to the *Spedalingo* is entered as well, and

58

get out the ledger with the folios[3] and then let me know the total amount I have there.

If you see the Herald, tell him to thank his lordship the Gonfalonier for me, and commend me to him. I haven't time this evening; I will write to him next Saturday. When you go to the *Spedalingo* take one of those brothers of yours with you and don't discuss it with others. That's all. Keep the chest locked, so that my clothes don't get stolen like Gismondo's. On the eleventh day of January.

MICHELANGELO DI BUONARROTA SIMONI SCULPTOR IN ROME

1. *For this and other transfers of money see Appendix 4.*

2. *Lanfredino Lanfredini (c.1446–c.1518), a Florentine banker who belonged to the Santo Spirito Quarter. He was later one of twenty citizens appointed to reform the government on the return of the Medici in 1512 (Sanuto, XV, 93, 105, and Mansfield, passim). For the management of his banking house in Rome see No. 58.*

3. *These folios, 'carte', may have been the equivalent of the modern pass-sheet, containing details of the customer's debit and credit account. It is possible that they were torn out from the main ledger. Cf. Edler, pp. 363 et seq.*

¶ TO BUONARROTO DI LODOVICO DI BUONARROTA SIMONI IN FLORENCE

58

*British Museum
Mil. lxxxvi
From Rome
January 26th
1511*

Buonarroto — Fifteen days ago to-day I sent you two hundred and twenty–eight broad gold ducats, which I gave to Francesco Perini[1] here in Rome. He drew up the bill of exchange for me, so that the money could be paid to you in Florence by one of the Orlandini, and the said bill I enclosed with one of my letters, and sent it to you. I should have had an answer yesterday; not having had it, I suppose the letter has not been delivered to you, and if in fact the one of fifteen days ago has not been delivered to you, it must have gone astray. Eight days ago to-day Francesco Perini drew the second bill of exchange on the same lines and I enclosed it with a letter of mine and sent it to you. So as soon as you get this, if you have not had the letter or the money, let me know without fail, and send the letters through Bonifazio Fazi, because he gives me a better service with them. And if you have had the money, go and take it to the *Spedalingo* and get him personally to enter it, with the last amount you paid into my account, and let me know.

I got the parcel. Also I agree about Baccio.[2] I am certainly in favour of renting them. I've no time for writing. Answer me without fail and as quickly as you can, because it is important to me. On the twenty-sixth day of January 1510.[3]

MICHELANGELO IN ROME

1. *Francesco Perini, presumably the Director of the Lanfredini banking house in Rome. He was still corresponding with Michelangelo in 1517 (Frey, Briefe, p. 80).*

2. *Probably Baccio Mariotto da Settignano. Michelangelo was in correspondence about certain lands bought from him in 1528 (Frey, Briefe, p. 295).*

3. *N.S. 1511.*

59

British Museum Mil. xxvii From Rome March (8th) 1511

¶ To Lodovico di Buonarrota Simoni in Florence

Dearest father — I did not answer your last, because I had told Buonarroto what I thought you should do if you can.[1] Then again, in the last one I wrote to Buonarroto, I said the same and asked him to read it to you, so I assume you have understood. Nevertheless, if you cannot, I make no demands. What I thought you should do was only the better to enable me to help, or rather to do as I have promised those brothers of mine. Do what you can, and do not be in any way upset by what I write, for I am disposed towards every one of you as I have always been.[2]

Your Michelangelo sculptor in Rome

1. *This certainly refers to the repayment of the money Lodovico had drawn from Michelangelo's account at Sta. Maria Nuova without permission. See No. 60.*

2. *The date, March 8th, on the face of the letter, is in Buonarroto's hand, but whether it is the date of receipt or dispatch is uncertain.*

60

British Museum Mil. xi From Rome June 1511

¶ To Lodovico di Buonarrota Simoni in Florence

Most revered father — A few days ago I sent you a hundred ducats from those I had put aside here for my living and working expenses; this I did, because I think they are safer there than here. I assume you have received them. Please will you take them to the *Spedalingo* and have them put to my account with the others. This leaves me eighty ducats here, which I think will last me four months, and I still have six month's work to do here before I am due to have any money from the Pope, so I am certain to be short, and I reckon that I shall be short by fifty ducats. I therefore beg you out of the hundred you have promised to repay me,[1] that you will repay fifty; the balance you can keep, on

60

condition that, whatever happens, you will have them [*i.e. the fifty*] ready within four months, as I shall need them here. The hundred I have sent you I want to try to save to return to the heirs of the Cardinal of Siena,[2] for you are aware that some of the money in Santa Maria Nuova is owed to them. Would you in any case look into the question of buying a farm, as I am told they are going cheap; since, when my painting here is finished, I still have a thousand ducats due to me from the Pope, and if it goes well, I hope to be paid without fail. So pray to God for him, for his good and for ours.

Write to me by return.

On the . . . of June.

YOUR MICHELANGELO SCULPTOR IN ROME

1. *Prior to becoming Podestà at San Casciano, Lodovico had used some of Michelangelo's money without permission, and had expressed his intention of repaying it (Frey, Briefe, pp. 16–18).*

2. *Francesco Piccolomini, afterwards Pope Pius III (d. 1503), with whom Michelangelo had entered into a contract in June 1501 for fifteen marble statues for his chapel in the Duomo in Siena (Milanesi, p. 616). The Cardinal advanced Michelangelo 100 gold ducats, but as the work was never completed he remained in debt to the Cardinal's heirs, a debt which was not liquidated until after his death (Tolnay, I, pp. 227 et seq.). See also Vol. II, No. 469 and Frey, Briefe, pp. 344, 382.*

¶ TO BUONARROTO DI LODOVICO SIMONI IN FLORENCE

61

Buonarroto — I learn from your letter that you would be glad to learn whereabouts I should like to buy. I learnt the same from Lodovico's last one, but I have not had time to write before.

Buonarroti Archives Mil. lxxxviii From Rome July (1511)

It seems to me that above all things we should look for a sound title, wherever the property may be, which makes no difference to me at all; what pleases you, pleases me likewise. Again, be careful to buy from people with whom, in case of trouble, the agent can deal personally. About Luigi Gerardini's I don't know what to say. If the property has neither a good income nor a sound title, I don't know what else there is to buy. In short, I'm not bothered at all as to the locality in which you buy, and about this there is no need to write further, provided it is a good proposition. And don't rush at it, that we may not be cheated. I think that's all. When you see Giovanni da Ricasoli, commend me to him.

MICHELANGELO SCULPTOR IN ROME
in July, I don't know what date.

62

*British
Museum
Mil. xxv
From Rome
(July 1511)*

⁋ To Lodovico di Buonarrota Simoni in Florence

Dearest father — I did not reply to your letter on Saturday, because I didn't have time. As regards the *Spedalingo*, it seems to me that it is all the same whether I do, or do not, write and tell him to pay you the money on demand, since he already knows perfectly well that you will not go and draw the money until you have decided to buy, and he will know exactly the same thing when I have written to him. However, let me know his name and how I should write to him, and I will see to it. As to the things you have on hand, I replied to Buonarroto that I'm not bothered as to whether they're nearby or some way off, provided the title is sound. As to Luigi Gerardini's thing, I am not confident, because if it were a good proposition, I reckon it would have been sold by now. I do not know why it should be reserved for us rather than for others; and it seems to me that his need of money has made him unreliable in this matter. I think that's all. Proceed slowly; perhaps it may come over the *Spedalingo* to offer us something.

Your Michelangelo sculptor in Rome

63

*British
Museum
Mil. xxiii
From Rome
October 4th
1511*

⁋ To Lodovico di Lionardo di Buonarrota Simoni in Florence

Father dearest — On Tuesday I went to see the Pope. I will tell you why when I have more leisure. It suffices that I went again on Wednesday morning and was paid four hundred broad ducats of the Camera in gold, of which I am sending three hundred to Florence, so that the three hundred broad ducats in gold, which I'm paying to the Altoviti[1] here, may be paid to you there by the Strozzi. So make out the proper receipts and take them [*i.e. the ducats*] to the *Spedalingo* and get him to enter them like the rest, and remind him about the farm, and if he prevaricates with you, try to buy from someone else, if you see that it is safe. I give you permission to spend up to one thousand four hundred ducats. Take Buonarroto with you, and ask the *Spedalingo* whether he is willing to be of service to us. Try to buy from him if possible, because it is safer.

I wrote and told you that none of my things, either the drawings or anything else, were to be touched by anyone. You have not replied to me about this. It seems that you do not read my letters. That's all. Pray God that I may be honoured here, and that I may satisfy the Pope, because I hope, if I satisfy him, that we shall receive some benefit at his hands. Again, pray God for him.

Your Michelangelo sculptor in Rome

1. *The banking house of Bindo Altoviti on the Tiber was not demolished until 1889 (Lanciani, p. 279).*

¶ To Lodovico di Buonarrota Simoni in Florence

64

British Museum Mil. xxiv From Rome October 11th 1511

Dearest father — On Saturday I sent you three hundred broad ducats in gold through the Altoviti, so that they might be paid to you in Florence by the Strozzi, so I assume you have received them and have done as I wrote you. So let me know about this, and let me know what the *Spedalingo* is up to, if he is prevaricating with you. That's all. I have no time for writing. Please keep me informed about things, because there are many tales going about here.[1]

On the eleventh day of October.

YOUR MICHELANGELO SCULPTOR IN ROME

1. *See Appendix 10.*

¶ To Lodovico di Lionardo di Buonarrota Simoni in Florence

65

British Museum Mil. xxvi From Rome (January 3rd) (1512)

Father dearest — I could not answer your letters before. I learn, I learn *[sic]* from your last one that you have a number of things on hand, but nothing good, as I should expect. I'm sure one cannot buy independently of Santa Maria Nuova without risk. Therefore, it seems better to bide our time for a few months more, because the *Spedalingo* is perhaps also biding his time before doing us this service. If however you find something sound and good in the meantime, take it and do not be particular as to the price, within a hundred ducats. And if you do not buy, either from the *Spedalingo* or from anyone else, I hope to be home this Easter and we will come to some decision; because I do not wish the *Spedalingo* to keep my money and to trifle with us. I had a letter from Buonarroto a few days ago and could not answer him then. Make my apologies. I will answer him when I can. I think that's all.

YOUR MICHELANGELO SCULPTOR IN ROME

¶ To Buonarroto di Lodovico Simoni in Florence

66

Buonarroti Archives Mil. lxxxv From Rome January 10th 1512

Buonarroto — A few days ago I had a letter of yours, from which I learnt exactly what you have in mind; but because it would take a long time to answer in detail, I will tell you briefly what I think. As to the shop, I have it in mind to do all that I have promised you when I return home, and although I have written about buying a property, I still have it in mind to set up the shop, because when I have finished here and have obtained what is due to me, I shall have the means to do as I have promised you.

As to your now having found someone willing to advance two or three thousand broad ducats to set you up with a shop, he has a larger purse than I have. It seems to me that you should certainly accept; but look out that you are not cheated, because one never finds anyone ready to do something for nothing. You tell me that this fellow wants to give you one of his daughters to wife; but I tell you that all the offers he makes you will be unfulfilled, except for the wife[1] once he has foisted her on you, and you will have more of her than you'll want. Again I tell you that I do not like your getting involved through avarice with men much more unscrupulous than yourself. Avarice is a deadly sin and nothing sinful can succeed. It seems to me that you had better put him off with plausible excuses and hold the matter in abeyance until I've finished here and can see how I'm placed. This will be in about three months or thereabouts. Now do as you think. I could not reply to you before.

On the 10th day of January.

MICHELANGELO SCULPTOR IN ROME

---

1. *Nothing is known about the date or circumstances of Buonarroto's first marriage, nor when his wife, Cassandra di Bernardo Puccini died. See No. 89, n. 2.*

67 ¶ To Lodovico di Lionardo di Buonarrota Simoni in Florence

British Museum Mil. xxviii From Rome (February 28th) 1512

Dearest father — I have received two of your letters and one of Buonarroto's to the same effect. Indeed, from Buonarroto's I learn that you have been to see a farm in the region of Prato, that it is a good property and that you are looking into the title and if it is sound that you will do a deal. I should be very pleased if it were possible to buy, but I know to whom it belongs and I fancy it is not an honest deal. So keep your eyes open and don't bother with it unless you're sure. As to affairs in Rome[1] there has been some apprehension and still is, but not so much. Things are expected to settle down – may they do so by the grace of God. That's all I have to tell you. I expect to be home this summer whatever happens.

YOUR MICHELANGELO SCULPTOR IN ROME

---

1. *While the Holy League was moving into action against the French invaders of Italy (see Appendix 10) Julius II, finding himself threatened by the intrigues of the pro-French elements in Rome, withdrew for a time to the fastness of the Castel Sant' Angelo. The city guard was strengthened and many arrests were made (Pastor, VI, p. 398).*

¶ To Lodovico di Lionardo di Buonarrota Simoni in Florence

68

British Museum Mil. xxix From Rome (March 6th) 1512

Dearest father — In my answer to your last letter I said that I fancied that the farm on the road to Prato did not have a sound title. Since then I am more fully informed, and it seems to me better, unless I am mistaken, not to bother with it. You again informed me that the *Spedalingo* had sent you to see one two miles outside Florence, and that you thought it very dear, and furthermore that it had come to nothing. I assure you that, if one were to buy a farm for fifty or a hundred ducats more from him, rather than from anyone else, one would not do badly. But I have no hope of it, because I believe he is an arrant rascal.[1] The one you say you have on hand in the plain of Fonte di Valdarno, if it were a good proposition, would not displease me. However, do as you think best, and buy what pleases you, because what pleases you will also please me, wherever it is, provided it has a sound title. That's all I have to tell you. This summer I shall certainly come home, God willing, and we will take the game out of the *Spedalingo*'s hands if he does not offer us something in the meantime. As to Francesco Consiglio[2] I don't want to hear about him, because his father did not do you such a good turn that I need do anything for him. Those who are ill disposed must take the consequences.

Your Michelangelo sculptor in Rome

When you write to me, do not any longer send my letters through the Altoviti. Send them, as you used to, to Balduccio's bank, and if you send them through other banks, write on the letter 'Deliver to the shop of Baccio Bettini', and it will be delivered to me.

1. *Michelangelo was correct in his surmise, the Spedalingo at this date being Leonardo di Giovanni Buonafè, who was later suspended for unethical practices. See Appendix 5.*

2. *Michelangelo's cousin. See No. 3.*

¶ To Lodovico di Lionardo di Buonarrota Simoni in Florence

69

British Museum Mil. xxx From Rome (March 13th) 1512

Dearest father — I told you about my enquiries here and what I had learnt; that is to say, that the thing was more risky than not, I mean the farm in the Prato region. However, you are on the spot and can see and judge better than I. Do as you think best. As to the authority you want me to make out for the *Spedalingo*, imagine that I am the *Spedalingo*, and make me out one exactly as you want it, with the address and everything and I will copy it exactly and will send it back to you; because I don't know his name and would not know how to do it. So have no qualms, because, should the

Spedalingo be unwilling to let you have the money when you have bought, I will come to Florence in person and will make him give it you. If you buy, do not take anything near the Arno or any other noisome river. Look into anything the *Spedalingo* is willing to offer you; if you can pull it off at a reasonable price, take it; again, if the price is a little more than it should be, but not too much so, I should be for taking it. I think that's all. Here there is no sign of the danger anticipated in Florence, and God grant things may go well.[1]

YOUR MICHELANGELO SCULPTOR IN ROME

Send me the copy of the authority exactly as you want it, and I will send it to you by return. Take it to the *Spedalingo* and I shall be glad of it, as he will see that we are in earnest about buying.

1. See Appendix 10.

70

British Museum Mil. xxxi From Rome (March 20th) 1512

¶ TO LODOVICO DI LIONARDO DI BUONARROTA SIMONI IN FLORENCE

Dearest father — Since I wrote to you I've been told that the *Spedalingo* would laugh at a mere note of authority from me. I have therefore had a power of attorney drawn up which I'm sending you with this which you can show to the *Spedalingo*, and as my attorney you can get him to pay you from my account whatever sum the purchase of the property amounts to. This I assume he will do. If it is not valid let me know.

The said power of attorney was drawn up here by a Florentine notary called Ser Albizo.[1] I'm making you my attorney in this matter, that is to say in order that you may demand from the *Spedalingo*, or rather get him to give you as much as the purchase of the property amounts to, together with the tax, from the money he holds for me, on this condition, that you do not spend a *quattrino* of mine on any other thing without my permission, nor draw more than is needed for the said purchase from the said *Spedalingo*. I assume that the provisions of the power of attorney are to this effect, because these were my instructions to the notary.[2]

If you buy, above all take care over the title and let me know what you do, or rather when you have bought. That's all. The longest I could delay would be until September, but I do not think it will be as long as that.

YOUR MICHELANGELO SCULPTOR IN ROME

1. *Albizo di Francesco di Ser Albizi of the Collegium scriptorum archivii Curiae Romanae. He it was who in 1516 drew up the Third Contract for the Tomb of Julius II (Milanesi, p. 648).*

2. *Michelangelo apparently knew no Latin, in which, like all legal documents of the period, the instrument was drawn up. Cf. Giannotti, p. 65.*

¶ To Lodovico di Lionardo di Buonarrota Simoni in Florence

71

British Museum Mil. xxxviii From Rome (March 27th) (1512)

Dearest father — I learn from your last letter that the interdict has been lifted,[1] which I was very pleased to hear. I learn also that the *Spedalingo* is encouraging and that you think it better to wait. I think so too, because one cannot rely on buying from others, and I do not think, as he has said several times that he will offer you something, that he will trifle with you. Therefore it is better to wait. Giovanni da Ricasoli is asking something of me, which I do not want to do, and I haven't time to write to him this evening, so please ask Buonarroto to make him my apologies and tell him not to expect anything of me. He will understand. Also please will you do me a kindness. It is this. There is a young Spaniard in Florence, named Alonso,[2] a painter, who, I understand, is ill. And because someone here, a relative of his or a Spanish friend, would like to know how he is, he has asked me to write to some friend of mine in Florence to find out and let him know. So please will you or Buonarroto make some enquiry of Granaccio, who knows him, as to how he is, and let me have a definite answer, so that I may show my willingness to oblige the man here. That's all.

YOUR MICHELANGELO SCULPTOR IN ROME

1. *In the middle of November 1511, the ban of excommunication, which the Pope had laid on Florence on September 23rd, was lifted. It was later reimposed, but was finally raised on March 21st 1512.*

2. *Alonso Berruguete. See No. 42.*

¶ To Lodovico di Buonarrota Simoni in Florence

72

British Museum Mil. xiii From Rome (April) 1512

Dearest father — I learn from your last that the *Spedalingo* has let you down and is prevaricating. Have patience and pretend not to notice, until I return and arrange everything. I reckon I shall have finished here within two months,[1] and then I will come home. I have nothing else to tell you. If I do not write to you more often, do not be surprised, because I cannot, and besides, I have no-one to take the letters. Do not write to me too often either, during the rest of the time I have to remain here, because I do not go for the letters myself and have to have them brought to me and to bother other people. Pray God that my thing here may end well.

YOUR MICHELANGELO SCULPTOR IN ROME

1. *Michelangelo always underestimated the time it would take him to complete any work on which he was engaged. He had estimated three months in January. See No. 66.*

73

British Museum Mil. xiv From Rome (April) 1512

¶ TO LODOVICO DI LIONARDO DI BUONARROTA SIMONI IN FLORENCE

Dearest father — I wrote to you last Saturday asking you not to put yourself to the trouble of writing to me too often; this I did because I live at a distance from the bank and more often than not, the letters have to be brought to me and seem to me to be more of a nuisance than anything else. Nevertheless, if you need to write to me, please do, and particularly if you were to buy, see that I know of it. I understand that you have been let down by the *Spedalingo*. I am not surprised, because if he were reliable he would not be kept in that position! Nevertheless, be polite to him and pretend not to notice. Perhaps he will be inclined to offer us something before I return. But if he does not, when I return we will take steps so that he may not benefit from both the money and the farm. That's all.

YOUR MICHELANGELO SCULPTOR IN ROME

74

British Museum Mil. xii From Rome (May) 1512

¶ TO LODOVICO DI BUONARROTA SIMONI IN FLORENCE

Dearest father — I learn from your last letter that the *Spedalingo* has offered you two farms, one belonging to him and the other to someone else. I would sooner buy from him than from someone else, but it does not matter to whom the farm belongs, so long as the Hospital guarantees it. The one at Pian di Ripoli, according to your description, is a fine property; I do not know whether it is a fine one because it is well maintained or because the soil is good. However, for my part, if it is good, it would please me as to price, because it is convenient, and particularly so as it has a good house for the owner. You are on the spot and can judge. I cannot advise you from here, but I assure you that whatever you buy will be satisfactory. Therefore, do not hesitate, provided the title is sound; and whatever you are pleased to take, will please me, because you have taken it, whichever it is. I think that's all. Do as you think best. I shall be home in any case when I have finished my painting here, which will be in two or three months.

YOUR MICHELANGELO SCULPTOR IN ROME

¶ TO LODOVICO DI LIONARDO DI BUONARROTA SIMONI IN FLORENCE

British Museum Mil. xxxiii From Rome (May) 1512

75

Dearest father — I have received two letters of yours to the same effect and have understood everything; that is to say, about the *Spedalingo* and about Raffaello the broker.[1] I do not know what I can say to you, because one can never judge without seeing for oneself. Therefore, do what you think best, and whatever you do will be satisfactory. I only remind you to take the greatest care over the title, because these are not the times to make a loss; for if that should happen, I do not think I could find a way to make it good any more. And if you do not see anything to suit you, have patience, since, as we have waited so long, we can wait another two or three months. That's all I have to say to you. Pray God my affairs may go well.

YOUR MICHELANGELO SCULPTOR IN ROME

1. *Raffaello di Giorgio Ubaldini da Gagliano, Lodovico's brother-in-law.*

¶ TO LODOVICO DI LIONARDO DI BUONARROTA SIMONI IN FLORENCE

British Museum Mil. xxxiv From Rome (June 5th) 1512

76

Dearest father — I learnt from your last letter about the farm[1] you've got from Santa Maria Nuova and that it is a sound proposition. I'm extremely pleased about it and although it is expensive, I assume you saw that it was worth it, and if we've paid a hundred ducats over and above, having the title it has, it is not dear. I thank God I am quit of this business. Now only one thing more remains for me to do and that is to set up those brothers of mine in a shop, for I think of nothing else day or night. Then, it seems to me I shall have discharged my obligations; and if more of life remains to me,[2] I want to live it in peace.

Giovanni da Ricasoli has written me a letter to which I haven't time to reply. Please make my apologies. I'll reply to him next Saturday. That's all.

YOUR MICHELANGELO SCULPTOR IN ROME

1. *In May 1512 Michelangelo bought a farm in the parish of Santo Stefano-in-Pane, called La Loggia. A month later he bought a plot of arable land in the same parish. The contract was drawn up by the notary, Ser Giovanni Romena. See Appendix 6.*

2. *Michelangelo was at this time thirty-seven years of age. Some fifty-two years of life remained to him, but never to the end of his days was he allowed to live life in peace.*

77 ❡ To Buonarroto di Lodovico Simoni in Florence

Buonarroti Archives Mil. lxxxvii From Rome July 24th 1512

Buonarroto — I haven't time to answer your letter because it's late and again, if I had time, I could not give you a definite answer until I see the outcome of my affairs here. I shall be home this September and will do all I can for you. I work harder than anyone who has ever lived. I'm not well and worn out with this stupendous labour and yet I'm patient in order to achieve the desired end. So you, too, can very well be patient for two months, being ten thousand times better off than I am.

MICHELANGELO SCULPTOR IN ROME

78 ❡ To Lodovico di Buonarrota Simoni in Florence

British Museum Mil. xxxv From Rome (July/August) 1512

Dearest father — I wrote to you about doing what I had promised for those brothers of mine and I have not thought better of it; on the contrary I care more about it than they do; but believe me this is not the time.[1] You will find many people ready to give you advice, but trust few of them. Having waited so long, it seems to me we may leave it, at any rate, for another three months. This is not so large an undertaking that it cannot be carried into effect. And if you were to see that we are running any risk with the money or that it is not safely deposited where it is, let me know. That's all. I have nothing else to add just now.

YOUR MICHELANGELO SCULPTOR IN ROME

1. *Florence stood in some danger from the vengeance of the Pope at this time. See Appendix 10. Cf. Sanuto, XIV, 454, and Landucci, pp. 319 et seq.*

¶ To Buonarroto di Lodovico Simoni in Florence

79

Buonarroto — I've had a letter of yours to which I'm replying briefly owing to lack of time. As to my returning home, I cannot return until I've finished this undertaking, which I expect to finish by the end of September. The truth is it's so great a labour that I cannot estimate the time within a fortnight. Let it suffice that I shall be home before All Saints in any case, if I do not die in the meantime. I'm being as quick as I can, because I long to be home.

MICHELANGELO SCULPTOR IN ROME

Buonarroti Archives Mil. lxxxix From Rome August 21st 1512

¶ To Buonarroto di Lodovico Simoni in Florence

80

Buonarroto — I have not written to you for some days, because I had no need. Now, hearing here how things are going in Florence it seems to me I ought to write and tell you what I think, which is this. As the Territory,[1] according to what is being said here, is in evil plight[2] I think you should all see about withdrawing to some place where you would be safe, abandoning your possessions and everything else, since a man's life is of more value by far than his possessions. And if you haven't the money to leave Florence, go to the *Spedalingo* and get him to give you some. And if I were with you, I would draw out all the money the *Spedalingo* holds for me and would go to Siena and take a house and remain there until things have settled down in Florence. I believe the power of attorney I gave Lodovico, enabling him to draw on my account, is still valid. Therefore, if need be, take the money and in time of danger such as this spend what you need. Keep the balance for me. As regards the Territory, don't get yourselves involved in any way, either by word or deed; act as in case of plague – be the first to flee. That's all. Let me have news as soon as you can, because I'm very concerned.

MICHELANGELO SCULPTOR IN ROME

Buonarroti Archives Mil. xc From Rome September 5th 1512

1. *i.e. Florence, the townships and rural communes of Tuscany.*

2. *See Appendix 10.*

9. *The Vault of the Sistine Chapel*

Michelangelo
The Vatican, Rome

81

¶ To Buonarroto di Lodovico Simoni in Florence

*Buonarroti
Archives
Mil. xci
From Rome
September 18th
1512*

Buonarroto — I learnt from your last letter that the Territory was in great danger which distressed me very much. Now there are fresh rumours that the Medici have entered Florence[1] and that everything is settled; on which account I assume that the danger, that is to say, from the Spaniards, is over and I assume there is no longer any need to leave. So stay quietly and do not make friends or intimates of anyone, save God, and do not speak either good or evil of anyone, because no-one knows what the outcome will be. Attend only to your own affairs.

The forty ducats that Lodovico drew from Santa Maria Nuova – I wrote and told you the other day that if your lives were in danger you could spend, not forty, but the lot;[2] but except for this I did not give you permission to touch them. I warn you I haven't a *grosso* myself and am, so to speak, barefoot and naked and I cannot have the balance that is owed me until the work is completed. I'm enduring the utmost discomfort and weariness. So if you are also putting up with some discomfort, don't be sorry for yourselves, and while you can support yourselves on your own money, don't touch mine, save in case of danger as I've said. If, however, you should have some great need, I beg you to tell me of it first, if you please. I shall soon be home. There is no doubt at all that I shall celebrate All Saints with you in Florence; if God wills.

On the 18th day of September.

MICHELANGELO SCULPTOR IN ROME

1. *Giuliano de' Medici reached Florence on September 1st, and Cardinal Giovanni, his elder brother (afterwards Pope Leo X), made a ceremonial entry a fortnight later (Ammirato, 6, xxix, pp. 5 et seq.).*

2. *This is the precise order of the original.*

82

¶ To Lodovico di Buonarrota Simoni in Florence

*British
Museum
Mil. xxxvii
From Rome
(October) 1512*

Dearest father — From your last letter I learnt how things are going in Florence, though I knew something of it before. We must be resigned and commend ourselves to God and recognize the error of our ways, through which alone these adversities come upon us, and particularly through arrogance and ingratitude; for never have I come across people more arrogant or more ungrateful than the Florentines. So if judgment comes upon us, it is not without cause.[1]

As to the sixty ducats which you tell me you have to pay,[2] it seems to me excessive and I'm very concerned about it. However, as long as it is pleasing to God we must be resigned. I'll write a couple of lines to Giuliano de' Medici, which will be enclosed with this. Read them over and if you're disposed to take them to him, take them and see whether they're any use. If they're of no use, consider whether it would be possible to sell what we've got and go and live elsewhere. Again, if you find that you fare worse than others, do all you can to avoid payment and let them rather take away what you've got. But if they treat others as they do you, be resigned and trust in God. You tell me you've provided up to thirty ducats. Take the other thirty from the money belonging to me and send me the balance here. Take it to Bonifazio Fazi who will make it payable to me here through Giovanni Balducci, and get Bonifazio to make you out a receipt for the said money and send it to me in your next letter.

Make the most of life and if you cannot share in the honours of the Territory[3] like other citizens, be satisfied that you have bread to eat and can live at peace with Christ and poorly as I do here. For I lead a miserable existence and reck not of life nor honour – that is of this world; I live wearied by stupendous labours and beset by a thousand anxieties. And thus have I lived for some fifteen years now and never an hour's happiness have I had, and all this have I done in order to help you, though you have never either recognized or believed it – God forgive us all. I am prepared always to do the same as long as I live, provided I am able.

YOUR MICHELANGELO SCULPTOR IN ROME

1. *This sentiment is typical of the period. Cf. Landucci, p. 324. 'It was almost incredible speed to have taken Campi on the 27th and Prato on the 29th. It happened, however, on account of our sins.'*

2. *Not a fine, as Tolnay states (I, p. 43), but Lodovico's liability in respect of the indemnity which the Florentines were required to pay in order to preserve their liberty after the fall of Prato. See Appendix 10.*

3. *By refusing to pay his share of the indemnity, Lodovico would become a debtor to the Commune and, like all those whose names were entered in the 'Libri dello Specchio' for failure to meet their obligations in respect of taxes, dues, etc., he would automatically be excluded from office and from the enjoyment of the 'onori della Città' or 'della Terra' (Marzi, pp. 169 et seq., and Staley, p. 190). Having been approved by the 'Squittino' or scrutiny of 1524, Lodovico again became eligible and was appointed Podestà of Castelfranco in the following year (Gotti, II, p. 18).*

¶ TO LODOVICO DI BUONARROTA SIMONI IN FLORENCE

83

Dearest[1] father — I learnt from your last letter that you've returned the forty ducats to the *Spedalingo*. You've done rightly, but should you hear that this is risky, please let me know of it. I have finished the chapel I have been painting;[2] the Pope is very well satisfied. But other things have not turned out for me as I'd hoped. For this I blame the times, which are very unfavourable to our art. I shall not be home for All

British Museum Mil. xv From Rome October 1512

Saints, because I have not the means to do what I want to do, but again this is not the time for it. Make the most of life and don't bother yourself about anything else. That's all.

YOUR MICHELANGELO SCULPTOR IN ROME

1. *There is some doubt among specialists in Renaissance handwriting as to the precise significance of the abbreviation used by Michelangelo at the beginning of this and some other letters. It may stand for 'Carissimo' or 'Karissimo', it may stand for 'Reverendissimo' or perhaps for 'Caro e Reverendissimo'. As it is a matter of opinion, Milanesi's reading has here been followed in a majority of instances.*

2. *This letter (the implications of which are discussed in Appendix 9) marks the end of the painting of the Sistine vault. In the Diary of Paris de Grassis, the Papal Master of Ceremonies, the entry for the eve of All Saints, October 31st, reads as follows – 'Vesperae in vigilia omnium sanctorum. . . . Hodie primum capella nostra, pingi finita, aperta est.' (Tolnay, II, p. 247).*

10. *Facsimile of Letter No. 83*   British Museum, London

V

LETTERS
84 - III

From Rome
1512 - 1515

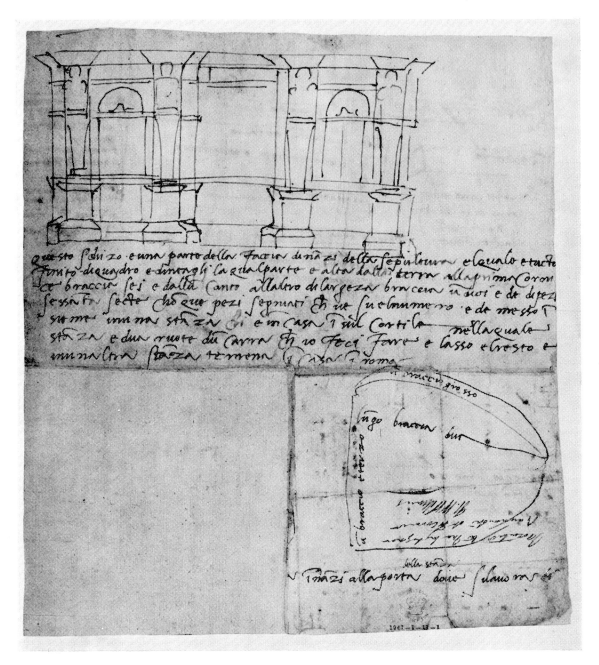

11. *Sketches connected with the Tomb of Julius II*

Michelangelo
British Museum, London

V. From Rome: 1512-1515

¶ To Baldassare

84

*Buonarroti
Archives
Mil. cccxlv
From Rome
(October 1512)*

Baldassare[1] — I am very surprised at you. Since you wrote me such a long time ago that you had so many marbles ready, since you have had so many months of wonderfully fine weather for sailing, since you have had of me a hundred gold ducats and are lacking in nothing, I do not know how it comes about that you do not serve me. Will you please ship the marbles you told me you had ready immediately, and the sooner you come the better. I will wait for you till the end of the month. After that, we shall proceed as we are advised by those who have more experience of these things than I have. Only I would remind you that you do wrong to fail in your agreement and to trifle with those upon whom you depend for your livelihood.

MICHELANGELO IN ROME

1. *Assumed by Milanesi to be the son of Giampaulo di Cagione, and the brother of Bartolomeo, called Il Mancino da Torre. The latter was concerned with other members of his trade in a dispute over Michelangelo's order for marbles, which had been given in May 1506. A judgment was delivered at Carrara on January 23rd 1511 (Milanesi, pp. 633–4).*

¶ To Lodovico di Buonarrota Simoni in Florence

85

*British
Museum
Mil. xxxvi
From Rome
(October) 1512*

Dearest father — I learn from your last that I should be careful not to keep money in the house or to carry it about on me; and also that it is said in Florence that I have spoken against the Medici.

As to the money, what I have I keep in Balduccio's bank; I do not keep it in the house nor on me, except what I need from day to day. As regards the Medici, I have never said anything against them, except what is said generally by everybody, as it was in the case of Prato;[1] for if the stones could have spoken of it, they would have done so. Afterwards many other things were said here, which, when I heard them, I repeated. If it is true that they did as is said, they did wrong; not that I really believe it; and God grant they did not. Again, a month ago an acquaintance of mine spoke very ill of them to me. But I replied saying that it was wrong to talk like that and that he was not to say any more to me about it. So I want Buonarroto to see if he can find out on the quiet whence the fellow had it that I had spoken against the Medici, in order to see if I can find out where it came from, so that, if it came from any of my acquaintances, I can be on my guard. That's all I have to tell you. I am not doing anything as yet, but am waiting for the Pope to tell me what to do.

YOUR MICHELANGELO SCULPTOR IN ROME

1. *The notorious sack of Prato, August 29th 1512. See Appendix 10.*

86

British Museum Mil. ix From Rome November 5th (1512)

¶ TO LODOVICO DI LIONARDO BUONARROTA SIMONI IN FLORENCE

Most revered father — I learn from your last that you have given Michele's[1] mother and his wife six bushels of corn at twenty-five *soldi* the bushel, and that you intend to give them what you can while they are in need. But I tell you that you are not to give them anything more; and if they ask for anything more, tell them in reply that you have no further instructions from me.

As to my clothes, I learn that you will be sending them soon. Please do, and write and tell me what you have spent and I will immediately send you the money for them and for the corn at the same time. Have the draft drawn up as you yourself know to be right and I will immediately send you the power of attorney and we will do as before agreed.

Also, I should be glad if you would see whether there is some lad in Florence, the son of poor but honest people, who is used to roughing it and would be prepared to come here to serve me and to do all the things connected with the house, such as the shopping and running errands when necessary, and who in his spare time would be able to learn. If you find anyone, let me know, because here only rascals are to be found, and I have great need of someone. That's all. I am well, thank God, and working. On the fifth day of November.

YOUR MICHELANGELO SCULPTOR IN ROME

1. *Michele di Piero di Pippo.*

¶ To Lodovico di Buonarrota Simoni in Florence

87

British Museum Mil. xxxii From Rome (November 1512)

Dearest father — I have learnt from your last that things are going well in Florence and that the power of attorney I sent you was in order. I find all this satisfactory.

Now I should be glad if you would find out from the *Spedalingo* of Santa Maria Nuova if he is willing to sell us a good property for two thousand broad ducats, because I have that amount here in Balduccio's bank, which is not bringing me in anything. It had been in my mind to invest the money here, to bring me in an income which would be a help to me in doing this work.[1] Afterwards I decided, when I have finished the marbles I have here, to come and do the rest in Florence. So it seems to me better to buy there. So make enquiries and answer me as soon as you can. And if you think I should transfer this money to Florence and deposit it in Santa Maria Nuova, before the agent buys, in order that he may sell to us more willingly later, let me know likewise.

Your Michelangelo sculptor in Rome

1. *i.e. the Tomb of Julius II. See Appendix 11.*

¶ To Lodovico di Buonarrota Simoni in Florence

88

British Museum Mil. xvi From Rome (January 1st 1513)

Dearest father — In my last I told you what I thought about buying; so if the farm about which you told me, belonging to Girolamo Cini, seems to you a good proposition and if it has a sound title, take it; and if you don't think so, buy from Santa Maria Nuova and spend all the money, if you can get something good; if not, let us leave it until something turns up. And if you find something let me know, so that I may send you the power of attorney. As to the business of the house, I think I can arrange it satisfactorily, so that the house[1] will be mine and I shall have a sound investment. That's all.

Your Michelangelo in Rome

1. *The implication of this reference is not entirely clear. See No. 89, n. 1.*

89

British Museum Mil. xvii From Rome January 5th 1513

¶ To Lodovico di Buonarrota Simoni in Florence

Dearest father — I wrote you in my last as to what I thought about buying. Now you inform me that you have on hand another farm at Pazolatica, besides the one belonging to Girolamo Cini. I would buy both of them, if the titles are sound, but be sure to keep your eyes open, so that there may be no disputes afterwards. Take every care over the titles. As regards the house,[1] they are prevaricating. It doesn't matter, as I know I only have to pay the rent during the time I'm here. I have no need to worry otherwise.

Buonarroto writes to me about taking a wife;[2] I am writing to you about what I have in mind, which is this. I am intending within five or six months to release you all from your obligations and to make you a gift of what you have had from me up to now; and afterwards you can do entirely as you like. In any event, I will always help you all as far as I can. But urge Buonarroto not to marry until the end of the summer. If I were with you, I would tell you why. As he has waited so long, he will not be much older by waiting another six months.

Buonarroto also wrote me that Bernardino di Pier Basso[3] wants to come here to work for me. If he wants to come, let him come now, before I take on others, because I want to get something started. I will give him the wage you mentioned, that is to say, three ducats a month and his expenses. It is true that I live simply in my own house[4] and intend to do so; tell him this, and not to delay; and if after a week he does not like my way of living, he can return home and I will give him enough money to return. I think that's all.

On the fifth day of January.

MICHELANGELO SCULPTOR IN ROME

1. *Michelangelo was negotiating for a house in which to execute the Tomb of Julius II. Although the Pope was prepared to purchase it for this purpose, Michelangelo was required to pay the rent. The house eventually acquired, in the Trevi ward, which may certainly be identified with the one in which he lived in the Macel de' Corvi, was afterwards granted to him rent free by the Contract of 1516 (Milanesi, p. 651 and Appendix 11).*

2. *Buonarroto married twice, but the date of his first marriage and of the death of his wife, Cassandra di Bernardo Puccini, who died s.p., is unknown. He married his second wife, Bartolomea di Ghezzo della Casa, who survived him, on May 19th 1516.*

3. *Bernardo di Pier Basso (d. 1551), a sculptor from Settignano.*

4. *He means, presumably, that he did not keep open house and possibly that he had no intention of emulating the courtly style of living adopted by Raphael and his circle.*

¶ TO LODOVICO DI BUONARROTA SIMONI IN FLORENCE

90

*British
Museum
Mil. xviii
From Rome
(February)
1513*

Most revered father — I replied to you as regards Bernardino that I wanted, as you know, to settle the matter of the house first, and I make the same reply now. I first sent for him because I was promised that the matter would be arranged within a few days and that I could begin work. Afterwards, I saw that it would be a long business and in the meantime I am looking for another house with a view to getting out of this one; I do not want to put any work in hand until I am settled. Therefore explain to him how the matter stands.

As to the lad who came here, that scoundrel of a muleteer swindled me out of a ducat. He took it swearing that it had been so agreed, that is, for two broad ducats in gold, but no-one gives more than ten *carlini* for the lads who come here with muleteers. I should not have been more annoyed if I had lost twenty-five ducats, because I see that it is the fault of the father, who wanted to send him grandly mounted upon a mule.[1] Upon my word, I was never so well off myself! Besides which, the father told me, and the lad too, that he would do everything and would look after the mule and would sleep on the floor if need be; but I have to look after him. This is the last straw after all the worry I have had since I returned.[2] For my apprentice, whom I left here, has been ill ever since I returned. It is true that he is better now, but his life was in the balance and despaired of by the doctors for about a month, so that I never went to bed. Besides all the other worries I have, I've now got this dunghill of a boy, who says who says [*sic*] that he does not want to waste time, that he wants to learn; and in Florence he told me that two or three hours a day would be enough for him; now the whole day is not enough for him and he wants to draw all night as well. The father has put him up to this. If I were to say anything, he would say that I did not want him to learn. I need to be looked after. If he is not disposed to do it, they should not have put me to this expense. But they are good for nothing, but they are good for nothing [*sic*] and have one end in view and nothing else. Please will you have him removed out of my sight, because I am so disgusted I can bear no more. The muleteer has had so much money that he can very well take him back home – he is a friend of his father's. Tell the father to send for him. I will not give him a *quattrino* more; for I have no money. I will have as much patience as I can till he sends for him; but if he does not send, I will send him away. Although I dismissed him the second day and on several other occasions, he did not credit it.

As regards the shop, I will send you a hundred ducats next Saturday, on this condition, that if you see that they mean to make a success, you can give them the money and they can make me their creditor, as I agreed with Buonarroto when I left. If they do not mean to make a success, put it to my account at Santa Maria Nuova. As to buying,[3] the time hasn't come yet.

YOUR MICHELANGELO IN ROME

If you speak to the lad's father, tell him kindly about the affair; say that he is a good lad, but that he is too refined and not suited to my service and that he must send for him.

1. *Mules were much ridden by the nobility. In Benozzo Gozzoli's fresco 'The Journey of the Magi' in the Riccardi Chapel, the first of the Three Kings, Joseph, Patriarch of Constantinople, is shown mounted on a mule.*

2. *Michelangelo returned to Rome, presumably at the end of December 1512, after a 'breve permanenza' of not more than two or three weeks in Florence.*

3. *i.e. a shop or partnership for his brothers.*

91

British Museum Mil. xix From Rome (February) 1513

¶ To Lodovico di Buonarrota Simoni in Florence

Dearest father — I am sending you a hundred broad gold ducats that you may give them to Buonarroto and the others and may see that they credit them to me at the shop. And if they mean to make a success, I will help them from time to time as far as I can. Tell them this. Therefore, when you get this go to Bonifazio, or to Lorenzo Benintendi,[1] you and Buonarroto, and he will pay them over to you. He will pay over a hundred broad ducats in gold, in exchange for what I gave Baldassare Balducci here. I replied to you as to buying that the time hadn't come. As to my affairs here, I will do the best I can.[2] God will help me.

I wrote you as to the lad that his father should send for him and that I would not give him any more money. And this I repeat. The driver has already been paid to take him home. The lad is well enough in Florence, where he can stay at home to learn and can live with his father and mother; here he is not worth a *quattrino*, and keeps me on the go all the time, and my other apprentice is not yet out of bed. It is true that I haven't got him in the house, because when I was worn out and could bear no more I got him a room with one of his brothers. I have no money. This which I am sending you is of my life's blood, and yet I do not think it legitimate to ask for any, because I have not put any work in hand and I am only working very little by myself. When I have settled this business of the house, I hope to begin work in earnest.

Michelangelo sculptor in Rome

1. *Lorenzo Benintendi, the banker. He had taken an active part in the reconstitution of the government after the return of the Medici in 1512 (Sanuto, XV, 94, 106).*

2. *Julius II had died during the early hours of February 21st. Until Michelangelo knew what decisions would be reached in regard to the Tomb under a new pontiff his future necessarily remained uncertain.*

¶ To Buonarroto di Lodovico Simoni in Florence

Buonarroti Archives Mil. xcii From Rome July 30th 1513

92

Buonarroto — Michele the *scarpellino* has come here to work with me and has asked me for some money for his people at home, and this I am sending you. So go at once to Bonifazio and he will give you four broad ducats. Give them to Meo di Chimenti,[1] the *scarpellino* who works in the *Opera* and give him and give him *[sic]* the letter addressed to him, that is enclosed with this, and get him to give you a receipt in his own hand that he has received them from me on behalf of Michele, and send it to me.

The said Michele tells me that you informed him that you had spent some sixty ducats at Settignano. I remember that at table here you also told me that you had spent many ducats of your own. I pretended not to understand you and was not at all surprised, knowing you. I suppose you wrote them down and kept account of them, so as to be able some day to ask for them back. And I should like to know from Your Ingratitude with what capital you were enabled to earn them. Another thing I should like to know is whether you kept account of those two hundred and twenty-eight ducats of mine you all borrowed from Santa Maria Nuova and of the many other hundreds I spent on the house and on the family, and of the discomforts and of the miseries I have endured in order to help you. I should like to know if you have kept account of them. If you had the intelligence to realize the true state of affairs, you would not have said 'I have spent so and so of mine', nor would you have come here to urge me about your affairs, seeing how I have always behaved towards you in the past. Instead, you would have said, 'Michelangelo is aware of what he wrote to us, and if he has not now done as he said, there must be something to hinder him, which we do not know about', and would have been patient. For it does no good to spur on a horse that is going as fast and faster than it can. But you have never known me and do not know me. God forgive you, for through His grace I have been able to bear what I bear, or rather have borne, that you might be helped. But you will know it, when you haven't got me.

I must tell you that I do not think I shall be able to come home this September, because I'm being pressed in such a way in such a way *[sic]* that I haven't time to eat. God willing, I can bear up. So I want to execute the power of attorney for Lodovico as soon as I can, as I wrote, because I haven't forgotten about it, and I want to advance you a thousand broad ducats in gold, as I've promised you, so that, with the others you have, you may begin to do business on your own. I do not want any of your profits, but

I want to be assured that at the end of ten years, if I'm alive, you will undertake to return me these thousand ducats in money or in kind, if I want them back. I do not think this will happen, but should I need them, I could have them, as I said. This will be a curb on you, that you do not waste them. The four hundred ducats you have of mine I want divided into four parts, each of you receiving a hundred, and on this basis I make you a gift of them – a hundred to Lodovico,[2] a hundred to yourself, a hundred to Giovansimone and a hundred to Gismondo, with this proviso with this proviso *[sic]* that you cannot use them except as a joint investment in the shop. That's all. Show this letter to Lodovico and decide what you want to do and give me the assurance I've asked for. On the thirtieth day of July. Remember to hand over Michele's money which I'm sending you.

MICHELANGELO SCULPTOR IN ROME

1. *Bartolomeo di Chimenti di Frossino da Settignano. He worked in the Opera del Duomo.*

2. *The letter is endorsed in Lodovico's hand 'about the 100 ducats he gave to his brothers and to me, which I never had'. Like many fathers of Lodovico's age, he seems not to have understood the transaction. The long-promised shop would appear to have been bought at this time.*

93

Buonarroti Archives Mil. xciii From Rome March 31st 1515

¶ To BUONARROTO DI LODOVICO SIMONI IN FLORENCE

Buonarroto — Enclosed with this will be a bill of exchange for nine hundred broad ducats in gold, which the Benintendi have to cash for me, that is, Lorenzo Benintendi, when this arrives. Try to get it accepted[1] in the meantime, if I haven't reached Florence, as I expect to leave to-morrow morning. On the last day of March.

MICHELANGELO SCULPTOR IN ROME

1. *See Appendix 4.*

94

British Museum Mil. xciv From Rome April 28th 1515

¶ To BUONARROTO DI LODOVICO SIMONI IN FLORENCE

Buonarroto — I have just arrived safely in Rome – thank God. Please will you send me that *perpigniano*[1] as soon as you can; cut me a length of that rich colour of which you showed me a pattern, and see, above all, that it is of a good quality; cut a length of five *braccia* and try to send it either by a messenger or by someone else, provided it arrives as soon as possible. Then find out from the *Spedalingo* if he can have those three hundred and ninety-five ducats transferred to me here and keep back from these the price of the said *perpigniano* and please send it as soon as possible and address it to me or to Domenico Buoninsegni[2] at the Cardinal de' Medici's residence in the palace. I have nothing else to add now. On the twenty 8th day of April.

MICHELANGELO IN ROME

1. *A type of jersey cloth, suitable for the making of tight-fitting hose.*

2. *Domenico Buoninsegni, Treasurer to the Cardinal de' Medici. He was connected by marriage with the Strozzi family. For his subsequent dealings with Michelangelo see Appendix 14.*

¶ TO BUONARROTO DI LODOVICO SIMONI IN FLORENCE

95

Buonarroto — I have received the *perpigniano:* it is nice and of a fine quality. The bill of exchange which you sent me is no use, because it says that the Gaddi[1] may pay me in ducats of the Camera, but I must have broad ducats, so I decided not to draw them and am sending the bill back to you with this. Have another one correctly made out and send it back to me. That's all. I have no time for writing.

MICHELANGELO IN ROME

*British
Museum
Mil. xcv
From Rome
May 19th
1515*

1. *Another famous Florentine banking house in Rome.*

¶ TO BUONARROTO DI LODOVICO SIMONI IN FLORENCE

96

Buonarroto — I have received the money from the Gaddi, that is to say, three hundred and ninety-three ducats. You write me that you want me to assist you over that matter[1] about which you spoke to me when I was in Florence. I hesitate to assist you in a matter like this, because I have no means of doing so here; if I had, I should assist my own case, in which much more is involved. As to writing to Florence to Filippo[2] I'm not sufficiently familiar with the business to do so and I know, too, that he wouldn't pay any attention to a letter from me. However, if you want me to write, write me out a letter in full as you want it and I will copy it exactly.

I will enclose with this a letter to be sent to Carrara. Please will you see that you send it secretly, so that neither Michele nor anyone at the *Opera* nor anyone else knows

*British
Museum
Mil. xcvi
From Rome
June 2nd
1515*

89

about it. See if Luigi Gerardini[3] has the means to send it directly and commend me to him and tell him I will reimburse him. That's all.

MICHELANGELO SCULPTOR IN ROME

1. *i.e. Buonarroto's appeal against his assessment for the 'Arbitrio', an unpopular tax upon the estimated earnings of citizens. The tax was abolished by the first Grand Duke, Cosimo I. See also Nos. 99 and 100.*

2. *Filippo Strozzi had been appointed Pontifical Treasurer in Florence after the coronation of Leo X in 1513. He was extremely influential at this period. Cf. Marzi, p. 315.*

3. *The family appears to have been connected with Pietra Santa (Milanesi, p. 643).*

97

British Museum Mil. xcvii From Rome June 16th 1515

¶ TO BUONARROTO DI LODOVICO SIMONI IN FLORENCE

Buonarroto — I have written the letter to Filippo Strozzi. See whether it pleases you and give it to him. If it is not very good I know he will excuse me, because it[1] is not my profession. All that matters is that it should be of use to you. I want you to see the *Spedalingo* of Santa Maria Nuova and to arrange to have transferred to me here one thousand four hundred ducats from the money which he holds for me, because I must make a great effort here this summer to finish the work[2] as soon as possible, because afterwards I anticipate having to enter the Pope's[3] service. And for this I've bought some twenty thousandweight of copper, in order to cast certain figures. I am in need of money, so as soon as you get this arrange with the *Spedalingo* to have it transferred to me. And if you can arrange with Pier Francesco Borgherini,[4] who is in Florence, to have it transferred from his own funds, I shall be very glad, because Pier Francesco is a friend of mine, and would accommodate[5] me. Do not go talking about it, because I want it to be transferred to me here without anyone knowing. Get proper security from the *Spedalingo* for what remains at Santa Maria Nuova. I have my reasons for this. I await the money. That's all.[6]

MICHELANGELO IN ROME

1. *Michelangelo's attitude was always that of a professional.*

2. *The Tomb of Pope Julius II, for which a second contract had been drawn up with his executors on May 6th 1513. See Appendix 11.*

3. *Leo X (Giovanni de' Medici). His pontificate lasted from 1513 to 1521.*

4. *Pier Francesco Borgherini, a Florentine banker resident in Rome. For his patronage of the arts, see Vasari, V, p. 26.*

12. *Pope Leo X with Cardinal Giulio de' Medici and Cardinal Luigi Rossi*

Raphael
Palazzo Pitti, Florence

5. *i.e. he would pay on presentation of the bill of exchange without waiting for the customary period of usance.*

6. *The date on the face of the letter is not in Michelangelo's hand.*

98

British Museum Mil. xcviii From Rome June 30th 1515

¶ To Buonarroto di Lodovico Simoni in Florence

Buonarroto — As I was passing the Borgherini bank to-day, the cashier told me that he has some money for me and that it was at my disposal. I did not wish to draw it until I had received a letter from you as to the amount. I wrote you the letter you asked me for. I know it was not very good, because it is not my profession and I have no head for things like this. I think that's all. A letter for Michele will be enclosed with this. Please give it to him himself.

MICHELANGELO IN ROME

99

British Museum Mil. xcix From Rome July 7th 1515

¶ To Buonarroto di Lodovico Simoni in Florence

Buonarroto — I have received the money from the Borgherini, who accommodated me. Now I would like you to withdraw the ledger with the folios for the rest of the money which he[1] has and to send it to me to keep by me, although I wish shortly to take what he holds for me out of his hands, for a very good reason; and that suffices.

I learn from your last that the letter I sent you was all right and that it might help in the matter of the *arbitrio*.[2] Pray God it may! In a recent letter to you I enclosed one to Michele. I would like you to get me an answer, so that I can come to some decision. Although it is no use depending on Michele for anything, I thought he at least knew the answer to my question, that is, whether I'm going to get marble from Pietra Santa[3] this summer, because here Domenico Buoninsegni told me that he heard that the road was nearly finished. So tell Michele to answer me. That's all. Look to your own interests, and particularly those of the soul, for in these days it seems imperative.[4]

MICHELANGELO SCULPTOR IN ROME

1. *i.e. the Spedalingo.*

2. *See No. 96, n. 1.*

3. *See Appendix 13.*

4. *See Appendix 12.*

¶ To Buonarroto di Lodovico Simoni in Florence

*British
Museum
Mil. c
From Rome
July 21st
1515*

100

Buonarroto — I recently informed you that I had received the money from the Borgherini. I also wrote that I wished shortly to withdraw the rest. So if you feel inclined to notify the *Spedalingo* that within a fortnight I shall need a further sum, I should be glad. I hear that the letter I wrote you for Filippo has helped to reduce the assessment. I'm pleased to hear it. When he comes here, I'll thank him. That's all. I've no time for writing.

MICHELANGELO IN ROME

¶ To Buonarroto di Lodovico Simoni in Florence

*British
Museum
Mil. ci
From Rome
July 28th
1515*

101

Buonarroto — I see from your last how things stand regarding the money, the ledger and the folios. I was glad of the information, although I'm thinking of withdrawing the money shortly, as I wrote you. When the time comes, I'll let you know.

A letter for Michele will be enclosed with this. See that he gets it. I write to him, not because I do not know that he's a fool, but because I'm in need of a certain amount of marble and do not know what to do. I do not want to go to Carrara myself, because I cannot, and I cannot send anyone as I need to, because if they are not fools, they are knaves and rascals, like that scoundrel Bernardino, who cost me a hundred ducats during the time he was here, besides going about tittle-tattling and complaining about me all over Rome, as I discovered on my return here. He is a proper scoundrel; shun him like the devil, and don't let him enter the house under any pretext whatsoever. I've strayed from the point. I think that's all. Will you give the letter to Michele.

MICHELANGELO IN ROME

¶ To Buonarroto di Lodovico di Lionardo Simoni in Florence

*British
Museum
Mil. cii
From Rome
August 4th
1515*

102

Buonarroto — As I myself have heard things here about the *Spedalingo* that I do not like, you who are near at hand in Florence can see, or rather, estimate the position better than I can. So if you think I am running any risk with my money, have it transferred to me here. Go to Pier Francesco Borgherini and he will have it transferred to me here. And if you think this should be done, do it at once as soon as you get this and have no scruples. If not, let me have a reply as to what you think. I should also be glad if you would make a few enquiries as to whether that road for the marble is being made by Michele, or by others, and would let me know. Please answer me as soon as possible because I am uneasy and let me know how Lodovico is, because it is some time since he wrote to me.

On the fourth day of August.

MICHELANGELO IN ROME

103

Buonarroti Archives Mil. ciii From Rome August 11th 1515

¶ TO BUONARROTO DI LODOVICO SIMONI IN FLORENCE

Buonarroto — I learn from your last that the *Spedalingo* has told you that he has not yet completed the realization of my money. This seems to me a bad sign. I make no doubt I shall have to take up the cudgels with him.

Since I returned from Florence I have done no work at all; I have devoted my attention solely to making the models and to preparing the work, in such a way that I can make one great effort with a host of workmen to finish the work in two or three years. And this I have undertaken to do and have incurred heavy expenses solely on the security of the money I have in Florence, as I counted on having it at my disposal, as is stipulated in the agreement and as is usual with deposits. And if I shouldn't get it now, I should be in a mess. Therefore, as soon as you get this, will you go to see the *Spedalingo* immediately and say that I must have it now without fail, and that I should have thought if he had not called mine in, he would have lent me the money and obliged me from his own account, having held so much money for such a long time without paying any interest at all. And if he is prepared to disburse it, have it transferred to me here through Pier Francesco Borgherini, or, if he wishes to arrange to transfer it to me here himself, let him do so, with the proviso that I have it at once. Answer me as to what ensues, and I will let you know what you must do; and intimate to the *Spedalingo* that I am proposing within four months to arrange to deposit with him six thousand ducats in gold. That's all.

As to the marbles of which you wrote me, it is not a matter you can deal with. I'll manage to get what I want in one way or another. I understand there is nothing doing in Florence. Rest content, accommodating yourselves to the times as best you can, and don't involve yourselves in affairs other than your own.[1] Let me have a reply as soon as possible.

On the eleventh day of August.

MICHELANGELO IN ROME

I'll enclose a letter to be sent to Zara[2] in Carrara, which I'll leave unsealed. Please write one or two on the same lines and send several copies for me, so that he may get at least one of them.[3] Then seal mine and send it as well by the best route you can.

1. *See Appendix 12.*

2. *Domenico di Alessandro di Bartolo Fancelli (1469–1519), a sculptor from Settignano. He executed the tomb of Don Juan, son of Ferdinand II of Aragon in the church of S. Tomás at Avila (Campori, p. 311 et seq.).*

3. *Communications with Carrara were difficult and uncertain.*

¶ To Buonarroto di Lodovico Simoni in Florence

104

British Museum Mil. civ From Rome August 18th 1515

Buonarroto — I have no time to write to you at length – only these two lines to tell you I'm expecting the money, as I wrote you in my last.

As to the fields you say Lodovico told you to mention, tell him I'll take them over, but let us allow a couple of months to elapse first. That's all. Try to make a success, because it is imperative.

MICHELANGELO SCULPTOR IN ROME

¶ To Buonarroto di Lodovico Simoni in Florence

105

British Museum Mil. cv From Rome August (27th) 1515

Buonarroto — I got both bills of exchange. The Borgherini have accepted it,[1] and have given me a receipt to the effect that they have the said money of mine on deposit and that it is at my disposal. I'll draw it next week. You write me that Pier Francesco will send me the balance. If Pier Francesco has no means of making it payable here to me without loss to himself, I instruct you to return it to Santa Maria Nuova immediately and to withdraw the ledger with the folios and send it to me. Please deal with this business without delay. And let me know how things stand with you and with the shop. Have patience and use every means to keep the capital you have intact. That's all. I didn't write on Saturday, because the courier was dispatched on Friday, without my knowledge.

MICHELANGELO SCULPTOR IN ROME

1. *i.e. the first one received. See Appendix 4.*

106

*Buonarroti
Archives
Mil. cvi
From Rome
September 1st
1515*

¶ To Buonarroto di Lodovico Simoni in Florence

Buonarroto — I got the bills and took them to the Borgherini and left the money on deposit there. To-day or on Monday I'll go and get it. Another time do not draw the money from Santa Maria Nuova unless you know beforehand that you can have it transferred to me here, and do not draw more than you can get transferred to me. So if you have not sent me the balance, return it to Santa Maria Nuova at once, and arrange to get the ledger with the folios and send it to me, and do it as soon as you can and do not leave my money in the hands of other people, for I do not trust a living soul.

You complain to me as regards the shop. Have patience; there are more troubles everywhere than you credit or are aware of. These are the times I have anticipated for some years now and because of this I have continually told you that it was not the time to enter upon a thing like this. However, strive to preserve your capital and look to the good of your soul, because things might become worse than you suppose.

In reply to Betto da Rovezzano's[1] father, say that I have no marble to work, or I would have taken him on willingly, and do not give him further hope. A letter will be enclosed with this, to be sent to Messer Antonio,[2] chancellor to the Marquis of Carrara. Expedite it and keep me informed.

MICHELANGELO IN ROME

1. *Benedetto di Bartolomeo da Rovezzano (1474–1552), a sculptor.*

2. *Antonio da Massa.*

107

*Buonarroti
Archives
Mil. cvii
From Rome
September 8th
1515*

¶ To Buonarroto di Lodovico Simoni in Florence

Buonarroto — I learn from your last that the balance of the money is in Santa Maria Nuova. I wrote telling you to return it, supposing, from what you wrote, that you had given it to Pier Francesco for him to send to me by a muleteer. And because I didn't like this, I told you to put it back where it was. Now you tell me you didn't withdraw it. So everything's all right and there's no need to say any more about it. When I have need of it I'll let you know.

You write me in a manner that suggests that you think that I care more for worldly things than one should. Oh come! I care for them more for your sakes than for my own, as I have always done. I do not go running after fictions and am not therefore quite crazy, as you all imagine. Sometime hence I think you'll appreciate the letters I've written during the last four years more than you do now, if I'm not mistaken. And if I am mistaken, I'm not mistaken in a bad cause, since I know that at all times it is wise

13. The Hospital of Santa Maria Nuova   *Florence*

to have a care for oneself and one's possessions. I remember some eighteen months ago – more or less, I don't remember – that you wanted to take a certain course and I wrote you that the time was not ripe and that you would be advised to let a year elapse. Recently, a few days after the King of France died,[1] you answered me, or rather wrote, that the King was dead, and that there was no further danger of any kind in Italy and that I went running after friars and fictions and you made a mock of me. You see, however, that the King is not dead and it would be much better for us had you been guided by me several years ago; and that suffices.

I had with yours a letter from Carrara from Zara, who is evidently anxious to oblige me. I am not giving him any answer, because I wrote to Messer Antonio da Massa, chancellor to the Marquis of Carrara, with the last one I sent you. I assume you sent it on to him, and I do not want to give any commissions to others until I've had an answer from him. That's all.

MICHELANGELO SCULPTOR IN ROME

1. *Louis XII died on January 1st 1515, and was succeeded by Francis I. Buonarroto's sanguine hopes that the threat of another French invasion of Italy was thereby removed proved unfounded, as Francis renewed his predecessor's claims to the Duchy of Milan a few months afterwards. See Appendix 12.*

108

British Museum Mil. cviii From Rome September (22nd) 1515

¶ TO BUONARROTO DI LODOVICO SIMONI IN FLORENCE

Buonarroto — I have often written and told you my views and I propose always to do so, because what I do I do for your good, and although you are of another opinion, this makes no difference. There is, in fact, no occasion to make a mock of anyone, and to be apprehensive in these days and to make provision for oneself, body and soul, can do no harm whatever.

I should be glad if you would have the money transferred to me here, if you hear that the time has come when he wouldn't lose anything on it.[1] That's all. Try to rest content; what can't be done, can't be. If the times are bad, one must have patience. And believe me, what I do, I do as much for you as for myself.[2]

MICHELANGELO IN ROME

1. *i.e. when the rate of exchange would not be against Pier Francesco in making the transfer from Florence to Rome.*

2. *These injunctions are in the plural ('voi') and are therefore addressed to the rest of the family as well, and not exclusively to Buonarroto. The date on the face of the letter is not in Michelangelo's hand.*

98

¶ To Buonarroto di Lodovico Simoni in Florence

109

*British
Museum
Mil. cxi
From Rome
October 6th
1515*

Buonarroto — You write me that you have spoken to the *Spedalingo* and that, when the exchange is favourable, he says he will do what is required. You tell me that you will go and see Pier Francesco's assistant and that you will arrange to have the transfer made to me here. I wrote you that, when you found it possible to have it transferred, you should do so. Pier Francesco says that he is not losing on it. I do not want him to stand a loss or to suffer on my account, because I do not want to be beholden to anyone. So if it is not convenient to him or anyone else, I'd sooner you left it where it is. I think that's all. The Pope has left Rome and is said here to be going to Florence.[1]

MICHELANGELO SCULPTOR IN ROME

1. *The Pope had just left for Viterbo, where he went to hunt. He did not make his ceremonial entry into Florence until November 30th. See Appendix 12.*

¶ To Buonarroto di Lodovico Simoni in Florence

110

*British
Museum
Mil. cix
From Rome
October 20th
1515*

Buonarroto — I wrote and asked you to have that money transferred to me here – and this I repeat – when it is advantageous to the banker through whom you have it transferred to me, because, as I wrote you, I want to be under as little obligation as I can. On the first transfer you had made to me here he made two per cent; on the second he made a loss, though this was inadvertent on my part, because I'm not knowledgeable about these things. I had supposed it would be at the same rate.

Now as to this transfer, do as you think best, provided it is made when you have the opportunity. Bear in mind that I do not want to impose on Pier Francesco Borgherini nor to bother him in any way, because I want to be under as little obligation to him as I can, as I have to do a painting[1] for him, and it might appear that I sought payment in advance. Therefore I do not want to be beholden to him; I have a regard for him and do not want anything from him. I wish to serve him as a pleasure and not as a duty and I'll serve him, if I can, more gladly than anyone I've ever served, for he is really a young man of honour and, if I'm not mistaken, without an equal among the Florentines here.

I hear that in Florence you will soon be celebrating the treaty.[2] I'm very glad to hear it, because I have the good of Florence very much at heart.[3] Nevertheless, confine yourself to your own affairs, and don't involve yourself in anything and do not make a mock of what I've written you in other letters. That's all.

A letter will be enclosed with this; please send it to Carrara safely.

MICHELANGELO IN ROME

1. *Michelangelo never executed this painting. It was undertaken by Andrea del Sarto to Michelangelo's design, but not to Borgherini's satisfaction.*

2. *The meeting between Leo X and Francis I took place in Bologna in December 1515. But the Pope stayed in Florence on his way to and from Bologna and tremendous preparations were accordingly made for his reception. See Appendixes 8 and 12.*

3. *Literally, 'nostro bene'.*

---

111   ¶ To Buonarroto di Lodovico Simoni in Florence

*British
Museum
Mil. cx
From Rome
November 3rd
1515*

Buonarroto — I got the bill of exchange for the balance of the money. I haven't been to the Borgherini bank yet – I'll go next week. I think they'll accommodate me as they did before. You write me that the *Spedalingo* complained about my having withdrawn so much money in so short a time. It seems to me he must indeed be a fool to complain about having to return me my own money, of which he has had the use for so long, and still more so, having placed at my disposal five hundred ducats of his own should they be needed. But I'm not surprised, knowing him.

You ask me for money and say that things are now settling down and that trade is beginning to recover.[1] I'm amused at what you've done and surprised at some of the things you tell me.[2] I do not want to comment on anything else for the present. As to the money, I cannot do anything about it, because I have another two years' work to do before I'm square with these people, as I've had so much money.[3] So accommodate yourselves to the times and you will not go short. Try to recover as much as you can of the money that is owing to you, but do not enter into further commitments this winter and do not give credit on anything. I have had to write to you about these matters, because, understanding them in this way, I feel obliged to do so. I'm well aware you'll make a mock of it. That's all.

Michelangelo sculptor in Rome

---

1. *In anticipation of the Pope's visit, business was beginning to improve and prices were rising. Cf. Nos. 15, 16.*

2. *As Buonarroto's letter is not available, we do not know to what Michelangelo refers – perhaps to the extravagant preparations being made for the Pope's reception.*

3. *Between May and October 1515 he had received 1,000 ducats on account for the Tomb of Julius II, but was in no position to dissipate them in loans or gifts (Milanesi, p. 564).*

VI

LETTERS
112 - 144

From Carrara, Pietra Santa,
Seravezza, Pisa and Florence
1516 - 1520

14. The Mountains of Carrara

VI. From Carrara, Pietra Santa, Seravezza, Pisa and Florence: 1516-1520

¶ To Lodovico di Buonarrota Simoni in Florence

British Museum Mil. xl From Carrara September 1516

112

Dearest father — Through a brother[1] of Zara's I recently had a letter from Gismondo, from which I learn that you are all well, except that Buonarroto still has a bad leg. I'm sorry about this, because I'm afraid remedies may make it worse; and, as I said to him, I should do nothing but keep it warm, look after myself and leave it to nature.

As to my affairs here, as yet I've done nothing. I've begun quarrying in many places and I hope, if it remains fine, to have all my marbles[2] ready within two months. Then I shall decide whether to work them here or in Pisa, or I shall go to Rome. I would gladly have stayed here to work them, but I have met with some unpleasantness, so that I should remain with some misgiving. That's all. Try to rest content, as I'm hopeful that things will go well. Please seal the letter enclosed with this and see that it is given to Stefano the saddler to send to Rome.

YOUR MICHELANGELO IN CARRARA

1. *Giovanni di Alessandro di Bartolo Fancelli (d. 1522), sculptor. He assisted his brother Domenico and the Spanish sculptor, Bartolomeo Ordognez, in the commissions undertaken in Spain. See No. 103, n. 2.*

2. *i.e. the marbles for the Tomb of Julius II on which he was still engaged.*

¶ To Buonarroto di Lodovico Simoni in Florence

British Museum Mil. cxii From Carrara November 23rd 1516

113

Buonarroto — I learn from your last letters[1] that Lodovico has been at the point of death, but that at last the doctor says that, if nothing else befalls, he is out of danger. This being so, I won't arrange to come home, as it would be very inconvenient for me. However, if there were any danger I should want to see him, whatever happened, before he died, if I had to die with him. But I have good hope that he will be all right, so I won't come. But if he should happen to have a relapse, which God forfend for him and for us, see that he lacks nothing for the welfare of his soul and that he receives the sacraments of the Church and get him to leave instructions if he wants us to do anything for the salvation of his soul. And for the needs of the body, see that he wants for nothing; because I have never exerted myself but for him, in order to help him in his need, as long as he lives; so arrange for your wife[2] to devote herself to looking after him, if he needs it, because I'll make it up to her and to all of you, if need be. Have no scruples if you have to spend whatever we've got. I think that's all. Rest content and keep me informed, as I'm very distressed and anxious.

Give the letter which will be enclosed with this to Stefano, the saddler, to send to Rome, care of the Borgherini. Get him to send it promptly, as it deals with important matters.

On the twenty-third day of November 1516.

[Unsigned]

1. *On November 12th 1516, Buonarroto had written to Michelangelo saying that their father, Lodovico, had been ill since the beginning of the month with a 'trabocco di scesa', and again on November 18th, saying that he was out of danger (Frey, Briefe, pp. 44, 45).*

2. *Bartolomea della Casa, whom he had married as his second wife on May 19th 1516.*

---

114 ¶ To Domenico [Buoninsegni in Rome]

Buonarroti Archives Mil. cccxlvi From Florence March 20th 1517

Messer Domenico — I came to Florence to see the model which Baccio[1] has finished and have found the same thing again, that is to say that it is a mere toy. If you think it should be sent, write me. I'm leaving tomorrow morning and returning to Carrara where I have agreed, with the aid of la Grassa,[2] to make a model in clay, based on the drawing, which I'll send to him. He assures me he will have one made that will be all right. I do not know how it will turn out; I expect in the end I shall have to do it myself. I regret this from the point of view of the Cardinal and the Pope.[3] I cannot help it.

I must inform you that, for a very good reason, I have terminated the partnership,[4] which I wrote and told you I had formed at Carrara and have commissioned from these same people a hundred cart-loads of marble at the prices of which I wrote you, or a little less. And from another partnership which I have got together, I have commissioned another hundred and they have a year in which to deliver it to me in barge-loads.

[Unsigned][5]

1. *Baccio d'Agniolo, the architect to whom Michelangelo had entrusted the making of a wooden model of the façade of San Lorenzo. See No. 144 and Appendix 14.*

2. *Francesco di Giovanni Nanni della Grassa, a scarpellino from Settignano. He had been employed by the Signoria in 1511 (Gaye, II, p. 132).*

3. *Cardinal Giulio de' Medici and Leo X.*

4. *A business partnership formed on February 12th 1517 to supply Michelangelo with the marble he needed for the façade of San Lorenzo. The second company was formed on March 14th 1517 (Milanesi, pp. 381, 662).*

5. *This, like other unsigned letters addressed to people other than members of the family, was presumably either a draft for, or a copy of, the letter sent.*

¶ TO DOMENICO BUONINSEGNI IN ROME   **115**

Messer Domenico — Bernardo Niccolini[1] informs me that he has forwarded some letters of yours, which I haven't received. I assume they deal with the matter of the model.

*Buonarroti
Archives
Mil. cccxlvii
From Carrara
April 1517*

Since I last wrote you I have had a small model made by an assistant of mine, a little one, to send to you.

[Unsigned]

1. *Bernardo Niccolini, Treasurer to the Archbishop of Florence, an office then held by the Cardinal Giulio de' Medici, afterwards Pope Clement VII.*

¶ TO DOMENICO [BUONINSEGNI IN ROME]   **116**

Messer Domenico — Since I last wrote to you, I have been unable to attend to the making of the model, as I wrote and told you I would. It would take a long time to explain the why and the wherefore. I had previously roughed out a little one in clay, for my own use here, which, although it is crinkled like a fritter, I want in any event to send you, so that this thing may not seem to be a figment of the imagination.

*Buonarroti
Archives
Mil. cccxlviii
From Carrara
(May 2nd 1517)*

I have several things to say to you; would you read on patiently for a little, because it is important. That is to say, I feel myself able to execute this project of the façade of San Lorenzo in such a manner that it will be, both architecturally and sculpturally, the mirror of all Italy, but the Pope and the Cardinal would have to make up their minds quickly as to whether they wish me to do it or not. And if they wish me to do it, they would have to come to some decision, that is to say, either to commission me to do it on contract and to rely upon me entirely for everything, or on some other basis, of which I am ignorant, which they may decide upon. I will explain why.

I, as I wrote you, and since I wrote you, have given commissions for many blocks of marble and have handed out money on this side and on that, and have begun quarrying in various places. And in one place where I laid out money, the marbles did not afterwards turn out to be any use to me, because things are deceptive, particularly with the big blocks which I need, if they are to be as excellent as I require them to be. And in one block, which I had already had cut, certain defects became apparent on the inner face, which couldn't have been anticipated, so that I did not get out of it the two columns I wanted and half the expense was wasted on it. And thus, with these mishaps, it is inevitable that, among so many, a few blocks run into some hundreds of ducats. But I cannot keep account and shall not be able ultimately to show proof of my expenditure, except for the actual amount of marble I shall deliver. I would willingly do as Maestro Pier Fantini[1] did, but I haven't enough ointment. Again as I'm an old man[2] it doesn't seem to me worth while wasting so much time in order to save the Pope two or three hundred ducats; and because I'm being pressed about my work in Rome[3] I must come to terms whatever happens.

The terms are these. If I knew that I had the work to do and the cost of it, I should not worry about wasting four hundred ducats, because I should not have to account for them, and I should select three or four of the best men here and should give them a commission for the marbles, which would have to be of the same quality as the marble I have already quarried, which is admirable, though I haven't much of it. For this, and for the money I advanced to them, I should take out a good insurance in Lucca, and should give orders to transport the marbles to Florence, together with those I've got, and should go and work there on the Pope's account and on my own. But if I did not come to the above arrangement with the Pope, it would be difficult for me, nor should I be able, if I wanted to, to transport the marbles for my work to Florence and then back to Rome afterwards, but should have to come to work in Rome as soon as possible, because I'm being pressed, as I've said.

The cost of the façade in the manner in which I intend to execute it and to put the work in hand, including everything – for the Pope would not need to concern himself about anything further – could not be less, according to the estimates I've made, than thirty-five thousand gold ducats, and for this I'll undertake to execute it in six years;[4] on this condition, that within six months I should have at least another thousand ducats in respect of the marble. But if the Pope is not disposed to do this, either the expenses which I have begun to incur for the aforesaid work must go towards my profit or loss and I must return the thousand ducats to the Pope, or he must engage someone to carry on the enterprise, because for a number of reasons I wish to leave here whatever happens.

As to the said price; should I realize, once the work is begun, that it could be done for less, such is my loyalty towards the Pope and the Cardinal, that I should advise them of it much sooner than if I were to incur a loss. But on the contrary, I propose to execute it on such a scale that the price may not be sufficient.

Messer Domenico, I beg you to let me have a definite answer as to the intention of the Pope and the Cardinal, which would be the greatest of all the kindnesses you have done me.

[Unsigned]

1. *Pier Fantini was a doctor who became proverbial, because he not only made no charge for his attendance, but supplied the ointment and bandages into the bargain.*

2. *He was only forty-two, but he undoubtedly felt old before his time, owing to the strain and the hardships he had undergone.*

3. *i.e. by the executors of Pope Julius, who were anxious about the completion of the Tomb, to which the phrase 'my work' invariably refers at this period. See Appendix 11.*

4. *The price eventually agreed in the contract of January 19th 1518 was 40,000 ducats and the time allowed eight years (Milanesi, p. 671).*

¶ To Lodovico di Buonarrota Simoni in Florence   **117**

Dearest father — I am sending my assistant Piero[1] to Florence for the mule. Please let him have it, and when he returns with it, I will come home for the whole of August, in order to make the model of San Lorenzo to send to Rome, as I've promised. That's all.

Your Michelangelo in Carrara

British Museum Mil. xli From Carrara July 1517

1. *Pietro di Annibale Urbano da Pistoia (b. 1495) was in Michelangelo's service from c. 1515 to 1521. He is constantly referred to by Michelangelo, but as 'Pietro' or 'Piero' indifferently.*

118   ¶ To Lodovico Buonarroti in Florence

*British
Museum
Mil. xlii
From Carrara
July 1517*

Dearest father — I have received a letter of yours through Maestro Andrea,[1] from which I learn that you haven't been very well, nor Buonarroto either. I'm sorry about this; however you must have patience. Take as much care of yourselves as you can. I've sent my assistant Pietro to Florence for the mule, because I want to leave here. So please let him have it. That's all. As to my affairs, I'm doing as best I can. I hope to be home within three weeks.

YOUR MICHELANGELO IN CARRARA

1. *Andrea Ferrucci da Fiesole (1465–1526). He left Florence on July 12th for Carrara, to receive Michelangelo's instructions about preparing the foundations for the façade of San Lorenzo (Frey, Briefe, p. 75).*

119   ¶ [To Domenico Buoninsegni in Rome]

*Buonarroti
Archives
Mil. cccl
From Florence
(Mid–March
1518)*

Domenico — As the marbles[1] have turned out to be excellent for me and as those that are suitable for the work at St. Peter's are easy to quarry and nearer the coast than the others, that is, at a place called Corvara; and from this place no expense for a road is involved, except over the small stretch of marsh land near the coast *[sic*[2]*]*. But for a choice of the marbles for figures, which I need myself, the existing road will have to be widened for about two miles from Corvara to Seravezza and for about a mile of it or less an entirely new road will have to be made, that is, it must be cut into the mountains with pickaxes to where the said marbles have to be loaded. Therefore, if the Pope is only prepared to undertake what is required for his own marbles, that is, the marsh, I haven't the means to undertake the rest and I shouldn't have any marble for my own work. If he does not undertake this, I cannot take any responsibility for the marbles for St. Peter's, as I promised the Cardinal, but if the Pope undertakes the whole of it, I can do all that I promised.

I've told you all about it in other letters. Now, you are experienced and discreet and are, I know, well disposed towards me; so I beg you to arrange the matter in your own way with the Cardinal and to reply to me quickly, so that I may reach a decision, and if nothing else eventuates, may return to Rome to what I was doing before. I could not go to Carrara, because in twenty years I shouldn't get the marbles I need, since, owing to this business, I've become an object of great hostility there and I should be compelled, if I return to Rome, to work in bronze, as we agreed.

I must inform you that the Commissioners[3] have already made great plans in regard to this business of the marbles since they got my report, and I believe that they have already fixed the prices, the duties and the dues and that the notaries, and arch-notaries, the purveyors and sub-purveyors are already resolved to wax fat on their profits there. So think it over and do whatever you can to prevent this affair falling into their hands, because later on it would be more difficult to get anything out of them than out of Carrara. I beg you to answer me quickly as to what you think I should do, and to commend me to the Cardinal. I am here as his agent, so I will not do anything, except what you tell me, because I assume that to be his wish.

If in writing to you I haven't written as grammatically as one should, or if I've some-times missed out the main verb, please forgive me, because I'm troubled with a ringing in my ears, which prevents my thinking as clearly as I'd like.

YOUR MICHELANGELO SCULPTOR IN FLORENCE

1. *i.e. those in the mountains of Seravezza, where he was now engaged in opening up the quarries. See Appendix 13.*

2. *See the apology for the omission of the main verb at the conclusion of the letter.*

3. *i.e. of the Opera del Duomo.*

¶ TO BUONARROTO DI LODOVICO SIMONI IN FLORENCE

120

British Museum Mil. cxiv From Pietra Santa April 2nd 1518

Buonarroto — Would you let me know if Jacopo Salviati[1] has got the Consuls of the Wool Merchants' Guild[2] to grant the concession[3] on the basis of the draft, as he promised me, and if he hasn't done so, ask him on my behalf to do so. And if you find that he doesn't want to, let me know, so that I may withdraw from here, as I'm on the highway to ruin and, in addition, I'm not getting on as I'd hoped. Nevertheless, if the promise made to me is kept I'm prepared to carry on with the enterprise, with its enormous expense and trouble, though as yet without any certainty of success.

About the business of the road here, tell Jacopo that I'll do whatever his Magnificence pleases and that he'll never find himself cheated over anything he entrusts to me, because in matters of this kind I do not seek my own advantage, but the advantage of my patrons and of my country. And though I've requested the Pope and the Cardinal to grant me the supervision of this road, I've done so merely to be in a position to give directions and to have it routed to those places where the best marbles are to be found, which are unknown to anyone. Neither have I made this request in order to profit by it, because I do not take such things into account. On the contrary, I beg his Magnificence Jacopo to have it made by Maestro Donato,[4] because for this he's invaluable and I'm sure he's to be trusted, and to give me the authority to have it made where and how I think best, because I know where the best marbles are and what kind of road is needed for carting them, and I think I can reduce the cost considerably for whoever does the paying. So acquaint the said Jacopo with what I've written to you, and commend me to his Magnificence and beg him to commend me to his agents in Pisa, so that they may do me the favour of finding barges to transport the marbles from Carrara.

I went to Genoa and got four barges sent to the quayside to load them. The Carrarese bribed the masters of the said barges and are bent on balking me, so that I achieved nothing, and to-day I'm thinking of going to Pisa to see about others. So commend me to him, as I've said, and write to me. On the second day of April.

MICHELANGELO IN PIETRA SANTA

Treat my assistant, Pietro, as you would treat me, and if he needs any money, give it to him and I'll settle with you.

1. *Jacopo Salviati (d. 1533), the banker, who was acting in the matter on behalf of Leo X, whose sister, Lucrezia de' Medici, he had married. He was a very good friend to Michelangelo, for whom he had a great liking, admiration and respect.*

2. *The wealthy Guild of Wool Merchants, the Arte di Lana, of which the Consuls were the chief officers, was responsible for the superintendence and financing of the building operations at the Cathedral of Santa Maria del Fiore, of which the Commissioners, the 'Operai del Duomo', were in charge.*

3. *The Guild entered into an agreement with Michelangelo for the excavation and transport of marbles from Pietra Santa and Seravezza, for which the construction of a new road was required. See No. 123, n. 1, and Appendix 13.*

4. *Donato Benti (1470–1536), a Florentine sculptor who acted as Michelangelo's deputy and agent at Carrara, Pietra Santa and Seravezza. The first contract made with him for the superintendence of the quarrying, blocking out and transport of the marbles is dated April 17th 1518 (Milanesi, p. 678).*

121

¶ TO PIETRO URBANO DA PISTOIA IN FLORENCE

Buonarroti Archives Mil. cccxlix From Pietra Santa April 2nd 1518

Pietro — I learn from a letter of yours that you are well and are trying to learn all you can. I'm very pleased about this. Work hard and don't on any account neglect your drawing and make the most of your opportunities. Ask Gismondo, on my behalf, for the money you need and keep account of it. I must tell you that I went to Genoa to enquire about barges to transport the marbles I have at Carrara and got them to Avenza,[1] but the Carrarese bribed the masters of the said barges and balked me, so that

I shall have to go to Pisa to order others and am leaving to-day. And when I have given orders for the transport of the marbles, I shall come back at once. I expect it will be in about a fortnight's time. Mind you behave yourself. There is no need for you to come here at present. That's all.

MICHELANGELO IN PIETRA SANTA

1.   *The port of Carrara.*

¶ TO BUONARROTO DI LODOVICO SIMONI IN FLORENCE

122

British Museum Mil. cxv From Pisa April 7th 1518

Buonarroto — I was balked, as I wrote you, about the transport of my marbles, but, through the good offices of Jacopo Salviati, when I arrived in Pisa I made an arrangement with a barge-master here who will serve me for a reasonable sum. It has all been done for Jacopo's sake by Francesco Peri,[1] as I've said. So please commend me to his Magnificence and thank him, because I'm grateful to him for this great service, which has placed us all under a lasting obligation to him. I have had a letter from him, but I'm not replying to it, as I am not equal to it, but I shall be in Florence in about a fortnight and hope to reply by word of mouth better than I can in writing.

I'm hoping the road and everything else will go well. Acquaint him with this, thank him, and commend me to him, as I've said. I'm now leaving for Pietra Santa and Francesco Peri is giving me a hundred ducats to take to the Commissary[2] at Pietra Santa for the road.

On the seventh day of April.

MICHELANGELO IN PISA

1.   *The Director of the Eredi d'Alamanno Salviati bank in Pisa. Immediately on receipt of Michelangelo's request for an introduction (see No. 120) Salviati had written to Peri, commending Michelangelo to him in the warmest terms (Frey, Briefe, p. 95).*

2.   *Messer Vieri de' Medici.*

123   ¶ To Buonarroto di Lodovico Simoni in Florence

*British
Museum
Mil. cxvi
From Pietra
Santa
April 18th
1518*

Buonarroto — I learn from yours that the concession[1] hasn't yet been granted, which worries me very much. I'm therefore sending one of my assistants post, solely so that he may wait till Thursday evening to see whether the concession is granted, and on Friday morning he will leave to bring me the answer. If the concession is granted as I requested, I'll carry on with the enterprise. If it isn't granted by Thursday evening, as you wrote me, I shan't assume that Jacopo Salviati[2] wasn't willing to arrange it, but that he wasn't able to, and I shall immediately take horse and go in search of the Cardinal de' Medici and the Pope and shall tell them how I'm placed. And I shall abandon the enterprise here and go back to Carrara, for they implore me to do so, as they would implore Christ.

These *scarpellini* whom I brought from Florence know nothing on earth about quarrying or about marble. They have already cost me more than a hundred and thirty ducats and haven't yet quarried me a chip of marble that's any use, and they go round bamboozling everyone into believing that they have made great discoveries and are seeking to execute work for the *Opera* and for others, at my expense. I don't know what support they're getting, but the Pope shall hear all about it. Since I've been here I've thrown away about three hundred ducats and haven't as yet got anything out of it for myself. In trying to tame these mountains and to introduce the industry into these parts, I've undertaken to raise the dead; for if, over and above the marbles, the Guild of Wool Merchants were to pay me a hundred ducats a month for doing what I'm doing, they wouldn't do badly, without failing me over the concession. So commend me to Jacopo Salviati and write to me by my apprentice as to how the matter goes, so that I may come to an immediate decision, because I'm being worn away here in this state of suspense.

Michelangelo in Pietra Santa

The barges[3] I hired at Pisa have never arrived. I think I've been gulled, and so it is with everything I do. Oh cursed a thousand times be the day I left Carrara! It's the cause of my undoing. But I shall soon return there. To-day it is a crime to do right. Commend me to Giovanni da Ricasoli.

1. *By an instrument dated April 22nd 1518 the Commissioners of the Arte di Lana (see No. 120, n. 2) granted Michelangelo a life concession for the quarrying of marble for his own use, in return for the opening up of the quarries at Pietra Santa and Seravezza, and for the supplying of the marbles required for the work at the Duomo (Milanesi, p. 679).*

2. *Jacopo Salviati was one of the six members of the Guild who were empowered to act on behalf of the Arte di Lana (Frey, Briefe, p. 99).*

3. *The marbles were not shipped until October (Frey, Briefe, p. 111) and had not reached Florence by the end of the year (No. 134).*

¶ To the Captain of Cortona

Buonarroti Archives Mil. cccliv From Florence (May) 1518

Lord Captain[1] — When I was in Rome during the first year of Pope Leo, there arrived there Maestro Luca da Cortona,[2] the painter, whom I met one day near Monte Giordano. He told me that he had come to request something of the Pope, I don't remember what, and that he had once nearly had his head cut off in the Medici cause and that this seemed to him, so to speak, not to have received recognition. He told me other things in the same vein, which I don't recall. And to crown these arguments, he asked me for forty julians[3] and indicated to me where I should send them, that is, to the shop of a shoemaker, where I believe he was lodging. And I, not having the money on me, offered to send it to him and this I did. As soon as I got home I sent him the said forty julians by an assistant of mine called, or rather named, Silvio,[4] who is now in Rome, I believe. Then a few days later the said Maestro Luca, who had perhaps not succeeded with his project, came to my house in the Macello de' Corvi, the house which I still have to-day, and found that I was working on a marble figure – upright, four *braccia* in height, which has the arms behind.[5] He grumbled away to me and asked me for another forty julians, because he said he wanted to leave Rome. I went upstairs to my room and fetched the forty julians for him, a Bolognese servant who was in my service being present, and I think the aforesaid assistant who had taken him the others, was also there. He took the said money and went with God. I have never seen him since. But as I was ill at the time, I complained about not being able to work, and he said to me, 'Doubt not but that Angels will come from heaven and take you by the hand and aid you'.

I'm writing to you about this, because if the said things were repeated to the said Maestro Luca, he would remember and not say he had repaid me . . . .
. . . .

[Only a fragment of the rest of the letter remains, but its substance is as follows:]

Your lordship wrote and told Buonarroto that he says he repaid them and you believe that he did. This is not true. You call me an arrant rascal, and so I should be, if I sought repayment of what I had already had. Your lordship may think what you like. They are owed to me, and this I swear. If you wish to do me justice, you can do so . . .[6]

1. *Captain and Keeper of the Public Peace, one of the three supreme magistrates in Tuscan cities.*

2. *Luca Signorelli (1441–1523).*

3. *See Appendix 3.*

4. *Silvio Falcone da Magliano nella Sabina, who before the date of this letter had been dismissed from Michelangelo's service (Symonds, II, p. 341).*

5. *One of the two 'Captives' for the Tomb of Julius II, now in the Louvre, which may accordingly be dated 1513/14. Plate 15.*

6. *He had been trying to recover this and another debt since the beginning of the year (Frey, Briefe, p. 90).*

125

*Buonarroti
Archives
Mil. ccclv
From Florence
July 15th
1518*

¶ [To the Cardinal Giulio de' Medici in Rome]

On the 15th day of July, 1518.

Most Reverend Monsignor — As I am expecting delivery of a fair amount of marble this year for the work at San Lorenzo in Florence, and as I have not found a place suitable for working it, either within the precincts of San Lorenzo or nearby, I opened negotiations for the purchase of a plot of land[1] near Santa Caterina from the Chapter of Santa Maria del Fiore in order to build one. This land is costing me some three hundred broad ducats in gold; and I have been after the said Chapter for two months to get possession of the said land. They made me pay sixty ducats more for it than it's worth,[2] pretending they regret it, but saying they cannot contravene the terms of the Bull of sale they had from the Pope. Now if the Pope is issuing Bulls granting licence to rob, I beg Your Most Reverend Lordship to get one issued to me too, because I have more need of it than they; but if this is not customary, I beg you to have justice done me in this wise; this land which I have taken is not large enough for my purpose; the Chapter has some more land behind it; I therefore beg Your Lordship to have another plot given me, whereby I may recover the amount by which they overcharged me for the one I've bought. And if anything is owing them, I want no favours.

As regards the undertaking, the beginnings are difficult . . . . .

[Incomplete and unsigned]

1. *On July 14th 1518 Michelangelo purchased from the Chapter of Santa Maria del Fiore a site in the Via Mozza for the purpose of building a workshop (Gaye, II, p. 254). On November 24th he paid one hundred and seventy ducats, presumably, for the adjacent land he required (Milanesi, p. 575). Milanesi's statement (p. 141) that the first purchase was made on April 17th 1517 does not appear to accord with the available evidence. In April 1517 Michelangelo was in Carrara (Milanesi, p. 664).*

2. *On July 29th the Cardinal wrote to Michelangelo, saying that he had ordered a reduction in the price; 'the Bull notwithstanding' (Steinmann and Wittkower, p. 440).*

126

*Buonarroti
Archives
Mil. ccclii
From Florence
July 1518*

¶ To my dear Maestro Donato Benti, sculptor, in Pietra Santa

My dear Maestro Donato — Please commend me to the Commissary and tell his lordship that I have carried out his instructions here.

As to our affairs, he, Ceccone,[1] has come here to me for money. I was unwilling to give him any, because I do not know what has been arranged there. So please tell them to let me know what they have arranged, because if they are to be paid, I am willing to pay them, as I'm never for contravening the terms of a contract.

15. *A Captive*
(Figure for the Tomb of Julius II)

Michelangelo
Musée du Louvre, Paris

Concerning your affairs, the said Ceccone tells me that you are behindhand with the measurements,[2] that they cannot get on, and that the men from Pietra Santa whom I set to quarrying have abandoned the undertaking and are doing nothing; which things I do not believe. I shall soon be with you. I commend me to you.

Your most faithful

MICHELANGELO SCULPTOR IN FLORENCE

1. *Francesco Lucchesini da Corbignano, a scarpellino, one of five to whom Michelangelo subsequently paid four ducats on account in respect of an unpublished contract mentioned in his 'Ricordi' (Milanesi, p. 573).*

2. *i.e. the measurements for the marble blocks.*

127   ¶ TO BUONARROTO DI LODOVICO SIMONI IN FLORENCE

British Museum Mil. cxvii From Seravezza August 12th 1518

Buonarroto — If I'm not home in time to pay the tax on the land I bought, see that it is so arranged that I may not suffer by default before I get back, which will be in about a month. I think my affairs here will go well, but not without the utmost trouble. I'm sending Michele to Florence to borrow certain things from the *Opera*.[1] If he needs a mule to convey them here, help him to find one, so that as little as possible is spent.

MICHELANGELO IN SERAVEZZA

1. *From an entry in the 'Ricordi' dated August 10th 1518, it appears that it was tackle for use at the quarries that Michele was sent to borrow from the Opera (Milanesi, p. 573).*

128   ¶ TO BUONARROTO DI LODOVICO SIMONI IN FLORENCE

British Museum Mil. cxviii From Seravezza August 1518

Buonarroto — Of the *scarpellini* who came here, only Meo and Ceccone remain. The others have taken themselves off. They had four ducats[1] from me here, and I promised to keep them supplied with money for their living expenses, in order that they might do what I require. They worked for a few days, and with such ill-will that that contemptible wretch Rubecchio[2] very nearly spoilt a column I had quarried. But I'm more upset about their going to Florence and, in order to exonerate themselves, giving me and the marble quarries such a bad name, that I shan't be able to get any men later on when I want them. I wish at least, since they've fooled me, that they'd keep quiet. I'm therefore informing you myself, so that you may make them keep quiet through fear of some sort, either of Jacopo Salviati, or as you think best, because these miserable money-grubbers are doing this enterprise a great deal of harm, and me too.

MICHELANGELO IN SERAVEZZA

1. *Money on account in respect of an unpublished contract (see No. 126). The terms were evidently generous.*

2. *Mazo di Simone di Matteo, called Rubecchio (d. 1525), a scarpellino from Settignano.*

¶ TO BERTO DA FILICAIA IN FLORENCE   *129*

Buonarroti
Archives
Mil. ccclvi
From
Seravezza
August 1518

Berto[1] — I commend me to you and thank you for the services and kindnesses I have received from you, and with all that lies in my power I am always at your command. Things here are going tolerably well. One may say that the road is finished, since there is little left to do. That is to say, there are a few boulders, or rather outcrops, to be cut away. One outcrop is where the road, which leads from the river, debouches on the old road to Rimagno; another outcrop is a little beyond Rimagno on the way to Seravezza, where a large boulder is lying across the road; and another is near the last houses in Seravezza, going towards Corvara. In addition, there are a few places to be levelled with small pickaxes. And all these being short jobs, could be done in a fortnight, if the *scarpellini* were worth anything. As to the marsh, it is about a week since I was there, when they were still filling in, to the worst of their ability. If they have gone on with it, I reckon they must have finished it by this time.

As to the marbles, I've got the quarried column safely down into the river-bed, fifty *braccia* from the road. It has been a bigger job than I anticipated to sling it down. Some mistake was made in slinging it, and one man had his neck broken and died instantly, and it nearly cost me my life. The other column was almost blocked out; I discovered a flaw in it, which left me short; it was necessary to cut back into the hillside again to the full width to avoid the flaw, and this I've done, and I hope that now it will be all right and I can block it out to the full length.

I think that's all, except to ask you, when you speak to his Magnificence, Jacopo Salviati, to make my excuses for not having written, as I have nothing as yet that I care to write about, so I'm not doing so. The site here is very rough to quarry and the men very inexperienced in an operation of this kind. A great deal of patience will therefore be needed for some months, until the mountains are tamed and the men trained; then

117

we shall get on faster. It is sufficient that what I have promised I shall perform without fail and shall produce the finest work that has ever been produced in Italy – with God's help.

Since I wrote I have had an answer from the men at Pietra Santa who undertook to quarry a specific amount of marble some six months ago; they will neither do the quarrying nor return me the hundred ducats I gave them. It seems to me that they have taken a bold course, which, as I see it, they would not have taken without support. So I intend to come to Florence to the Eight[2] and to demand damages from them for this dishonesty. I don't know whether this can be done. I hope his Magnificence Jacopo Salviati will help me to get justice.

[Unsigned]

1. *In a letter dated August 14th 1518 (Frey, Briefe, p. 112) Buonarroto had spoken highly of Berto da Filicaia, who was in a position of authority at the Opera del Duomo, and had emphasized the excellence of his disposition towards Michelangelo. He it was who lent the tackle which Michele was sent to Florence to borrow (No. 127).*

2. *The 'Otto di Guardia e Balia', a tribunal delegated to the investigation of criminal offences. As noted in his 'Ricordi', Michelangelo recovered ninety of the hundred ducats he had advanced (Milanesi, p. 565). For a comparable application to the Eight for an infringement of contract see Vasari, III, p. 262.*

130   ¶ To Buonarroto di Lodovico Simoni in Florence

*British
Museum
Mil. cxix
From
Seravezza
September 2nd
1518*

Buonarroto — I gather from a letter of yours that Donato Capponi[1] has made you an offer of a certain property and also that the Chapter[2] is willing to sell the rest of that plot. I cannot reply to you as to the one or the other, because I'm undecided. We'll talk it over together in Florence later.

The *scarpellini*[3] who came here have not discharged their obligations. They worked only to the value of the small amount I paid them and then went with God. It's true that Meo and Ceccone would have stayed on and done what they could, but on their own like this they couldn't do anything, so I've given them leave.

Even Sandro[4] has left here. He lived here in style for several months with a big mule and a little one, intent on fishing and philandering. I've thrown away a hundred ducats on him. He has left a certain quantity of marbles here, with witnesses to the fact that I may take what suits me. I cannot find twenty-five ducats' worth among them that's any use to me, because they're a swindle. Either through malice or through ignorance he's treated me very badly. When I get back I intend to obtain satisfaction, whatever happens. That's all. I think I'll be here for another month.

MICHELANGELO IN SERAVEZZA

Please seal the letter that will be enclosed with this and put in a cover addressed – 'To Maestro Piero Rosselli,[5] architect in Rome' – and direct it to the Borgherini Bank in Rome.

1. *Donato di Francesco Capponi (1469–1524). He was a Consul of the Mint, no doubt in his capacity as a banker, for a period of six months during this year (Litta, X, tav. xvi, and Staley, p. 566).*

2. *i.e. the Chapter of Santa Maria del Fiore.*

3. *For the contract made with them on March 15th 1518, see Milanesi, p. 673.*

4. *Alessandro di Giovanni di Bertino Fancelli (1457–1521), who had entered into a contract on May 22nd 1518 to supply Michelangelo with a stipulated amount of marble. According to the terms of the contract, if he failed to do so he would forfeit the hundred ducats he had received in advance. Hence the reference to witnesses (Milanesi, p. 683).*

5. *Piero Rosselli, son of the more famous Domenico. His design for the shrine for the head of St. John the Baptist in San Silvestro in Rome was submitted to Michelangelo for his approval. He it was who raised the marble, destined for the 'Hercules slaying Cacus', when it fell into the Arno (Vasari, VI, p. 150, and Appendix 14, pt. III).*

¶ TO PIETRO URBANO [IN FLORENCE]

131

*Buonarroti
Archives
Mil. ccclvii
From
Seravezza
September 1518*

Pietro — If your finger is better and you think it's all right to come here with Michele, you can come and bring me two shirts. If you don't think so, send them by Michele and let me know how you are.[1]

MICHELANGELO IN SERAVEZZA

1. *Pietro had written to Michelangelo on September 3rd, telling him that his finger was all right again. In a previous letter, dated August 19th, he said that the doctor at Santa Maria Nuova had prevented him from leaving Florence on account of the injury (Frey, Briefe, pp. 113, 114).*

132

TO BUONARROTO DI LODOVICO SIMONI IN FLORENCE

British Museum Mil. cxx From Seravezza September 16th 1518

Buonarroto — I learn from your letter that you have a farm on hand near Fiesole, and that it is a good proposition, and also that Pier Francesco Borgherini has spoken to you about the house.

As to Pier Francesco's house, I say to you that I am in favour of taking it at a reasonable price, if the air is all right.[1] As to the farm, I am in favour of taking it also, if it seems to you a good proposition, so if you can hold things in abeyance, do so until I get home. I expect to return within two or three weeks.

As to Ceccone, you tell me that if I want him to come now, he has recovered and would come willingly. Tell him that winter is now coming on here, that it does nothing but rain, and that one can't stay and work in the mountains, so I don't think he should come at present, because we should waste both time and money.

I'm writing to Berto[2] about what I need. Commend me to him.

Let me know when you write to me how Gismondo is, and tell Pietro to try to apply himself and that I shall soon be home.

MICHELANGELO IN SERAVEZZA

1. *A necessary proviso in a city without proper sanitation. The house was situated near Sta. Maria del Carmine (Frey, Briefe, p. 116).*

2. *Berto da Filicaia.*

133

TO BUONARROTO IN FLORENCE

British Museum Mil. cxxi (From Settignano) (October) 1518

Buonarroto — I should be grateful if you would find out how many *staiora*[1] those plots near Santa Caterina[2] comprise and what they cost. I don't mean the plots we are going to look at, but those beyond. I have pointed them out to Piero and he will show you which they are. And this I beg you to do at once, because I must reply to Giovanni da Ricasoli, who is reserving them for me.

As to Pier Francesco's house, if I were certain of getting it, I would wait several months; but the contract would have to be drawn up now and I would put down the money on deposit at once. If not there is nothing more to be said about it. Answer me as soon as you can.

MICHELANGELO

1. *A staiora = an area sufficient for the sowing of one bushel of seed.*

2. *See No. 125, n. 1.*

¶ To my dear friend, Lionardo, saddler, with the Borgherini in Rome

134

*Buonarroti
Archives
Mil. ccclix
From Florence
December 21st
1518*

Lionardo[1] — You exhort me in your last letter to press on; I appreciate this, because I see that you do it for my good. But I must make it clear to you that such exhortations are, nevertheless, so many knife-thrusts, because I'm dying of vexation through my inability to do what I want to do, owing to my ill-luck. A week ago this evening my assistant Pietro returned from Porto Venere with my assistant, Donato, who is in charge of the transport of the marbles at Carrara, leaving a loaded boat at Pisa, which has never appeared because it hasn't rained and the Arno is completely dried up. Another four boats are commissioned for the marbles in Pisa, which will all come loaded when it rains, and I shall begin work in earnest. On this account I am more disgruntled than any man on earth. I am also being pressed by Messer Metello Vari about his figure[2] which is likewise there in Pisa and will be in one of the first boats. I have never replied to him, nor do I wish to write to you again, until I have started work: because I'm dying of anguish and seem to have become an impostor against my will.

I have an excellent workshop in preparation here, where I shall be able to erect twenty figures at a time. I cannot roof it because there is no wood here in Florence, nor likely to be any until it rains, and I don't believe it will ever rain again from now on, unless to do me some mischief.

As to the Cardinal,[3] I'm not asking you to say anything further to him, because I know he has a bad opinion of my conduct; but he will soon have proof to the contrary. Commend me to Sebastiano[4] and to you do I commend myself.

Your Michelangelo in Florence

1. *Lionardo di Compagno, a Florentine who had matriculated in the Guild of Saddlers, and was afterwards employed by the Borgherini in Rome. He was a great friend of Michelangelo's and often wrote to him urging him to press on with the work on the Tomb of Julius II (Frey, Briefe, pp. 30 et seq.).*

2. *The 'Risen Christ' which Metello Vari, a Roman gentleman, had commissioned under a contract dated June 14th 1514 (Milanesi, p. 641). The figure was eventually completed by Federigo Frizzi and placed in the church of Santa Maria sopra Minerva in 1521. Vari had written an importunate letter to Michelangelo on November 24th 1518 (Frey, Briefe, p. 125).*

3. *The Cardinal Aginensis, who was continually pressing Michelangelo about the completion of the Tomb of Julius II.*

4. *Sebastiano Luciani, afterwards called from his office, Sebastiano del Piombo (c. 1485–1547), the Venetian painter with whom Michelangelo was on intimate terms.*

135

*Buonarroti
Archives
Mil. ccclx
From Florence
December 22nd
1518*

❡ To Francesco Peri, Director of the Salviati in Pisa

My dearest Director[1] — I haven't come to agree the accounts, as you've asked me to several times, because I haven't been well. I'm now fit and strong and as soon as I get an answer I'm awaiting from Rome, which is of great importance to me – as soon as I get it, I'll mount my horse and come to Pisa and agree the accounts and do whatever you wish. May I beg you, as you've been so patient, to be patient a few days longer, and not to be surprised at my shortcomings, because I couldn't help it.

I'm well aware of the services you've done me and of all the trouble you've had; and recognizing this and being eternally obliged to you, I make you an offer of myself, small though this offering may be, with all that I have and am. And as I've said, I will be with you in a few days and with your guidance we'll arrange matters, so that you may not be put to any more trouble.

On the twenty-second day of December.

Your Michelangelo sculptor in Florence

1. *'Carissimo Maggiore' in the original. The term 'Maggiore' means the Senior Partner or Director of a company – in this case the Director of the branch of the Salviati bank in Pisa. Peri had been instrumental in arranging for the transport of the marbles (Frey, Briefe, pp. 109 et seq.).*

136

*Buonarroti
Archives
Mil. ccclxi
From Florence
December 26th
1518*

❡ To Maestro Donato Benti in Seravezza

Donato — I wrote you through Domenico, called el Zucca, Andrea's partner,[1] that I should be with you directly after the festival. Now as Francesco Peri, who is here, tells me that he wishes to remain here for another four to six days, on account of certain business affairs of his, and as I have to agree the accounts with him in Pisa, I've agreed to wait for him, in order to go with him to Pisa and from there I'll come on to you. Since in the meantime I'm delayed here, I'm sending you ten broad ducats by the aforesaid Zucca, Andrea's partner, so that, if the weather's fit for carting, you can get on with it. Francesco Peri assures me that the freight for as much marble as you will be conveying there will be paid for in Pisa.[2] And I, within these next few days, will leave here with Francesco and agree the accounts in Pisa, and then come on to you and will give you the money you want.

I've written to Rome about the Pisan customs duty, as you advised me, and also as to how you are being treated there;[3] and I hope to have a reply before I leave. I've recently heard from Francesco Peri of the efforts you are making – though I knew of them and was grateful for them before. I thank you for this and remain most obliged to you and, if this Pope survives, I'm sure that this enterprise will redound to your good.

On the 26th day of December 1518.

YOUR MICHELANGELO SCULPTOR IN FLORENCE

1. *Domenico di Matteo Moregli and Andrea di Giovanni del Luchesino were both scarpellini from Settignano, working in Seravezza (Milanesi, p. 579).*

2. *There is another draft of this letter up to this point (Mil. ccclxii) so nearly the same as to add nothing. It has therefore been omitted.*

3. *In the matter of exempting the marbles from duty. The Pope undertook to pay if the concession could not be obtained (Frey, Briefe, p. 134).*

¶ [TO MESSER DOMENICO BUONINSEGNI IN ROME]

137

*Buonarroti
Archives
Mil. ccclxiii
From Florence
January 1519*

Messer Domenico — I perceive from your letter that Bernardo Niccolini has written and told you that I was indignant with him about a report[1] of yours, which said that the Lord of Carrara was making numerous charges against me and that the Cardinal was complaining about me. The reason I was indignant is this; because he read it to me in a haberdasher's shop in public, as if it were a formal indictment, so that thereby everyone knew that I was condemned to death; that was the reason why I said to him 'Why doesn't he write to me?' I note that you do write to me. So do write to him, or to me just as it suits you, but after the execution, if it takes place, I beg you for the honour of our country not to disclose the reason!

I understand from your last that I had better place commissions for the marbles for San Lorenzo. I have already placed three commissions and have been cheated over all three. This is because the *scarpellini* from here have no understanding of marble and as soon as they saw their lack of success, they went with God. And thus I've thrown away some hundreds of ducats there. For this reason I had to stay there from time to time, to set them to work, and to show them the lines of the marbles and what things to avoid, which marbles are the poor ones, and even how to quarry, because in things of this kind am I skilled.

It was even necessary for me to remain there in the end.

[Unsigned]

1. *The letter in question, addressed to Bernardo Niccolini, is dated December 21st 1518. The Cardinal referred to was Cardinal Aginensis, who was said in the letter to be 'furious about the tomb of Pope Julius' (Frey, Briefe, p. 128).*

138   ¶ To Pietro Urbano in Florence[1]

*Buonarroti
Archives
Mil. cccli
From Florence
March 29th
1519*

Pietro — You are to pay the boatmen, when they come and deliver you a letter from Donato, and you are to give them the amount stated in the letter in my hand, which each of them will have. Keep the letters from Donato which they give you.

You will also pay the cartwrights – when they bring large blocks at the rate of thirty-five *soldi* the thousandweight, and for the small blocks twenty *soldi*.

Pay the duty of ninety *lire* to the *Contratti*[2] and get the ledger with the folios.

Give Baccio di Puccione[3] the money he asks you for and make a note of it.

Buy some canes and train the vines in the garden, and if you can get either earth or other dry material to fill in the workshop *[floor]*,[4] do so.

Buy a piece of rope thirty *braccia* long that won't rot, and pay for it, and make a note of it.

Go to confession, apply yourself and take care of the house.

Settle the account with Gismondo and pay him and get him to give you the reckoning.

I'm leaving you forty ducats to-day, this twenty-ninth day of March.

[Unsigned]

1. *This is clearly not a letter, in the ordinary sense of the word, but a list of instructions left for Pietro on March 29th, the day Michelangelo left Florence for Pietra Santa (Milanesi, p. 516).*

2. *i.e. the 'Magistrato sulla Gabella de' Contratti', the office responsible for the collection of dues of all kinds.*

3. *The carpenter in charge of building the workshop on the site in the Via Mozza, which Michelangelo had bought in November 1518.*

4. *The workshop presumably had a beaten earth floor.*

139   ¶ To Pietro Urbano, in the house of Michelangelo, sculptor, in Florence

*Buonarroti
Archives
Mil. ccclxiv
From
Seravezza
April 20th
1519*

Pietro — Things have gone very badly. That is to say, on Saturday morning, having made great preparations, I set about having a column lowered and nothing whatsoever was lacking; but after I had lowered it about fifty *braccia* one of the rings of the tackle attached to the column broke and the column fell into the river in a hundred pieces. The said ring Donato had had made by a colleague of his, Lazzaro,[1] a smith; and as to its being adequate, had it been properly made, it could have carried four columns and looked at from the outside there was no doubt about it. After it broke we saw the utter rascality of it, for it was not solid inside at all, and the iron in it was no thicker than the back of a knife; so much so that I marvel it withstood so much. Those of us who were anywhere near were in imminent danger of our lives; and a splendid block was ruined. I left the superintendence of the ironwork to Donato during the Carnival, that he might go to the forge and procure good malleable iron. You see how he's treated me. And the blocks of the pulley he had made for me were likewise all split at the ring in lowering this column and are also about to give way and they are twice as big as those used by the *Opera*; because, had they been of good iron, they would have withstood an unlimited weight. But the iron is brittle and poor and could not be worse forged. And this is because Donato keeps in with this colleague of his and sent him to the forge and has served me as you see. I suppose one must have patience. I shall be home this Easter and we'll begin work, if God wills. Commend me to Francesco Scarfi.[2]

On the twentieth day of April.

MICHELANGELO IN SERAVEZZA

1. *Lazzaro della Corvara. He is mentioned several times in the 'Ricordi'.*

2. *Francesco Scarfi was referred to by the Commissioners of the Opera as 'our colleague'. His father-in-law, Francesco Vettori (1474–1539), dedicated his 'Sommario della Storia d'Italia' to him. As Michelangelo was in correspondence wih the Commissioners over the said column, it was, presumably, intended for the Duomo (Frey, Briefe, p. 140).*

¶ TO PIETRO URBANO IN FLORENCE

140

Buonarroti Archives Mil. ccclxvi From Florence May 10th 1519

Pietro — You are to go to Pietra Santa to Ser Giovan Badessa and get him to give you the formal contract[1] I made with the Carrarese, that is with Pollina and with Leone and with Bello, for eight figures they have to do for me, that is to say, marble for eight figures,[2] four of four and a half *braccia* and four of five *braccia*, of the width and thickness stipulated in the contract. The said contract says, or rather I think it says, that by the middle of May I have to give the said Carrarese thirty broad gold ducats, on condition that they must have quarried by the said time four of the aforesaid figures, two of four and a half *braccia* and two of five. Get him to read you the said contract and you will understand better what you have to do. And if they have not quarried the said four figures, you do not have to give them the money. And you can tell them to quarry them, and then to inform me of it, and I will pay them the money. And if they have quarried them in accordance with the contract give them thirty ducats as stipulated by the contract, and pay them to them in Pietra Santa, and get a contract[3] made out for them by the said Giovanni Badessa, and in Carrara get a declaration made with witnesses that

125

you were there in the middle of May, ready to pay the said quarrymen in fulfilment of the contract.

Get in touch with Marco,[4] who has had two ducats for blocking out the stone I have at Sponda and making a figure from it of four or five *braccia*; and see whether he has blocked it out and if you can get him to transport it to the coast and to arrange about the cartage of what is on the shore, which I got from Leone, do so. And Marco will find the barges to transport them to Pisa at the usual rate. Also a figure of two *braccia*, that I got from Cagione. Donato tells me that he gave the money to Marco to transport them to the coast. Ser Giovan Badessa has had three *barili* for transcribing the aforesaid contract.[5] Complete the payment, which I think will come to about one ducat. Do the best you can.[6]

[Unsigned]

1. *The contract drawn up by Ser Giovanni del Paolo della Badessa on April 13th 1519, with Jacopo di Tomeo, called Pollina, Antonio di Jacopo Polliga de Puliga, called Leone, and Francesco di Jacopo Vannelli di Torano, called Bello (Milanesi, p. 689). Needless to say, the blocks were not ready and Pietro made the required declaration on May 18th 1519, having refused to pay for them (Milanesi, p. 692).*

2. *The four blocks of four and a half braccia were for the four seated figures to be placed above the first cornice of the S. Lorenzo façade; the four of five braccia were for those flanking the three main doors (Milanesi, p. 673).*

3. *Although 'contratto' is the word used, it may have been a slip of the pen for 'quitanza' i.e. 'receipt', which one would expect in the context.*

4. *Probably Marco di Bernardo Girardi with whom Michelangelo is known to have had dealings at a later date (Milanesi, p. 696 and Tolnay, III, p. 228).*

5. *The three barili had been paid to Badessa on April 13th (Milanesi, p. 577).*

6. *Though written in the form of a letter, this is really a list of instructions given to Pietro prior to his departure. Michelangelo gave him forty-four ducats in respect of this journey on May 10th (Milanesi, p. 578).*

141

¶ To Girolamo del Bardella in Porto Venere

Buonarroti Archives Mil. ccclxvii From Seravezza August 6th 1519

Girolamo[1] — Having recently returned from Rome,[2] I found a letter of yours in Florence, written from the Salviati in Pisa, to which you haven't had a reply from me, owing to my not having been where I could get it. Now as I understand your proposal, from the said letter, that is to say, that you would have undertaken to transport my marbles from Avenza and Pietra Santa to Pisa, I thought it as well, as I am here in Pietra Santa,[3] to write you these few lines, in order to learn whether you are still prepared to undertake the said transport; and if you are prepared to do so, I am in Seravezza.[3] Would you kindly let me know where I should go, so that we may meet, as I think we can come to an agreement. Please let me have a decisive answer as soon as possible.

On the sixth day of August.

YOUR MICHELANGELO SCULPTOR IN SERAVEZZA

1. *Girolamo del Bardella was the barge-master who had shipped the previous consignment of marbles in October 1518 (Frey, Briefe, p. 122).*

2. *This is, apparently, the only evidence we have that Michelangelo went to Rome at this period.*

3. *Where, in fact, was he, and did they succeed in meeting?*

¶ TO PIETRO, ASSISTANT TO MICHELANGELO, SCULPTOR, IN SERAVEZZA **142**

Pietro — Certain *scarpellini*[1] are coming to Seravezza and will remain one day to see the quarry. When they return, let me know how you are and when you want me to send you the mule. Let me know without fail, and if you cannot write, see that I get a message, because I'm anxious, as you were not as well as I should have liked when I left. That's all. Take care of yourself.[2]

MICHELANGELO IN FLORENCE

Buonarroti Archives Mil. ccclxxii From Florence September (12th) 1519

1. *Possibly those sent initially by the Commissioners of Santa Maria del Fiore. See No. 144.*

2. *This letter belongs to the Buonarroti Collection purchased from the Portuguese Consul in Civitavecchia, Cavaliere Bustelli, in 1861 (Giornale Storico, V, p. 938).*

¶ TO PIETRO URBANO IN PISTOIA **143**

Pietro — I'm sending you the jerkin, a pair of hose and the riding cloak, by a man called the Turk, who works in Buonarroto's shop. Let me know how you are[1] and if you need anything. I would have come to Pistoia to see you, but I'm so busy I cannot leave. However, if there is any need for me to come, let me know. And when you feel able to leave send someone trustworthy from there for the mule, and write and tell me what I should give him and I'll pay it. Keep up your health and spirits and, if you're able to, write and acknowledge receipt of the clothes mentioned above.[2]

On the seventeenth day of September.

MICHELANGELO SCULPTOR IN FLORENCE

Buonarroti Archives Mil. ccclxviii From Florence September 17th 1519

1. *Having been sent to Carrara to pay for certain work in connection with San Lorenzo, Pietro was taken seriously ill there. As soon as Michelangelo heard of it, he rode post from Seravezza to Carrara to see him. In the 'Ricordi' he notes that the cost of the journey, of having Pietro carried from Carrara to Seravezza, of the doctor and the medicines, in addition to the money he gave to Pietro, amounted to thirty-three and a half ducats. In Seravezza Michelangelo left him in the care of the scarpellino known as Topolino until he was fit enough to go on to his home in Pistoia to recuperate (Milanesi, p. 578).*

2. *Pietro acknowledged the clothes on the following day, September 18th (Frey, Briefe, p. 147).*

144

British Museum Mil. ccclxxiv From Florence (March) 1520

¶ [TO MESSER . . . . .][1]

When I was in Carrara on business of my own, that is to say, obtaining marbles to transport to Rome for the Tomb of Pope Julius, in fifteen hundred and sixteen, Pope Leo sent for me with reference to the façade of San Lorenzo, which he wished to execute in Florence. I therefore left Carrara on the fifth day of December and went to Rome, and there I did a design for the said façade, on the basis of which the said Pope Leo commissioned me to arrange for the quarrying of the marble at Carrara for the said work. Then, when I had returned to Carrara from Rome on the last day of the aforesaid December, Pope Leo there sent to me, through Jacopo Salviati, for the purpose of quarrying the marbles for the said work, a thousand ducats, which were brought by a servant of Salviati's called Bentivoglio. I received the said money about the eighth of the following month, that is to say, of January, and I accordingly gave a receipt for it.

Then, the following August, having received instructions from the Pope aforesaid about the model of the said work, I came to Florence from Carrara to execute it. I accordingly made it to scale in wood, with the figures in wax, and sent it to Rome. As soon as he saw it he ordered me to go there. So I went and undertook the said façade on contract, as appears from the covenant[2] with His Holiness, which I have. And as, in order to serve His Holiness, I had to transport the marbles I needed in Rome for the Tomb of Pope Julius to Florence, as I have done, and then to transport them, when they had been worked, back to Rome, he promised to indemnify me for all the expenses, that is to say, the dues and the freight, which is an outlay of about eight hundred ducats, although the written agreement doesn't say so.

On the sixth day of February, fifteen hundred and seventeen,[3] I returned to Florence from Rome, and as I had undertaken the façade of San Lorenzo aforesaid on contract, defraying all the expenses, and as the said Pope Leo had to pay me four thousand ducats in Florence on account of the said work, as appears in the agreement, I received from Jacopo Salviati on about the twenty-fifth day eight hundred ducats for the same, and gave a receipt and went to Carrara. But as they had not fulfilled the contracts and

16. *The Church of San Lorenzo*   *Florence*

previous orders for the marbles for the said work, and as the Carrarese were bent upon balking me, I went to have the said marbles quarried at Seravezza, a mountain near Pietra Santa in Florentine territory. And then, when I had already blocked out six columns, each eleven and a half *braccia*, and many other marbles, and had there begun the workings that are to-day established, for no quarrying had ever been done there before, I went to Florence on the twentieth day of March, fifteen hundred and eighteen[4] for money to begin transporting the said marbles, and on the twenty-sixth of March, fifteen hundred and nineteen,[5] the Cardinal de' Medici had paid to me on behalf of Pope Leo for the said work, through the Gaddi of Florence, five hundred ducats, for which I accordingly gave a receipt. Afterwards, in this same year,[6] the Cardinal, by order of the Pope, told me not to proceed further with the work aforesaid, because they said they wished to relieve me of the trouble of transporting the marbles, and that they wished to supply me with them in Florence themselves, and to make a new contract. And thus the matter stands, from that day to this.

Now at this time, the Commissioners of Santa Maria del Fiore, having sent a certain number of *scarpellini* to Pietra Santa, or rather to Seravezza, to take possession of the new workings and to take away from me the marbles I had quarried for the façade of San Lorenzo, in order to use them for the paving of Santa Maria del Fiore, while the Pope was willing to continue the façade of San Lorenzo, and the Cardinal having allocated the marbles for the said façade to everyone but to me, and having handed over to those who had taken charge of the transport my new workings at Seravezza, without coming to terms with me, I was very upset, because neither the Cardinal nor the Commissioners were empowered to interfere in my affairs until I had first terminated the agreement with the Pope. And the said *[façade]* of San Lorenzo having been abandoned in agreement with the Pope, and the expenses incurred and the money received having been accounted for, the said workings and the marbles and equipment would of necessity have belonged either to His Holiness or to me; and after this, the one party or the other could have done with it as he chose.

Now concerning this, the Cardinal has told me to account for the money received and the expenses incurred and has said that he wishes to release me, so that he may take over, both for the *Opera* and for himself, those marbles he wants from the aforesaid workings at Seravezza.

I have therefore shown that I received two thousand three hundred ducats, in the manner and at the times herein stated, and have also shown that I spent one thousand eight hundred ducats. That of these, about two hundred and fifty were spent in consideration of the freight up the Arno of marbles for the Tomb of Pope Julius, which I had transported here in order to serve Pope Julius *[sic]* in Rome, which will amount to some five hundred ducats. I am not charging to his account, over and above, the wooden model of the said façade which I sent to him in Rome. I am not charging to his account, over and above, the space of three years I have lost over this; I am not charging to his account the fact that I have been ruined over the said work for San Lorenzo; I am not charging to his account the enormous insult of having been brought here to execute the said work and then of having it taken away from me; and I still do not know why. I am not charging the loss, amounting to five hundred ducats, on my house in Rome, which I left, including marbles, furniture and completed work. Without charging the aforesaid items to the account, out of two thousand three hundred ducats, I am left with not more than five hundred ducats in hand.

Now we are agreed. Pope Leo takes over the new workings, with the said marbles, that have been quarried, and I the money which remains to me in hand, and I am left free. And I propose to have a brief drawn up which the Pope will sign.

Now you know exactly how the matter stands. Please draw up a draft of the said brief for me, and set forth the money received for the said work at San Lorenzo, in such a way that it can never be demanded of me, and also set forth how in exchange for the said money, which I have received, Pope Leo takes over the aforesaid workings, the marbles and the equipment . . . . .

[Incomplete and unsigned]

1. *The superscription of this letter, as given by Milanesi, reads 'Al Sebastiano del Piombo? in Roma'. This makes no sense at all, since Sebastiano was not appointed Frate del Piombo until 1531, and in any case there would be no reason for addressing such a letter to him. It was probably addressed to Ser Bonaventura di Leonardo, a Florentine notary who had drawn up other documents connected with the enterprise.*

2. *Milanesi, p. 671.*

3. *N.S. 1518.*

4. *N.S. 1519.*

5. *Correct by both Old and New Style, as by the former the new year had begun on the previous day, viz. March 25th.*

6. *See Appendix 14.*

VII

LETTERS
145 - 182

From Florence
1520 - 1527

17.   *Cardinal Bernardo Dovizi da Bibbiena*   *Raphael*
Palazzo Pitti, Florence

VII. From Florence: 1520-1527

¶ [To the Cardinal Bernardo Dovizi da Bibbiena in Rome]   **145**

Buonarroti
Archives
Mil. ccclxxiii
From Florence
(May/June)
1520

Monsignor[1] — I beg your Most Reverend Lordship - not as a friend nor as a servant for I am unworthy to be either the one or the other – but as a man of no account, poor and foolish, to obtain Bastiano Veneziano,[2] the painter, some share in the work at the Palace, now that Raphael is dead. But should Your Lordship think that the favour would be thrown away on a man like me, I think that one might still find some pleasure in granting favours to fools, just as one does in onions as a change of diet, when one is surfeited with capons. You are always granting favours to men of esteem; I beg Your Lordship to try out the change with me. The said Bastiano is a capable man and the favour would be considerable, which, though it might be wasted on me, would not be so on him, as I'm sure he will do credit to Your Lordship.

[Unsigned]

1. *For the implications of this curious letter of recommendation see Appendix 15.*

2. *Sebastiano Luciani, sometimes called Veneziano.*

¶ [To Messer Domenico Buoninsegni in Rome]   **146**

Buonarroti
Archives
Mil. ccclxxi
From Florence
(March) 1521

Domenico — I'm always ready to risk life and limb, *if need be,*[1] for the Cardinal de' Medici. I refer to the Tombs[2] and to the matter of the marbles which have been commissioned, or rather ordered, to be quarried at Carrara. You *know* the Cardinal's wish concerning this much better than I do. So *let me know* how much you think I should do and I'll do it. I myself haven't the means to go riding round nor money of my own to spend.[3] Though if I had the means, I *should do* what I think would be useful and pleasing to the Cardinal without *saying anything more about it.*

[Unsigned]

1. *The draft is defective. The missing words, printed in italic, are supplied from Milanesi's conjectural restoration of the Italian text.*

2. *The Medici Tombs in the New Sacristy at San Lorenzo. See Appendix 16.*

3. *On April 9th Michelangelo received 200 ducats from Domenico Buoninsegni to enable him 'to go to Carrara for the said marbles for the Cardinal' (Milanesi, p. 582).*

147

¶ To Giusto di Matteo, shoemaker, in Pistoia

*Buonarroti
Archives
Mil. ccclxxv
From Florence
March (16th)
1521*

Giusto — I learn from your letter that Masina's husband, that is to say, Julio Forteguerri, would sell the house which he has here in the Via Mozza, if he got his price. It must be a year now since I spoke to you about it, and not having heard anything since then, I began walling in a garden which I have next to it. Now, if the said Julio and Masina are prepared to sell the said house for a reasonable price, I'll take it and will stop building the wall. So please will you answer me at once and let me know what they want for it, and I'll have it valued, and if the price is reasonable, I'll go ahead with it. I think that's all. I imagine that Pietro[1] will reach Rome this evening, but I expect he'll soon be back.

On the . . . . day of March.

Your Michelangelo sculptor in Florence

1. *With characteristic consideration, Michelangelo gives his correspondent news of Pietro Urbano, who came from Pistoia and may have been a friend or relative of Giusto's. Pietro had been sent to Rome in connection with the completion of 'The Risen Christ', which had been executed to the order of Metello Vari and was subsequently erected in the church of Santa Maria sopra Minerva.*

148

¶ To the Most Reverend Monsignor de' Medici in Rome

*Buonarroti
Archives
Mil. ccclviii
From Florence
(June) 1521*

Most Reverend Monsignor — They are quarrying hard at Pietra Santa for the work at San Lorenzo,[1] and as I am finding the Carrarese more submissive than they used to be, I have also placed an order for the quarrying of a large amount of marble there, so that when the weather breaks I expect to have a good part of it in Florence, and I do not think I shall fall short of anything I have promised. May God be gracious to me, for I care for nothing in the world so much as pleasing you. I think that within a month I shall need a thousand ducats. I beg Your Most Reverend Lordship not to let me lack for money.

I must also inform Your Most Reverend Lordship that I have searched for, but never found, a house large enough in which to do the whole of this work, that is to say the figures in marble and in bronze. But Matteo Bartoli[2] has recently found me an admirable site, suited to the building of a workshop for an undertaking like this; and that is the piazza in front of the church of Ognissanti. The Brethren,[3] according to what Matteo tells me, are prepared to sell me the rights they hold, and the whole parish is agreeable to it, according to the said Matteo, who is one of the Syndics.[4] There is no-one else one has to deal with, except the officials of the Towers[5] who are the authorities in charge of the Arno wall, on to which all the houses in the Borg' Ognissanti abut. They will grant me permission to abut on to it also with the workshop I shall build. All that remains is that the Brethren would appreciate a letter from Your Most Reverend Lordship, indicating that this matter is according to your pleasure, and everything would be arranged. Therefore, if you think fit to have a couple of lines sent, either to the Brethren or to Matteo, would you do so.[6]

Your Most Reverend Lordship's servant,

MICHELANGELO

1. *The newly commissioned work on the New Sacristy and the Medici Tombs.*

2. *Matteo Bartoli was the father of the more famous Cosimo Bartoli (1503–1572), the author of 'Ragionamenti Accademici'. Matteo had held office as Podestà of Pistoia in the autumn of 1513.*

3. *The 'Umiliati', or Humble Fathers of St. Michael of Alexandria.*

4. *The Syndics were inspectors appointed by the Priors in each of the 'sestiere' or wards of Florence.*

5. *The 'officials of the Towers', or, as Villani calls them, 'officials of the Walls', were those originally responsible for the construction and later for the upkeep of the city walls and their towers for defensive purposes.*

6. *See Appendix 17.*

¶ To Lodovico in Settignano

149

*British
Museum
Mil. xxxix
From Florence
September/
October 1521*

Dearest father — I was amazed at your conduct the other day, when I did not find you at home;[1] and now, when I hear that you are complaining about me and saying that I've turned you out, I'm still more amazed; for I'm certain that never to this day, since the day I was born, has it ever occurred to me to do anything, either great or small, opposed to your interest; and all the toils and troubles I've continually endured,

charissimo padre io mi maravigliai molto de chasi vostri i laltro di
quandio no mi trovai i chasa e adesso se te do ch voi vi dolete di me
e dite ch io vo chacciato via mi maraviglio piu assai p ch io so certo
ch mai daldi che io naqui p insino adesso ch nelanimo mio
di far chosa nepichola negrande che fussi chotra divoi e so
pre tucte le fatiche ch io o soportate lo soportate p nostro amore
epoi ch io sono tornato darroma ifireze sapete ch io lo sempre
presa p voi e sapete ch vo rafermo cio ch io c e no e p molti
di quande noi avevi male che io vidissi epromessi dino vi machar
mai ch tutte lemia forze mentre ch io vivo e chosi mi rafermo
ora mi maraviglio ch voi abiate sipresto dimetichato ogni cosa
noi mouete pure sperimetato gia treta anni voi e vostri figluoli
e sapete ch io o sempre pesato e factovi quandio o potuto delbene
chome adate voi dicedo ch io vo chacciato via no vedete voi fama
ch voi mi date ch si dicha che io vo chacciato via no mi machan
alt vo oltragha farmi ch io o dellaltre chose e tucti gho p nostro
amore voi mene redete buo merito ora sia lachosa chome si vuo
le io voglio darmi adintetere dauervi chacciato e dauermi facto
sempre vergognia edanno e chosi chome se io lauessi facto io vi
hieggo pdonaza fate choto di pdonare un nostro figluolo chsia
sempre vissuto male e che nabi facti tucti emali che si possono
fare me vesto modo e chosi dimouo vi prego ch voi mi pdonate
chome un tristo ch io sono e no vogliato darmi cho stassu quesa
fama ch io nabbi chacciato voi p ch lamporta piu ch voi no
credete io so pur vostro figluolo

laportatore diquesta sara rafaello dagagliano io vi prego p lamore
didio e no p mio che voi vegniate isino afireze p che o andar mi
e oi adire chosa ch importa assai e no posso venire cho stassi
e ch io omeso p dipietro ch sta mecho p le sua parole proprie certe
chose che no mi piacciono io lo mado stamani apistoia e no tor
nera piu dove me p ch io no voglio ch esia laro vina di chasa
nostra e voi tucti ne sapeni ch io no sape vo e sua portameti
do veni piu tepo fa avisarvi e no savebe nato tato cha do lo
io so sollecitato dadar via e no so p partirmi se io no vi parlo e no vi lascio
qui in chi io vi prego ch vos lasciate adare triste le passioni e chuoi vegniate

Vostro michelagnolo in fireze

18. *Facsimile of Letter No. 149 (verso and recto)*
    British Museum, London

I've endured for your sake. And you know that since I returned to Florence from Rome, I've always taken care of you and you know that I have assured you that what I have is yours. After all, it was only a few days ago, when you were ill, that I talked to you and promised you that to the best of my ability I would never fail you as long as I live, and this I reaffirm. I'm now astonished that you should so soon have forgotten everything. You have, besides, made trial of me, you and your sons, these thirty years and you know that I've always considered you and done well by you whenever I could.

How can you go about saying that I've turned you out? Don't you see what a reputation you give me, that it should be said that I've turned you out? This is the last straw, added to the worries I have about other things, all of which I endure for your sake. A fine return you make me!

However, be it as it may, I'll try to imagine that I've always brought shame and trouble upon you and thus, as if I'd done so, I ask your forgiveness. Imagine that you are forgiving a son of yours who has always led a bad life and has done you every possible wrong on earth. And thus again, I beg you to forgive me, like the reprobate I am, and not to take away my reputation up there by saying that I've turned you out, for it matters more to me than you think. After all, I am your son!

The bearer of this will be Rafaello da Gagliano. I beg you for the love of God, and not for my sake, to come down to Florence, because I have to go away and I have something very important to tell you and I cannot come up there. And because, on his own telling, I've heard several things from my assistant Pietro,[2] which displease me, I'm sending him back to Pistoia this morning and he will not return to me any more, as I do not wish him to be the ruin of our family. And you, who all knew what I did not know about his behaviour, should have informed me long ago and so much misunderstanding would not have arisen.

I'm being urged to go away, but I'm not prepared to leave without seeing you and leaving you here at home. I beg you to put aside all rancour and to come.[3]

YOUR MICHELANGELO IN FLORENCE

1. *In the Biblioteca Angelica in Rome there is a copy of an undated letter from Lodovico that appears to relate to this incident. It is a pathetic letter and was obviously occasioned by some misunderstanding (Wolf, p. 71).*

2. *Pietro Urbano had also behaved very badly in Rome, when sent there to finish 'The Risen Christ' (Milanesi, Corr., p. 30). On his return to Florence Michelangelo dismissed him from his service, either at the end of September or the beginning of October 1521. From Vettorio Ghiberti's letter to Michelangelo, written on November 28th of the same year, we learn that Pietro had already been in Naples for a month (Frey, Briefe, p. 183). Nothing further is known of him.*

3. *This letter is endorsed in Lodovico's hand, 'When he made me go to Florence, he and Raffael da Gagliano, and then Michelangelo told me about the beating of his Piero at the workshop'.*

150

Buonarroti Archives Mil. ccclxxvii From Florence (January 1522)

¶ TO MY DEAR SER GIOVAN FRANCESCO, CHAPLAIN IN SANTA MARIA DEL FIORE, FLORENCE

My dearest Ser Giovan Francesco[1] — Since, as you know, the first tailor couldn't come, and since this last one I've got is a friend of yours, please would you commend me to him and tell him not to do next Sunday as he did last, for he never let me try on the doublet, which he could perhaps have altered and made to fit me. I've worn it these last few days and it's much too tight for me, particularly across the chest. I don't know whether he skimped it in order to cheat me over the cloth,[2] though he seemed to me a man to be trusted with it. This is now done with; as regards my other things, please would you have a word with him, and tell him to have his eyes about him next time he measures me; as I should not like to have to change shops again. I rely on you for this renewed favour.

At the eleventh hour, each one of which seems to me a year.[3]

Your most faithful sculptor
in Via Mozza near the Canto
all' *[drawing of a millstone]*[4]

1. *Messer Giovan Francesco di Antonio di Benedetto Fattucci, a chaplain at Santa Maria del Fiore. While resident in Rome on ecclesiastical business, he acted as Michelangelo's representative in the protracted negotiations over the Tomb of Pope Julius II.*

2. *Actually 'rubarne'.*

3. *His depression may have been due to anxiety over the outcome of the conclave of 1521/22. In the event of the election of a cardinal other than the Cardinal de' Medici, he anticipated being in an invidious position (which proved to be the case), owing to his non-fulfilment of the Contract for the Tomb of Julius.*

4. *Perhaps the drawing is an oblique reference to the phrase 'essere alle macine', meaning to be in want or distress. Alternatively it may refer simply to the Canto della Macina which is at the junction of the Via Ginori and the Via Guelfa.*

¶ To the prudent young man, Gherardo Perini, in Pesaro

151

*Buonarroti
Archives
Mil. ccclxxvi
From Florence
February 1522*

All your friends, including myself, are delighted, my dearest Gherardo,[1] and especially those who you know are especially fond of you, to learn from your last letter, delivered by the ever faithful Zampino, of your good health and well-being. Although the kindness shown in the said letter compels me to reply, I do not really feel able to do so. I will only say this to you, that we, your friends, are the same, that is to say we are well and we all commend ourselves to you, and particularly Ser Giovan Francesco[2] and Piloto.[3] As I learn that you are shortly having to come here, I hope to reply to you more fully by word of mouth, and to satisfy myself about every particular, because it is a matter of concern to me.[4]

On the I know not what day — of February, according to my servant.

Your poor and ever faithful friend

*[Signed with a rebus – a sketch of an angel,
i.e. a winged head and three balls]*

1. *Gherardo Perini, probably a member of the banking family of that name. Papini's suggestion that he may be identified with Gherardo di Domenico Perini (1480–1564) is unacceptable (Papini, p. 243). This letter is clearly addressed to a young man. At some time or other Michelangelo presented him with three sheets of drawings in black haematite (Vasari, VII, p. 276).*

2. *Ser Giovan Francesco Fattucci.*

3. *Giovanni di Baldassare (Giusti ?), called Piloto, a goldsmith and a friend of Michelangelo's, who accompanied him to Venice shortly before the siege of Florence. He was stabbed to death in Florence in 1536 (Vasari, V, p. 607).*

4. *Tolnay somewhat naïvely imagines this to be a love letter; whereas it is only typical of the kind of affectionate correspondence which Michelangelo carried on with several young men, as for example with Andrea Quaratesi, who was devoted to him. Gherardo Perini had written on January 31st (Frey, Dicht., p. 504), begging Michelangelo to let him know whether he could be of the least service to him – a desire which seems to have been cherished by almost everyone with whom he came in contact.*

152 ¶ [TO SER GIOVANNI FRANCESCO FATTUCCI IN ROME]

*British
Museum
Mil. ccclxxix
From Florence
(April 1523)*

Ser Giovanni Francesco — It is now about two years since I returned from placing orders in Carrara for quarrying the marbles for the Cardinal's Tombs and when I went to discuss them with him he told me to find some sound solution for doing the said Tombs quickly. I wrote and sent him an account of all the ways of doing them, as you know, since you read it; that is to say, that I would do them either on contract, or for a monthly or a daily salary, or without payment, as his lordship might please, because I was anxious to do them. None of my offers was accepted. It was said that I had no mind to serve the Cardinal.

Then, when the Cardinal reopened the matter I offered to make the models in wood to the full size that the Tombs are to be, and to put in all the figures in clay and shearings[1] to the full size, and finished exactly as they are to be, and I pointed out that this would be a quick and inexpensive way to do them. That was when we wanted to buy the Caccini garden.[2] Nothing came of it, as you know. Then, as soon as I heard that the Cardinal was going to Lombardy I went to see him, because I was anxious to serve him. He told me to expedite the marbles and to get the men and to do everything I could, so that he might see something completed without my consulting him further; and that if he survived, he would also do the façade and that he was leaving orders to Domenico Buoninsegni to arrange about all the money required.

As soon as the Cardinal left I wrote and gave Domenico Buoninsegni an account of all that he had said to me and I told him that I was ready to do everything the Cardinal desired. I kept a copy of this, which I had witnessed, so that everyone might know that it was not my responsibility. Domenico immediately came to see me and told me he had no authority whatever and that if I wanted anything, he would write to the Cardinal about it. I told him I did not want anything. Finally, on the Cardinal's return, Figiovanni[3] told me he wanted to see me. I went at once, supposing he wished to discuss the Tombs. He said to me, 'For these Tombs we should require at least one good piece, that is to say, something by your own hand.' He did not say that he wanted me to execute them. I left, and said that I would return to discuss them with him when the marbles arrived.

Now you know that in Rome the Pope[4] has been informed about this Tomb of Julius[5] and that a *motu proprio* has been drawn up for him to sign, in order that proceedings may be taken against me for the return of the amount I received on account for the said work, and for the indemnity due;[6] and you know that the Pope said that this should be done 'if Michelangelo is unwilling to execute the Tomb'. It is therefore essential for me to do it, if I don't want to incur the loss, which you see is decreed. And if, as you tell me, the Cardinal de' Medici now once again wishes me to execute the Tombs at San Lorenzo, you see that I cannot do so, unless he releases me from this affair in Rome. And if he releases me, I promise to work for him without any return for the rest of my life. It is not that I do not wish to execute the said Tomb, which I'm doing willingly, that I ask to be released, but in order to serve him. But if he does not wish to release me, but wants something by my hand for the said Tombs, I'll do my best, while I'm working on the Tomb of Julius, to find time to execute something to please him.

[Unsigned]

1. *This was in fact the method ultimately adopted. If the full-scale models were made, the work could be more swiftly and accurately carried out by a large body of assistants working under Michelangelo's supervision.*

2. *See Appendix 17.*

3. *Giovanbattista Figiovanni (d. 1544) canon and Sub-Prior of the church of San Lorenzo (Cianfogni, p. 232), who, though frequently referred to as the Prior, only succeeded to that office in 1534 on the death of his predecessor, Francesco Compagno who was Prior at this time. Figiovanni was also a canon of S. Maria del Fiore (Salvini, Cat. p. 83). He was a staunch adherent of the Medici and a self-appointed guardian of their interests in Florence.*

4. *Adrian VI, Pope from January 9th 1522 to September 14th 1523. He succeeded Leo X, who had died on December 1st 1521.*

5. *See Appendix 11.*

6. *'Danni e Interessi', the technical term for a penalty on an unfulfilled contract, in the form of interest to be paid on the money advanced.*

153

*British
Museum
Mil. xliii
From Florence
June 1523*

⁋ To Lodovico Buonarroti at Settignano

Most revered father — A letter of yours brings me good news this morning, which is that you don't appear to me to be satisfied with the agreement[1] recently made between us. I am still less satisfied with it, and beg you to consent to other conditions, because I'm always prepared to cancel it, as I haven't the means to pay Gismondo the money and would never have consented to such an agreement, if you hadn't promised me to help to pay him. So it turns out that, of your own accord, without going to officials you are doing me a great favour and extricating me from an extraordinary labyrinth; and there will be no need for you to go to any other official, because I have more need of money than of your farms. I'm not answering you as to the other things, except that you may do just whatever you like.

Your Michelangelo in Florence

Not having anyone else, I'm sending Mona Angelo up to you solely for this purpose – to let you know at once that this contract is greatly to my disadvantage; you may as well know that I was not in a position to enter into it, but I did so in order to do you a good turn. If it is no use to you, please cancel it, as I have need of my money, as I've said.

1. *The agreement under discussion concerned the dowery of Lodovico's second wife, Lucrezia Ubaldini, who died in July 1497. Apparently Lodovico enjoyed a life interest in the capital, which was invested in the Monte. By an agreement drawn up by Ser Niccolò di Antonio Parenti on June 16th 1523, relating to Gismondo's share of the said capital, Michelangelo entered into an agreement to pay him 500 florins within two years, in exchange for the right to certain farms. As this sum was disbursed within the specified two years, the agreement was evidently not cancelled (Milanesi, p. 54). Unfortunately the implications of the transaction are not clear, but it may have had some connection with the security for the loan made by Michelangelo to Buonarroto and Giovansimone in 1513. See Nos. 92 and 154.*

154

*British
Museum
Mil. xliv
From Florence
June 1523*

⁋ To Lodovico Buonarroti in Settignano

Lodovico — I'm not replying to your letter, except about those matters which seem to me essential; as to the others, I treat them with contempt. You say you cannot draw the interest on the capital, because I've had it registered in my name. This is not true, and on this point I must reply to you, to warn you that someone on whom you are relying may be deceiving you and has perhaps drawn it and made use of it himself, and has given you to understand this for his own ends. I have not had the capital registered in my name, nor could I do so, if I wanted to. But it is certainly true that the notary said to me, in the presence of Rafaello da Gagliano, 'I should not like your brothers to enter into any commitments involving this capital, as a result of which you might not find it here after your father's death',[1] and he took me to the Monte and made me put down fifteen *grossoni* and there had a clause inserted that no-one might dispose of it during your lifetime. You are the beneficiary during your lifetime, as stated in the agreement, as you know.

I've made the position about the contract clear to you, that is to say about cancelling it, if you like, since you are not satisfied with it. I've always entered into agreements and cancelled them as you wished; I don't know what more you want of me.

If my existence is a cause of annoyance to you, you have found the way to remedy it and you will inherit the key to that treasure which you say I have; and you will prosper. For all Florence knows the fine rich man you were, and how I have always robbed you and deserve to be punished. You will be highly commended! Publish it abroad and say what you like about me; but don't write to me any more,[2] because you prevent me from working, since I must make good what you have had from me for the past twenty-five years. I would rather not have said this to you, but I cannot help but say it. Take care of yourself, and beware of those of whom you must beware. For man only dies once, and does not return to put right what he has done amiss. Even in a matter like this you have delayed until the hour of death. May God help you.

MICHELANGELO

1. *As an addition to an entry of 1514 in the 'Libro del Monte' (C.2, N. 976) there is a clause, dated June 22nd 1523, to the effect that in respect of some 312 florins, the brothers might not enter into any agreement concerning the reversion without Michelangelo's consent (Milanesi, p. 55).*

2. *This is the last extant letter addressed by Michelangelo to his father, whom, notwithstanding his wrath on this occasion, he never abandoned. Numerous letters written by the old man to his son during the ensuing years have survived and are preserved, either in the original or in copies, in the Casa Buonarroti in Florence and in the Biblioteca Angelica in Rome. For another version of the opening paragraph to this letter see Draft 1.*

¶ TO MY DEAR FRIEND, BARTOLOMEO ANGIOLINI, IN ROME

155

Bartolomeo,[1] dearest friend — I have received a letter from the Cardinal,[2] enclosed in one of yours. It surprised me that for so small a thing you should have got him to write, and in such a hurry. I will reply as before, because I cannot do so as decisively as I should like. To you I make the same reply as in my last, that is to say, that I am desirous of serving his Most Reverend Lordship and will do my best when I can and as soon as I can.

*Buonarroti
Archives
Mil. ccclxxviii
From Florence
July 1523*

I have a great task to perform, but I'm old and unfit; because if I work one day I have to rest for four in consequence. I'm not confident, therefore, about making definite promises. I'll do my best, at any rate, to be of service and to prove to you that I recognize the affection you have for me. I think that's all. I am yours always. Commend me to Sebastiano Veneziano.

YOUR MICHELANGELO SCULPTOR IN FLORENCE

1. *Bartolomeo Angiolini, a writer of madrigals and sonnets, was a great friend of Michelangelo's. He corresponded with him frequently between 1521 and 1533. Some time after Michelangelo returned to Rome in 1534 he took over the management of his business affairs.*

2. *The Venetian Cardinal, Domenico Grimani (1460-1523), Patriarch of Aquila and Bishop of Prato, on whose behalf Angiolini had written to Michelangelo in June, asking for a work by his hand. Michelangelo had apparently suggested a small picture. The commission was not executed, as the Cardinal died in August of the same year.*

156

*Buonarroti
Archives
Mil. ccclxxx
From Florence
November 25th
1523*

¶ To my dear friend Maestro Domenico, called Topolino, sculptor, in Carrara

My dearest Maestro Domenico[1] — The bearer of this will be Bernardino di Pier Basso,[2] who is coming to Carrara for some blocks of marble which he needs. Please will you direct him to where he will be well and quickly served. I commend him to you wholeheartedly. I think that's all on this point.

You will have heard that Medici is made Pope,[3] which I think will rejoice everyone. I expect, for this reason, that as far as art is concerned many things will be executed here. Therefore work well and faithfully, so as to gain honour.

On the twenty-fifth day of November.

YOUR MICHELANGELO SCULPTOR IN FLORENCE

1. *Domenico di Giovanni Bertino Fancelli (b. 1464), a scarpellino from Settignano who was under contract to Michelangelo for the supplying of marble from Carrara. He had a great fancy to be a sculptor. To please him Michelangelo, who was vastly amused by his efforts, here addresses him as 'maestro'. See also Vasari, VII, p. 283.*

2. *Cf. No. 101. It seems that Michelangelo bore him no grudge.*

3. *Following the death of Adrian VI in September, Cardinal Giulio de' Medici was elected Pope on November 19th 1523 and took the name Clement VII. His election was universally acclaimed. On November 30th, for example, Baldassare Castiglioni wrote to the Marquis of Mantua saying, 'it seems that everyone expects all that is best of this Pope'. His pontificate proved, however, to be so disastrous that at his death everyone, likewise, rejoiced (Segni, II, p. 45).*

19. *Pope Clement VII*
(prior to the sack of Rome)

Sebastiano del Piombo
Museo Nazionale, Naples

157   ¶ To Ser Giovan Francesco Fattucci in Rome

*Buonarroti
Archives
Mil. ccclxxxiii
From Florence
December
1523*

Messer Giovan Francesco — You ask me in one of your letters how my affairs stand regarding Pope Julius.[1] I assure you that if damages could be claimed I should expect rather to be the creditor than the debtor. Because when he sent for me from Florence, which was, I believe, in the second year of his pontificate, I had undertaken to execute half the Sala del Consiglio of Florence, that is to say, to paint it, for which I was getting three thousand ducats; and I had already done the cartoon, as is known to all Florence, so that the money seemed to me half earned. And of the twelve Apostles that I also had to execute for Santa Maria del Fiore, one was blocked out, as can still be seen, and I had already transported the greater part of the marble. But when Pope Julius took me away from here I got nothing either for the one or for the other.

Then when I was in Rome with the said Pope, and when he had given me a commission for his Tomb, into which a thousand ducats' worth of marbles were to go, he had the money paid to me and sent me to Carrara to get them. I remained there eight months to have the marbles blocked out and I transported nearly all of them to the Piazza of St. Peter, but some of them remained at Ripa. Then, after I had completed the payment for the freight for the said marbles, I had no money left from what I had received for the said work, but I furnished the house I had in the Piazza of St. Peter with beds and household goods out of my own money, in anticipation of the Tomb, and I brought assistants from Florence, some of whom are still living, to work on it, and I paid them in advance out of my own money. At this point Pope Julius changed his mind and no longer wanted to go on with it. But I, not knowing this, went to ask him for money and was turned away from the audience chamber. Enraged at this, I immediately left Rome, and what I had in the house went to pieces and the said marbles, that I had transported, remained in the Piazza of St. Peter until the election of Pope Leo, and in one way and another they came to grief. Among other things which I can prove, two pieces of four and a half *braccia*, which had cost me over fifty gold ducats, were stolen from me by Agostino Chigi;[2] these could be recovered, because there are witnesses. But to return to the marbles, from the time that I went for them and stayed in Carrara, until I was turned away from the Palace, more than a year went by and during that time I never had anything and it cost me several tens of ducats.

Then the first time that Pope Julius went to Bologna I was forced to go there, with a rope round my neck, to ask his pardon, whereupon he gave me his figure to do in bronze, which was about seven *braccia* in height, seated. When he asked me what it would cost, I replied that I believed it could be cast for about a thousand ducats; but that it was not my trade and that I did not want to be obliged to do it. He replied, 'Set to work and cast it over and over again till it succeeds, and we will give you enough to content you.' To be brief, it was cast twice, and at the end of the two years I had stayed there I found myself four and a half ducats to the good. And from that time I never had anything more. But all the expenses I had in the said two years were included in the thousand ducats for which I had said it could be cast, and these were paid me in instalments by Messer Antonio Maria da Legnia[me], a Bolognese.

When I had set up the figure on the façade of San Petronio and returned to Rome, Pope Julius still did not want me to do the Tomb, and set me to paint the vault of Sixtus and we made a bargain for three thousand ducats. The first design for the said work was for twelve Apostles in the lunettes and the usual ornamentations to fill the remaining area.

After the work was begun it seemed to me that it would turn out a poor affair, and I told the Pope that if the Apostles alone were put there it seemed to me that it would turn out a poor affair. He asked me why. I said, 'because they themselves were poor.'[3] Then he gave me a new commission to do what I liked, and said he would content me and that I should paint down to the Histories below. Meanwhile, when the vault was nearly finished the Pope returned to Bologna; whereupon I went there twice for money that was owed me, but effected nothing[4] and wasted all that time until he returned to Rome. When I returned to Rome I began to do the cartoons for the said work, that is for the ends and the sides round the said chapel of Sixtus, in the expectation of having the money to finish the work. I was never able to obtain anything; but one day when I was complaining to Messer Bernardo da Bibbiena[5] and to Attalante[6] that I couldn't remain in Rome any longer but must go with God, Messer Bernardo told Attalante that he would remind him that he intended to have money paid to me in any case. And he had two thousand ducats of the Camera paid to me, which, together with the first thousand for the marbles, they are putting to my account for the Tomb. But I reckoned that I was owed more for the time I had lost and the works I had done. And from the said money, as Messer Bernardo and Attalante had saved my life, I gave the former a hundred ducats and the latter fifty.[7]

Then came the death of Pope Julius and at the beginning of Leo, as Aginensis wished to increase the size of his Tomb, that is, to execute a larger work than the one I had first designed, a new contract was drawn up. And when I did not wish them to put to the account the three thousand ducats I had received, and showed that I was owed much more, Aginensis called me an impostor.[8]

[Unsigned]

1. *See Appendix 11.*

2. *Agostino Chigi (d. 1520), the fabulously wealthy Sienese banker who lived in Rome. On January 9th 1524 Lionardo, the saddler, wrote to Michelangelo saying he would be reimbursed for the stolen marbles (Frey, Briefe, p. 205).*

3. *According to Vasari, when the Pope suggested that the figures should be touched up with gold, Michelangelo answered, 'Holy Father, in those days they did not wear gold . . . they were holy men, who despised wealth.' But whether he actually said this, as is quite possible, or whether it is an embellishment of the story, which improved with the years, it is hard to say.*

4. *His memory plays him false, as this is not strictly accurate. See Nos. 57 and 59.*

5. *Afterwards the Cardinal Dovizi da Bibbiena.*

6. *Attalante (b. 1466) was a natural son of Manetto Migliorotti, a Florentine. From 1513 onwards he was one of the superintendents of the fabric of St. Peter's. Nothing is heard of him after 1535.*

7. *For this episode, see Appendix 9.*

8. *For another version of this letter, see Draft 2.*

158

British Museum Mil. cdxcv From Florence January 7th 1524

¶ [To Giovanni Spina]

Giovanni[1] — The bearer of this will be Antonio di Bernardo Mini,[2] my assistant. Will you pay him fifteen ducats in gold in respect of the models of the Tombs for the Sacristy of San Lorenzo, which I'm doing for Pope Clement.

On the seventh day of January one thousand five hundred and twenty-three.[3]

YOUR MICHELANGELO SCULPTOR IN FLORENCE

1. *Giovanni di Francesco Spina was employed in the Salviati bank in Florence and transacted the financial business connnected with the New Sacristy, the Library and the Medici Tombs. He belonged to an eminent banking family.*

2. *Antonio Mini (d. 1533) appears to have been engaged in December 1523 (Frey, Briefe, p. 197) by Piero Gondi (see No. 161), who was acting at this time as Michelangelo's intermediary. Mini remained in his service until November 1531. On his departure to France, and in order that he might furnish doweries for his two sisters, Michelangelo gave him the 'Leda' and many cartoons and drawings as well (Vasari, VII, p. 202, and Tolnay, III, p. 190 et seq.).*

3. *N.S. 1524.*

159

Buonarroti Archives Mil. ccclxxxv From Florence January 1524

¶ To Ser Giovan Francesco Fattucci in Rome

Messer Giovan Francesco — I learn from your last that His Holiness Our Lord wishes the design for the Library[1] to be by my hand. I have no information about it nor do I know where he wants to build it. Although Stefano[2] spoke to me about it, I did not give my mind to it. When he returns from Carrara I'll inform myself through him and will do what I can, although it's not my profession.

As to the stipend about which you write me, I do not know how I shall feel in a year's time, so I don't want to promise something I might regret.[3] As to the salary, I've written to you about it.

[Unsigned]

1. *The Laurentian Library, built to house the famous Medici collection of books and early MSS. Michelangelo began work on the building in the autumn of 1524, but left it unfinished when he returned to Rome in 1534. The work was completed under Vasari's supervision in 1568.*

2. *Stefano di Tommaso Lunetti (1465–1534), miniaturist. He was trained as an illuminator, but on the death of his master and father-in-law, Bartolomeo Gherardo, in 1498 he left illuminating for architecture (Vasari, III, p. 241). Initially, he and Michelangelo were together concerned with the designs for the Laurentian Library. He acted as clerk of works at the New Sacristy, but seems not to have proved satisfactory. He is known to have been in Carrara in January 1524.*

3. *See Appendix 18.*

¶ To Pope Clement VII in Rome

160

Most Blessed Father — As intermediaries are often the cause of grave misunderstandings, I have, accordingly, made bold to write to Your Holiness without their intervention,[1] about the Tombs here at San Lorenzo. I declare that I know not which is preferable – a disadvantage which proves to be a benefit, or an advantage which proves to be a hindrance.[2] I am certain, idle and unreasonable though I am, that had I been left to carry on as I began, all the marbles for the said work would be in Florence to-day, blocked out as required, and with less expense than has so far been incurred, and they would be of a quality as admirable as the others I brought here.

Now I see that it is going to be a long business and I do not know how it will proceed. Therefore, should matters turn out to be displeasing to Your Holiness, I desire to be exonerated; since I have no authority here, I do not think I should have the blame either. If Your Holiness wishes me to accomplish anything, I beg You not to have authorities[3] set over me in my own trade, but to have faith in me and give me a free hand. Your Holiness will see what I shall accomplish and the account I shall give of myself.

Stefano[4] has finished the lantern of the chapel of the said San Lorenzo here and has uncovered it. It is universally admired by everyone, as I hope it will be by Your Holiness, when You see it. We are having the ball[5] which surmounts it made about a *braccia* in diameter and, in order to vary it from the others, I decided to have it made with facets, and this is being done.

Your Holiness's servant

Michelangelo sculptor in Florence

*Buonarroti Archives
Mil. ccclxxxi
From Florence
(January) 1524*

20. *The Lantern and Faceted Ball of the New Sacristy*

Michelangelo
San Lorenzo, Florence

1. *Michelangelo was not the only one who found it necessary to disregard the protocol and write direct to the Pope himself. When Nuncio to the Court of Charles V, Baldassare Castiglione likewise found it imperative to adopt this unusual course (Cartwright, Cast. II, p. 288). Throughout his letter Michelangelo addresses the Pontiff in the third person singular, but unfortunately it is not possible to render the effect of this polite form in English. At this period the usual form of address was the second person plural.*

2. *A cryptic sentence. He means to contrast the disadvantages of having to quarry the marbles himself, but getting what he wanted, with the advantages of not having to quarry it, but not getting what he wanted.*

3. *Bernardo Niccolini and Domenico Buoninsegni, who did everything in their power to exasperate and obstruct him in the work. See Appendix 14.*

4. *Stefano Lunetti is generally supposed to have completed the lantern of the New Sacristy in January 1524. With reference to this lantern, Michelangelo, when told by people that he should improve upon Brunelleschi's design for the Old Sacristy, replied, 'I might make alterations – not improvements' (Vasari, VII, p. 192).*

5. *Piloto, the goldsmith, was the maker. The ball has seventy-two facets.*

¶ [To Piero Gondi in Florence]

161

*Buonarroti
Archives
Mil. ccclxxxvii
From Florence
January 26th
1524*

Piero[1] — It is characteristic of the poor ingrate that if you assist him in his time of need, he says you can well afford it, whatever you give him. If you put him into some job in order to do him a kindness, he always says that you were forced to do so, and that you put him into it because you did not know how to do it yourself. And all the benefits he receives he attributes to his benefactor's need of him. And when the benefits received are obvious and not to be denied the ingrate, in order to rid himself of the obligation under which he feels himself to be, waits until his benefactor happens to make some mistake publicly, and then takes this opportunity of speaking ill of him and being believed. This is what has always happened in my case. For no-one has ever had dealings with me, I mean workmen, for whom I have not wholeheartedly done my best. Yet because they say they find me in some way strange and obsessed, which harms no-one but myself, they presume to speak ill of me and to abuse me; which is the reward of all honest men.

It is about yesterday evening's discussion and with reference to Stefano[2] that I am writing to you. Up to now I haven't put him in charge, although if I wasn't able to be there myself, I haven't found anyone else among them to put in charge. I've done everything to help him, not for my benefit, but for his, as in this instance. What I'm doing I'm doing for his good, because I gave an undertaking[3] to help him and I cannot go back on it. But let him not think or say that I do it for my own convenience since, thank God, I do not want for men. And if I've spurred him on recently more than usual, I've done so because I've been more than usually spurred on myself. But I must find out whether he can or whether he will or whether he knows how to serve me, in order that I may decide about my arrangements. And as I do not really know how he is disposed, I asked you yesterday evening, as you were the go-between, to let me know his views, and if he knows how to do what I require, whether he either can or will, or whether he knows and will and can *[sic]* and to find out from him how much he wants a month to be in charge of the assistants and to teach them the process and to do what I order. I'm responsible for paying the assistants myself. I asked you about this yesterday evening and again I beg you to let me know his views as I've said. And don't be surprised that I've sat down to write to you about it, because it is of some importance to me for a number of reasons and particularly because, if I were to omit to justify myself and were to put others in his place, I should be proclaimed among the Piagnoni[4] as the most perfidious man on earth, although I might be in the right. So please would you oblige me. I'm putting you to this trouble with confidence, because you have given me proof of your goodwill towards me.

On the twenty-sixth day of January 1523.[5]

MICHELANGELO SCULPTOR IN FLORENCE

1. *Piero di Filippo Gondi (1501–1556). The Gondi belonged to the Santa Maria Novella quarter of Florence. Michelangelo gave him the key of the New Sacristy during the scare prior to the sack of Rome, in order that he might conceal some of his possessions (Milanesi, p. 598).*

2. *The question under discussion appears to concern Stefano's capability of supervising the interior decoration of the Sacristy. Michelangelo apparently made him clerk of works in the following February, but his name disappears from the 'Ricordi' in April, so he evidently proved unsatisfactory.*

3. *It is possible that it was to Giovan Francesco Fattucci that Michelangelo had given an undertaking to help Stefano. From one of Fattucci's letters (Frey, Briefe, p. 202) it may be conjectured that Stefano was on intimate terms with Fattucci's family.*

4. *The Piagnoni was the name originally given to the followers of Savonarola (1452–1498). They survived as a bigoted political faction among the ranks of the Popolani, to whom the aristocratic Ottimati were opposed.*

5. *N.S. 1524.*

162 ¶ TO GIOVANNI SPINA IN FLORENCE

Archive unknown Mil. ccclxxxviii From Florence February 6th 1524

Giovanni — The bearer of this will be Stefano the miniaturist. Will you give him fifteen ducats in respect of the models I'm making for Pope Clement, as I told you in the other note.

On the sixth day of February, fifteen hundred and twenty-three.[1]

YOUR MICHELANGELO SCULPTOR IN FLORENCE

1. *N.S. 1524. In the nineteenth century this letter was included among the Ashburnham MSS., which have since been dispersed. All efforts to trace its present whereabouts have so far proved abortive.*

¶ [TO MEO DELLE CORTE]

163

Meo[1] — I am again being urged to begin work and to send as soon as I can to replace the marble that is faulty. So please will you be in the Piazza of San Lorenzo to-morrow morning a little earlier than usual, so that we can examine two pieces of marble that are there for any flaws, before we are bothered by the sun, so that we can move them inside and you can leave. Get some of the others to come with you; and send for Forello,[2] so that we can move them inside with the tackle.[3]

YOUR MICHELANGELO

Buonarroti
Archives
Mil. ccclxix
From Florence
(July 1524)

1. *Bartolomeo delle Corte appears to have been one of Michelangelo's senior assistants. See Milanesi, pp. 595, 597, etc.*

2. *Forello da la Porta alla Croce, one of the many scarpellini employed on the marbles for the Medici Tombs. See Milanesi, p. 584.*

3. *Two other drafts of this short note exist, both incomplete. Michelangelo was obviously interrupted when writing it. The three versions indicate his anxiety to make himself clear and to give a courteous explanation for making an earlier appointment. See Draft 3.*

¶ TO MESSER GIOVAN FRANCESCO FATTUCCI IN ROME

164

Messer Giovan Francesco — In view of your last letter I went to see Spina to find out whether he has authority to pay for the Library as well as for the Tombs. And seeing that he hasn't, I haven't begun on the said work, as you advised me *[not to]*; since it cannot be undertaken without money. If it is to be undertaken, however, please would you make arrangements in Rome for Spina to make the payments here, because one couldn't find anyone more obliging, or anyone who would deal with a matter of this kind with greater courtesy and kindness.

As to beginning on the work, I must wait until the marbles arrive, though I don't believe they ever will, such is the order that prevails! I could tell you things that would stupefy you, but I wouldn't be believed; it is enough to say that it's the ruin of me. Because, if I were further on with the work than I am, perhaps the Pope would have settled

Buonarroti
Archives
Mil. ccclxxxix
From Florence
July 1524

21. *Interior of the Laurentian Library*

Michelangelo
Florence

my affair[1] for me and I should be rid of this anxiety. But much more work is involved in breaking than in making.

Yesterday I went to see someone who told me to go and pay, otherwise by the end of the month I shall incur penalties. I didn't think there were penalties other than those of hell or a couple of ducats fine if I kept a shop as a silk merchant or gold-beater[2] and lent the rest of my money at usury. We have paid taxes in Florence for three hundred years. For once at least I might have been bailiff to the Proconsul![3] However, they must be paid. Everything I have will be seized, because I haven't the wherewithal, and I shall betake myself to Rome. If the matter had been settled for me, I should have sold something and invested in the Funds, which would have enabled me to pay the taxes, and I could at least have remained in Florence.

[Unsigned]

1. *i.e. the matter of the Tomb of Pope Julius. See No. 157.*

2. *The gold-beaters were members of the Guild of Silk Merchants, but were not licensed money-lenders.*

3. *The Proconsul was the chief magistrate of the Guild of Judges and Notaries, and bailiffs were attached to his staff for the collection of debts. What Michelangelo means is that for once he might have been exempt.*

❡ To Giovanni Spina in Florence

165

Buonarroti Archives Mil. cccxc From Florence August 8th 1524

Giovanni — The bearer of this will be Niccolò di Giovanni, called il Surdo. Will you pay him three ducats for the building stone he has undertaken to quarry for the Library of San Lorenzo. Pay them to him on account. From the first loads we'll see how he serves us both with regard to the fairness of the price and the quality of the stone. I will stand surety for the said three ducats.

YOUR MICHELANGELO AT SAN LORENZO

❡ To Giovanni Spina

166

Buonarroti Archives Mil. cccxci From Florence August 29th 1524

Giovanni — Since leaving you yesterday I've been reconsidering my position and realizing how much the Pope has this work for San Lorenzo at heart and how hard I am being pressed by His Holiness, who has voluntarily granted me a good salary,[1] in order that I may have a better opportunity of serving him quickly; and realizing that not to draw it is a hindrance to me and that I should have no excuse whatever for not serving him, I've changed my mind. And whereas up till now I haven't asked for it, I

157

now do so, as I think it would be much better and for more reasons than I need mention, but particularly in order that I may take up residence in the house you've taken for me at San Lorenzo and may establish myself there like a man of honour, since not to reside there gives occasion for gossip and does me a lot of harm. So I should like you to tell me the amount of the salary due to me since the day it was granted up till now. And if you have authority to pay it, would you inform my assistant, Antonio Mini, the bearer of this, and when you wish me to call for it.[2]

[Unsigned]

1. *See Appendix 18.*

2. *The words 'Copy made on the day of the Decollation of St. John' are written in capitals in red chalk at the foot of the letter. The Decollation of St. John the Baptist is commemorated on August 29th. The page on which the copy was made also contains lists of payments for the work at San Lorenzo, entered in another hand. As these properly belong to the 'Ricordi' they have been omitted.*

167

Buonarroti Archives Mil. cccxciii From Florence December 24th 1524

¶ [TO MESSER GIOVAN FRANCESCO FATTUCCI IN ROME]

Messer Giovan Francesco — From your last letter I learn that you will soon be through and will come home, as you long to. I beg you to return now and not to delay, since my affairs[1] cannot be satisfactorily settled unless I am there in person. It is now nearly a year since I began to write to you saying that if you had no other business in Rome but mine, you should abandon it and return, as I do not want it to be said that I kept you there for the sake of what might eventuate. Then, seeing that you did not return, I made you write to Ser Dino[2] saying that your mother[3] wasn't feeling well and that you should return to see her as soon as possible. Finally, I sent word through Messer Riccardo del Milanesi[4] to say that you should return in any case and should abandon my affairs, and a few days ago, through Lionardo, the saddler, I sent, making the same request. So, if you haven't any other business but mine, I again beg you to abandon it and to return at once.[5]

YOUR MICHELANGELO IN FLORENCE

1. *i.e. the negotiations over the Tomb of Julius II.*

2. *Almost certainly Francesco d'Antonio Dini (d. c.1541), a senior canon of San Lorenzo. He had been appointed to a prebend in 1510 (Cianfogni, p. 235).*

3. *In his letters to Michelangelo Fattucci often asked him to go and see his mother. With his usual consideration, Michelangelo did so from time to time. Cf. No. 173.*

4. *Riccardo di Giovanbattista di Baldassare del Milanesi (d. 1542), a canon of S. Maria del Fiore. He held office in Rome as an Apostolic Protonotary and as a member of the College of Abbreviators during the pontificates of Clement VII and Paul III (Salvini, Cat., p. 79).*

5. *At the head of this draft there is a note in Michelangelo's hand 'On the 24th December. Copy of one sent to Ser Giovan Francesco in Rome in 1524'.*

¶ [To Giovanni Spina in Florence]

Giovanni — I don't think there is any necessity to send a power of attorney[1] in respect of the Tomb of Pope Julius, because I don't want to go to law. They can't go to law if I admit that I'm in the wrong. I'll assume that I've been to law and have lost and must pay up. This I'm prepared to do, if I can. Therefore, if the Pope will help me in this matter, which would be a great favour, seeing that, whether through old age or ill-health, I cannot finish the said Tomb, he, as an intermediary, can make it known that he wishes me to return what I've received for its execution, so that I can be quit of this burden; and the relatives of the said Pope, having obtained restitution, can have it done to their satisfaction by someone else. In this way His Holiness Our Lord can assist me greatly. And also in this, that I may have to return as little as possible, by having some of my arguments taken into consideration, though without departing from the principle, such as the time I wasted without remuneration when the Pope was at Bologna and on other occasions, as Ser Giovan Francesco, who is fully informed, is aware.

As soon as I'm clear as to how much I have to return, I'll review my resources. I'll sell out and so arrange things that I'll make restitution and be able to give my mind to the Pope's concerns and get on with the work, since as it is I do not live life at all, much less do I work. There is no course that could be taken that would be safer for me, nor more acceptable to me, nor a greater relief to my mind, and it could be done amicably and without going to law. And I pray God that the Pope may be willing to settle it in this way; since I don't think it will be an imposition on anyone. So would you please write to Messer Jacopo[2] and put it in the best way you can, so that the matter may proceed and I may be able to work.[3]

MICHELANGELO SCULPTOR IN FLORENCE

Buonarroti Archives Mil. cccxciv From Florence April 19th 1525

1. *Michelangelo had received a letter, dated April 8th, from Lionardo the saddler, asking him to send a power of attorney to Rome, as the Executors of Julius II were about to take legal proceedings against him (Frey, Briefe, p. 249).*

2. *Jacopo Salviati.*

3. *There is a note in Michelangelo's hand, following the conclusion, 'Copy of a draft I made for Giovanni Spina so that he might write to Rome. On the 19th day of April 1525.'*

169

*Buonarroti
Archives
Mil. cccxcvi
From Florence
April 1525*

¶ [To Sebastiano Veneziano, painter, in Rome]

Sebastiano, colleague and dearest friend — A picture by your hand,[1] painted for Anton Francesco degli Albizzi, is here awaited, not only by me, but by others who are attached to you or who know you through the excellence of your reputation. We imagine that it is finished and are longing to see it. . . . .[2]

[Unsigned]

1. *This painting has not been identified. Anton Francesco degli Albizzi was associated with Michelangelo during the siege of Florence (Gaye, II, pp. 206, 212). He was executed in the Bargello, together with other Republicans, by Cosimo I in 1537 (Nardi, II, p. 310).*

2. *Michelangelo wrote this letter at the behest, presumably, of Sebastiano's patron or his agents. In his reply, dated April 22nd, Sebastiano expressed himself as being very angry, not with Michelangelo for his tactful reminder, but with those who had dared to bother him with such a matter (Milanesi, Corr., p. 32).*

170

*Buonarroti
Archives
Mil. cccxcvii
From Florence
(May) 1525*

¶ [To Sebastiano Veneziano, painter, in Rome]

My dearest Sebastiano — Yesterday evening our friend Captain Cuio[1] and several other gentlemen kindly invited me to go and have supper with them, which gave me the greatest pleasure, as I emerged a little from my depression, or rather from my obsession. I not only enjoyed the supper, which was extremely pleasant, but also, and even more than this, the discussions which took place. But later on my pleasure in the discussions increased on hearing the said Captain mention your name. Nor was this all; still later I was infinitely delighted when, on the subject of art, I heard the said Captain say that you were altogether unique and were held to be so in Rome. So that, had it been possible to be more cheerful, I should have been. Seeing, then, that my opinion is justified, don't say, henceforth, that you are not unique,[2] when I write and tell you that you are, because there are too many witnesses and there is a picture here, thank God, which proves, to anyone who has eyes to see, that I'm right.

[Unsigned]

1. *Capitano, a civic title. Cuio Dini was killed in the sack of Rome on May 7th 1527 (Dorez Nouv. Rech., LXXVIII, p. 209).*

2. *Sebastiano's reply to this contention of Michelangelo's was that it was Michelangelo who was truly unique – unique above all others (Milanesi, Corr., p. 34).*

¶ To Ser Giovan Francesco Fattucci in Rome

171

*Buonarroti
Archives
Mil. ccclxxxvi
From Florence
(June) 1525*

In order to give you a little news, since there is so much I haven't told you, I must tell you that Guidotto who, as you know, had a thousand business concerns, died after a few days' illness and has left his dog free of debt to Donato,[1] and Donato has bought a gown of masculine cut to wear as mourning, which you will see if he comes to Rome, as it's also suitable for riding.

I think that's all. As regards my affairs, since you are my attorney[2] at the Pope's wish, I beg you to do well by me, as you have always done, for you know I'm more indebted to you for kindnesses I've received than the crucifixes of Santa Maria del Fiore to Noca the shoemaker,[3] as we say in Florence.[4]

[Unsigned]

1. *Probably Donato del Sera, a relative of Michelangelo's on his mother's side. He is mentioned several times in Fattucci's letters at this period, and in July 1525 had a fall from his horse on the way to Rome (Frey, Briefe, p. 255).*

2. *By an instrument, dated June 14th 1525, Fattucci was formally appointed as Michelangelo's attorney to act for him in the negotiations over the Tomb of Pope Julius (Milanesi, p. 699).*

3. *Noca, whose real name was Andrea di Cristoforo, was a confidant of Leo X as well as his shoemaker (Milanesi, p. 432).*

4. *This draft is written at the back of a letter from Lionardo, the saddler, dated January 21st 1525 (Frey, Briefe, p. 245).*

¶ To Ser Giovan Francesco Fattucci in Rome

172

*Buonarroti
Archives
Mil. cccxcv
From Florence
(August)
1525*

Ser Giovan Francesco — As it is not to be supposed that I have to execute a new Tomb for the two thousand ducats stipulated in the contract,[1] I want you to make Ser Niccolò understand that the said Tomb is more than half finished and of the six figures mentioned in the contract, four are done as you know, since you've seen them in my house in Rome, which they are giving me, as the contract shows.

[Unsigned]

1. *A new contract was being negotiated, but was not completed owing to the political events which culminated in the sack of Rome and the siege of Florence. The terms mentioned above were eventually incorporated in the Contract of 1532. See Appendix 11.*

173   ¶ [To Messer Giovan Francesco Fattucci in Rome]

*Buonarroti
Archives
Mil. cccxcviii
From Florence
September 4th
1525*

Messer Giovanfrancesco — I've written to Rome several times saying that as I am obliged to serve Pope Clement in the execution of things which will take a long time to complete, and as I am an old man, I have no hope of being able to execute anything else and that for this reason, being unable to execute the Tomb of Julius, I desire to give satisfaction – if I am obliged to give satisfaction for what I have received – in money rather than in work, because I should not have time to do otherwise. I don't know what else to say to you in reply, because I'm not acquainted with the position nor do I understand the details as you do.

As to executing the said Tomb of Julius as a wall tomb, like those of Pius,[1] I am agreeable to the method, which is quicker than any other.

I think that's all, except for saying this to you – abandon my affairs and your own and come home, because I hear the plague is again raging and I would rather have you alive than my affairs settled. So come home. If I die before the Pope there will be no need for me to settle anything further; if I live, I'm sure the Pope will settle the matter – if not now, some other time. So come home. I spent yesterday evening with your mother and in the presence of Granaccio and Giovanni the turner, I advised her to get you to come home.

On the 4th day of September 1525.[2]

YOUR MICHELANGELO IN FLORENCE

1. *The Tombs of Pius II and of Pius III.*
2. *Copy in Antonio Mini's hand.*

174   ¶ [To Messer Giovan Francesco Fattucci in Rome]

*Buonarroti
Archives
Mil. cd
From Florence
October 24th
1525*

Messer Giovan Francesco — In reply to your last letter the four figures[1] begun are not yet finished, and there is still a considerable amount to do. The four others, representing Rivers, are not yet started, because we've got no marbles, although they've arrived here. I'm not saying why, because it's none of my business.

As to the affairs of Julius, I'm agreeable to doing a tomb like that of Pius in St. Peter's,[2] as I wrote you. I'll have it done here little by little, sometimes one piece and sometimes another, and I'll pay for it myself, if I have my salary and if I retain the house, as you wrote me; that is to say, the house in which I was living there in Rome, together with the marbles and other things in it. That is to say, if, in order to discharge my obligations as to the Tomb, I haven't got to give them, I mean the heirs of Pope Julius, anything other than I had to give them up till now – that is the said Tomb like that of Pius in St. Peter's,[3] and if I'm allowed a reasonable time, I'll do the figures myself. And as I've said, if I'm given my salary, I'll always go on working for Pope Clement with such powers as I have, which are slight, as I'm an old man – with this proviso, that the taunts, to which I see I am being subjected, cease, because they very much upset me and have prevented me from doing the work I want to do for several months now. For one cannot work at one thing with the hands and at another with the head, particularly in the case of marble. Here it is said that they are meant to spur me on, but I assure you they are poor spurs which drive one back.[4] I haven't drawn my salary for a year now, and I'm struggling against poverty. I have to face most of the worries alone, and there are so many of them that they keep me more occupied than my work, since I cannot employ anyone to act for me,[5] as I haven't the means.[6]

[Unsigned]

1. *See Appendix 16.*

2. *The Tomb of Pius II formerly in St. Peter's; but now in Sant' Andrea della Valle.*

3. *We hope this was clear to Fattucci. The Italian text is somewhat involved.*

4. *See Appendix 14, pt. III.*

5. *The phrase 'tenere chi mi governi' is sometimes translated as 'to keep someone to look after me', meaning that he was without a personal servant. This is incorrect, because Niccolò da Pescia was in his service at this time (Milanesi, p. 597).*

6. *The words 'This is a copy of the letter which Michelangelo, sculptor, has sent to-day, this 24th day of October 1525 to Pope Clement, and I, Antonio di Bernardo Mini have made this copy with my own hand', are appended at the foot of the page.*

❡ [To Messer Giovan Francesco Fattucci in Rome]

175

*Buonarroti
Archives
Mil. cdi
From Florence
(October 1525)*

Messer Giovan Francesco — Piero Gondi has shown me one of your letters, which is an answer to one he wrote you several days ago, from which I learn that you wanted to know by whom I've been approached, as Piero, who has told you the truth, wrote you.[1] I've been approached by several people, but among those whose province it is, Lorenzo Morelli[2] is one who has sought to learn my mind in this connection. Francesco da Sangallo[3] came and told me that the said Lorenzo would be glad to learn if I would be prepared to serve them, if he were to move in the matter. I replied that, although I recognized their kindness and that of the whole people, I couldn't repay them, except by doing it and doing it as a gift, if the Pope were agreeable; as I was already committed, since, being committed to him, I could not work on anything else without his permission. Messer Luigi della Stufa[4] has also enquired the same of me several times himself, and I made the same reply. I've never discussed it apart from this, nor would I have broached it, but being asked, I was forced to reply. Recently, also, several people have again told me that the Commissioners have agreed that they would be agreeable to waiting two or three years until I had finished serving the Pope, provided I would do it.

[Unsigned]

1. *i.e. about the execution of a statue of 'Hercules slaying Cacus', which the Republic wished to have placed as a companion piece to the 'David' in front of the Palazzo Vecchio. See Appendix 14, pt. III.*

2. *Lorenzo di Matteo Morelli is mentioned by Varchi (p. 5) as being one of the 'maggiori cittadini'. In 1523 he went with others to congratulate Clement VII on his elevation.*

3. *Francesco di Giuliano da Sangallo (1494-1576), the sculptor. He executed part of the frieze of masks in the New Sacristy (Milanesi, p. 596).*

4. *Luigi della Stufa took a prominent part in civic affairs. During the 'Squittino Generale' of 1531 he held office as one of the 'Accoppiatori' (Varchi, p. 467 et seq.).*

176

Buonarroti
Archives
Mil. cccxcix
From Florence
(December)
1525

¶ To my dear friend Messer Giovan Francesco, priest of Santa Maria del Fiore in Florence, in Rome

Messer Giovan Francesco — If I had as much strength as I have had amusement from your last letter I should believe I could complete, and quickly too, all the things about which you write to me, but as I haven't, I'll do what I can.

As to the colossus of forty *braccia*,[1] which you inform me is to go, or rather to be put at the corner of the loggia of the Medici garden, opposite Messer Luigi della Stufa's corner, I've considered it not a little in that position, as you instructed me. It seems to me that at the said corner it would not be well placed, because it would take up too much of the roadway; but at the other corner where the barber's shop is, it would in my opinion, look much better, because it has the piazza in front and would not be such a nuisance to the street. And since there might be some objections to doing away with the said shop, owing to the income it provides, I thought that the said figure might be made to sit down and the said work being hollow beneath – which can be conveniently done with blocks – its seat could come at such a height that the barber's shop could go underneath and the rent would not be lost. And as at present the said shop has an outlet for the smoke, I thought of putting a cornucopia, which would be hollow inside, into the hand of the said statue to serve as a chimney. Then, as I would have the head of such a figure hollow like the other members, I believe it, too, could be put to some use, for there is a huckster[2] here in the piazza, a great friend of mine, who suggested to me in confidence that a handsome dovecot could be made inside. Another idea also occurred to me, which would be even better, but the figure would have to be considerably larger – which it could be since a tower is made up of blocks – and that is that the head might serve as a much-needed campanile for San Lorenzo. And with the bells clanging inside and the sound issuing from the mouth the said colossus would seem to be crying aloud for mercy, especially on feast days when there is more ringing and with larger bells.

As to bringing in the marbles for the said statue unbeknown to anyone, I thought of bringing them in by night, well covered up, so as not to be seen. There would be a little risk at the gate, but for this too we'll find a way; at the worst the San Gallo gate won't fail us, because the postern is kept open all night.

As to doing or not doing the things which are being done, which you tell me are to be held over, they had better be left to whomsoever will have to do them, because I shall have so much to do that I'm not bothering with them any more. For me this will suffice – that the thing should be imposing.

I'm not replying to you about everything, because Spina is shortly coming to Rome and will do better by word of mouth than I by writing and in more detail.

YOUR MICHELANGELO SCULPTOR IN FLORENCE

1. *In a letter dated October 14th Fattucci had written expressing the Pope's desire to erect a colossus and had emphasized his notion of constructing it by means of blocks (Frey, Briefe, p. 260). Michelangelo, who thought that the Pope was presuming to teach him his own trade, twice refers to this possibility. The letter is throughout a typical piece of Renaissance 'double entendre'. By thus ridiculing the idea from the outset, Michelangelo effectually put a stop to this absurd proposal, despite the Pope's insistence that it was not a joke (Frey, Briefe, p. 271).*

2. *This is a sarcastic reference to Figiovanni, who had been appointed 'Provveditore della fabbrica' at San Lorenzo in 1520 (Cianfogni, I, p. 204). He was always making mischief and had written to Rome saying that Michelangelo was building the Library like a dovecot (Frey, Briefe, p. 237).*

¶ [TO MESSER GIOVAN FRANCESCO FATTUCCI IN ROME]   *177*

Messer Giovan Francesco — This coming week I shall have the figures[1] that are blocked out in the Sacristy covered up, because I want to leave the Sacristy free for the *scarpellini* working on the marbles, as I want them to begin building in the other Tomb opposite the one that is built in, which is aligned, or very nearly. And while they are building it in I thought the vault might be done and supposed that, with enough men, it could be done in two or three months, but I don't know. At the end of next week

*Buonarroti
Archives
Mil. cdii
From Florence
June 17th
1526*

Our Lord can send Messer Giovanni da Udine[2] whenever he wishes, if he thinks the vault should be done now, as I shall be ready.

As to the recess, four columns have been built in this week – one of them was built in before. The tabernacles will be a little behindhand; however, I think it will be finished in four months from to-day. The framework of the floor should be begun by now, but the limes are not yet seasoned; we'll hasten the drying process as much as possible.

I'm working as hard as I can, and in a fortnight's time I shall get the other 'Captain' started; then of the important things, I shall have only the four 'Rivers' left. The four figures on the coffers, the four figures on the ground, which are the 'Rivers', the two 'Captains', and 'Our Lady' which is going into the Tomb at the top end, are the figures I want to do myself. And of these, six are begun. I feel confident about doing them within a reasonable time and having the others, which are not so important, done in part. I think that's all. Commend me to Giovanni Spina and beg him to send a note to Figiovanni[3] to beg him not to call off the cartwrights from here in order to send them to Pescia, because we should be left without stone, and likewise not to use his charms to ingratiate himself with the *scarpellini* here by saying to them, 'These people have no consideration for you, making you work until dusk, now that the nights last only two hours.'

We are hard put to it with a hundred eyes to keep one of them at work, and even that one has been spoilt for us by these bowels of compassion. Patience! God forbid that what does not displease him should displease me!

[Unsigned]

1. *For a discussion of the figures intended for the Medici Tombs in the New Sacristy see Appendix 16.*

2. *Giovanni da Udine (1494–1564). See Appendix 20.*

3. *Figiovanni, as usual, was making mischief and spreading it abroad that Michelangelo was not working. On one occasion, when this was repeated to Pope Clement in Rome, he replied, 'He really is a beast; he would do better to tittle-tattle less' (Frey, Briefe, p. 293).*

178   ¶ [To Messer Giovan Francesco Fattucci in Rome]

Buonarroti Archives Mil. cdiii From Florence November 1st 1526

Messer Giovan Francesco — I know that Spina has recently written very heatedly to Rome about my affairs regarding this Julius affair. If he made a mistake, in view of the times in which we are living,[1] it is my mistake, because I implored him to write. Perhaps anxiety caused me to be too insistent. I had recently had a notification from Rome about the said affair of mine, which has filled me with alarm. This is because of the ill-will the relatives of Julius bear me – and not without reason – and because

22. *The Tomb of Lorenzo de' Medici, Duke of Urbino*
The New Sacristy

Michelangelo
San Lorenzo, Florence

23. *The Tomb of Giuliano de' Medici, Duke of Nemours*
The New Sacristy

Michelangelo
San Lorenzo, Florence

the suit is proceeding and they are demanding such damages that a hundred such as I would not suffice to discharge them. This has put me in a great turmoil and has made me wonder where I should find myself if the Pope were to fail me, since I should be unable to exist in this world. This is the reason I got him to write, as I've said. Now I only want what pleases the Pope; I know he has no wish to see me ruined and put to shame.

I have observed that building is being slowed down here and I realize that public expenses are being curtailed and I realize that a house is being rented in San Lorenzo for me and that my salary is being paid as well – which are not slight expenses. If it would be advantageous to curtail these expenses also and to give me leave, so that I might begin something, either here or in Rome, for the said work of Julius, I should be very glad, because I desire to be rid of this obligation more than to live. None the less, I'm never disposed to depart from the will of the Pope – provided that I comprehend it. So, as you know my mind, I beg you to write and tell me what the Pope's wishes are and I won't contravene them. And I beg you to find out from him and to write and tell me on his behalf, so that I may the better and more readily obey, and also so that one day, should it befall, I may be able to justify myself by means of your letters. I think that's all.

If I haven't been able to make myself clear to you, don't be surprised, because I'm completely distraught. You know my mind; you will know his, who must be obeyed. Reply I beg of you.

On the first day of November 1526.

YOUR MICHELANGELO SCULPTOR AT SAN LORENZO IN FLORENCE

1. *See Appendix 19.*

¶ [TO GIOVANNI SPINA IN FLORENCE]

179

Giovanni — It seems to me that Piero Buonaccorsi[1] should be given permission to go, because there is no longer need of him here. If you want to keep him on to do him a good turn, keep him on as long as you think fit. I'm telling you this, because I don't want to be the one to keep him on, nor to be the one to throw away the Pope's money, as I've been said to do.[2] So please would you tell him, and the sooner the better, so that he may decide about his arrangements and may not then have cause to complain that he wasn't informed.

YOUR MICHELANGELO, who commends himself to you

*Buonarroti
Archives
Mil. cdiv
From Florence
November 10th
1526*

1. *See Appendix 20.*

2. *Michelangelo was being asked to cut down expenses owing to the threat of war (Frey, Briefe, p. 289).*

180

*Buonarroti
Archives
Mil. ccclxxxii
From Florence
(December
1526)*

¶ To the Director,[1] Giovanni Spina

My dear Giovanni — Because the pen is always bolder than the tongue, I am writing to say what I haven't had the courage to say by word of mouth in view of the times, on several occasions recently. It is this: realizing as I've said, that the times are unfavourable to this art of mine,[2] I do not know whether I have any further expectation of my salary. If I were certain about not having it any longer, I should not cease on that account to work for the Pope and to do everything I could; but in view of the obligation you know that I am under, I should not go on keeping open house, as I have somewhere else to live with much less expense, and it would also relieve you of having to pay the rent. If, however, my salary is to be continued, I'll stay here as I am and do my best to fulfil my obligations. So please would you tell me what you intend to do about it, so that I can consider my arrangements. I remain much obliged to you, and will see you again at the coming festival[3] in Santa Maria del Fiore.

Your Michelangelo at San Lorenzo

1. *Whether Spina had recently been appointed to a directorship in the Salviati bank, or whether Michelangelo happened on this occasion to use the formal mode of address 'mio maggiore' cannot be ascertained.*

2. *Owing to the political and international situation which culminated in the sack of Rome in May 1527. See Appendix 19.*

3. *Probably Christmas 1526, though it might be Epiphany 1527.*

181

*Buonarroti
Archives
Mil. cxxii
From Florence
August 22nd
1527*

¶ To Buonarroto in Settignano

Buonarroto — I have to-day been offered an appointment as clerk extraordinary to the *Cinque del Contado.*[1] They say it lasts a year and is worth four ducats a month and the holder can pass it on to whomsoever he likes. I know nothing about it and cannot attend to it. I must either decline it or give it away, or rather, pass it on to someone else. See whether it suits you, though in these times I don't advise you to come to

Florence.[2]   However I wanted to let you know about it before I decline it, as I have fourteen days' grace. Let me have an answer.

On the 22nd day of August 1527.

MICHELANGELO IN FLORENCE

1. *The Five Commissioners for the Countryside were responsible for the administration of affairs in Tuscan territory beyond the city walls.*

2. *Owing to a severe outbreak of plague.*

¶ To Buonarroto in Settignano

Buonarroto — I've been to see Messer Antonio Vespucci.[1] He tells me that according to law I cannot pass on the appointment I've been offered to someone else, and that, though this is done, it is done by custom and not by law; that if I want to risk accepting it to pass it on to someone else, I can risk it, but that I could be denounced[2] and get into trouble over it. So I think it best to decline it, not so much for this, as on account of the plague, which seems to me to go from bad to worse. I would not like you to risk your life for a song of forty ducats. I will help you as far as I can.[3] Answer me at once as to what you think I should do, as I must decide tomorrow so that they can appoint someone else if I decline.

MICHELANGELO IN FLORENCE

British Museum Mil. cxxiii From Florence September 4th 1527

Don't handle the letters I send you.[4]

1. *Antonio Vespucci, Notary to the 'Tratte', the office responsible for the drawing of the names of those eligible for the various appointments in the Commune. He had served in the department since February 1498 and was pensioned, without cancellation of his appointment, in May 1528, being considered by this time 'quasi inutile' owing to his advanced age (Marzi, pp. 284, 322, and Varchi, p. 144).*

2. *The verb used is 'tamburare', i.e. to accuse a citizen secretly by placing a note in the box – tamburo – which stood at the entrance of a government office.*

3. *In view of this remark and also because Buonarroto was apparently not working in Florence, it seems probable that the shop which he had set up in partnership with Jacopo Gianfigliazzi had proved a failure. On February 16th 1528 Lodovico sent Michelangelo a list of debtors and creditors (Steinmann and Wittkower, p. 445). See also Wolf, p. 69.*

4. *On account of the plague. This is the last extant letter to Buonarroto, who died of plague on July 2nd in the following year.*

VIII

LETTERS
183 – 198

From Florence,
Venice and Rome
1529 - 1534

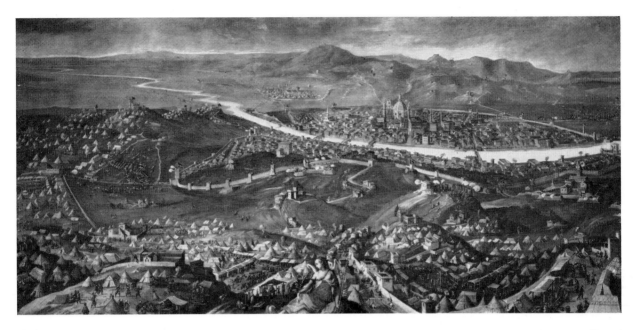

24. The Siege of Florence

Vasari
Palazzo Vecchio, Florence

VIII. From Florence, Venice and Rome: 1529-1534

¶ To Ser Marcantonio del Cartolaio

183

*Buonarroti
Archives
Mil. cdv
From Florence
(January 1529)*

Ser Marcantonio[1] — I'm sure you will know how to choose an honest and capable man[2] much better than I should. I therefore willingly delegate my vote, with this proviso, that I retain the right to exercise it myself another time.[3]

YOUR MICHELANGELO BUONARROTI

1. *Ser Marcantonio was secretary to the 'Nove della Milizia', the Council of Militia, formed prior to the anticipated siege of Florence. Michelangelo became a member of this body on January 10th 1529.*

2. *Pagolo di Benedetto Bonsi was elected Provveditore, the office in question (Milanesi, p. 456).*

3. *See Appendix 21.*

¶ To my dear friend Battista della Palla in Florence

184

*Buonarroti
Archives
Mil. cdvi
From Venice
September 1529*

Battista, dearest friend[1] — I left Florence, as I believe you know, and intended to go to France, but when I reached Venice and made enquiries about the route I was told that going from here one has to pass through German territory which is difficult and dangerous. I therefore decided to find out from you, if you would be so good as to let me know, whether you were any longer disposed to go, and to beg you, as I do, to inform me if you are and where you wish me to wait for you, and we'll go together. I left without taking leave of any of my friends and in a very haphazard fashion. But although, as you know, I wanted to go to France in any case, and several times asked permission, but never got it, it was not because I had not resolved to see the war[2] through first without any fear whatsoever. But on Tuesday morning, the twenty-first day of September, someone came out from the San Niccolò gate to the bastions where I was, and whispered in my ear that to remain any longer would be to risk my life. And he came home with me, where he had dinner, and he brought me mounts and never left me till he got me out of Florence, assuring me that this was for my good. Whether he were god or devil I know not.

I beg you to answer me as to the first part of this letter and as quickly as you can, because I'm consumed with impatience to be off. But if you're no longer disposed to go, I still beg you to let me know, so that I may arrange to go as best I can by myself.[3]

YOUR MICHELANGELO BUONARROTI

1. *Giovanni Battista della Palla da Lucca was an agent of Francis I for the purchase of works of art in Italy. Among other things, he bought an unfinished statue of Hercules by Michelangelo from the steward of Filippo Strozzi in 1530, and sent it to France. His extant letters to Michelangelo, urging him to return, are filled with moving confidence in the justice of the Florentine cause and with affectionate concern for Michelangelo's welfare (Gotti, I, p. 195). On the return of the Medici, he was imprisoned in the Castle of Pisa, where he died of poison, probably administered by his own hand.*

2. *See Appendix 21.*

3. *The letter is endorsed in the hand of Michelangelo the Younger, 'Given me, I do not remember by whom – I think by Canon Nori.'*

185   ❡ TO GIOVAN SIMONE BUONARROTI IN SETTIGNANO

*Buonarroti
Archives
Mil. cxxix
From Florence
(Summer) 1531*

Giovan Simone — Mona Margareta[1] hasn't understood the point. When speaking about you and Gismondo in front of Ser Giovan Francesco the other morning I said that for the sake of all of you I had always done more than I would have done for myself and had endured many hardships, in order that you might not endure any, and that you had never done anything but speak ill of *[me]* all over Florence. That is what I said. Would it were not so in your own interest, since you merely earned yourselves a bad name.

As to your staying up there, I should be glad if you would stay there at your ease and try to get well;[2] as I'll always do what I can for you, because I care more about fulfilling my obligations than about the things you say. I should be very glad if you would settle down there, so that Mona Margareta could stay there too, because when he was dying my father commended her to my care, and I'll never abandon her.

MICHELANGELO IN FLORENCE

1. *Mona Margareta had previously been in his father's service.*

2. *This letter was written shortly after Lodovico's death. All the brothers had been ill after the raising of the siege.*

¶ [TO FRA SEBASTIANO DEL PIOMBO[1] IN ROME]

186

*Buonarroti
Archives
Mil. cdvii
From Florence
November
(25th) 1531*

My dear Sebastiano — I'm giving you too much trouble. Bear with it patiently, reflecting that it is surely more glorious to raise the dead than to produce figures which appear to be alive. Concerning the Tomb of Julius, I've thought it over several times, as you told me to, and it seems to me that there are two ways of freeing oneself from the obligation. One is to do it; the other is to give them the money to have it done themselves. Of these two courses, only the one agreeable to the Pope can be taken. To do it myself will not, in my opinion, be agreeable to the Pope, because I should not be able to devote myself to his things. Therefore they'll have to be persuaded – I mean whoever is acting for Julius – to take the money and get it done themselves. I would supply the drawings and models and whatever they want, together with the marbles that have been done for it. With the addition of two thousand ducats I think a very fine tomb could be produced; and among the young men there are some who could do it better than I could myself. If this latter course – that of giving them the money to get it done – is taken, I could put down a thousand gold ducats now and the other thousand somehow or other later on – provided they resolve on something that is agreeable to the Pope. And if they're prepared to put this last into effect I'll write and tell you how the other thousand ducats can be raised, which I think will not be unacceptable.

I'm not writing about my position in detail, because there's no need. I'll only tell you this, that the three thousand ducats that I took to Venice in gold[2] and silver became fifty, when I returned to Florence and the Commune borrowed from me some one thousand five hundred of them.[3] So I can't do more. But a means will be found, I hope, if the Pope fulfils his promise. Sebastiano, dearest colleague, I stand firm by the courses proposed and beg you to pursue them to the end.

[Unsigned]

1. *Sebastiano Luciani, also known as Veneziano, was appointed to the office of Piombatore sometime after October 3rd and before November 21st 1531. His undated letter to Michelangelo announcing the appointment is characteristic. See Milanesi, Corr., p. 44.*

2. *Vasari (VII, p. 109) states that Michelangelo and his two companions, Piloto and Antonio Mini, took with them 12,000 scudi, sewn into their doublets. On the face of it, the sum is absurd, by reason of the weight of the specie alone, even apart from the fact that Michelangelo would not have been able to put his hand on so large an amount at a moment's notice.*

3. *This was a forced loan, known as a Prestanza, and was neither a gift nor a fine, as has generally been supposed. From the thirteenth century onwards the Commune of Florence had been adept at devising new forms of taxation, mostly oppressive. See Staley, pp. 188 et seq. Clement VII subsequently ordered some 500 ducats to be restored to Michelangelo (Milanesi, Corr., p. 114).*

25. *Sebastiano del Piombo with Cardinal Ippolito de' Medici*

School of Sebastiano del Piombo
National Gallery, London

¶ [To Fra Sebastiano del Piombo in Rome]   *187*

Frate Sebastiano, dearest colleague — I've had three letters from you. I replied to the   *Buonarroti*
first two. The reply to the first I sent you, by arrangement with Messer Bartolomeo   *Archives*
Angiolini, to a friend of his in Rome, who wrote saying that he had given it to you him-   *Mil. cdviii*
self. Then, the second reply – the one to your second letter – I sent through the man   *From Florence*
you suggested, which I understand from you is the only one you've received.[1]   *(March 1532)*

[Unsigned]

1. *In a letter dated April 29th 1531, Sebastiano had complained about a letter of Michelangelo's, which
   he found on receipt had been opened. He therefore consulted Bartolomeo Angiolini, who was employed in the Customs. Angiolini accordingly arranged to send Sebastiano's letters with his own,
   while Michelangelo was advised to send his through Lorenzo Mannucci, a vestment-maker who lived
   in the Piazza in Florence (Symonds, II, p. 388). See The Dating and Sequence of the Letters.*

¶ [To Fra Sebastiano del Piombo in Rome]   *188*

Frate Sebastiano — Please would you for pity's sake tell Messer Lodovico del Milanesi,[1]   *Buonarroti*
or rather ask him, to send Ser Giovan Francesco his stipend.[2] You will be doing me a   *Archives*
very great favour, and him a greater, because he has a good deal of money to pay out   *Mil. cdix*
and he hasn't the means. I commend him to you.[3]   *From Florence*
                                                                                            March 1532
[Unsigned]

1. *Lodovico del Milanesi was presumably employed in the Datary's office and was in all probability a
   brother of Riccardo del Milanesi. See No. 167, n. 4.*

2. *With characteristic courtesy and consideration, Michelangelo was always disposed to do his friends
   and even his acquaintances a kindness when it lay in his power.*

3. *Sebastiano replied to this request on March 25th, saying that Ser Giovan Francesco Fattucci would
   have to send an affidavit to the effect that he was still alive, a fact which Lodovico del Milanesi's
   superior, the official responsible for the payment, being desirous of retaining the money in question,
   preferred not to believe (Milanesi, Corr., p. 86).*

189 ❡ To Giovan Simone Buonarroti in Florence

*Buonarroti
Archives
Mil. cxxviii
From Florence
April (8th/9th)
1532*

Giovan Simone — I have to go to Rome this morning about a matter of some importance to me.[1] So I'm sending you four ducats by Mona Margareta, for your own use, and if you should need anything while I'm away get someone to write and tell me, and I'll always help you wherever I am. I can't come to see you, because I haven't time. Pray to God for me, and be as light-hearted as you can.

MICHELANGELO AT SAN LORENZO

1. *i.e. the negotiations for the Third Contract for the Tomb of Julius II.*

190 ❡ [To Andrea Quaratesi in Pisa]

*Buonarroti
Archives
Mil. cdx
From Florence
(May 1532)*

My dear Andrea[1] — I wrote and told you about a month ago that I had had the house surveyed and the amount for which it could be offered in these times assessed. I also wrote and said that I did not think you would manage to sell it. As I have to pay out two thousand ducats for my affair in Rome, which, with some other items, will amount to three thousand, I meant to sell houses and lands and to let them go at half price in order not to be stark naked, but I did not and have not managed to do so. I think, therefore, that it will be better to wait than to rush ahead.

[Unsigned]

1. *Andrea di Rinieri di Giovanni Quaratesi (1512–1585) belonged to the well-known banking family and later held several public offices. He was greatly attached to Michelangelo (Wilde, p. 96).*

191 ❡ [To Messer Tommaso de' Cavalieri in Rome]

*Buonarroti
Archives
Mil. cdxii
From Rome
January 1st
1533*

Most inadvisedly I was prompted to write to your lordship,[1] and had the presumption to be the first to move, as though I had a debt to pay in replying to a letter of yours. Afterwards I recognized my error the more, so much did I enjoy reading your reply,[2] for which I thank you.

Far from being a mere babe, as you say of yourself in your letter, you seem to me to have lived on earth a thousand times before. But I should deem myself unborn, or rather

26. *Andrea Quaratesi*

Michelangelo
British Museum, London

27. *Ideal Head*

Michelangelo
H.M. The Queen, Windsor Castle

stillborn, and should confess myself disgraced before heaven and earth, if from your letter I had not seen and believed that your lordship would willingly accept some of my drawings. This has caused me much surprise and pleasure no less. And if you really esteem my works in your heart as you profess to do in your letter, I shall count that work much more fortunate than excellent, should I happen, as I desire, to execute one that might please you.

I'll say no more. Many things that might be said in reply remain unwritten, lest you be wearied and because I know that Pierantonio,[3] the bearer of this, can and will supply what I lack. On the, for me, happy first day of January.

> Though it is usual for the donor to specify what he is giving to the recipient, for obvious reasons it is not being done in this instance.[4]

> *[Unsigned]*[5]

1. *Tommaso de' Cavalieri, a young nobleman whom Michelangelo met in Rome sometime towards the end of 1532. See Appendix 23.*

2. *See Symonds, II, p. 138.*

3. *Pierantonio Cecchini, a member of Cardinal Niccolò Ridolfi's household. He seems to have received some instruction in carving from Michelangelo, with whom his name is coupled in a motu proprio of Paul III, dated February 14th 1540, by which both, together with other unnamed 'statuarii' working for the Curia Romana, were exempted from the authority of the Guild of Scarpellini (Guasti, Motu. p. 151, et seq.). See also Giannotti 'Dialogi'.*

4. *Michelangelo was apparently sending a portfolio of drawings, from which Cavalieri was free to choose what he liked. According to Vasari (VII, p. 271) Michelangelo executed for him a number of 'carte stupendissime, designate di lapis nero e rosso, di teste divine', of which Plate 27 may perhaps be one (Popham and Wilde, p. 257).*

5. *There are two other drafts of this letter. One is almost identical and has therefore been omitted; the other is longer and is included among the Drafts (Draft 4).*

❡ To Francesco Galluzzi

192

Francesco[1] — The bearer of this will be Bernardo Basso, clerk of works at San Lorenzo, to whom I beg you to pay the rent you owe me, of which I am in great need. Payment will be appreciated.[2] I commend me to you.

On the 19th day of March 1532.[3]

YOUR MICHELANGELO BUONARROTI AT SAN LORENZO

Buonarroti Archives Mil. cdxiv From Florence March 19th 1533

1. *From 1525 onwards Francesco di Bernardo Galluzzi rented the house in the Via Ghibellina which Michelangelo had himself previously occupied. He paid twenty-two broad gold ducats a year for it, and was always in arrears with the rent.*

2. *'Saranno ben pagati.' According to Edler (p. 201) the phrase 'ben pagato' (lit. well paid) means either 'paid promptly' or 'paid in an acceptable medium'. From its use in certain contexts it would appear to be a polite form of indicating that payments were overdue – as in this instance.*

3. *N.S. 1533. This is the only evidence we have that Michelangelo was in Florence at this time. He had generally been supposed to have been resident in Rome until the early summer.*

193 ¶ [TO MESSER TOMMASO DE' CAVALIERI IN ROME]

*Buonarroti
Archives
Mil. cdxvi
From Florence
July 28th
1533*

My dear lord — Had I not believed that I had convinced you of the immense, nay, boundless love I bear you, the grave apprehension shown by your letter that I might have forgotten you, as I haven't written to you would seem to me neither strange nor surprising. But there is nothing unusual in this, nor in being alarmed, when so many other things go wrong, lest this too should come to grief; since what your lordship says to me, I would have said to you. But perhaps you did this in order to try me, or in order to kindle anew a greater flame, if a greater were possible. But be that as it may, I realize now that I could *[as soon]* forget your name as forget the food on which I live – nay, I could sooner forget the food[1] on which I live, which unhappily nourishes only the body, than your name, which nourishes body and soul, filling both with such delight that I am insensible to sorrow or fear of death,[2] while my memory of you endures. Imagine, if the eye were also playing its part, the state in which I should find myself . . . . .[3]

[Unsigned]

1. *Though not exactly paralleled, the simile is strongly reminiscent of Dante. Cf. Paradiso, xvi.69.*

2. *At this time Michelangelo feared for his life, owing to the enmity of Duke Alessandro de' Medici.*

3. *There are two versions of the second half of this draft (written on the same sheet) and another version of the opening (Draft 5). From Cavalieri's reply, dated August 2nd 1533 (Symonds, II, p. 139), it is clear that the sentiments expressed in the above draft were included, together with a reference to other matters, in the letter Michelangelo finally sent. This version is therefore given here instead of being placed with the other drafts, as approximating most nearly to the actual letter, which is no longer extant.*

[To Fra Sebastiano del Piombo in Rome]

M y dear Colleague — I have received the two madrigals[1] and Ser Giovan Francesco[2] has had them performed several times; according to what he tells me, they are considered wonderful things to sing; the words didn't merit such a setting. It's what you wanted and has been a source of the greatest pleasure to me. Please will you let me know what I should do for the master who wrote the music, so that I may not appear more ignorant and ungrateful than need be.[3]

Buonarroti Archives Mil. cdxv From Florence August 1533

As to the work here,[4] I'll say no more for the moment, as I think I've said enough about it recently, but I've done my best to imitate Figiovanni's manner and style in every particular,[5] as it seems to me well suited to anyone who wants to have a say in everything. Don't show this letter.[6]

You tell me you have given a copy of the above-mentioned madrigals to Messer Tommao.[7] I'm very grateful to you for having done so. If you see him, I beg you to commend me to him a thousand times, and when you write to me tell me something about him to put me in mind of him, because if he were to fade from my memory I think I should instantly fall dead.

[Unsigned]

1. *Both madrigals were by Michelangelo. One had been set to music by Constanzo Festa of Piedmont (1490–1545) who in 1517 became a member and later 'maestro di cappella' of the Sistine Choir. His Te Deum is still sung at the election of a new Pope and on other traditional occasions. According to Dr. Burney, his madrigals were characterized by extraordinary 'rhythm, grace and facility'. The other madrigal had been set by Giacomo Concilion, or Consiglium (d. 1535), a French musician who was also a member of the Papal Choir.*

2. *Fattucci may perhaps have been a 'cappellano cantore'.*

3. *Michelangelo's anxiety to recognize and reward such services is notable. He expressed the same desire when others of his poems were set to music by Arcadelt a few years later. See Vol. II, Nos. 216, 217.*

4. *The Medici Tombs at San Lorenzo.*

5. *Figiovanni was always trying to ingratiate himself with everyone, while making trouble at the same time (see No. 177, n. 3). He was Michelangelo's 'bête noire' and from Sebastiano del Piombo's letter of July 17th 1533 (Milanesi, Corr., p. 106) it is clear that he and Michelangelo were trying to get at him, apparently by taking a leaf out of his own book.*

6. *i.e. to the Pope, who always wanted to read Michelangelo's letters.*

7. *i.e. Tommaso de' Cavalieri.*

195

*Buonarroti
Archives
Mil. cccliii
From Florence
(September
1533)*

¶ To Niccolò in Florence

Niccolò[1] — I could not answer you decisively yesterday evening at the Canto de' Bischeri,[2] as I had it in mind to do, because, as the man on whose behalf you spoke to me was there and as you may perhaps have given him some hope of obtaining what he desired of me, I was afraid of causing you embarrassment. Therefore, although I burned to do so several times, I did not say precisely what I would have said had you been alone. But I am now writing to make the position clear to you, namely, that for a very good reason I cannot take on any apprentice, much less a foreigner. I therefore told you that I was not prepared to do anything for two or three months, so that he could decide – that is to say, so that your friend should not leave his son here, expecting anything of me. But he did not see the point and answered, saying, that if I were but to see him I should pursue him not only into the house, but into bed. I assure you that I'll deny my-self that consolation, which I have no wish to filch from him. Therefore, will you get rid of him for me? I'm sure you'll know how to do it, and will do it in such a manner that he won't go away disgruntled. I commend me to you.

Your Michelangelo in Florence

1. *Probably Niccolò di Raffaello de' Pericoli, known as il Tribolo. See Appendix 24.*
2. *The corner of the Palazzo Bischeri, the junction of the Piazza del Duomo and the Via dell' Oriuolo.*

196

*Buonarroti
Archives
Mil. cdxix
From Florence
October 15th
1533*

¶ [To Messer Giovanbattista Figiovanni in Florence]

Messer Giovanbattista, my dear patron — On the last day of this month the four months since I arrived in Florence on the Pope's business will be completed. During the first of the said four months you brought me my salary. I did not want it, and told you to keep it for me. You answered me that if you had to write to the Pope you would say that I had had it. I told you to tell the truth. Afterwards you showed me a letter from the Pope which said that you should pay no attention to what I said and should give it to me. I now wish to raise as much money as I can to expedite my affair in Rome, and by tomorrow night I shall have finished the two small models I'm making for Tribolo,[1] and on Tuesday I want to leave without fail. So I beg you to give me the salary I told you to keep for me – that is to say, would you give me two months' salary and I'll make the Pope a present of the other two months. You will be doing me a great favour, for which I shall always remain obliged.

On the 15th day of October 1533.

Your Michelangelo in the casa i' Macciagnini in Florence

1. *Tribolo was commissioned to execute the flanking figures, 'Heaven' and 'Earth', for the Tomb of Giuliano, Duke of Nemours, after the models supplied by Michelangelo, but he fell ill and, on the death of Clement VII, the work was abandoned. He copied the four allegorical figures in clay and gave the 'Night' to Figiovanni as a return for having admitted him to the Sacristy (Vasari, VI, p. 66).*

¶ [TO GIOVAN SIMONE]

197

Giovan Simone — I have a young man in view for Ceca.[1] He belongs to the Sacchetti family and is named Benedetto. He has one brother[2] whose wife is a Medici, and another[3] who is a prisoner in the fortress of Pisa; another of them, named Albizo, died in Rome. If you know him I should be glad to learn what you think of him before I go any further. You can send and tell me by Mona Margareta, and don't discuss it with others.

MICHELANGELO AT SAN LORENZO

Buonarroti
Archives
Mil. cxxx
From Florence
(July 1534)

1. *Francesca, the daughter of Michelangelo's brother Buonarroto. She eventually married Michele di Niccolò Guicciardini in 1537.*

2. *Niccolò Sacchetti, who married Margherita di Giuliano de' Medici (Litta II, tav. xvii).*

3. *Lionardo Sacchetti, who died in prison where he had been incarcerated since 1530. He was described by Varchi (p. 452) as a 'giovane di buona presenza, ma cattivo cervello'. If his brother, Benedetto, resembled him in this respect he would certainly not have been acceptable to Michelangelo.*

¶ TO FEBO

198

Febo[1] — Although you have conceived for me a great hatred – I do not know why – I certainly do not believe that it is owing to my affection for you, but owing to what other people say, which you ought not to believe, having made trial of me; I cannot but write and tell you this however. I am leaving tomorrow morning and going to Pescia to meet Cardinal Cesis[2] and Messer Baldassare.[3] I shall go with them to Pisa and then to Rome. And I shall not return here any more.[4] I want you to understand that as long as I live and wherever I may be I shall always be ready to serve you with loyalty and with affection, as much as any other friend you may have in the world.

Buonarroti
Archives
Mil. cdxx
From Florence
September 1534

I pray God that in some way He may open your eyes, so that you may recognize that he who desires your good more than his own welfare knows how to love and not, like an enemy, to hate.

[Unsigned]

1. *Febo di Poggio, a young friend of Michelangelo's, who according to his own telling had always looked upon him as a father (Symonds, II, p. 403).*

2. *Cardinal Paolo Emilio Cesis (1481–1537), a man revered by the poor and the outcast no less highly than he was esteemed for his singular qualities by the learned and the great (Cardella, IV, p. 57).*

3. *Baldassare Turini da Pescia (1485–1543). He had held office as Datary to Leo X from 1517–1521 and had later been appointed principal secretary to Clement VII. Under the succeeding Pope, Paul III, he served as a clerk of the Camera and as Nuncio to Charles V (Puccinelli, p. 366).*

4. *Michelangelo never again returned to Florence. See Appendix 25.*

DRAFTS
I – 6

From Florence and Rome
1523 - 1533

Drafts 1-6. From Florence and Rome: 1523-1533

¶ [To Lodovico Buonarroti at Settignano][1]

Lodovico—I'm replying to you about those matters to which reason demands that I should reply to you; as to the others, I treat them with contempt. You say that I have had the capital registered in my name and that you cannot draw the interest. It is not true that I've had the capital registered in my name, nor could I do so without you, and I cannot prevent you from drawing the interest. Therefore go and get it and you will see for yourself that I'm telling the truth. It is certainly true that you cannot dispose of the capital, because you have made it over to me. As to the other things, do as you propose, since all Florence knows the rich man you were and that I have always robbed you and deserve to be punished. . . . .

1. Draft of No. 154.

Draft 1

British Museum Mil. xlv From Florence June 1523

¶ To Messer Gio. Francesco Fattucci in Rome[1]

In the first years of Pope Julius, I believe it was the second year, I went and entered his service; after many designs for his Tomb, one of them pleased him, on the basis of which we made a bargain. And I undertook to execute it for ten thousand ducats. And as a thousand ducats were going into the marbles, he had them paid to me, I believe by the Salviati in Florence, and sent me for the marbles.

I went and brought both marbles and men to Rome and I began to work on the frame and the figures – and some of the men who worked on it are still there. But at the end of eight or nine months the Pope changed his mind and did not want to go on with it, and when I complained to him, because I found myself involved in heavy expenses, His Holiness, not wishing to pay for the said work, got tired of it and had me turned away from the audience chamber. I immediately left Rome in a rage and all the preparations I had made for a work on this scale were upset. A disruption such as this cost me more than three hundred ducats of my own money, without counting my time and the six months I was at Carrara, when I never had anything. And the said marbles remained in the Piazza of St. Peter.

Draft 2

British Museum Mil. ccclxxxiv From Florence December 1523

191

After about seven or eight months which I spent practically in hiding through fear, for the Pope was furious with me, I was forced, not being able to remain in Florence, to go and sue to him for mercy at Bologna. That was the first time he went there, where he kept me for about two years to execute his statue in bronze, which was six *braccia* in height, seated. And this was the agreement. When Pope Julius asked me what the said figure would come to, I said bronze casting was not my trade, but that I believed it could be cast for a thousand ducats, but that I did not know if I should succeed. He said to me 'Cast it over and over again until it succeeds and we will give you as much money as is necessary'. And he sent for Messer Antonio Maria del Legnia*[me]* and told him to pay me a thousand ducats at my convenience. I had to cast it twice. I can show that I spent three hundred ducats on wax, that I employed many assistants and that I had to pay Messer Bernardino, who was Master of the Ordnance to the Signoria of Florence, thirty ducats a month and his expenses, and I employed him for several months. In short, at the end, when the figure was in place at the end of two years, and having endured the utmost misery, I found myself better off by four and a half ducats. Hence I reckon for the said work alone I could justly demand from Pope Julius more than a thousand gold ducats, because I never had anything but the first thousand, as I've said.

Then when I returned to Rome he still did not want me to go on with the Tomb, but wanted me to paint the vault of Sixtus, on which we were agreed for three thousand ducats for all my expenses, for a few figures only. Then when I had done some designs it seemed to me that it would turn out a poor affair. Thereupon he gave me a fresh commission down to the Histories below and said that I should do what I liked in the vault, which amounted to about as much again. And thus we were agreed. Then when the vault was finished and it came to the emolument, it was not increased, so that I reckon I am owed several hundreds of ducats. . . . .

1. *Draft of No. 157.*

Draft 3   ¶ [To Meo delle Corte]¹

*Buonarroti
Archives
Mil. ccclxx
From Florence
(July 1524)*

Meo — I have again had letters telling me to begin work on the marbles I have and to send at once to get the marble that is faulty replaced. So please be a little earlier than usual, so that we may not be bothered by the sun in examining for flaws the two pieces that are there, so that we can move them inside and you can leave.

1. *One draft of No. 163.*

Meo — Please would you be at San Lorenzo tomorrow morning a little earlier than usual, so that we may not be bothered by the sun in examining the marble for flaws.

1. *Another draft of No. 163.*

¶ [To Messer Tommaso de' Cavalieri in Rome][1]

Draft 4

*Buonarroti
Archives
Mil. cdxi
From Rome
(January 1st)
1533*

Inadvisedly, Messer Tommao, my dearest lord, I was prompted to write to your lordship, not in answer to any letter I had received from you, but being the first to move, thinking, as it were, to cross a little stream dry-shod, or rather what was apparently, from its shallow water, a ford. But after I left the bank I found it was not a little stream but the ocean, with its overarching billows, that appeared before me; so much so that, had I been able, I would willingly have returned to the bank whence I came, to avoid being completely overwhelmed.[2] But since I've got so far we'll take courage and go on. And if I haven't the skill to steer a course through the surging sea of your brilliant endowments, you will, on that score, forgive me and neither scorn the disparities between us nor expect from me what I do not possess, since he who is unique in all things can have no companions in any. Your lordship cannot therefore rest content with the work of anyone else, being matchless and unequalled – light of our century, paragon of the world.[3] If, however, any one of the things which I promise and hope to perform were to please you, I should count that work much more fortunate than excellent. And if, as I've said, I were ever to have the assurance of pleasing your lordship in anything, I would devote to you the present and the time to come that remains to me, and should very deeply regret that I cannot have the past over again, in order to serve you longer than with the future only, which will be short, since I'm so old. That's all I have to say. Read the heart and not the letter, since 'affection exceeds the compass of the pen'.[4]

I must offer my apologies for having expressed such wondering amazement at your rare quality in my first letter which I do, as I afterwards realized the extent of my error; since there is no more cause for wonder that Rome should produce men who are divine, than that God should perform miracles. And for this the world can vouch.

1. *This draft was evidently written before Michelangelo had received Cavalieri's answer to his first letter, but was presumably abandoned in favour of No. 191, which is clearly an answer to Cavalieri's, though embodying some of the ideas contained in this first draft.*

2.   *For the style and choice of metaphors in these passages, cf. the first canto of Dante's 'Inferno'. Michelangelo was much influenced by the 'Divina Commedia'.*

3.   *For this type of extravagant compliment cf. Ariosto, I, s.3, l.2.*

4.   *'la pena al buon voler non po gir presso . . .' (Petrarch, Canzone XXIII, 'Nel dolce tempo', l.91).*

Draft 5   ¶ [To Messer Tommaso de' Cavalieri in Rome][1]

*Buonarroti
Archives
Mil. cdxvi
(second and
third parts)
From Florence
July 28th
1533*

. . . and were you certain of this, as I was, we ought both to reflect that he who loves has a retentive memory and can as soon forget the thing he fervently loves as a hungry man the food on which he lives – nay, much less can a man forget the things he loves than the food on which he lives, because the former nourish the body and the soul, the body with perfect temperance, the soul with blissful tranquillity and an expectation of eternal felicity. . . . .

. . . Nay, much rather can a man forget the food on which his body lives and is nourished – because in the end it frequently leads him into pain and misery – than he can forget the things he loves, which in tranquil bliss hold for him the promise of eternal felicity. . . . .

Mil. cdxvii

Messer Tommao, my dear lord—Although I have not answered your last letter, I do not believe that you believe that I had forgotten, or could forget, the food on which I live, which is none other than your name. Therefore I do not think, although I speak very presumptuously being much inferior, that anything could hinder our friendship.

1.   *For another and more complete version of these drafts, see No. 193.*

Draft 6   ¶ [To Bartolomeo Angiolini in Rome][1]

*Buonarroti
Archives
Mil. cdxviii
From Florence
July 28th
1533*

The cat and . . . .
peace or truce . . . .
that my animals . . . .
to be surprised at . . . .
I should be there if I were able . . . .
but merely to live . . . .

my soul to Messer Tommao . . . .
to imagine to what extent I can remain with it . . . . for the first time
given the heart . . . . you can also consider . . . .
how I could remain and how I could live, being so far away from the one . . . .
therefore, if I long day and night, as it were, without any intermission to be in Rome, it
is merely in order to return to life, which is impossible without the soul. And since the
heart is in truth the abode of the soul, and my heart being for the first time in the hands
of him to whom you have confided my soul, the natural impulse was for it to return to
its own abode;

[or]

the natural impulse has caused it to return to its proper place.[2] Would that you had been
able to do so with the body, which would willingly have gone to the same place as its
soul, and I should not be here in a state of such restlessness and distress. But as it has
not been *[i.e. in the same place]*, may it soon be, the sooner the better, nor may it live
eternally elsewhere.

My dear Bartolomeo, although I may seem to jest with you, please realize that I am
also serious in saying that I have aged twenty years and lost twenty pounds since I've
been here, and I don't know when the Pope is leaving Rome,[3] what he wants of me,
nor where he wishes me to be.

1. *This draft has unfortunately been torn, which is the more regrettable as it is the only reply extant to any of the numerous letters he received at this time from Angiolini, who kept him informed about his house in Rome, about the ripening of the grapes in the garden and the figs in the courtyard, about the hens and 'messer gallo triomfano' the cock, and about the cats, which (like his friends) lamented his absence, though without loss of appetite.*

2. *Apparently only a variant of the preceding phrase.*

3. *Clement VII left Rome for Marseilles on September 9th 1533, to celebrate the marriage on October 26th of his young relative, Catherine de' Medici, to the Duke of Orleans, afterwards Henry II. Michelangelo had an interview with the Pope during his progress, at San Miniato del Tedesco on September 22nd.*

The Dating and Sequence of the Letters

The Dating and Sequence of the Letters

Notes on the emendations made in the present edition

In arranging Michelangelo's letters for publication Milanesi divided them into two main groups: (i) those addressed to members of his family; (ii) those addressed to his other correspondents. The first group he further subdivided into letters addressed (a) to Michelangelo's father, Lodovico; (b) to his brother, Buonarroto; (c) to his brother, Giovansimone; (d) to his brother, Sigismondo; (e) to his nephew, Lionardo.

This method of grouping, a method typical of the archivist as opposed to the historian, obviously simplified a task which even Michelangelo himself might have regarded as a *grandissima fatica*, yet at the same time it inevitably confused the issue when it came to the question of ascribing dates to undated or partially dated letters. By grouping them with reference to the recipients Milanesi obscured the chronological sequence, and was thereby led into a series of errors, many of which might have been avoided by a different arrangement of the material.

But while subsequent authorities have found it easy to point out Milanesi's mistakes, they have found it less easy to correct them, so that there is still a considerable divergence of opinion, even in the light of more recent research, as to the correct dating of certain letters. To differ from Milanesi in arranging (or rather in attempting to arrange) them in chronological order, irrespective of the recipients, is therefore neither to belittle his scholarship nor to minimize his contribution.

For purposes of dating, the letters fall into the following clearly defined categories: (i) those that are dated in full by Michelangelo; (ii) those that are endorsed with the date of receipt by the person addressed; (iii) those that are partially dated; (iv) those that are undated.

Unfortunately, as Michelangelo became more and more overwhelmed by the artistic demands made upon him and by the immensity of the tasks with which he was faced, he tended to be uncertain about the precise date on which he was writing, the 29th instead of the 31st being, for instance, as near as makes no matter, 'the last day of July'.

But even when the letters are dated in full, as was usually the case in the earlier years, the chronological problem is not automatically solved, owing to the different methods of dating current in Italy during Renaissance times. Thus in Florence it was customary to date the year according to the Style of the Incarnation, that is to say, from Lady Day, March 25th, whereas in Rome it was customary to date it either according to the Style of the Nativity, that is from Christmas Day, December 25th, or according to the *stile comune*, that is from January 1st. And in this connection it is interesting to observe that in his diary Paris de Grassis, Papal Master of

199

Ceremonies to Julius II and Leo X, used both systems indifferently, though perhaps more frequently the latter, the *stile comune*, which appears to have been the more general practice and was, incidentally, that almost invariably followed by Michelangelo himself when he was living in Rome.

The use of two calendar systems, whereby the legal or civil year began on March 25th and the historical year on January 1st was also current in England at this time and continued in use until 1752, when the change from the Old Style, Julian Calendar to the New Style, Gregorian Calendar was made. The English term, New Style (N.S.) has therefore been used throughout this translation to indicate the change in the dating of the year that has had to be made, in order to conform to the modern practice of dating the year from January 1st, in the case of those letters which were written between January 1st and March 24th and dated according to the old Florentine system. In a majority of instances Milanesi has, of course, made the necessary adjustment, but in one or two he has failed to observe the necessity of doing so and on at least one occasion has made an adjustment where no adjustment is required.

As Michelangelo was extremely erratic, and as often as not omitted to date his letters at all, and as the character of the handwriting is by no means an infallible guide to the period during which they were written, it is fortunate that his brother, Buonarroto, and his nephew, Lionardo, were both in the habit of endorsing the letters, not only with the date of receipt, but also with the date (either known or assumed) on which they were despatched. Yet even so, it has not always been possible to supply the dates that are wanting in the family correspondence, since, unlike Michelangelo, both Buonarroto and Lionardo wrote a notarial and somewhat illegible hand, so that even when not blurred or obliterated, the endorsements have often proved difficult and sometimes impossible to decipher.

In some instances the dates of undated or partially dated letters can be supplied or completed from known or ascertained facts to which the letters refer; in others the required information can occasionally be obtained by the simple expedient of *thinking* – usually the last resort, but finally the most stimulating and the most rewarding.

Of the four hundred and ninety-five letters published by Milanesi a few have been omitted in the present translation; namely those that are too fragmentary to be of interest and those which are merely duplicate drafts of a single letter which differ from one another only in minute particulars. Apart from these, two letters, which were accepted by Milanesi, have been excluded, as they were not written by Michelangelo.

The first of these is one addressed to Buonarroto *(Milanesi, xlvi)* which is not, as Milanesi supposed, a letter written by Michelangelo in a disguised hand and under an assumed name, but a letter written by his assistant, Piero Paesano d'Argento, on March 10th 1498 (N.S.) *(Poggi, p. 113 et seq.)*. The second is a letter to Pope Paul III *(Milanesi, cdxli)* relating to the proposed cornice for the Farnese Palace, which, though it exists in a copy in Michelangelo's hand, does not, as was formerly supposed, embody Michelangelo's criticism of Sangallo's cornice, but Sangallo's criticism of Michelangelo's. This is obvious even on the most cursory reading of the letter in question. In the first place, it is completely different in style, composition and content from anything ever written by Michelangelo; in the second, the criticism is not applicable to the cornice designed by Sangallo *(Clausse, II, p. 97)*, though it might be thought to be applicable to Michelangelo's, which is less classical and more original in conception; and finally, never in the whole of his existence did Michelangelo propose to kiss anybody's feet, the feet of His Holiness not excepted. What, then, is the explanation for the letter in Michelangelo's hand? It can only be supposed that Sangallo, being understandably enraged by the Pope's desire to select a cornice for the palace of which he himself was the architect from designs submitted by others, wrote to the Pope, as soon as Michelangelo's had been chosen, condemning the design in the strongest and most opprobrious terms. Thereupon the Pope presumably showed the letter to Michelangelo, who evidently took a copy of it. This conclusion – namely that the letter is not by Michelangelo – is fully supported by Armando Schiavo, following S. Meller, who published a paper on the subject in 1909 *(Schiavo, p. 113)*.

In all cases where there is no evidence or presumption to the contrary, I have accepted Milanesi's conjectural dating of undated or partially dated letters; where this has not proved possible, I have given my reasons for emending the dates which are in doubt. These revised dates fall into three categories: (i) those that have been 'corrected' and are certainly right; (ii) those that have been 'ascertained' and are presumably right; (iii) those that have been 'assumed' and are approximately right. The arguments in support of these revised dates are given below.

Sequence of Letters the dates of which have been emended

All dates, whether whole or in part, shown in brackets are assumed dates

4	Assumed	.... *(1497)* .... *(October)*	.... —
	Milanesi	.... *(1497)* .... *(March)*	.... —

As this letter refers to advice concerning Lodovico's affairs given to Buonarroto during his visit to Rome in the summer of 1497, October seems a more likely month for it than March.

5	Assumed	.... *(1499)* .... *(August)*	.... —
	Milanesi	.... *(1508)* .... *(August)*	.... —

The date of this letter is problematical. But the first Roman period is to be preferred to the third on the following grounds: (i) the character of the handwriting; (ii) the evidence that he was occupied, but uncertain as to his future movements, which suggests the completion of a commission – in this case the *Madonna della Febbre*, which was due for delivery in August 1499; (iii) the fact that he had sufficient money to allow him to expend five ducats, or rather four and a half, on charity; (iv) the fact that he required so small a quantity of the finest varnish, which he may have needed for some slight repair to the marble.

6   Corrected   . . . .   *1506*   . . . .   *January* *31st*

    Milanesi   . . . .   *1507*   . . . .   *January* *31st*

Milanesi's adjustment of the date, which he supposed to be *ab Incarnatione*, is unnecessary. The letter was written in Rome and dated according to Roman usage. In January 1507 Michelangelo was not in Rome but in Bologna.

7   *Assumed*   . . . .   *(1506)*   . . . .   *(February/March)*   . .   —

    Milanesi   . . . .   *(1508)*   . . . .   *(July)*   . . . .   —

As this letter refers to the payment for consignments of marble from Carrara, on Michelangelo's return to Rome in December 1505, it seems more likely that this letter belongs to 1506 than to 1508, when he was engaged on the Sistine vault.

40   *Ascertained*   . . . .   *1508*   . . . .   *February*   . . . .   *(13th)*

    Milanesi   . . . .   *1508*   . . . .   *February* *18th*

The endorsement in Buonarroto's hand indicates that February 18th was the date of receipt, not of despatch. Five days would be a reasonable time for a normal delivery from Bologna to Florence. The letter was written at the beginning of the week, and from what Michelangelo says about his anticipated movements from January 5th onwards, the 13th seems a more probable day than the 6th. The bronze statue of Julius II was moved into San Petronio on Tuesday, February 15th.

46   *Corrected*   . . . .   *1509*   . . . .   *June*   . . . .   —

    Milanesi   . . . .   *(1508)*   . . . .   *(June)*   . . . .   —

Michelangelo received 500 ducats on account for the Sistine vault on May 10th 1508. As he here states that he has received no payment for thirteen months, this letter must belong to June 1509. The reference to Mona Cassandra's lawsuit for the return of her dowery renders it impossible that it should belong to June 1508, since her husband did not die until June 18th of that year.

47	Corrected	. . . .	1509	. . . .	(June)	. . . .	—
48	Milanesi	. . . .	(1508)	. . . .	(July and	. . . .	—
49					August)		

These letters all refer to the lawsuit with Mona Cassandra and are otherwise interrelated. They must therefore be assigned to 1509.

50	Corrected	. . . .	1509	. . . .	September	. . . .	15th
	Milanesi	. . . .	(1510)	. . . .	September	. . . .	15th

This letter is endorsed in Lodovico's hand 'On the 18th of September 1509 from Rome'. In any case the contents suggest 1509.

52	Corrected	. . . .	1510	. . . .	(July)	. . . .	—
	Milanesi	. . . .	(1509)	. . . .	—	. . . .	—

As Lodovico held office as Podestà at San Casciano from September 22nd 1510 to March 22nd 1511, this letter obviously belongs to 1510. The notice allowed in respect of appointments to the office of Podestà was approximately two months (*cf. Frey, Briefe, pp. 61, 69*).

56	Ascertained	. . . .	1510	. . . .	November	. . . .	23rd
	Milanesi	. . . .	1510	. . . .	—	. . . .	23rd

Buonarroto's endorsement, 'February 1510' cannot be correct and must have been added at a later date, since it conflicts with Michelangelo's statement in No. 57 that he received the required payment on his return to Rome on January 7th, after a second visit to Bologna, whence the Pope had, in any case, departed on January 2nd. As December is obviously excluded, the only possible date for this letter is Saturday, November 23rd.

60	Corrected	 1511	....	*June*	.... —
	Milanesi	.... (1509)	....	*June*	.... —

From the contents of the letter it is clear that it must have been written in 1511 and not in 1509 for the following reasons: (i) it refers to the repayment of 100 ducats drawn from Michelangelo's account without his consent by Lodovico in 1510; (ii) it infers that the end of the painting of the Sistine vault is in sight; (iii) it contains the first reference to the purchase of farms during this period.

61	*Assumed*	.... (1511)	....	*July*	.... —
& 62	*Milanesi*	.... (1512)	....	*July* —	.... —

These letters refer to the negotiations for the purchase of farms first mentioned in No. 60 and must therefore be assumed to be the sequel to it.

63	Corrected	 1511	....	*October*	.... 4th and 11th
& 64	*Milanesi*	.... (1510)	....	*October*	.... (3rd) and 11th

Both these letters belong not to 1510, but to 1511. In any case the audience referred to in No. 63 could not have taken place in October 1510, as the Pope was then in Bologna. The change from the 3rd to the 4th has been made because October 4th was a Saturday.

65	*Assumed*	.... (1512)	....	*(January)*	.... (3rd)
	Milanesi	.... (1512)	....	—	.... —

This letter precedes the one to Buonarroto dated January 10th. For the dating arguments for this letter and Nos. 67–70 and 72–76, see below, under Nos. 72–76.

66	Corrected	 1512	....	*January*	.... 10th
	Milanesi	.... (1511)	....	*January*	.... 10th

According to Milanesi this letter is endorsed in Buonarroto's hand '1510 from Rome: received on the 15th day of January' [*i.e. 1511*]. This must be a misreading of

Buonarroto's notoriously difficult hand, for it could not have been written on January 10th 1511, as Michelangelo wrote to his brother announcing his safe arrival from Florence on January 11th 1511 *(No. 56)*. The balance of evidence is in favour of 1512, since the estimate of time required for the completion of the Sistine vault agrees with that given in No. 65.

67	Assumed	1512	*(February)*	*(28th)*
	Milanesi	*(1512)*	—	—
68	Assumed	1512	*(March)*	*(6th)*
	Milanesi	*(1512)*	—	—
69	Assumed	1512	*(March)*	*(13th)*
	Milanesi	*(1512)*	—	—
70	Assumed	1512	*(March)*	*(20th)*
	Milanesi	*(1512)*	—	—

See below, Nos. 72–76.

71	Assumed	*(1512)*	*(March)*	*(27th)*
	Milanesi	*(1512)*	*(October)*	—

Florence had been placed under an interdict by Julius II on September 23rd 1511. This ban was lifted temporarily in November, but was reimposed shortly afterwards. It was finally lifted on March 21st 1512. From the rest of the context this letter appears on balance to belong rather to March 1512 than to November 1511, but there is no certainty about it. The 27th was a Saturday, the day of the week on which Michelangelo usually wrote letters to the family.

72	Assumed	1512	*(April)*	—
	Milanesi	*(1509)*	*(September)*	—
73	Assumed	1512	*(April)*	—
	Milanesi	*(1511)*	*(September)*	—

74	Assumed	. . . .	1512	. . . .	(May)	. . . .	—
	Milanesi	. . . .	(1509)	. . . .	—	. . . .	—

76	Ascertained	. . . .	1512	. . . .	(June)	. . . .	(5th)
	Milanesi	. . . .	(1512)	. . . .	(May)	. . . .	—

All these letters, together with No. 65 and Nos. 67–70, refer to negotiations for the purchase of a farm or farms. At least two purchases were finally made, one on May 28th and the other on June 20th 1512 *(see Appendix 6)*. The order of this series has long been in dispute and it is impossible to make dogmatic assertions as to the sequence. No arrangement is entirely satisfactory, as Michelangelo's own estimates as to the probable date of the completion of the Sistine vault and of his return to Florence were characteristically over-optimistic and are therefore no guide. The letters have accordingly been arranged in what can only be claimed to be the least unconvincing order, having regard to the political events mentioned, the payments recorded, the names of the bankers included, etc. etc.

78	Assumed	. . . .	1512	. . . .	(July/August)	. . . .	—
	Milanesi	. . . .	(1512)	. . . .	—	. . . .	—

This letter would appear to belong to the summer of 1512, following Michelangelo's return to Rome, after his brief visit to Florence in June *(see Appendix 9)* and prior to the completion of the Sistine vault.

83	Corrected	. . . .	1512	. . . .	October	. . . .	—
	Milanesi	. . . .	(1509)	. . . .	(October)	. . . .	—

This letter refers to the completion of the whole Sistine vault, which was uncovered on the eve of All Saints, October 31st 1512. By some extraordinary aberration Milanesi assigns the uncovering, after 'seventeen months and twenty days work', to 1509.

84	Assumed	. . . .	(1512)	. . . .	(October)	. . . .	—
	Milanesi	. . . .	(1512)	. . . .	—	. . . .	—

From its contents this letter was evidently written in the autumn, probably in October on the completion of the Sistine vault.

86	Assumed	. . . .	(1512)	. . . .	November	. . . .	5th
	Milanesi	. . . .	(1508)	. . . .	November	. . . .	5th

This letter, which is assigned by Frey as well as by Milanesi to 1508, and by Thode and Spahn to 1511, may confidently be assigned to 1512, the date also preferred by Pogatscher, for the following reasons: (i) because this is the first reference to the boy whom Michelangelo afterwards engaged during his brief visit to Florence in December 1512, and subsequently dismissed shortly after his arrival in Rome at the beginning of the following year *(see No. 90)*; (ii) because the power of attorney mentioned is again referred to in No. 87; (iii) because the price of corn – 25 *soldi* the bushel – would be likely to be high owing to the political troubles of the months immediately preceding; (iv) because Michelangelo's request that his clothes might be sent may be referred back to his remark in No. 81.

87	Assumed	. . . .	(1512)	. . . .	(November)	. . . .	—
	Milanesi	. . . .	(1512)	. . . .	—	. . . .	—

This letter is related to No. 86, in addition to which the 2,000 ducats referred to may be assumed to have been paid to Michelangelo at about this time. See Appendix 9.

88	Assumed	. . . .	(1513)	. . . .	(January)	. . . .	(1st)
	Milanesi	. . . .	(1509)	. . . .	(December)	. . . .	—
89	Corrected	. . . .	1513	. . . .	January	. . . .	5th
	Milanesi	. . . .	(1510)	. . . .	January	. . . .	5th
90	Corrected	. . . .	1513	. . . .	(February)	. . . .	—
	Milanesi	. . . .	(1510)	. . . .	(January)	. . . .	—
91	Corrected	. . . .	1513	. . . .	(February)	. . . .	—
	Milanesi	. . . .	(1510)	. . . .	(January)	. . . .	—

These letters are interrelated, but Milanesi's conjectural dating of the group is unacceptable, because at that period Michelangelo was occupied with the painting of the Sistine vault and was not concerning himself with the engagement of *scarpellini* or with the acquisition of a house in which to execute the Tomb of Julius II, on which work was resumed in January 1513.

100	Assumed	. . . .	1515	. . . .	July	. . . .	(21st)
	Milanesi	. . . .	1515	. . . .	July	. . . .	28th
101	Corrected	. . . .	1515	. . . .	July	. . . .	28th
	Milanesi	. . . .	1515	. . . .	August	. . . .	1st

Both these letters are endorsed as having been written on July 28th and received on August 1st. As this is manifestly incorrect the dates have been conjecturally emended.

| 105 | Assumed | . . . . | 1515 | . . . . | August | . . . . | (27th) |
| | Milanesi | . . . . | 1515 | . . . . | August | . . . . | 25th |

This letter, like No. 104, is endorsed as having been written on August 18th and received on August 25th, the date which Milanesi took to be the date of writing. Close attention to the contents of Nos. 105 and 106 leads to the conclusion that it was probably written on Monday, August 27th.

| 109 | Corrected | . . . . | 1515 | . . . . | October | . . . . | 6th |
| | Milanesi | . . . . | 1515 | . . . . | November | . . . . | 6th |

This minor correction is made in accordance with the endorsement.

| 121 | Corrected | . . . . | 1518 | . . . . | April | . . . . | 2nd |
| | Milanesi | . . . . | (1518) | . . . . | (March) | . . . . | — |

As this letter was written on the same day as the one addressed to Buonarroto on the same subject *(No. 120)*, it must be dated April 2nd.

| 126 | Ascertained | . . . . | 1518 | . . . . | July | . . . . | — |
| | Milanesi | . . . . | (1518) | . . . . | — | . . . . | — |

This letter may be assigned to July for the following reasons: (i) it was written shortly before Michelangelo left Florence for Seravezza, as witness the words, 'I shall soon be with you'; he is known to have been in Florence in July and in Seravezza in August; (ii) he refers to a contract to which Ceccone was a party, the precise terms of which were unknown to him. This contract is mentioned in a *ricordo* of August 4th, in respect of which he paid four ducats on account to each of the five *scarpellini* mentioned *(Milanesi, p. 573).*

133   *Assumed*   ....   *1518*   ....   *(October)*   ....   —

      Milanesi   ....   *(1518)*   ....   —   ....   —

      Michelangelo reached Pistoia on September 25th on his way back to Florence, where he remained until October 30th, presumably recuperating from his recent illness. The letter, which was very probably written in Settignano, must therefore be assigned to October, particularly as the mention of Pier Francesco Borgherini's house relates it to No. 132.

137   *Ascertained*   ....   *1519*   ....   *January*   ....   —

      Milanesi   ....   *(1519)*   ....   —   ....   —

      The communication to Bernardo Niccolini referred to is dated December 21st 1518. Michelangelo's letter may accordingly be assigned to the beginning of January 1519.

138   *Corrected*   ....   *1519*   ....   *March* *29th*

      Milanesi   ....   *(1518)*   ....   *March* *29th*

      Michelangelo left for Pietra Santa on March 29th 1519 *(Milanesi, p. 576).* In March of the previous year he was already in Pietra Santa by this date. Further confirmation that this letter belongs not to 1518 but to 1519 is provided by the reference to the workshop, the site for which was not purchased until July 1518.

140   *Ascertained*   ....   *1519*   ....   *May* *10th*

      Milanesi   ....   *(1519)*   ....   *(May)*   ....   —

      This letter giving Pietro Urbano instructions for his journey to Pietra Santa and Carrara can be dated precisely, because Michelangelo gave him forty-four ducats in respect of this journey on May 10th *(Milanesi, p. 578).*

142 *Ascertained* . . . . 1519 . . . . *September* . . . . *(12th)*
     Milanesi . . . . *(1519)* . . . . *(October)* . . . . —

Frey is undoubtedly right in supposing that this letter antedates No. 143. It was evidently written shortly after Michelangelo's return to Florence from Seravezza, where he had left Pietro Urbano, who had not completely recovered from his recent illness *(Milanesi, p. 578)*.

144 *Assumed* . . . . 1520 . . . . *(March)* . . . . —
     Milanesi . . . . *(1520)* . . . . — . . . . —

As the contract for the façade of San Lorenzo was cancelled on March 10th 1520, this draft was presumably drawn up at about the same time.

146 *Assumed* . . . . 1521 . . . . *(March)* . . . . —
     Milanesi . . . . *(1519)* . . . . — . . . . —

This letter cannot belong to 1519, as it refers to the Medici Tombs, which were not under discussion until the autumn of 1520. As it was written prior to the payment of two hundred ducats made to Michelangelo on April 9th 1521 for marbles that had already been ordered *(Milanesi, p. 582)*, the most probable date for it is March 1521.

147 *Ascertained* . . . . 1521 . . . . *March* . . . . *(16th)*
     Milanesi . . . . *(1521)* . . . . *March* . . . . —

The probable date of this letter is March 16th, as we know, from a letter addressed to Michelangelo by Lionardo the saddler on March 22nd, that he had already informed him of Pietro Urbano's arrival in Rome at about this time *(Frey, Briefe, p. 166)*.

148 *Corrected* . . . . 1521 . . . . *(June)* . . . . —
     Milanesi . . . . *(1518)* . . . . *(September)* . . . . —

This letter refers to negotiations for the purchase of a further workshop in which to carry out the work on the Medici Tombs. The reasons for assigning it to 1521 are fully discussed in Appendix 17.

149   *Corrected*   . . . .   *1521*   . . . .   *September/*   . . . .   —
                                                  October

       Milanesi   . . . .   *(1516)*   . . . .   —   . . . .   —

Michelangelo dismissed Pietro Urbano from his service on Pietro's return from Rome, either at the end of September or the beginning of October 1521. Pietro was still in Rome, prior to his return to Florence on September 14th and had been in Naples for one month on November 19th *(Frey, Briefe, pp. 179, 183)*. As this letter was written the night before Pietro was sent back to Pistoia, it must belong to the autumn of 1521.

150   *Assumed*   . . . .   *(1522)*   . . . .   *(January)*   . . . .   —

       Milanesi   . . . .   *(1522)*   . . . .   —   . . . .   —

From Michelangelo's concluding remark, 'At the eleventh hour, each one of which seems to me like a year', it is clear that this letter was written during a period of suspense, perhaps that prior to the election of the Flemish Pope, Adrian VI, on January 9th 1522. Only the election of a Medici Pope would have been in his favour, owing to his non-fulfilment of the 1516 Contract for the Tomb of Julius II.

152   *Assumed*   . . . .   *(1523)*   . . . .   *(April)*   . . . .   —

       Milanesi   . . . .   *(1523)*   . . . .   —   . . . .   —

The approximate date generally assigned to this letter by authorities other than Milanesi is November 1522, owing to Jacopo Salviati's letter of November 18th concerning the Tomb of Julius II *(Frey, Briefe, p. 193)*. This conflicts, however, with Michelangelo's opening statement that it was now about two years since he returned from Carrara, having ordered the marbles for the Medici Tombs, which was at the end of April 1521 *(Milanesi, p. 582)*. In addition, it seems likely that the *motu proprio* mentioned, which had not yet been signed by the Pope, was drawn up by the heirs of Julius II at about this time, as the Duke of Urbino was invested with his estates on March 26th 1523 *(Sanuto, XXXIV, 54)*. Whether the brief was actually signed (and it seems probable that it was not) cannot be ascertained until the Registers of Adrian VI have been published.

157   *Ascertained*   . . . .   *1523*   . . . .   *December*   . . . .   —

       Milanesi   . . . .   *(1524)*   . . . .   *(January)*   . . . .   —

This letter cannot have been written in January 1524, because reference to the matters contained in it is made in two of Giovan Francesco Fattucci's letters, written on December 22nd and December 30th respectively *(Frey, Briefe, pp. 198, 201)*. December 1523 would therefore seem to be the most probable date for it.

160   *Assumed*   ....   *1524*   ....   *(January)*   ....   —

      Milanesi   ....   *(1524)*   ....   —   ....   —

January 1524 – and not July 1525, as Frey suggests *(Frey, Briefe, p. 239)* – seems to be an acceptable date for this letter. The lantern is generally supposed to have been uncovered at this time, and in any case by February 1524 scaffolding was being erected inside the New Sacristy *(Milanesi, p. 585)*, which indicates that the exterior work was complete.

163   *Assumed*   ....   *(1524)*   ....   *(July)*   ....   —

      Milanesi   ....   *(1519)*   ....   —   ....   —

Bartolomeo (Meo) delle Corte and Forello da la Porta alla Croce were both employed by Michelangelo at this period. The marble in question was certainly marble quarried for the work in the New Sacristy, and not for the façade. In two letters, one dated July 9th and the other July 21st 1524 *(Frey, Briefe, pp. 232, 233)*, Michelangelo had been urged by Fattucci to replace the defective marbles. This note to Meo delle Corte and Draft 3 have accordingly been dated to this period.

171   *Corrected*   ....   *1525*   ....   *(June)*   ....   —

      Milanesi   ....   *(1524)*   ....   *(January)*   ....   —

Notwithstanding the date of Lionardo the saddler's letter, namely January 21st 1525, on the back of which this draft was written, it certainly belongs to the time at which Giovan Francesco Fattucci became Michelangelo's *procuratore* at the Pope's wish in June 1525 *(Milanesi, p. 699)* – a view which is also supported by Frey *(Briefe, p. 245)*.

172   *Assumed*   ....   *1525*   ....   *(August)*   ....   —

      Milanesi   ....   *(1525)*   ....   —   ....   —

August 1525, the date proposed by Frey *(Briefe, p. 257)* seems a not improbable date for this note.

176   *Assumed*   . . . .   *1525*   . . . .   *(December)*   . . . .   —

     Milanesi   . . . .   *(1525)*   . . . .   *(October)*   . . . .   —

    The Pope's desire to erect a colossus was first conveyed to Michelangelo by Giovan Francesco Fattucci in his letter of October 14th 1525 *(Frey, Briefe, p. 260)*. Although this letter of Michelangelo's appears to be an immediate answer to Fattucci's, it can scarcely have been written prior to December, as in his letter of November 29th Fattucci asks him to let him have his views about the project, as 'Our Lord is much surprised that you have made no reply' *(Frey, Briefe, p. 267)*.

180   *Assumed*   . . . .   *(1526)*   . . . .   *(December)*   . . . .   —

     Milanesi   . . . .   *(1524)*   . . . .   —   . . . .   —

    The political events referred to are those prior to the sack of Rome in May 1527 *(cf. Landucci, p. 367)*. The coming festival mentioned by Michelangelo was presumably either Christmas 1526 or Epiphany 1527, but more probably the former.

183   *Assumed*   . . . .   *(1529)*   . . . .   *(January)*   . . . .   —

     Milanesi   . . . .   *(1529)*   . . . .   —   . . . .   —

    This letter cannot be dated precisely. Michelangelo became a member of the *Nove della Milizia* on January 10th 1529. On the assumption that this note betrays a certain unfamiliarity with the proceedings and may have been written shortly after his appointment, it has been tentatively assigned to January 1529.

184   *Corrected*   . . . .   *1529*   . . . .   *September*   . . . .   —

     Milanesi   . . . .   *1529*   . . . .   *September* *25th*

    Milanesi does not state on what grounds he assigns this letter to the 25th September, but as Michelangelo did not leave Florence until the 21st, and stayed at Ferrara on the way, it seems unlikely that he could have reached Venice and made enquiries about the route to France in time to have written this letter on September 25th. The day of the month has therefore been omitted.

185   *Assumed*   . . . .   *1531*   . . . .   *(Summer)*   . . . .   —

     Milanesi   . . . .   *(1533)*   . . . .   —   . . . .   —

There are no means of dating this letter precisely. As it was evidently written shortly after the death of Lodovico Buonarroti, it must be assigned to 1531, for the reasons set forth in Appendix 22, but the time of the year can only be assumed.

186	Corrected	. . . .	1531	. . . .	November	. . . .	(25th)
	Milanesi	. . . .	*1531*	. . . .	*June —*	. . . .	*26th*

Milanesi supposed this to be the letter to which Sebastiano del Piombo replied on July 22nd 1531. But there is no doubt that it is the one which Sebastiano received on December 1st and acknowledged on December 5th *(Milanesi, Corr., p. 74)*.

187	Assumed	. . . .	(1532)	. . . .	(March)	. . . .	—
	Milanesi	. . . .	*(1531)*	. . . .	*(July)*	. . . .	—

Whatever the date of this draft, it cannot be July 1531, because Sebastiano Luciani was not appointed to the office of *Piombatore* until the late autumn of 1531. From the wording of the letter it suggests that Bartolomeo Angiolini was not in Rome and that in his absence letters were being sent through a friend of his. That being so, and the gap in the correspondence with Angiolini, as given by Symonds *(II, pp. 386–399)*, extending from the end of August 1531 to the end of August 1532, the *terminus ante quem*, as determined by Sebastiano's appointment, and the *terminus post quem* by Angiolini's letter of August 26th 1531, leaves a period of approximately nine months, within which Michelangelo might have written the draft in question. This period can, however, be narrowed still further, as Michelangelo was himself in Rome in April, while Sebastiano was absent from June 9th until shortly before July 15th *(Milanesi, Corr., pp. 96, 98)*. The choice therefore rests between January, February, March, or May 1532.

Frey, on the other hand, relates the draft to Sebastiano's letter of August 23rd 1533 *(Milanesi, Corr., p. 116)*, but this concerns Michelangelo's non-receipt of letters, not Sebastiano's, which is little help. The sonnet written on the back of the draft, '*Se 'l foco alla bellezza fusse equale*' *(Dicht., p. 337)* being addressed to Tommaso de' Cavalieri, is later in date, but this does not invalidate the present argument, because Michelangelo was in the habit of using old letters in this way. Cf. No. 171, n. 4.

The balance of evidence is therefore in favour of March 1532, a period during which the delivery of letters in Rome is known to have been uncertain *(Milanesi, Corr., p. 88)*. Despite the subtlety of this reasoning, the date assigned may nevertheless be entirely wrong, but who shall say?

189   *Ascertained* .... *1532* .... *April* .... *(8th/9th)*
      Milanesi .... *(1532)* .... *(April)* .... —

When Sebastiano del Piombo's letter of Saturday April 6th reached Florence, Michelangelo had already left for Rome *(Gotti, I, p. 222)*. As Sebastiano's letter was written on Saturday night, it can scarcely have been despatched before Monday, April 8th, and probably did not reach its destination before April 10th/11th, by which time Michelangelo would have reached Rome, supposing he left Florence on April 8th/9th.

194   *Corrected* .... *1533* .... *August* .... —
      Milanesi .... *(1533)* .... *(July)* .... —

This letter is a reply to Sebastiano del Piombo's of July 25th *(Milanesi, Corr., p. 108)*. As the madrigals referred to had been sung 'several times' it seems hardly possible that the letter was written before the beginning of August.

195   *Assumed* .... *(1533)* .... *(September)* .... —
      Milanesi .... *(1518)* .... — .... —

For the arguments relating to the assumed date of this letter see Appendix 24.

197   *Assumed* .... *(1534)* .... *(July)* .... —
      Milanesi .... *(1533)* .... — .... —

The date of this letter is problematical. It must have been written at some date between the beginning of August and the end of October 1533, or between June and September 1534, as Michelangelo was not in Florence during the intervening period. On the whole July 1534 seems a not improbable date, as his niece, Francesca Buonarroti, would have been about seventeen years of age at this time, and Michelangelo might well have been anxious to arrange a suitable marriage for her before his final departure from Florence. Nothing came of the proposed betrothal and Francesca was not married until 1537.

198   *Corrected* .... *1534* .... *September* .... —
      Milanesi .... *(1533)* .... *December* .... —

For the arguments in favour of dating this letter to September 1534 rather than to December 1534 see Appendix 25.

Draft
6   *Corrected* . . . . 1533 . . . . *July* *28th*

Milanesi . . . . 1533 . . . . *October* *14th*

This is manifestly the draft of the letter acknowledged by Angiolini on August 2nd 1533 *(Symonds, II, p. 393).* Milanesi's conjecture that it relates to Angiolini's letter of October 18th *(ibid., p. 398)* is therefore incorrect.

APPENDIXES
1 - 25

Appendix 2

Part I

the Medici Family : 1360-1589

Lorenzo = Ginevra
1395–1440 | Cavalcanti

*(The younger branch –
see Table on verso)*

Giuliano
1453–1478

Piero Ridolfi

GIULIO
(POPE CLEMENT VII)
1478–1534

LÒ   LORENZO   ALESSANDRO = MARGARET
FI   RIDOLFI   *Duke of Florence*   *ill. d. of Charles V*
50   1503–1576   1511–1537   1521–1586

Appendix 2

Part II

Genealogical Table of the Your

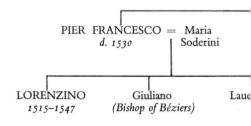

Giovanni di Bicci = Pi
de' Medici
1360–1428

Cosimo   = Contessina
'Pater Patriae'   de' Bardi
1389–1464

*(The elder branch – see
Table on recto)*

PIER FRANCESCO = Maria
d. 1530   Soderini

LORENZINO   Giuliano   Lauc
1515–1547   *(Bishop of Béziers)*

Genealogical Table of the Elder Branch o

```
Giovanni di Bicci  =  Piccarda
    de' Medici          Bueri
    1360–1428
```

```
        Cosimo       =  Contessina
    'Pater Patriae'      de' Bardi
      1389–1464          d. 1473
```

```
  Piero      =   Lucrezia                      Giovanni   =   Ginevra
'il Gottoso'     Tornabuoni                    1421–1463      degli Albizzi
 1416–1469       1425–1482
```

```
                                          Nannina  =  Bernardo
)RENZO    =   Clarice                                 Rucellai
Magnificent'   Orsini
49–1492      1453–1487
```

```
erte    Maddalena = Francesco    Lucrezia  =  JACOPO      Maria      Contessina
·oy     1472–1519    Cibo                     SALVIATI    d. 1487
524                                            d. 1533
```

```
          Innocenzio          Giovanni      Maria     =  Giovanni de' Medici    NICC
             Cibo             Salviati     1499–1543      delle Bande Nere       RIDC
          (Cardinal)         (Cardinal)                    1498–1526            1501–
          1492–1550          1490–1553
```

```
                                           COSIMO I
                                       (see Table on verso)
```

arda
ueri

Lorenzo = Ginevra
1395–1440 Cavalcanti

Pier Francesco = Laudomia
1415–1476 Acciajuoli

Lorenzo = Semiramide   Giovanni
1463–1507 d'Appiano   *1467–149*

Averardo   Vincenzo   Ginevra   Laudomia   G
=   *delle*
                                                                               14

nia = Piero   Maddalena = ROBERTO
     Strozzi   STROZZI
I   *d. 1558*   *d. 1566*

Maria   Joanna (1) = Francis I = Bianca (2)   Isabella =
1540–1557   *of Austria* *1541–1587* Capello   *1542–1576*
               1547–1578 *Grand Duke* *1543–1587*
                            of Tuscany
                            1574–1587

nd I = Christine   Pietro = Eleonora
609   of Loraine   1554–1604   d. of Garzia
Duke   1565–1636   of Toledo
cany   1556–1576
609

The later Grand
       Dukes

```
        ┌─────────────────────────────────────
Maria  =  Leopetto
          Rossi
   │
   │
   │
Luigi  Rossi                    PIETRO
 (Cardinal)                     'The Un
 1474–1519                       1471
┌──────────────────────────────────────
│
LORENZO  =  Madeleine de la
Duke of Urbino │ Tour d'Auvergne
1492–1519  │   1501–1519
           │
           │
CATHERINE  =  Henry II
 de' Medici │  of France
 1519–1589 │  1517–1559
           │            - - -
      Francis II
       of France
      1543–1560
```

Bianca = Guglielmo de' Pazzi

L(
'The
1.

MEDICI = Alfonsina   GIOVANNI   GIULIANO   =   Phili
unate'   Orsini   (POPE LEO X)   *Duke of Nemours*   of Sa
603   *1472–1519* *1476–1521*   *1479–1516*   *1498–*

Clarice   = FILIPPO   Ippolito
de' Medici   STROZZI   *(Cardinal)*
1493–1528   *1488–1538* *1509–1535*

Piero = Laudomia   ROBERTO   = Maddalena   Leon   *six othe*
Strozzi de' Medici STROZZI   de' Medici   Strozzi   *children*
d. 1558   *d. 1566*   *1515–1545*

Filippo
Strozzi
1541–1583

```
            =   Caterina
                Sforza
                1462–1509


ovanni      =   Maria
ande Nere       Salviati
8–1526          1499–1543


     COSIMO I      =   Eleonora
      1519–1574        di Toledo
     Duke of Florence  1522–1562
       1537–1569
  Grand Duke of Tuscany
       1569–1574


Paolo       Giovanni      Lucrezia   =   Alfonso       Garzia       Ferd
Orsini      1543–1562     1544–1561      d'Este        1547–1562    154
                                         Duke of                    Gra
                                         Ferrara                    of
                                                                    158
```

Appendix 1

Part I

e Buonarroti Family : 1228-1458

```
                    Buonromano = Bellastella di
                      fl. 1246  |   Borgagnone
 opo          Bene          Bernardo        Zetto
1259        fl. 1286        fl. 1256      fl. 1268
            Merchant    Member of Council


         Lapo
        fl. 1340
i

 a di Filippo         Andrea
  agnesi         Enrolled Arte di
 45  d. 1376        Lana 1352


 Piero di Maso    A daughter = Matteo di Gualterrotto
 della Antella                    Catellini


 dra di Brunaccio      Lisa      Michele    Francesco
   Brunacci          d. 1400   1403–1471   fl. 1426
 1432 d. 1494                    Prior       Priest


     Piera              Brigida             Selvaggia
   m. 1466             m. 1470                 m.
 Ser Giovanni    Consiglio d'Antonio   Filippo di Tommaso
                       Cisti            di Nardaccio
```

Appendix 1

Part II

Genealogical Table of the Buon

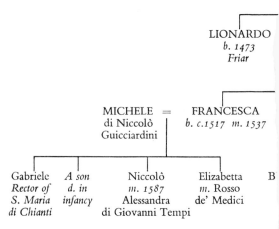

LIONARDO
b. 1473
Friar

MICHELE = FRANCESCA
di Niccolò   *b. c.1517 m. 1537*
Guicciardini

Gabriele	*A son*	Niccolò	Elizabetta	B
Rector of	*d. in*	*m. 1587*	*m. Rosso*	
S. Maria	*infancy*	Alessandra	de' Medici	
di Chianti		di Giovanni Tempi		

(The order of birth of the children is not known, but the eldest
was born in 1538 and the youngest in 1545)

Genealogical Table of th...

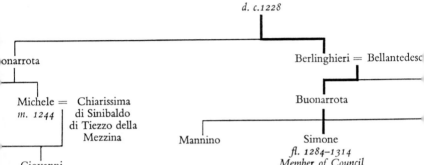

Bernardo
d. c.1228

...onarrota

Berlinghieri = Bellantedesc...

Michele = Chiarissima
m. 1244   di Sinibaldo
di Tiezzo della
Mezzina

Buonarrota

Mannino

Simone
fl. 1284–1314
Member of Council

Giovanni
fl. 1313
...cil   *Clerk*

Buonacorso = Agnese
Passerini

Michele
fl. 1325

Buonarrota = Tessa di
Prior 1343   Giacomin...
d. 1348   de' Tebald...

di Lapo = Giana
...nelli   *m. 1332*

Filippo = Lapa di
d. 1348   Franceschino
Pepi

Simone = Tac...
d. 1373
3 times Prior   *m...*

...a di = Buonarrota = Selvaggia di Antonio
...eruzzi   *1355–1405*   dei Rossi
.1374   *Banker, 3 times*
Prior

Tessa
m. 1364

Simone
1374–1428
Merchant

Piera
Nun in Convent
of S. Francesco

Piera di Andrea di = Lionardo = Ales...
Guido Portinari   *1399–1458*
Banker, Prior

...assandra = Francesco
Cosimo   *1434–1508*
...Bartoli   *Banker*

Buonarrota
d. in infancy

Lisa
m. 1449
Giusto Giusti

LODOVICO
1444–1531

(See Table on ver...

arroti Family : 1399-1684

Neri di Miniato = Bonda
del Sera | Rucellai

Lionardo di =
Buonarrota Simone | Brı
1399–1458. Banker | m

(1) Francesca = LODOVICO = (2) Lucrezia
m. 1472 d. 1481 | 1444–1531
m.

MICHELANGELO
1475–1564
Jac Sculptor, Painter, Architect,
Poet

Cassandra =
di Bernardo Puccini
d.s.p.

BUONARROTO =
1477–1528
Wool Merchant, Prior

Bartolomea
Ghezzo della
m. 1516 d. 1

LIONARDO = CA
1519–1599 di D

ɔc

ARROTO =
4–1628
B
1.

Alessandra di
Andrea Macinghi

MICHELANGELO
b. & d. 1555

A daughter
b. & d. 1556

A daughter
b. & d. 1558

ALI
b.

Lionardo
1602–1684

↓

*Direct
descent
to the
19th century*

Cosimo Buonarroti
d. 1858
*bequeathing the Casa
Buonarroti and its
contents to the City
of Florence*

```
 ┬─────────────┐
terina      Francesco
1592        1574–1632
Chericini
```

Alessandra di
naccio Brunacci
1432 d. 1494

di Antonio Ubaldini
a Gagliano
1485 d. 1497

di	GIOVAN	SIMONE	SIGISMONDO
Casa		1479–1548	1481–1555
93			

SSANDRA
nato Ridolfi
m. 1553

Simone
b. c.1521 d. c.1530

SSANDRA	Lucrezia	Bartolomea	Michelangelo	Lodovico	
& d. 1560	m. 1581	Nun in S. Agata	'The Younger'	d. 1600	
	Tommaso		1568–1647		Pier
	Corsi		Poet, Playwright		

Bu

Bugliotto
fl. 1255

Feo
fl. 1304
Member of Cour

Niccol
Sp

Elizabet
Alberto I
m. 1373

C
d

Appendix 3

Italian Renaissance Coinage

Arbitrary statements as to the value of any particular coin current in Italy during the lifetime of Michelangelo are apt to be misleading. References to most encyclopaedias and dictionaries, for instance, may be rewarded by obtaining the incorrect information that the ducat and the gold florin were 'worth' nine shillings and fourpence, a 'valuation' based on the fact that the actual gold content of these coins was slightly less than that of the English half-sovereign current in the nineteenth and early part of the twentieth century.

Such comparisons are economically invalid, since they take no account of the processes of inflation and deflation and of the consequent variations in the ratio of gold to silver, nor of the changes in the relative standards of living at various periods, upon which the whole price system is based.

In attempting to assess the purchasing value of any Renaissance Italian coin, or to judge the scale of payments made for salaries and wages, houses and lands, it is therefore essential to understand something of the complex monetary system of the period and to bear in mind the different ratio between the cost of services and commodities which existed prior to the Industrial Revolution. In the Middle Ages and the Renaissance, moreover, wide differentials existed between the remuneration of the townsman and the peasant, the skilled craftsman and the labourer, and even between the salaries and fees paid to artists of almost equal standing. These questions which can be better discussed in relation to the whole range of business transactions noted by Michelangelo in his *Ricordi*, are here mentioned in passing, since they are relevant to a comprehension of those payments referred to in the Letters.

The immense complexity of the fiduciary issues in the Italian city states of the Renaissance was to a large extent due to the almost endemic inflation in the price of gold and the devaluation of silver and base metal in relation to it. The constant efforts to achieve stability or to induce some measure of deflation were rarely successful for more than a few months or a few years at most; and political and economic crises were usually accompanied by a deliberate debasement of the coinage. To meet the conditions brought about by inflationary pressure, moreover, new denominations were frequently introduced and repeated attempts were made to ensure a standard metal content for existing ones.

Long before the end of the Middle Ages the system of international coinage, introduced throughout the Empire of Charlemagne and based upon the *Libra, Solidus* and *Denarius*, had been disrupted by this instability. In many Italian states the old standard was still nominally preserved in the 'moneys of account', and merchants and contractors continued to quote their terms, keep their books and send out their bills in *lire, soldi* and *denari*, although of these only the *denari piccioli* were any longer represented by actual silver coins and the standard, being based upon silver, had constantly to be revalued in terms of the gold currency.

When in 1252 the Florentine Mint for the first time issued the famous gold florin, it set a new standard of reliability for the whole of Europe, since 'until then no other coin but the Byzantine *hyperper* had had a stable value and had been internationally accepted' *(Origo, p. 23)*. At that time the florin had a content of 3.53 grammes of fine gold and by a decree of 1301 its value was 'fixed' at 1 *lira*, 9 *soldi*, an attempt to effect a reconciliation between the old '*lira* system' and the new gold standard, which could not be maintained owing to inflationary pressure. Thus, at the end of the fourteenth century the gold florin, *fiorino d'oro*, though subject to fluctuations, was worth roughly two and a half *lire*, whereas in Michelangelo's day it had risen to seven *lire*. Variations in the gold content and the practice by unscrupulous speculators of clipping the coins, led to a long series of monetary reforms, culminating in the introduction of the *fiorino di suggello*, issued in a sealed purse, against which suspect coins could be weighed. This florin itself was later superseded by the larger 'broad gold florin', *fiorino largo d'oro*, of which seventy, as Michelangelo notes in his *Ricordi*, were worth one hundred of the sealed type.

As a rival to the Florentine coin, the Doge, Giovanni Dandolo, issued the first gold ducat in Venice as early as 1284, and these two thereafter became the standard gold coins for the whole of Italy, ducats being later issued by both Roman mints, the one attached to the civil authority of the Senate, and the other to the ecclesiastical authority of the Papal Camera.

Eventually, on the establishment of the Florentine Duchy, the ducat officially replaced the florin in Florence itself, although ducats had been in circulation much earlier, and, despite fiscal reforms, the use of the florin apparently persisted long after the downfall of the Republic, since in 1547 Michelangelo remarks, albeit with surprise, on the fact that the price of a house for which negotiations were in train was being quoted in florins *(No. 289)*.

In the latter part of Michelangelo's life the florin and the ducat were both officially superseded by the *scudo*, a gold coin of slightly higher value, which was established under a decree of Pope Paul III in 1540.

The relationship of the gold standard to the silver and base metal coinage was constantly changing. Nevertheless, with the exception of the 'small change', in the form of such coins as *denari* and *quattrini* and the Florentine *crazie* and *barili*, most silver pieces were directly related to the gold ones, and bore therefore varying values in terms of the *lira* system. This statement takes no account of the fact that, owing to the age-old habit (particularly among the illiterate *contadini*) of hoarding, gold, silver and base metal coins of earlier denominations and even of different states, remained in circulation side by side with those of later issues and added still further to the general monetary chaos which the reforms of the Popes, and in particular those of Julius II and Paul III, were designed to remedy.

The fact that the various city states minted their own coinage, as we have seen, adds still further to the difficulty inherent in any classification of Italian coinage at this period. Coins of equal value frequently appear under different names, while coins of the same name may be found to have had different values. In this connection one may instance the *bolognino*. The term originally denoted any Bolognese coin, but during the sixteenth century it was applied exclusively to one, which for all practical purposes had the same value as the Roman *baiocco*; the Florentine ducat, the Roman state ducat and the Roman papal ducat of the Camera, on the other hand, varied slightly from and fluctuated relatively to each other. An even more extreme instance of this in modern times may be seen in the wide differences which exist between the values of the French, Belgian and Swiss *franc*. Fluctuations of this kind in the fiduciary issues of different states were naturally dependent upon the economic vicissitudes to which they were subject, and it was upon such fluctuations that the whole elaborate system of exchange operated by the principal banking houses was founded. It is therefore interesting to note that on several occasions, when he was arranging for transfers of money between Rome and Florence, Michelangelo refers to these variations in exchange rate, which, if we may judge by the proviso expressed in his letter about the transfer to be made by Francesco Borgherini, must have fluctuated both sharply and suddenly *(Nos. 105, 110)*.

The enormous complexity of the silver and base metal coinage and its rapid depreciation had led, long before the beginning of the sixteenth century, to the mercantile practice of conducting international trade and making large-scale transfers in gold. It is in this practice that we find the reason for Michelangelo's constant insistence on the term 'gold florins (or ducats, or *scudi*, as the case might be) *in gold*'. Only so could an exact and equitable exchange rate between Florence and Rome be assured.

The following glossary of coins current in Florence and Rome during the first sixty years of the sixteenth century makes no claims to being complete, but covers only those coins and moneys of account mentioned by Michelangelo in his letters and records. When referring to it, it must be borne in mind that the values of all the coins were subject to fluctuation and that the definitions are not, in consequence, necessarily accurate for the whole period. The information given is based in the main on Eduardo Martinori's exhaustive standard work, *La Moneta*, and on the useful table of Florentine coins given in W. A. Shaw's *History of Currency*, but in certain instances evidence drawn from Michelangelo's own *Ricordi* has led me to differ from these authorities, and I am also indebted to Dr. Kent, of the Coin Room of the British Museum for his comments on the complex problems raised by a consideration of the *grosso* and *grossono*.

Glossary

*Moneys of account, not represented by
actual coins, are enclosed in brackets.*

Baiocco	A Roman silver coin equivalent to the *bolognino* and related to the florin and ducat systems, and not to the *lira* system. With certain fluctuations, it was generally equivalent to one hundredth part of the *fiorino largo d'oro*.
Barile	A purely Florentine silver coin, with a small proportion of alloy, first minted in 1505, when its value was 12 *soldi*, 6 *denari*. By 1531 its value had risen to

13 *soldi*, 4 *denari*, so that it was worth two-thirds of a *lira*. At this rate 10½ *barili* were equivalent to 1 *fiorino largo d'oro*, so that the value of the *barile* was only slightly less than that of the *carlino* etc.

Bolognino	A silver coin equivalent to the *baiocco*, see above. It was current not only in the Romagna, but elsewhere in Italy as well.
Carlino	A silver coin, current in various states (originally issued by rulers of the name of Charles) and having approximately the same value as the *coronato*, the *giulio* and some issues of the *grosso*, that is to say one tenth of a *fiorino largo d'oro* or a *ducato*.
Coronato	A silver coin having the same value as the *giulio* and the *carlino*.
Crazia	A purely Florentine copper coin, containing a small amount of silver, and equal in value to 5 *quattrini* or 20 *denari*. Martinori incorrectly states that it was first minted in the reign of Cosimo I, whereas its circulation as early as 1518 is attested in Michelangelo's *Ricordi*.
Denaro or *Picciolo*	The smallest coin, largely of copper, with a small admixture of silver. By the fourteenth century it was the only surviving coin in Florence of the old *lira* system and was the basic 'penny', worth one twelfth of a *soldo* and one two-hundred-and-fortieth part of a *lira*.
Ducato largo d'oro	The broad gold ducat, a standard gold coin, usually of 24 carats, current throughout most of Italy. It was derived from the Venetian *ducato* first minted in 1284. In 1422 the Florentine Mint had brought the gold content of the re-issued *fiorino* into line with it. During the sixteenth century it gradually replaced the *fiorino*, and was officially issued by the Florentine Mint under Alessandro de' Medici in 1531 and under Cosimo I in 1534, when its value was fixed at 7 *lire*, 10 *soldi*, 8 *denari*. In Rome, where it had been issued under the civil authority of the Senate, it was officially replaced by the *scudo* by a decree of Paul III in 1540 though it still continued in use.
Ducato di Camera, or *Papale*	The papal version of the basic gold coin, issued under the authority of the Camera. It was slightly smaller than the *ducato largo d'oro*, which was generally rated at 1 *ducato di Camera* + 2½%.
Fiorino largo d'oro	The broad gold florin, the standard Florentine gold coin of 24 carats, based on the original gold *fiorino* first minted in 1252. It was later enlarged in size, and many attempts were made to maintain its primacy as the leading

instrument of international trade. In its final form it contained 72 gr. of pure gold, and in 1501 was valued at 7 *lire*, and in 1508 at 7 *lire*, 2 *soldi*. On the establishment of the Duchy it was officially replaced by the *ducato largo d'oro*, but was still in circulation in Florence fifteen years later.

Fiorino di Sugello — The sealed florin represented one of the many Medieval attempts to maintain the standard of the currency. It was apparently still in circulation as late as the early sixteenth century, since Michelangelo in his *Ricordi* mentions that 100 *fiorini di sugello* were equal to 70 *fiorini larghi d'oro in oro*.

Giulio — The julian, a Roman silver coin, issued under the authority of Julius II, and equivalent to the *carlino*, the *coronato* and to certain of the *grossi* or *grossoni* (see below). 10 *giulii* equalled 1 *ducato di moneta*, i.e. a ducat's worth of small change in silver and base metal, and on the introduction of the *scudo*, that coin was valued at 11 *giulii*. 10 *giulii* per month was regarded by Michelangelo as a generous wage for a man or woman servant resident in his house.

Grosso and *Grossono* — The name given to a variety of silver groats of differing weights and values. The *grosso* current in the sixteenth century in Florence was generally equivalent to between a twentieth and a twenty-fourth part of a *fiorino d'oro*, and was therefore worth at that time about 6 *soldi*, 8 *denari* or 7 *soldi*. In 1503 a larger *grossono* minted in Florence appears to have been worth double the current *grosso* at a value of 14 *soldi*, that is, one tenth of a *fiorino largo d'oro*, and was therefore equivalent to the *giulio*, *carlino* and *coronato*. The whole history of the *grosso* and *grossono* is, however, so obscure that it is extremely difficult to make any categorical statement regarding either.

[Lira] — The old *libra* of the original Carolingian system, which had ceased to be represented by any actual coin in the early Middle Ages, and had become a 'money of account'. It was made up of 240 *denari piccioli*, and in the sixteenth century was accounted for at the rate of about 7 to 1 *fiorino* or *ducato*.

Quattrino — A copper coin with a small silver content, worth 4 *denari*.

Scudo — The standard gold coin which in both Roman and Florentine trade superseded the *fiorino largo d'oro* and the *ducato largo d'oro* in the mid-sixteenth century. In 1544 Paul III fixed its value at 11 *giulii*. On May 2nd 1542 a mercantile declaration made before the Governor of Rome decreed that debts contracted in non-gold currencies *(moneta)* between 1538 and 1540 should be settled in gold *scudi* at 5% discount, those contracted between 1540 and

1542 at $7\frac{1}{2}\%$ discount, and all debts contracted thereafter at 10% discount, an eloquent testimony to the continuing depreciation of silver.

[Soldo]   A money of account (see *Lira*) worth 12 *denari*.

M.E.E.

Appendix 4

The 'Monte' and the Banking System

I T is to Italy that most of our contemporary fiscal and banking practices owe their immediate origin, since the commercial supremacy of the Italian city states and the financial genius of their citizens in the early Middle Ages provided a model for the rest of Europe. As early as the eleventh and twelfth centuries the complex system of international trade, operated through the medium of the great Florentine banking houses, was well established, and Venice had already laid the foundation of her political and maritime power upon the prosperity of her merchant princes.

Florentine Taxation and the Public Funds

In the following centuries, while the techniques of banking and accountancy were being perfected by the mercantile houses, a rationalized system of fiscal administration was being developed by the Republic of Florence. The city was at first dependent for its special revenues upon a variety of forced and voluntary loans – *prestanze* – levied upon banks and wealthy private citizens, to supplement the more regular income derived from the *gabelle* (customs dues) and the *catasto* (a property tax assessed on schedules of houses, shops and lands). Both the *gabelle* and the *catasto* were still regular imposts in the time of Michelangelo and are referred to in his letters *(e.g. Nos. 17, 127)* and in the return of his property made in 1534 *(Appendix 6)*. Various special taxes were imposed from time to time, amongst which one of the most unpopular was the *arbitrio*, a form of income tax which was abolished, after a duration of only seventy years, in the reign of Cosimo I. The assessment for the *arbitrio* would appear to have been based on the possession of revenue-producing property beyond a certain size or value, since no mention is made of it in connection with Michelangelo's affairs. Buonarroto, however, appealed against his assessment in 1515 *(No. 96 et seq.)* and the fact that a certain property was subject to it was considered by Michelangelo as a serious objection to its purchase.

In order to reduce the number of special *prestanze*, the Florentine Public Debt was funded in 1222 and in 1344, the operations being financed by the institution of the *Monte Commune* or 'Public Pile', usually alluded to as *il Monte*, and best translated as the Funds. In the Funds, which normally bore interest at 5% and were secured upon the State revenues, the private citizen could hold shares, which were negotiable at fluctuating rates, according to the rise or fall in State credit. Shares were bought and sold in the Mercato Nuovo, and could be exchanged or pledged as security for private loans *(Staley, pp. 190 et seq.)*. The Buonarroti family holdings in the Funds are alluded to by Michelangelo *(e.g. Nos. 3 and 145)* and the method of recording an individual holding in the *Monte* Register is given in a footnote to No. 154.

The Banking System in Florence and Rome

The banks, to which such frequent reference is made by Michelangelo, were those of the fourth and most important class listed by de Roover *(pp. 1–5)*, namely the great merchant banks *(banchi grossi)* which conducted their business indoors *(dentro)* in their own offices, and not at tables in the open Mercato Nuovo. They combined extensive foreign trade with large-scale exchange and banking operations. Although this type of bank did offer certain deposit facilities to important customers, whether in the form of current or deposit accounts on which interest was sometimes, though not invariably, payable, Michelangelo did not normally avail himself of this branch of their services, apparently regarding his capital as being more secure in the safe-keeping of the Hospital of Santa Maria Nuova *(Appendix 5)*.

On two occasions at least, however, funds were held to his credit on deposit in Roman banks. In the first instance he temporarily banked the sum of 2,000 ducats which he had received ostensibly in payment for the completion of the Sistine vault *(Appendix 9)*, but he soon made arrangements for its withdrawal, on the grounds that it was earning no interest and would be better invested in land in Florence *(No. 87)*.

In the second instance, it would appear that the amount due to him upon the completion of the Tomb of Julius II was placed to a special account by the Pope's heirs in the bank of Salvestro da Montaguto and Partners (who seem to have worked in close association with the Covoni bank), from which withdrawals could be made by Michelangelo upon special authorization, consisting of a countersignature by Hieronimo Tiranno, the Duke of Urbino's envoy *(Nos. 247 et seq.)*.

The more usual transactions recorded in the letters take the form of transfers of money from Rome to Florence and, less frequently, from Florence to Rome, to Pisa or to Lucca. These transfers were made by bills of exchange *(lettere di cambio* or *di pagamento)*, a type of financial instrument which had been invented at least as early as the fourteenth century *(Origo, p. 146)*. In making such transfers, Michelangelo would pay the required sum in gold into one of the Roman or Florentine banks, and a bill for the amount in the golden state currency (ducats in Rome, florins and later broad ducats in Florence) was then drawn up by one of the senior members of the bank staff. The bills were holograph and only certain members of the staff were empowered to draw them up *(de Roover, p. 39)*. More than one copy of each bill was usually made (though not necessarily on the same day) and each was despatched by different messengers to ensure that at least one copy would escape the hazards of the bandit-infested roads and arrive at its destination. Each copy was marked with its number as a 'first', 'second', 'third *[bill]* of exchange' *(prima, seconda, terza di cambio)*, and payment could be demanded on whichever came first to hand. This practice is alluded to in No. 58. In No. 93 Michelangelo expresses a doubt as to whether payment would be made at sight, because he was availing himself of the exchange facilities of two banks with which he did not often transact business, and he was therefore allowing for the possibility that the Florentine establishment might insist upon the full period of usance in order to permit them to confirm his credit with their Roman correspondents.

In this connection two points are worthy of note. The first is that Michelangelo constantly varied the banks through which he made his remittances, no less than thirteen Roman houses and nine Florentine ones being mentioned in the letters. The reason for this we may infer from his constant admonitions to his family to keep secret his financial transactions, which, in a small city like Florence, must have been a common subject of speculation. It is therefore understandable that he should prefer not to satisfy the curiosity of his friends and acquaintances, and one of the best means of ensuring privacy in the matter was to use not one but several banks.

The other point of note is that each bank, whether in Rome or Florence, Lucca or Pisa, had its regular correspondent or correspondents in other cities. Where banks had branches in more than one place, transfers were made from one branch to the other, but the vast Medici establishment, which had had, during the fifteenth century, a head office in Florence and branches not only in Rome, Venice and Milan, but also in Geneva, Avignon, Bruges and London, had collapsed before the end of the century, and had no later parallels on a comparable scale. Jacopo Salviati, brother-in-law to Pope Leo X, headed a firm which had at least two branches, one in Florence and one in Pisa. As Salviati himself was frequently resident in Rome, the business of the Florentine branch was in the hands of Giovanni Spina, though whether he was a junior partner or a paid manager *(fattore)* is not clear. In one letter only is he accorded the title *maggiore*, the term usually reserved for partners. In Pisa the office was managed by Francesco Peri who, since he is addressed by Michelangelo as *Maggiore (No. 180)* was presumably a partner. Transactions with the Borgherini bank suggest that transfers were made from the Roman house to a Florentine branch of the same firm, and that Michelangelo's friend, Francesco Borgherini, was a partner in both. The Salviati and the Borgherini seem, however, to have been the exception rather than the rule at this period, for in making transfers from the Gallo bank in Rome, for instance, the bills were sometimes drawn upon Bonifazio Fazzi in Florence, but the earliest transfer recorded in the letters was made in 1497 by Baldassare Balducci, at that time a partner or employee of the Gallo bank, to the Strozzi in Florence. The bank headed by Bonifazio Fazzi, who became a member of the Signoria in October 1529 *(Varchi, p. 239)*, was a business of long standing, since Bonifazio first appears in the letters in 1497 and received a remittance from the Balducci bank on Michelangelo's behalf as late as 1540. A table of the Roman and Florentine banking houses used by Michelangelo is given below.

Remittances between the independent Italian city states, no less than between the Italian cities and foreign centres such as Bruges and Geneva, involved an exchange transaction, since each city state issued its own currency *(see Appendix 3)*. These currencies did not stand at par, but fluctuated according to the individual credit of the states, which in turn depended upon political contingencies and upon the market ratio between gold and silver *(de Roover, p. 59)*.

All important settlements, between states and between different countries, were made in gold, and it was in gold that all Michelangelo's remittances were reckoned. Even when ducats were involved in both sides of a transaction, the number paid in Rome seldom corresponded exactly to the number cashed in Florence, a point which is emphasized both by the mention of a fraction of a *scudo*, and in the direction which Michelangelo almost invariably gives to his family to make out their receipts for the amount shown on the face of a bill (i.e. for the amount in Roman currency) and not for the actual amount received in Florence *(e.g. No. 211).* The discount payable for the use of the bank's transfer facilities would have to be taken into account as well, but the cost of this is nowhere mentioned in the Letters. Even allowing for a discount, however, it was still possible for a bank to make a loss, or a further profit, upon the transaction, and this possibility was envisaged by Michelangelo in Nos. 105 *et seq.*, where, in the case of a transfer from Florence to Rome, he expressed his anxiety that payment should be deferred until the exchange rate was in the Borgherini's favour.

Another service which was offered by the banking houses, and one of which Michelangelo availed himself throughout his life, was that of the transport of mails. In the absence of a state postal service, the bank couriers, who plied regularly between the principal Italian cities, were entrusted with the carriage of private as well as of business letters. We have, unfortunately, no evidence as to the cost of carrying a letter from Rome to Florence, but from the fact that it was Michelangelo's custom to enclose several letters under cover of one to his family, we may assume that the charge was made for the carriage of a single letter packet, irrespective of weight. The time allowed between Rome and Florence varied from three to six days, and it would seem that the letters were usually collected by the recipient from the bank *(No. 72).* The specific direction to Buonarroto 'at the shop of Lorenzo Strozzi, Arte di Lana, in Porta Rossa' appears to contradict this supposition, but it may be remembered that the Strozzi were bankers, and that the wool warehouse in which Buonarroto worked was a subsidiary company of the main banking establishment, to which the mails would be sent in the first instance.

In order to maintain the courier service, each bank must have had a considerable staff of messengers, and a large stable, and it may therefore be conjectured that Lionardo the saddler, a friend of Michelangelo's, who was an employee of the Borgherini bank, although a member of the Guild of Saddlers, was retained by the bank to act as post-master. This must have been a post of considerable responsibility, for speed in the transmission of letters and news was of the utmost importance to the business houses, and it is known that, as the couriers neared their destination, there was frequently a race between them, since the bank which first received news of the sack of Prato or the victory at Pavia, for instance, was in a favourable position to make money on exchange.

The Organization of Business Houses and the Role of Private Investment

Complex as was the organization of the banks, with senior and junior partners, managers, clerks, post-masters and couriers, they remained, like the rest of the business houses in late Medieval and Renaissance Italy, private companies, whose structure was based upon the partnership system. Partnership agreements, of which many are still extant *(de Roover, pp. 5 et seq.)*, were drawn by notaries in accordance with the statutes and customs of the Guild under which the company was operating. In these agreements the amount of the capital *(corpo)* with which the company was to trade was laid down, as was the proportion of each partner's share. Such agreements, made for a term of two or at most three years, were frequently renewed upon different terms upon their expiry. By this means it was possible to get rid of an unsatisfactory junior partner without actual dismissal, or to limit his power, since the variation of the terms might include alteration in the personnel of the company, an increase or decrease of the total capital, or a variation of the partners' shares.

'Subsidiary companies' in the modern sense did not exist. Branches carrying on the same business in different cities, or different businesses in the same city, were in fact separate companies with the same senior partner or partners. Thus, the branches of the Salviati bank in Florence and in Pisa, the Strozzi banking house and wool warehouse, both in Florence, were separate companies. In the latter case, it is clear that Michelangelo envisaged the possibility of obtaining a junior partnership in the wool warehouse for his brother Buonarroto, who later formed his own partnership, as did his son Lionardo, in the wool trade.

The possibility of investing 'in the wool trade' is mentioned several times by Michelangelo in his earlier letters to his nephew *(No. 243)*. Here it is clear that he is not contemplating an opening for Lionardo's employment in the trade, but an investment of capital, to be made in the joint name of the young man and his uncles. This is in accordance with the occasional practice of some partnerships, whereby additional capital was accepted from outside investors. The money so invested was *fuori di corpo* or *sopra corpo*, and was not regarded as forming part of the actual capital. Unless the *sopracorpo* had been invested by the partners themselves (as sometimes happened) and unless it carried no fixed rate of interest but was subject to the normal hazards of profit and loss, such investment tended to be frowned on by the Church, as being usurious in tendency, and it will be noted that throughout his life Michelangelo preferred investment in lands, the revenues from which were never in similar danger of being branded as usurious.

Michelangelo and the Conduct of his Business Affairs

The diversity of financial transactions and business methods reflected in Michelangelo's letters provide an interesting commentary on the economic aspects of an artist's life in Renaissance Italy. Despite his assertion, *'Non è mia professione'*, made when consenting to intervene with Filippo Strozzi on Buonarroto's behalf in the matter of the *arbitrio* assessment *(No. 97)*, Michelangelo is shown to have been both wise and business-like in the administration of his affairs, relying, where his own knowledge failed, upon the advice of business men like Angiolini and del Riccio. In his old age he displayed a certain contempt for income earned by trade and expressed his preference for the display of the family fortune in mansions and landed estates *(No. 272)*, but to the end his business transactions show him to have remained a true Florentine at heart, mindful perhaps that the great patrons of the arts, including the Medici themselves, had founded their fortunes upon business and upon trade.

M.E.E.

Tables of the Roman and Florentine Banks
used by Michelangelo are given on the two following pages.

Roman Bankers and their Florentine Correspondents

Bank	Partners and/or members of staff	First and last date of mention		Florentine Banks
ALTOVITI	Bindo Altoviti	1511	1549	STROZZI; CAPPONI
BALDUCCI	Baldassare Balducci; Giovanni Balducci	1497	1512	FAZZI; BENINTENDI; STROZZI
BANDINI	Francesco Bandini	1556	1561	CAPPONI
BORGHERINI	Pier Francesco Borgherini; Lionardo di Compagno, *called sellaio, post-master*	1515	1518	BORGHERINI
BUSSOTTI	Bartolomeo Bussotti	1555	1555	RINUCCINI
CAVALCANTI & GIRALDI	Bartolomeo Bettini	1496	1549	SALVIATI; STROZZI
COVONI	Antonio Covoni	1542	1545	CAPPONI
GADDI	—	1515	1515	—
GALLO	Jacopo Gallo; Baldassare Balducci	1497	1497	FAZZI
LANFREDINI	Lanfredino Lanfredini; Francesco Perini	1511	1511	ORLANDINI
MONTAGUTO	Salvestro da Montaguto	1542	1545	CAPPONI
RUCELLAI	Pagolo Rucellai	1496	1496	—
STROZZI-ULIVIERI	Luigi del Riccio	1542	1547	ULIVIERI; CAPPONI

Florentine Bankers and their Roman and other Correspondents

Bank	Partners and/or members of staff	First and last date of mention		Roman and other Banks
BENINTENDI	Lorenzo Benintendi	1513	1515	BALDUCCI
BORGHERINI	Pier Francesco Borgherini	1515	1518	BORGHERINI
CAPPONI	Pier di Gino Capponi	1542	1552	ALTOVITI; BANDINI; COVONI; MONTAGUTO STROZZI-ULIVIERI
FAZZI	Bonifazio Fazzi	1497	1540	BALDUCCI; GALLO; Correspondent in Lucca
ORLANDINI	—	1511	1511	LANFREDINI
RINUCCINI	Simone Rinuccini	1555	1555	BUSSOTTI
SALVIATI	Jacopo Salviati; Giovanni Spina	1518	1542	CAVALCANTI & GIRALDI; EREDI di ALAMANNO SALVIATI in Pisa (Francesco Peri, *Maggiore*)
STROZZI	Lorenzo Strozzi; Francesco Strozzi	1511	1542	ALTOVITI; CAVAL-CANTI & GIRALDI
ULIVIERI	Giovanni Ulivieri; Francesco Salvetti; Lionardo del Riccio	1542	1542	STROZZI-ULIVIERI

Appendix 5

The Hospital of Santa Maria Nuova

THE Hospital of Santa Maria Nuova, which still stands, and is situated slightly to the northeast of the Duomo in Florence, was founded in 1285 by Folco Portinari, the father of Dante's Beatrice. In 1329 a formal constitution was drawn up for the Hospital, under which two wards, one for men and one for women, were established. At a later date a medical school was attached to the foundation, which was further enlarged by the addition of a medical library, a museum of drugs and an anatomical theatre. In 1448 the Hospital was expressly charged by the Signoria with the duty of attempting to prevent outbreaks of plague, of caring for the sick and of burying the dead in the event of the plague becoming rife *(Staley, p. 539)*.

Besides the care of the sick and the aged, the Hospital was also entrusted with the welfare of foundlings and with the distribution of food and alms to the poor. Its administration was in the hands of a *Spedalingo* or Warden, who, in accordance with the terms of the constitution, was a priest. He was assisted by a staff of *Conversi* who, though not even in minor orders, were men and women vowed to poverty and celibacy.

As the institution was under the patronage of the Greater Guilds, its revenues were large and at one period of the fifteenth century its Governors were in command of an annual income of over fifteen thousand gold florins. These revenues were mainly the result of investment in land, and in the late fourteenth century a salary of ten florins a month was paid to Ser Lapo Mazzei, the notary who transacted the Hospital's extensive legal business connected with the acquisition, management and sale of land *(Origo, p. 206)*.

The financial security of the Hospital funds was far greater than that which could be enjoyed by the funds of any private institution or of the State itself, since at that time not even 'the greatest rascal on earth would have dared to lay rapacious hands upon money dedicated to the maintenance of the poor'. It therefore became the custom for many Florentine citizens, who sought a safe deposit for their money, allied to a reasonable rate of interest, to 'lend' their capital to the Hospitals of S. Maria Nuova and S. Maria degli Innocenti. In return they received interest at a rate of 5% or more and were able to make withdrawals either on demand or at short notice *(Passerini, Stab., pp. 335–6)*.

This form of deposit account was of particular advantage to artists, architects and other professional men, whose business necessitated long periods of absence from Florence, during which they were not in a position to exercise a personal supervision over their capital, and its desirability had undoubtedly been greatly emphasized by the number of bank failures which had occurred in the latter half of the fifteenth and at the beginning of the sixteenth century. The political uncertainties of the period, moreover, and the constantly renewed threats of

French or Spanish invasion, further reinforced the arguments in favour of 'lending' one's funds to God's poor.

Leonardo da Vinci availed himself of the deposit facilities of S. Maria Nuova and in his Will he bequeathed to his brothers the money deposited there, while Giorgio Vasari, by his Will dated May 25th 1568, left the sum of '500 *scudi*, deposited in the Hospital of the Innocenti in Florence', to the son of a servant, and directed that a further sum of 200 *scudi*, destined for the dowery of his niece, Vittoria, should be deposited at the same hospital at 6% interest, there to accumulate until she was seventeen *(Gaye, II, pp. 502 et seq.)*.

As will be seen from constant references in his letters, Michelangelo likewise used S. Maria Nuova as a deposit bank. His statement in No. 103 that on so large a sum he had never received any interest whatsoever would appear to contradict the statements quoted above, but it is possible that it may be explained by suggesting that the money which Michelangelo had in mind in this instance was a particular sum, deposited on special terms, in order that he might be able to withdraw it on demand.

As the Hospital funds, whether derived from charitable bequests or from private deposits, were largely invested in real estate, the title deeds of which must have been carefully scrutinized by the legal advisers of the two Hospitals, the advantage of purchasing farms and land from or through the Hospitals rather than from private individuals was considerable, since the security of title for properties which had passed from father to son through generations of illiterate peasant proprietors could hardly be guaranteed. Thus, from the Letters it is apparent that by the beginning of the sixteenth century at least, S. Maria Nuova was discharging the dual functions of a deposit bank and of an estate agency, and was in some ways comparable to a modern building society.

The doubts which Michelangelo frequently expressed as to the honesty and helpfulness of the *Spedalingo* receive interesting confirmation in the story of the events which led up to the closing of the deposit facilities at S. Maria Nuova in 1553. As early as 1527 the then *Spedalingo*, Lionardo di Giovanni Buonafè (who had been elected in 1500), was temporarily suspended after an investigation which revealed that he had been lending deposit funds carrying interest at 5% to 8% to his friends, who in turn lent these funds to the State at 12% to 14%. Incidentally, this disgrace did not prevent him from being consecrated Bishop of Cortona in 1531 *(Cantini, VIII, p. 122)*. Permission to renew the practice of receiving deposits was not again granted to S. Maria Nuova until 1666, but apparently no scandal had attached to S. Maria degli Innocenti, which was able throughout the period to offer facilities to depositors.

M.E.E.

Appendix 6

The 'Denunzia de' Beni' of 1534

THE *Denunzia de' Beni* was a form of tax return made for the purpose of the *catasto*, a property tax originally introduced in Florence in 1427. The name of the tax was derived from the verb *catastare*, to accumulate. The returns were entered in ledgers, many of which are still preserved in the Florentine Archives *(Staley, p. 192)*.

Amongst the returns so preserved is that made by Michelangelo in 1534. The main part of it, dealing with the purchase of properties, is given below, but the years, in those cases where they refer to dates between January 1st and March 25th, have been adjusted to conform to New Style usage. The valuations are shown in *fiorini* (f.), *soldi* and *denari*.

Michelangelo di Lodovico di Lionardo di Buonarrota Simone

Inheritance

A farm situated in the parish of Sta. Maria Nuova at Settignano, with house for landowner and labourer and arable land, etc.

22 f.

Properties Acquired and Bought

A farm with labourer's house and arable land, vines, fruit trees and woodland, situated in the parish of St. Stefano at Pazzolatica, a property called Capiteto, bought by me on 27th January 1506.

34 f. 8

A house situated in Via Ghibellina, in the parish of S. Pier Maggiore, bounded on one side by a street and on the other by the hereditament of Ser Alberto and other buildings, for my own occupation.

Another small house adjoining the said house, bought by me from Benedetto d'Andrea Bonsi.

2 f. 1 6

A plot of arable land comprising 8 *staiore [i.e. sufficient for the sowing of 8 bushels of seed]* in the parish of S. Stefano-in-Pane, a property called Stradello, bought by me on 20th June 1512.

3 f. 16

A farm situated in the parish of S. Maria at Settignano, house for labourer, bought 1515.

16 f. 8 3

A farm with house for landlord and labourer, situated in the parish of S. Stefano-in-Pane, a property called La Loggia, bought 28th May 1512.

42 f. 14

A plot of land with a peasant's cottage in the parish of S. Maria at Settignano. I bought it myself 1520.

2 f. 8

A farm with house for labourer, with arable land, vines, in the parish of S. Michelangelo at Rovezzano, a property called Fitto, bought 27th October 1519.
A house in Via Ghibellina, parish of Pier Maggiore.

18 f. 11

A building site situated in Via Mozza, parish of S. Lorenzo, bought from the Chapter of S. Maria del Fiore, 14th July 1518.   *[amount omitted]*

Total —   216 f.   14   3

(For the 'Denunzia dei beni della famiglia de' Buonarroti' in full see Karl Frey in 'Jahrbuch d.p. Kunstsammlungen', VI, 1885, pp. 189–201; for the document in part, as above, together with other notes, additions and details of properties let to various lessors, see Giovanni Gaye 'Carteggio d' Artisti' II, p. 253.)

The Italian Hours

THROUGHOUT the whole of the Renaissance the system employed in Italy for computing time was that known as 'The Italian Hours' – *Ore Italiane*. The day was regarded as beginning at sunset and was divided into twenty-four equal parts. Thus, the beginning of each day, and consequently of each hour, varied every day, and eight hours or fifteen hours, for instance, represented a quite different time in spring, summer, autumn and winter. The hours of daylight were, moreover, broadly divided into *mattina* and *sera*, the former being 'morning' and the latter 'afternoon', rather than 'evening', as in modern Italian. When, therefore, Michelangelo stated that the Pope had been to see him at twenty-one hours in the *sera*, this has to be rendered, having regard to the time of sunset on January 29th in the latitude of Bologna, as three o'clock in the afternoon. The exact equivalent is, in fact, nearer to half-past two, but (perhaps owing to the inaccuracy of the contemporary clocks, which were subject to an error of about fifteen minutes per day) times are normally given by Renaissance writers in whole hours.

In theory the daily variation in the time of sunset necessarily implied, under this system, that the actual minutes in a day varied likewise, increasing with the approach of the summer solstice, and decreasing once it was passed. The natural consequence of this would have been that the length of the hours of each day would have varied proportionately and that only at the equinoxes would the hour have measured exactly sixty minutes. In practice, in order to overcome the difficulty, it is probable that clocks and watches were only readjusted once a week. Such readjustments were made with the aid of the sundial. Sixteenth century portable sundials are included in many horological collections, and the Science Museum in London contains examples made in the latitudes of Rome and Florence, having twenty-four hour dials and adjustments to allow for latitudinal variations in the time of sunset.

The services of the Church were timed according to the Italian hours, and the Ave Maria, sung half an hour after sundown, was therefore the first religious exercise of the new day. This convention served to ensure the maintenance of so awkward and inaccurate a method of time-keeping in Italy long after it had been superseded elsewhere, and even after it had been abandoned in the rest of Italy it was maintained in the Papal States. As late as 1829 Stendhal, in *Les Promenades dans Rome*, remarked on the extreme inconvenience of the system.

M.E.E.

Appendix 8

The Cartoon for 'The Battle of Cascina'

IN 1504 Piero Soderini, who had been appointed Gonfalonier for life, commissioned Michelangelo to paint the second of the two frescoes for the decoration of the great Council Chamber, La Gran' Sala del Consiglio, in the Palazzo della Signoria, or Palazzo Vecchio, as it is now called. The first had already been commissioned from Leonardo da Vinci, who chose as his subject 'The Fight for the Standard' at the Battle of Anghiari (1440), while as a complementary piece, Michelangelo proposed to execute 'The Battle of Cascina' (1364), an episode in the war with Pisa. Both cartoons were completed, but neither fresco was carried out. Leonardo began work on his, but abandoned it to return to Milan before he had got very far, while Michelangelo never proceeded beyond the stage of the finished cartoon.

On being summoned to Rome by Pope Julius II in 1505 Michelangelo was obliged to leave the cartoon unfinished, but during his seven months' stay in Florence after his flight from Rome in April 1506 he was able to complete it. The cartoon was executed in a room assigned to him in the Hospital of the Dyers at Sant' Onofrio and 'when finished, was carried', as Vasari relates, 'to the Pope's Hall *[i.e. the Sala del Papa in Santa Maria Novella]* amid the excitement of artists and to the glory of Michelangelo'. And here, according to Condivi, he left it. It is not therefore to the Gran' Sala del Consiglio that Michelangelo is assumed to refer in two of his letters *(Nos. 42 and 43)* but to the Sala del Papa, the keys of which were held by the Commissary, Tommaso Balducci, and, in his absence, by the second Herald, Messer Angelo di Lorenzo Manfidi da Poppi.

The whereabouts of the cartoon between 1506, when it was completed, and 1515/16, when it disappeared, is however in dispute. In his *Memoriale*, which was published in 1510, Francesco Albertini mentions 'the horses of Leonardo and the designs of Michelangelo' as being in the Gran' Sala del Consiglio, but in his *Il Riposo*, Raffaello Borghini says that Michelangelo's cartoon was first in the Sala del Papa and afterwards in the Casa Medici, to which, according both to Vasari and to Condivi, it was later removed, presumably on the expulsion of Piero Soderini and the return of the Medici to power in 1512. Tolnay's assumption that it was at this date that the cartoon was taken to the Sala del Papa is therefore surely unfounded. Benvenuto Cellini, on the other hand, when speaking of the two cartoons, says that 'one was placed in the Medici Palace and one in the Pope's Hall and while they could be seen there they were the school of all the world'. It may, accordingly, have been Leonardo's cartoon that was taken back at this time to the Pope's Hall, where he had originally worked on the design.

With regard to the disappearance of Michelangelo's cartoon in 1515/16, Vasari, somewhat disingenuously, has provided two accounts of what happened, of which the first has been generally accepted. One is that 'in the great hall of the Medici Palace . . . it was entrusted too freely to the artists, for during the illness of Duke Giuliano *[de' Medici, Duke of Nemours]* it was cut to pieces and scattered in many places'. In the second account he says that it was torn to pieces by Baccio Bandinelli out of hatred and jealousy of Michelangelo – a much less convincing explanation.

That it was 'cut to pieces and scattered in many places' cannot be doubted, but it seems less likely that the work disappeared merely in the absence of Duke Giuliano, who died at the Badia at Fiesole on March 17th 1516, than that it was divided up and used as a basis for some of the fabulous decorations that were erected in honour of the Medici Pope, Leo X, when he made 'his magnificent and triumphal entry into Florence' on November 30th 1515. As Lucca Landucci relates in his *Diario*, for over a month the whole city was given over to preparations for the Pope's arrival, 'holidays and workdays, night and day alike, the noise and commotion went on. . . . Several thousand men were employed and there was not the most humble painter of any kind in Florence whose aid was not required in some way.' In these circumstances, when everyone was preoccupied and invention was at a premium, what could be more probable than that some of the many artists who had access to the great hall of the Medici Palace should have profited by the opportunity to cut up or section the cartoon, in accordance with normal workshop practice, since with the change of regime in Florence and the banishment of Soderini, it might conveniently be assumed that the cartoon would no longer be wanted for execution in fresco. Michelangelo, moreover, had not been resident in Florence for some ten years and the adaptation of his designs to some of the many *archi trionfali con ornati emblemi e figure, opere dei grandi Artisti che aveva Firenze (Capponi, II, p. 323)* which decorated the streets of the city, may well have seemed almost permissible and not wholly out of place.

Appendix 9

Payments for the Painting of the Vault of the Sistine Chapel

THE amount Michelangelo received for the painting of the vault of the Sistine Chapel has been variously computed. According to Condivi, who must have obtained the information from the master himself, and to Vasari likewise, he received 3,000 ducats, some 20 or 25 of which he expended on colours; according both to Pastor and to Dr. Tolnay, whose statements are based on their interpretations of his letter of December 1523 to Ser Giovan Francesco Fattucci *(No. 157)*, of which there are two drafts, he received 6,000 ducats.

In the first version of this letter *(Draft 2)*, on which Tolnay relies initially, Michelangelo wrote as follows – 'Then when I returned to Rome . . . he *[Pope Julius II]* wanted me to paint the vault of Sixtus, on which we were agreed for three thousand ducats *[including expenses]* for a few figures only. Then when I had done some designs it seemed to me that it would turn out a poor affair. Thereupon he gave me a fresh commission . . . *[to]* do what I liked in the vault, which amounted to about as much again. And thus we were agreed.' The second and fuller version is worded slightly differently – 'When I returned to Rome Pope Julius . . . set me to paint the vault of Sixtus and we made a bargain – *patto* – for three thousand ducats. The first design . . . was for twelve Apostles in the lunettes and the usual ornamentations to fill the remaining area. After the work was begun it seemed to me that it would turn out a poor affair. He asked me why. I said, "because they themselves were poor". Then he gave me a new commission – *commissione* – to do what I liked and said he would content me.'

That a formal agreement for the first project originally existed we know from Michelangelo's own *ricordo* dated May 10th 1508 *(Milanesi, p. 563)*. In this entry, recording the receipt of 500 ducats, he notes that he was beginning work 'in accordance with the terms and conditions set forth in a written agreement'. This document, which was countersigned by Michelangelo, was signed on the Pope's behalf by Francesco Alidosi da Pavia, the cardinal who had negotiated with the Signoria about Michelangelo's submission to the Pope at Bologna two years before. Unfortunately it has not survived, so that we know nothing of the terms and conditions laid down in respect of the first project. As to the second, which was merely an extension of the first, we know from a reference in one of Fattucci's letters *(Frey, Briefe, p. 199)* that this was undertaken on the basis of a gentlemen's agreement between Michelangelo and Pope Julius himself.

Although 6,000 ducats is nowhere mentioned (though it might conceivably be argued that an approximate sum is implied), Dr. Tolnay is categorical in his statement on the point. 'We know from Michelangelo's letter to Fattucci', he writes, 'that the artist was to receive according to the first contract 3,000 ducats, which amount was raised to 6,000 ducats in the second contract' *(Tolnay, II, p. 191)*.

All that we know for certain about the payments is that which emerges from Michelangelo's own *Ricordi* and from his letters to his family, in which the sums are either specified or may be inferred on the basis of the amounts he remitted to Florence to be credited to his account at Santa Maria Nuova. These amounts are as follows those shown in brackets being assumed –

Milanesi, p. 563 1508	....	May	....	500 ducats
No. 50 1509	....	September	....	(500)ducats .... 350 remitted
No. 55 1510	....	October	....	500 ducats
No. 57 1511	....	January	....	(500)ducats .... 228 remitted
No. 63 1511	....	October	....	400 ducats
				2,400 ducats

This would leave a balance of 600 ducats to be paid either before or on completion of the work, assuming that he only received the 3,000 ducats recorded by his contemporaries. How, then, does Tolnay account for the additional 3,000 ducats which he says that Michelangelo received? To the 2,400 ducats, which are not in dispute, he adds the undermentioned amounts –

Brought forward			2,400 ducats
(i) *Condivi xxxix* 1510	....	May	500 ducats
(ii) *No. 60* ... 1512	....	January	100 ducats
(iii) *No. 60* ... 1512	....	January	1,000 ducats
(iv) *No. 157* ... 1512	....	May	2,000 ducats
			6,000 ducats

This handsome total is not reached, however, without considerable ingenuity, requiring, as it does, an alteration of Michelangelo's own facts and figures, in the first place, and a disregard of certain qualifying statements he makes about them, in the second. Although I have listed these additional payments in the chronological order preferred by Dr. Tolnay, I propose to comment on them in what I believe to be their correct chronological order, namely this: ii – iii – i – iv.

(ii) This sum of 100 ducats, which is the sum mentioned by Michelangelo in a letter to his father *(No. 60)* as having been remitted to Florence a few days previously, Tolnay believes to be part of the payment he received in October 1511. On this occasion Michelangelo says he received 400 ducats, but Tolnay thinks he must have been wrong, and that he actually received 500, because forsooth, 'he usually received 500 ducats at one time'. He therefore adds in this additional 100 to make up the required amount. In point of fact this 100 ducats is part of the payment made in January 1511, of which 228 ducats had already been remitted to Florence *(No. 57)*. Nor, indeed, would Tolnay ever have been led into supposing that they had anything to do with the October payment, had he not been pleased to imagine that in addition to being wrong in the matter of the amount he received in October, Michelangelo was also wrong in the dating of the said letter, supposing it to be June when in reality it was January, since, as Tolnay puts it, 'Although Michelangelo wrote *giugnio* the content points rather to January'!

(iii) This disingenuous manoeuvre is worth vastly more than a mere 100 ducats, however, since while supporting Tolnay's preference for a later date for 'the June letter', it also improves his calculation, inasmuch as it enables him to add a further sum of 1,000 ducats, the sum which Michelangelo mentioned in the same letter as being due to him on completion of the vault. Now as the said letter is, in fact, dated June *[1511]* and does not belong to the following January, the 400 ducats he said he received in October 1511 must undoubtedly be regarded as being a payment, in part, of the said 1,000 ducats, of which, for reasons that will be given below, the 500 ducats listed in item (i) must similarly be regarded as a part.

(i) The circumstances in which Michelangelo received this sum are related by Condivi. Once, when wishing to go to Florence for the Feast of St. John the Baptist, Michelangelo went to seek leave of the Pope and to ask him for money. In reply to this request Pope Julius demanded when he would finish the painting of the Chapel, to which enquiry Michelangelo replied, as he was wont, 'When I can', whereupon the Pope, who was quick-tempered, struck him with a staff he was holding, saying angrily, 'When I can, when I can, indeed.' But when Michelangelo had returned to his house to make preparations for his departure, Pope Julius fearing what he might do and being anxious only to placate him, sent Accursio *[Francesco de Accurtis]*, a favoured chamberlain, after him with 500 ducats to make the Pope's apologies. These Michelangelo accepted and, as Condivi concludes, 'betook himself to Florence'.

That we may accept this incident as authentic goes without saying, since Condivi can only have learnt of it from Michelangelo himself, and Tolnay is therefore perfectly correct in adding the amount to the undisputed sum of 2,400, thus making a total to date of 2,900 ducats. The only problem in connection with this episode that remains outstanding is that as to the time when it took place. As the Feast of St. John the Baptist, the great Florentine festival, is celebrated on June 24th, this famous interview with Pope Julius must have taken place in the late spring of either 1510, 1511 or 1512.

Taking Frey as his authority *(Studien, p. 99)*, Tolnay accepts 1510 as being the year in question, because according to Frey, Michelangelo was in Florence in the May of that year. He adduces as evidence of this a letter addressed to Michelangelo 'in Florence' by the Cardinal of Pavia, who wrote from Ravenna on the May 3rd 1510. Apart from the fact that Michelangelo's arrival in Florence at the beginning of May for the celebration of the Feast of San Giovanni at the end of June would seem to lack verisimilitude, seeing that he habitually worked under enormous pressure, there is nothing in the Buonarroti correspondence to suggest that he was in Florence at this time, but much to show that he was not, as, for instance, a letter from his father dated June 28th complaining that he had received no answer to his recent letters *(Tolnay, II, p. 229)*. One may therefore wonder whether the Cardinal did in fact address himself to Michelangelo in Florence, when he would, more naturally, expect him to be in

Rome; and on further investigation one finds that he did not. The address, which is given in full by H. Pogatscher in Steinmann *(Sixt. II, p. 714)* shows that it was not addressed to 'Michelangelo in Florence', but to 'Michelangelo, Florentine', thus –

> *Excell. viro d^{mo} Michelangelo Florent [inus] in pictura ac statuaria*
> *arte principi nobis dilectissimo.*

But the year 1510 is ruled out in any case, as is the year 1511 also, because the Pope, being engaged in a prolonged campaign against the French, was absent from Rome between August 17th 1510 and June 27th 1511, so that Michelangelo would have had no opportunity to ask him either for leave or for money at the relevant time.

This leaves us with the year 1512 as the only possibility. From a letter written early in that year *(No. 65)* we know that Michelangelo was hoping for leave and expected to be in Florence for Easter. But while it is clear from the correspondence that he was not there in April there is more evidence than not, indirect though it may be, that he returned home for a brief period in June. Firstly, though this is by no means definitive, there is a gap in the extant correspondence between the letter approving the purchase of the farm from Santa Maria Nuova *(No. 76)* and the next letter *(No. 77)* which is endorsed July 24th 1512. Secondly, we know from the *Denunzia de' Beni (Appendix 6)* that on June 20th 1512 he bought a piece of land in the same parish, which presumably adjoined the farm purchased in May. Now as there is no correspondence dealing with this additional purchase, it seems more than probable that he was in Florence for a *breve permanenza* in June, partly in order to be present at the celebrations on the 24th, and partly in order to inspect the newly acquired property. Moreover, as there is no reason to doubt the truth of the statement that the Pope sent him 500 ducats by Accursio, and as there are no letters dealing with the transfer of all or part of the said money, it seems equally probable that he took at least part of it with him to Florence and himself paid it into his account at Santa Maria Nuova.

(iv) We now come to Tolnay's last item, the exceedingly complicated affair of the 2,000 ducats. In his letter of December 1523, in which he gave Fattucci a somewhat abbreviated account of the last stages of the work on the vault and of the difficulties he had in obtaining the necessary money, Michelangelo referred to the circumstances in which they were paid in these words: '. . . one day when I was complaining to Messer Bernardo da Bibbiena and to Attalante that I could no longer remain in Rome, but must go with God, Messer Bernardo reminded Attalante that he had money to give me in any case. And he had two thousand ducats of the Camera paid to me . . .' As this sum was paid to him shortly after the painting of the vault had been completed, as will be shown later, it seems certain that the Pope had intended 'to content him', not indeed with a payment double the amount originally agreed, but with 2,000 ducats over and above the stipulated 3,000 ducats, a payment with which Michelangelo would undoubtedly have been satisfied. But while initially he accepted the money as being paid in respect of the vault, he afterwards found that he had been tricked and that it had been charged, together with the first 1,000 he had received for the marbles, to the account of the Tomb.

This 2,000 ducats which Tolnay seeks to attribute to the vault cannot, therefore, on Michelangelo's own showing be included among the Sistine payments. We are left, accordingly, with the 2,900 ducats so far reached in our calculations, to which, since there is no question but that he received the agreed 3,000 in full, we must add the outstanding 100 ducats, which we may assume he received immediately on the completion of the work, either at the end of September or the beginning of October 1512. That this must have been the case and that he had not at that point received the 2,000 ducats and had been, albeit temporarily, under the impression that they had been paid in respect of the Sistine, is confirmed by the concluding words of the first draft of the letter to Fattucci and by the bitter disillusionment evident in the letter he wrote to his father on completion of the vault. In the draft he makes this statement, which could not possibly be misunderstood, 'Then when the vault was finished and it came to the emolument, it was not augmented, so that I reckon I am owed several hundreds of ducats . . .'; while in the letter he wrote as follows: 'I have finished the chapel I have been painting; the Pope is very well satisfied; but otherwise things have not turned out for me as I'd hoped. For this I must blame the times which are very unfavourable to our art. I shall not be home for All Saints, because I have not the means to do what I want to do.' In other words, he had not, at this point, received the rewards he had expected at the hands of the Pope, rewards to which he had referred in a letter to his father written a year before *(No. 63)*. And not having the means to set his brothers up in a shop, as he had long promised to do, he had neither the heart nor the courage to return home for the family festival of All Saints. For this, however, he blamed the times as being unfavourable – unfavourable, that is to say, from a financial point of view, as indeed they were. After a protracted campaign against the French in Italy, Julius, who, as Pastor reminds us *(VI, p. 395)*, 'had strained his financial resources to their utmost limit' in his efforts to equip a sufficient army, had inevitably emerged, albeit as the liberator of Italy, with depleted coffers. Though these, incidentally, he did not scruple to replenish, not only by the customary sale of offices and benefices, but, at the instigation of his Datary, Lorenzo Pucci, by the granting of occasional Indulgences.

Although Michelangelo had been disappointed initially, it would appear that Julius, whose regard for him is not in question, had nevertheless intended to reward him for his labours by the payment of an additional 2,000 ducats. The responsibility for seeing that the Pope's wishes in the matter were carried out rested, of course, with the Datary. But that this money was due to him and had not been paid was known, not only to Attalante, a superintendent of St. Peter's, who eventually made the payment (just as it was from Melighini, who held a comparable office, that Michelangelo was accustomed to receive his salary many years later – *see No. 252*), but also to Bernardo Dovizi da Bibbiena, a member of the immediate entourage, who had himself been concerned with the raising of money for the French campaign earlier in the year.

Speculation as to whether or not this payment had been deliberately withheld or might never have been made but for Dovizi's intervention (which Michelangelo himself seems to have thought, if we may judge, not so much by the scale of the 'rake-off' he handed out both to Dovizi and to Attalante, as by the fact that he handed out a 'rake-off' at all), would be pointless, were it not that he subsequently found that he had been tricked. But this being so, it is to the character of Pucci and to the relationship in which he afterwards stood to Michelangelo that we must look for a solution of the problem.

Lorenzo d'Antonio Pucci (1458–1531), who was raised to the purple by Leo X and thereafter became better known as Cardinal Santiquattro *[Coronati]*, was a man highly endowed both physically and intellectually, but his fine appearance and excellent abilities were marred by an avarice that knew no bounds. He was notorious for the sale of Indulgences and during the pontificate of Adrian VI was actually charged with peculation *(Cardella, IV, p. 2)*. He was, however, restored to favour by Clement VII, who in 1524 appointed him to the office of Grand Penitentiary, an office which he did not fail to exploit to the full, as is shown, for example, by a private letter of his to a friend, which was discovered in the Strozzi archives *(Litta, x, tav. v)*. But while it cannot be asserted that he intended to appropriate the money for his own use or for some other purpose, knowing that Michelangelo was unaware of the Pope's intentions and that the Pope himself was virtually dying, it is at least pertinent that at the time Michelangelo received the money, probably towards the end of October 1512, Pucci himself was incurring enormous expense at his villa at Uliveto in the entertainment of Maximilian's ambassador, Matthias Lang, Bishop of Gurk, who was on his way to Rome to receive the Cardinal's hat *(Cambi, II, p. 338)*.

All this, though indicative, is scarcely sufficient to prove that he originally intended to cheat Michelangelo; but taken in conjunction with the fact that he was shortly afterwards appointed as one of the Pope's executors and as such, together with the Pope's nephew, Lionardo Grosso della Rovere, became responsible for the completion of the Tomb of Julius, it becomes more significant.

On this basis it can only be concluded that the 2,000 ducats were paid to Michelangelo, possibly during Pucci's absence from Rome, certainly without his knowledge or authority; that they were entered into the papal accounts as having been paid to him, but without specification as to the work in respect of which they were paid; and that being in a position to do so, Pucci later took advantage of this and proceeded to charge what had been meant as a retrospective payment for the Sistine vault as a prospective payment for the Tomb of Julius.

It may therefore be stated categorically that Michelangelo received 3,000 ducats for the painting of the vault of the Sistine Chapel, as recorded by Condivi and Vasari, and *not* 6,000 ducats, as alleged by Pastor and Tolnay; the payments being made up as follows –

Milanesi, p. 563	1508	May	. . . .	500 ducats
No. 50	1509	September	. . . .	(500) ducats
No. 55	1510	October	. . . .	500 ducats
No. 57	1511	January	. . . .	(500) ducats
No. 63	1511	October	. . . .	400 ducats
Condivi xxxix	1512	(June)	. . . .	500 ducats
—	1512	(October)	. . . .	(100) ducats
				3,000 ducats

In conclusion, it may be observed that had he been paid at the rate of 1,500 ducats a year, that is 6,000 ducats in all, he would have had no cause for complaint, since he would have been in receipt of a higher salary than he later received, when as supreme architect, painter, and sculptor to Pope Paul III he did not receive more than 1,200 ducats a year, a salary with which he was well content.

Appendix 10

The Historical Prelude to the Sack of Prato

I N November 1494, two years after the death of his father, Lorenzo the Magnificent, Piero de' Medici, called the Unfortunate, was banished from Florence for life, the populace having turned violently against him, though 'why this should be', Lucca Landucci remarked in his *Diario*, 'the Lord alone knows'. The revolt against Piero was, however, merely the culmination of an increasing and largely justifiable hostility.

During the next few years, and particularly after the execution of Savonarola in 1498, the city remained without a leader and became, as a result, a scene of ever-growing tumult and strife until in 1502 the Republic was finally reduced to the hitherto unthinkable expedient of appointing a Gonfalonier for life, which it did in the person of Piero Soderini.

During this period Italy was the battleground, under one pretext or another, for the contending claims to domination in the peninsula of Maximilian, the Emperor-elect, of Louis XII of France and of Ferdinand II of Spain, while to add to the general confusion Julius II, the warrior Pope, who had succeeded to the pontificate, was intent upon reasserting the temporal power of the Church and extending her possessions. With this end in view he continually entered into alliances, first with one side and then with another. Having first of all been allied in the League of Cambrai with the Empire and France against Venice, the Pope, having subdued the Republic, then changed sides and entered into the Holy League (Holy because the Pope *qua* Pope was the head of it) and together with the Empire and Spain turned against France. In revenge Louis lent his support to certain disaffected cardinals in an attempt to summon an Oecumenical Council to depose Julius, which with Florentine permission (Florence and Ferrara being allied with France) they proposed to hold at Pisa. The Pope was furious and immediately placed first Pisa and then Florence under an interdict. In the case of Florence this was lifted two months later, towards the end of November 1511, but was reimposed, 'the city remaining under the severe displeasure of the Pope, who was determined to reduce her to obedience and to impose his will'. As soon as he had driven the French from Italy, which, despite reverses, he succeeded in doing by the end of July 1512, he accordingly turned his attention to Florence and ordered the advance into Tuscany of his Spanish allies under the command of Raimondo da Cardona, Viceroy of Naples. Cardona immediately laid siege to Prato which, after a resistance of only twenty-four hours, fell to the besiegers. The carnage which followed became a byword in Italy; for such were the atrocities committed by the Spaniards and such the number and size of the ransoms they demanded that they were said to be without parallel in history.

In order to save Florence from a like fate, the Signoria instantly despatched messengers to

247

the Viceroy to treat for terms. These had been previously agreed with the Holy League and admitted of no compromise. As the price of their exemption from attack the Florentines were required to join the Holy League and to pay an indemnity of sixty thousand florins, which amount was subsequently raised to one hundred and fifty thousand in all; to dismiss the Gonfalonier, Piero Soderini, and to permit the Medici to return to Florence, for only thus, it was thought, could the Florentine alliance with France be severed once and for all. These terms the city had no option but to accept.

Thus it was that after the exile of eighteen years the Medici again returned to Florence in the persons of Giuliano, third son of Lorenzo the Magnificent, who arrived on September 1st, and of his elder brother, Cardinal Giovanni de' Medici (afterwards Leo X), who on September 14th made a formal entry into the city.

The Tomb of Pope Julius II : 1505-1545

Part I 1505-1532

THE Tomb of the della Rovere Pope, Julius II, was commissioned in 1505 and completed in 1545. During the forty years, throughout which Michelangelo was under contract to Julius and his heirs, the project underwent one change after another, until in the end the monument erected in San Pietro in Vincoli emerged as little more than a travesty of the original design. In addition to the preliminary agreement for its execution, there were four contracts and prolonged negotiations for another, which came to nothing. The Tragedy of the Tomb, as Condivi called it, was thus the great tragedy of Michelangelo's life.

1505-1513. The Original Commission

The history of this commission, which is told by Michelangelo himself in various letters written at various times during its execution, began in March 1505 or perhaps a little earlier. At that time he was under contract to the Signoria in Florence, whence he was summoned to Rome by Pope Julius II and entrusted with the execution of his Tomb.

If a written contract for the work was ever drawn up, it has not survived, and we are therefore dependent upon Condivi for what we know of the original design. From him we learn that the monument, which was to be free-standing and was to include more than forty figures, was conceived on so stupendous a scale that the Pope would be satisfied with nothing less than the rebuilding of St. Peter's to contain it. Despite the ambitious nature of the undertaking, the time stipulated for its completion was five years (*No. 8*) and the price estimated ten thousand ducats (*Draft 2*).

Having accepted the commission, Michelangelo left for Carrara, where he remained from April to December 1505, to supervise the quarrying of the immense amount of marble he required. Part of this he had transported to the Piazza of St. Peter, while part of it remained at the Ripa, where it was unloaded. At the beginning of the following year he began work. Scarcely had he done so, however, when the first act of the Tragedy began.

Finding himself without money to defray the heavy costs with which he was faced on his return to Rome, he naturally sought an audience with the Pope, by whom he had previously been treated with unusual cordiality. But after several unsuccessful attempts to gain admission to the audience chamber, he was finally turned away by the express order of the Pope himself *(Nos. 8 and 227)*. This was more than he could brook; so, having given orders for the sale of his goods, he immediately took horse and rode post to Florence, which he reached in the middle of April 1506. For six months he defied the Pope's command to return, but by order of the Signoria he was eventually compelled to make his submission, which he did at Bologna in the following November. During the next six years, while remaining in the service of the Pope, he was occupied first of all in Bologna with the execution of the colossal bronze statue of the Pontiff for the façade of San Petronio, and then in Rome with the painting of the Sistine vault.

According to Michelangelo, it was through the envy of Bramante and of his compatriot, Raphael of Urbino, that the Pope had been persuaded to suspend work on the Tomb in 1506, the pretext being that it was not propitious to proceed with it during his lifetime. Six years later, however, circumstances had changed. By the early summer of 1512 Julius was already aware that his days were drawing to a close, and on the eve of Pentecost he informed his Master of Ceremonies, Paris de Grassis, that he no longer felt able to officiate at public ceremonies. On the completion of the Sistine vault Michelangelo was accordingly required to return to the project of the Tomb, which the Pope now wished to have executed on a smaller scale. There is therefore little doubt that it was upon the drawings for a revised version that he was engaged when on November 5th he wrote to his father saying, 'I am well, thank God, and working' *(No. 86)*.

At the beginning of 1513, after a brief visit to Florence, he opened negotiations for the acquisition of a house in the Macello de' Corvi (the house in which he lived, when in Rome, for the rest of his life), which was purchased for him at the expense of the della Rovere family. Here it was proposed that he should work the marbles for the Tomb which the Pope desired, after all, to have erected in the former Sistine Chapel where his uncle, Sixtus IV, was buried. A bull to this effect was issued on February 19th, but two days later, in the early hours of Monday, February 21st, Julius expired. In his will he left a sum of 10,000 ducats for the execution of his monument, which was not, however, to be completed until thirty-two years later.

1513-1516. *First Contract with the Heirs of Julius II*

On May 6th 1513, two months after the elevation of Giovanni de' Medici as Pope Leo X, Michelangelo entered into a new contract for the execution of the Tomb with the heirs and executors of the late Pope. These were his nephew, Lionardo Grosso della Rovere, Bishop of Agen, who was commonly known as Cardinal Aginensis, and Lorenzo Pucci, the papal Datary, who as Cardinal Santiquattro Coronati figures amusingly in Fattucci's correspondence with Michelangelo as S4°.

According to Condivi, the executors 'had new designs prepared, the first one appearing to them to be too large'; but in two of his letters *(Nos. 157 and 227)* Michelangelo categorically states that the work was to be on a larger scale, that is, larger than the one that had been proposed for erection in the former Sistine Chapel. It was still to include forty colossal figures, but instead of being free-standing, it was to be attached to the wall by one of the four faces. The price was increased from 10,000 to 16,500 ducats and the time specified for its completion extended to seven years. The main condition imposed in the contract was that Michelangelo should undertake no work that would interfere with the fulfilment of his obligations *(Milanesi, p. 635)*.

At first all went well. Leo X was on excellent terms with Francesco Maria della Rovere, a nephew of Pope Julius and reigning Duke of Urbino, and Michelangelo was left in peace to proceed with the work from 1513 to 1516. During this time he executed the great *Moses*, which forms part of the Julius monument in San Pietro in Vincoli, and the two *Captives*, which are now in the Louvre. In 1515, however, the good relations between the Pope and the Duke were disrupted by the latter's refusal to support the Pope in his war against the French in Lombardy. In revenge Leo excommunicated him and, having deprived him of his Duchy, bestowed it upon his own nephew, Lorenzo de' Medici, who was henceforth known as the Duke of Urbino. This was in March 1516.

1516-1522. *Second Contract with the Heirs of Julius II*

Whether it was primarily this reversal of the della Rovere fortunes which led to the cancellation of the first contract with the heirs remains obscure. More probably this was only one of several reasons which contributed to the drawing up of a new agreement on July 8th 1516 between the executors, Cardinals Aginensis and Santiquattro, on the one hand, and Michelangelo, on the other *(Milanesi, p. 644)*.

According to the terms of the new contract the monument was to be drastically reduced in size. A new model of entirely different proportions was agreed upon, while instead of forty, only twenty-two figures were specified. It must be to this contract, therefore, and not to the previous one, that Condivi was referring when he said that the scale of the first project appeared to the executors to be too large. Notwithstanding this curtailment of the project, the time allowed for its completion was extended to nine years as from the date of the former contract, that is to say, as from May 6th 1513, though the amount stipulated for Michelangelo's remuneration and expenses remained the same, of which amount, namely 16,500 ducats, he acknowledged receipt of 3,000. In addition, the house in the Regione di Treve, near Santa Maria di Loreto, was placed rent free at his disposal for the purpose of working the marbles for the Tomb, though he was left free to execute the work elsewhere, in Florence, in Pisa, or in Carrara, as he pleased. Incidentally, it should perhaps be added that this house and the one in the Macello de' Corvi are one and the same and not two separate properties, as has hitherto been supposed, the situation of the first being identical with that of the second, as may easily be ascertained by anyone who takes the trouble to search out the matter. Finally, prominence was again given to the clause whereby Michelangelo promised not to accept any work on a scale large enough to interfere with the completion of the Tomb within the specified time.

As far as the executors were concerned, there may well have been other reasons besides a reversal of family fortune which led them to seek a revision of the first contract. In the first place, they may have come to the conclusion (now that Julius had been dead for three years) that the first project was altogether too grandiose; secondly, they may have realized the difficulties they would probably encounter in erecting a monument on so large a scale, either in St. Peter's or elsewhere; thirdly, they may have doubted Michelangelo's ability to complete so formidable a task in anything like the stipulated time; and lastly they may have anticipated Leo's desire to employ the greatest master in Europe on some enterprise other than that of perpetuating the glories of a house with which he was now at enmity. Thus there are plausible reasons for thinking that it was the heirs and executors and *not* the artist who sought a revision of the first contract. The very terms of the preamble, as summarized for Michelangelo in the Italian version, are, moreover, such as to suggest this – '*E volendo detti reverendissimi Cardinali come esecutori prefati transigere e fare nuova convenzione . . . e di nuovo convenire sopra le cose premisse . . .*' (*Milanesi, p. 649*), quite apart from the terms of the contract, such as that whereby no reduction was made in the price, while Michelangelo was left free to execute the monument wherever he chose.

As to Michelangelo's part in the affair, we know from a letter to Buonarroto, dated June 16th 1515 *(No. 97)* in which he says, 'I must make a great effort here this summer to finish the work as soon as possible, because afterwards I anticipate having to enter the service of the Pope', that he already feared some interruption of his work on the Tomb, now that the good relations which had existed between the Pope and the Duke were at an end. Perhaps Leo had already intimated his desire to employ him on some enterprise of his own, though the façade of San Lorenzo was not, of course, in question at this time, since it was only after the Pope's visit to Florence at the end of 1515 and the beginning of 1516 that the project was mooted.

According to Tolnay, who is at pains to discredit Michelangelo whenever possible, it was Michelangelo himself 'who took the initiative, probably at the end of September 1516, and himself expressed the wish to execute the façade' *(Tolnay, IV, pp. 44 et seq.)*. He then goes on to say that as Michelangelo could not execute two such projects as the Tomb and the façade, 'it became necessary for him to have the Tomb reduced to dimensions which would enable him to work on both simultaneously. The contract of July 1516 . . . was drawn up for this purpose.'

Now assuming Tolnay's thesis to be correct, what exactly does it amount to? Briefly this – that as soon as Michelangelo learnt of the Duke's discomfiture, self-interest prompted him to turn his attention to serving the Pope, as he felt that 'he could no longer continue to work exclusively for the destitute della Rovere family'. Wishing to undertake the façade (though having, be it understood, no guarantee of obtaining the commission) he therefore entered into negotiations with the heirs of Julius for a new contract in July 1516. Yet, having obtained the required concessions in respect of the Tomb, if Tolnay is to be credited, he apparently made no move in the matter of the façade until the end of September, notwithstanding the fact that several of the leading architects had already been invited to submit designs; among them 'Baccio d'Agnolo, Architect of the Cathedral *[i.e. architect to the Duomo]*, Antonio da San

Gallo, Andrea and Jacopo Sansovino'. We are assured, however, that although he succeeded in his efforts to obtain the commission, 'the artist paid a high price for this compromise', since in the end 'he neither went on with the Tomb, nor did he execute the façade'. So much for Tolnay's thesis. How, then, does it fit the facts, in so far as these can be ascertained?

As we have already seen, there are clear indications that it was the heirs, and not Michelangelo, who opened negotiations for a new contract, the first clause of which is to the effect that Michelangelo promised to undertake no work on a scale to interfere with the completion of the Tomb within the specified time – '*Michael Angelus promisit aliquod opus non capere saltim magni momenti, quo mediante, impediatur fabrica prefata, sed prius sepultura prefata facere et finire infra certum tempus*' *(Milanesi, p. 645)*. Now, even if everything we know of Michelangelo's character were not opposed to the view that he would give an undertaking to this effect, when in fact (as Tolnay supposes) he was negotiating the new contract with the express purpose of accepting the commission for the façade, it would still be somewhat anomalous, under the (assumed) circumstances, that prominence should be given to this clause.

In order to clarify the position in regard to Michelangelo's intentions at this time, we must first of all consider his movements after the negotiation of the new contract. Shortly after its terms had been agreed Michelangelo left for Florence en route for Carrara in order to quarry the new marble he required for the Tomb. Thereafter, he went backwards and forwards between Florence and Carrara, where on September 5th he rented a house from Francesco da Pellicaia, with the intention of executing some of the work there. But towards the end of the month he wrote to his father *(No. 112)* saying that owing to some unpleasantness he had encountered, his movements were undecided, and that he might go either to Pisa or back to Rome. At this time, therefore, Michelangelo's attention was still fixed on the Tomb, though there is no disputing that he stood in need of a good deal of encouragement to proceed with it after yet a third change in the specifications, if we may judge from the tenor of the letters he received from his friend, Lionardo the saddler, during this period. On August 9th, for instance, shortly after Michelangelo's departure from Rome, Lionardo wrote urging him to set himself to the task wholeheartedly, 'in order to give the lie to those who say you have gone off and will never bring it to completion' *(Frey, Briefe, p. 30)*.

At this time the question of the façade of San Lorenzo and of the masters likely to be asked to undertake it was still a matter of speculation, but on October 7th the question appeared to be settled, when Domenico Buoninsegni wrote to Baccio d'Agnolo signifying the Pope's intention of entrusting it to himself and Michelangelo jointly *(Frey, Briefe, pp. 35 et seq.)*. This letter, which was written at Montefiascone whither the Pope had betaken himself to indulge his passion for the chase (greatly to the consternation of his Master of Ceremonies, Paris de Grassis, 'without a stole, without a rochet, and what is worse in boots'), was forwarded by Baccio to Michelangelo, who apparently received the announcement with a storm of protest. For although Michelangelo's letter, the most crucial document of the whole correspondence, has not survived, much can be gathered from Buoninsegni's reply to it, written in Rome on November 3rd. In this letter Buoninsegni seems anxious to placate him, saying that from what he has heard the Pope would be satisfied if the principal figures were by his hand, the rest being allocated to others, if he supplied the models. He also notes that Michelangelo had informed Baccio that he might do as he pleased with the actual façade.

Although the necessity of proceeding to Rome to discuss the project had been impressed upon him from October onwards (Baccio having declined to go alone), Michelangelo delayed his departure until the beginning of December. On his arrival he was constrained to prepare designs of his own for the façade, and these having been approved by the Pope, he was required to undertake the commission. At this 'he made all the resistance he could, saying that he was bound to Cardinals Santiquattro and Aginensis and could not fail them. But the Pope, who was determined in this matter replied, "Leave me to deal with them; I will content them".' Then, as Condivi, who like Vasari was at pains to emphasize Michelangelo's unwillingness to undertake the task, goes on to say, 'he sent for both of them and made them release Michelangelo, much to the sorrow of himself and the Cardinals. . . . In this fashion, weeping, Michelangelo left the Tomb and betook himself to Florence' *(Condivi, xxxix)*. The only concession that he and the Cardinals were able to obtain was that the marbles for the Tomb should be transported to Florence at Leo's expense, so that Michelangelo could work on them in such time as remained at his disposal – an added proof that it was at the Pope's wish and not of his own volition that he entered upon the undertaking.

This account of what happened is at variance, however, with that given by Justi and accepted in turn by Pastor, Tolnay and others, who base themselves unreservedly upon the letter which Domenico Buoninsegni addressed to Michelangelo from Rome on November 21st 1516. In this letter Buoninsegni reminds him that it was he who took the initiative when they were in Florence together and had himself expressed a desire to execute the façade and that, in accordance with this expressed desire, he, Buoninsegni, had spoken to the Cardinal, who had consulted the Pope, who had immediately intimated his intention of entrusting the work to Baccio jointly with Michelangelo himself.

In view of this unequivocal statement there can be no denying that Tolnay, like others before him, is fully justified in asserting that Michelangelo himself took the initiative in the matter of the façade, but like everyone else, he seems to have overlooked the fact that there is more to Buoninsegni's letter than this, since it is mainly concerned with reproaching Michelangelo *for having changed his mind*, delayed his journey to Rome and sought to decline the commission for the actual façade in favour of Baccio – all no doubt extremely tiresome and provoking for Buoninsegni, who prided himself on not having lost his temper *(Frey, Briefe, p. 47)*.

So that while Michelangelo cannot be entirely exonerated, inasmuch as it was he who approached the Pope in the first instance, neither he nor Leo is deserving of the blame that has commonly been attached to each of them, since the history of the commission, as generally related, is confused and in many respects inaccurate.

The position in regard to the allegations that have been made can now be summarized as follows. *(i)* The new contract for the Tomb of Julius, which was drawn up in July 1516, was negotiated at the instance of the heirs and not at Michelangelo's request, and was in no way connected with the façade of San Lorenzo. *(ii)* Leo did not originally approach Michelangelo in respect of the commission for the façade and had no wish, as is generally asserted, either to prevent him from fulfilling his obligations to the heirs or to keep him in Florence. *(iii)* While in Florence, prior to leaving for Carrara, Michelangelo, perhaps on a sudden impulse, certainly in a rash moment, expressed a desire, either to execute the façade as a whole (since we have only Buoninsegni's word for it, and that, as we know, is not entirely to be trusted) or more probably to execute some of the figures for it. The latter, though not the former proposal, would have been entirely consonant with the terms of the newly concluded contract, which did not preclude him from accepting other commissions, but only such as might be likely to *impede* the completion of the Tomb within the stipulated time. *(iv)* On receiving the commission jointly with Baccio, Michelangelo did everything in his power to repudiate it, either because he now realized the rashness of the move he had made, or because he found himself more closely associated with it than he had ever intended to be, which seems the more likely interpretation of what occurred. *(v)* But Leo, having embraced an unlooked for opportunity to employ Michelangelo in his service, was not thereafter to be denied.

1522-1526. Negotiations for a Third Contract

From the end of 1516 onwards Michelangelo, contrary to his original inclinations, was kept wholly occupied with the Pope's affairs; first of all with the quarrying of the marbles for the façade of San Lorenzo, and then, after the cancellation of this contract in March 1520, with the work at the New Sacristy. It is therefore small wonder that except for the blocking out of various figures for the monument, the Tomb of Julius was no nearer completion when the contract expired than it had been nine years earlier. It was therefore singularly unfortunate that the Medici Pope, Leo X, on whose support Michelangelo might have counted, died suddenly in December 1521, five months before the Tomb was due to be completed. With the demise of Pope Leo the position of the della Rovere family was greatly strengthened. Shortly afterwards Francesco Maria regained his Duchy, in which he was later confirmed by the new Pope, Adrian VI. So that, when the 1516 contract expired on May 6th 1522, the dissatisfied heirs of Julius lost little or no time in pressing their claims and demanded, not unreasonably, that if Michelangelo could not complete the Tomb, he should repay the money he had received, plus the accumulated interest.

Michelangelo, who had neither the wish nor the intention to default, and who as early as 1518 had himself said that he had become an impostor against his will, was completely distraught. His friends in Rome intervened on his behalf, and in November 1522 Jacopo Salviati wrote to him in terms of affectionate regard, assuring him of his full support and telling him of the interviews he had had with Girolamo Staccioli da Urbino, protonotary of the heirs of Cardinal Aginensis, who had died on September 27th 1520. Unfortunately for Michelangelo, the new Pope was in sympathy with the heirs, who prepared a *motu proprio* for his signature, probably in April 1523 when the Duke was invested with his estates *(Sanuto, xxxiv, 54)*. It seems probable that the *motu proprio*, ordering Michelangelo to fulfil his obligations in one way or in the other, was never, in fact, signed, but this cannot be established until the Registers of the pontificate of Adrian VI are published. Negotiations were then opened between Cardinal Santiquattro, acting for the Duke of Urbino, and Jacopo Bartolomeo della Rovere, brother of Aginensis, on the one hand, and the Florentine, Giovan Francesco Fattucci, a chaplain of Santa Maria del Fiore, who had been appointed to act for Michelangelo, on the other.

A protracted correspondence between the parties ensued and during the four years, throughout which negotiations were carried on, various demands, proposals and concessions were made on both sides. Happily, in Clement VII, who had succeeded Adrian VI in November 1523, Michelangelo found a powerful ally whose influence was such that, after an interview with the Pope, Cardinal Santiquattro, who had formerly been hostile, virtually became Michelangelo's advocate, for, as Lionardo the saddler told him in his letter of March 21st 1524 *(Frey, Briefe, p. 217)*: 'Pucci wants everything you want, and will find a way to reach an honourable and advantageous settlement.'

Despite Santiquattro's goodwill, a lawsuit was nevertheless threatened the following year, whereupon Michelangelo became so desperate that he wrote to Giovanni Spina *(No. 168)* proposing to assume that he was in the wrong and had lost the case, and offering to repay at least some part of the money he had received in order that the heirs might employ others to execute the work. Unfortunately for his peace of mind, as it afterwards proved, his friends, notably Jacopo Salviati and Lionardo the saddler, dissuaded him from pursuing this course and the matter dragged on.

Of the 16,500 *scudi* which Michelangelo was to receive for the Tomb, 8,500 had been paid and one of the matters in dispute concerned the payment of the balance. For Michelangelo it was contended that the work could not proceed unless the remaining 8,000 were deposited; for the della Rovere family that they were unwilling to pay a *quattrino* more. There was also the question of the house in the Macello de' Corvi, which Clement maintained that Michelangelo should have in lieu of the payments he would have received from Cardinal Aginensis, had Aginensis not died when he did. Finally, however, these matters were agreed in Michelangelo's favour and in September 1525 he expressed himself as being agreeable to the suggestion that he should execute a wall tomb on the basis of those of Pius II and Pius III, which were then in St. Peter's and are now in Sant' Andrea della Valle. There was then some delay, while Fattucci had drawings made of the tombs, which were to serve as prototypes, and a further delay while Michelangelo prepared a new design for the approval of the Duke and of Messer Bartolomeo della Rovere. Once they had approved these designs, as Fattucci assured him on October 30th 1525, they would annul the contract of Aginensis and draw up a new one *(Frey, Briefe, p. 262)*.

Notwithstanding the pressure of work on the Medici Tombs and on the Library at San Lorenzo, Michelangelo seems to have been an unconscionable time in preparing the new design, which was not sent off until the middle of October of the following year. He addressed it to Jacopo Salviati, who, immediately on receiving it, went in search of Girolamo Staccioli, the Duke's agent, whom he found ill in bed. For this reason the matter was temporarily held in abeyance. By the middle of November Staccioli was still not well enough to proceed with it and, as Michelangelo's ill luck would have it, it was already too late. On December 8th,

Fattucci wrote to Giovanni Spina saying, 'Michelangelo's affairs remain the same, owing to the present troubles'. That is to say, everything was by this time at a standstill, owing to the course of political events, which culminated in the terrible sack of Rome in May of the following year. Thus, after four years of anxious negotiation, and at a time when agreement on all points had virtually been reached, Michelangelo failed at the last moment to obtain the release from the so-called 'Aginensis Contract' of 1516, which he had so passionately desired.

1526-1532. *The Third Contract with the Heirs of Julius II*

Owing first of all to the sack of Rome, and then to the siege of Florence *(see Appendixes 19 and 21)*, there were no further developments in the Julius affair until 1532, but as soon as things began to settle down again the old anxieties were renewed and negotiations over the Tomb were once more reopened. This time Michelangelo's friend and *compar*, Sebastiano Luciani, acted as his go-between with Girolamo Staccioli, who continued to act as the Duke of Urbino's agent.

In a letter dated April 29th 1531 *(Milanesi, Corr., p. 42)*, Sebastiano wrote as follows, 'On my way to Rome I met a painter at Pesaro, who is in the service of the Duke of Urbino, called Girolamo Genga. He is an honest man and obviously cherishes an affection for you. As he believes I have a good deal of influence with you, he told me he could be a means of the Duke's coming to terms with you over the Julius affair, which his lordship seems to have much at heart. I replied that the work was well advanced, but that 8,000 ducats were wanting to complete it, and there was no-one who could be applied to for the money. He answered me that the Duke would advance it, but that he feared to lose both the money and the work, and appeared to be very angry about it. After a long discussion he asked me whether the work couldn't be reduced, so as to satisfy both parties. I replied that he must discuss it with you.' After further correspondence, Sebastiano, who had by this time been appointed to the office of *Piombatore*, wrote reporting his negotiations with the Duke's agent, who had returned to Rome from Urbino, as follows: 'He treated me to a spate of words, and said in conclusion that he had offered His Excellency the Duke a choice – that you were willing to complete the Tomb of Julius according to the terms of the contract made with Aginensis, that is the large project, but that you must be provided with the rest of the money. The Duke replied that he could not provide the rest and would be better satisfied if you would put the second project into execution, that is to say, that the work should be reduced to the value of the amount you have received . . . and that the Duke wished you to do a design of the project on the basis of which he would decide. I replied stoutly . . . that you were not a man to provide designs of projects, models and such like bagatelles, and that His Excellency the Duke could very well rest content to see you disposed to execute the work according to the existing design.' In this view the agent concurred and Sebastiano went on to outline the terms of the new contract provisionally agreed. A further stipulation was also made, to the effect that the figures for the Tomb, which had been blocked out in Florence, should be brought to Rome, where the Tomb was to be completed. In reply to this letter, which was written some time between October 30th and November 21st 1531 *(Milanesi, Corr., p. 45)*, Michelangelo wrote expressing his desire to hand over the work to others and to be quit of the whole thing *(No. 186)*. This greatly upset Sebastiano, who, in a letter dated December 5th *(ibid., p. 74)*, assured him that the heirs would never agree to such a proposal and that without a 'little of your shadow', they would never reach agreement. The correspondence continued until April 1532 when Michelangelo finally left for Rome. He remained there until the 29th, the day on which, in the presence of Clement VII a third contract with the heirs of Julius was drawn up. All former contracts were annulled, Michelangelo agreed to execute the smaller project within the space of three years and to deliver six figures, which had been blocked out either in Rome or in Florence, finished by his own hand, the rest of the work being allocated to others. He was to contribute 2,000 ducats from his own purse, part of this sum being represented by the capital value of the house, including the marbles, in the Macello de' Corvi; the same terms, in short, that had previously been negotiated for him by Fattucci. The Pope agreed to allow Michelangelo to come to Rome for at least two months each year to supervise the work. A penalty clause was added, whereby, if he failed to fulfil the terms of this contract, it should be declared null and void and he would then be held liable under the former contract of 1516. This contract *(Milanesi, p. 702)* was witnessed on April 29th 1532 and the Duke's ambassador in Rome, Giovan Maria della Porta, acknowledged receipt of the ratification two months later.

In this connection Tolnay *(IV, p. 55)*, following Gotti and Venturi, specifically states that Michelangelo was not present at the proceedings on April 29th, as he left 'at the request of Clement one day before'. But in his letter addressed to Cardinal Farnese *(No. 227)* Michelangelo does not say that he left the day before, but that 'Clement sent me to Florence the same day'. There is, therefore, nothing to imply that he did not leave immediately *after* the proceedings. Indeed, there are two statements which show incontrovertibly that he was present. Firstly, the contract itself establishes this fact – *Maestro Michelagnolo quivi presente:* secondly, in a letter to the Duke of Urbino, dated June 19th 1532 *(Gotti, II, p. 80)* his ambassador, Giovan Maria della Porta, speaking of the choice of the church in which the Tomb was to be erected – whether in Santa Maria del Popolo, which the Duke would have preferred, or in San Pietro in Vincoli, which was ultimately chosen as being more spacious and better lit – says that he discussed the matter 'with Michelangelo himself, in the presence of His Holiness, on the day of the contract'. We must therefore disabuse our minds of the commonly accepted notion that he was not present on the occasion – a notion that has, in any case, always appeared strangely anomalous.

For the fourth and last Contract for the Tomb of Julius II,
see Volume II, Appendix 28.

Appendix 12

The Historical Situation during the Pontificate of Leo X : 1513-1521

POPE Julius II, who vastly extended the States of the Church and had succeeded in driving the French from Italy in the summer of 1512, died, after a short illness, on the night of February 21st 1513. He was succeeded on March 11th by Cardinal Giovanni de' Medici, whose attitude to his elevation to the throne of St. Peter, as Leo X, may best be expressed in the remark he made to his cousin, Cardinal Giulio – 'God has given us the Papacy; let us enjoy it'.

Despite the victories of his warlike predecessor and his own desire for tranquillity in Europe, Pope Leo was not long left free to enjoy the fruits of office in peace.

In the spring of 1513 Louis XII, who had entered into a treaty of alliance with the Venetians, which was signed at Blois in March of that year, again attacked the Milanese in support of his claim to the Duchy through his descent from Valentina Visconti. In this attempt, however, he was unsuccessful, the French under la Tremouille being defeated and routed at the Battle of Novara on June 6th 1513. Although Louis had no intention of relinquishing his claim to Milan, he deemed it politic at this juncture to compose his differences with Rome (the ban of excommunication imposed by Julius II still being operative) and, on the last day of December 1513, he was received back into the Church, the Pope, with the consent of the Lateran Council, granting him 'full absolution for all his past offences against the Holy See'.

Although the war being conducted by the Emperor-elect, Maximilian, and Ferdinand of Aragon, King of Spain, against Louis's allies the Venetians, continued to drag on, with appalling devastation of the Venetian provinces, the year 1514 remained comparatively peaceful. Louis was preoccupied with negotiating both an Anglo-French treaty and a secret alliance with the Pope who, in return for certain concessions calculated to enhance the power and prestige of the Medici, was prepared to acquiesce in Louis's designs upon Milan. In these projects both Leo and Louis were disappointed, as Louis died on January 1st 1515 and was succeeded by his cousin, Francis I.

The new monarch (contrary to Buonarroto's expectations) lost no time in pursuing his claim to Milan (ostensibly by virtue of the inheritance of his wife, Louis's elder daughter). In August 1515 he crossed the Alps into Lombardy and on September 14th, a fortnight after Michelangelo had written to his brother about the political situation *(No. 107)*, the French won a decisive victory at the famous Battle of Marignano.

As soon as the triumph of French arms was known, Leo hastened to enter into negotiations with the French king and early in October (as mentioned by Michelangelo in his letter *(No.*

109) of October 6th 1515) he left Rome on a hunting expedition prior to his meeting with Francis at Bologna at the beginning of December. On his way thither, he made a formal entry into Florence, where he stayed both before and after his meeting with the French king.

As a result of this meeting, and in return for certain concessions to Leo's Medici ambitions, Francis was confirmed in his possession of the Duchy of Milan, to which Parma and Piacenza were also annexed.

For the next few years, therefore, Leo remained outwardly friendly to France, but with the election of Charles V of Spain as Holy Roman Emperor in June 1519, his attitude began to change and in 1520 he entered into secret negotiations with Charles for the expulsion of the French from Lombardy.

Leo's jubilation at the news of the fall of Milan to the Papal and Imperial arms in November of the following year was, however, short-lived, as he died suddenly and unexpectedly on the night of December 1st 1521.

Appendix 13

Michelangelo and the Marble Quarries of Pietra Santa

No clear, coherent and unequivocal account of Michelangelo and the marble quarries of Pietra Santa is anywhere to be found – at least so far as I am aware. The facts themselves are difficult to come by and in consequence a number of ill-founded and misleading generalizations have been made, which have contributed to our being left with an impression that is, in many important respects, false. By a careful analysis of the available material and by a systematic co-ordination of statements made in Michelangelo's letters, in the *Ricordi*, in the contracts and in other relevant correspondence, it is possible, however, to acquaint ourselves with the sequence of events, if not beyond a peradventure, at any rate with sufficient accuracy to clarify the position and to correct certain misconceptions.

The abbreviated and somewhat naïve account of the affair given by Condivi, a primary source of our information, is not entirely borne out by the documents belonging to the period in question, partly because it is abridged, and partly because it is based on the master's recollection of what had occurred some thirty years before, a recollection inevitably tinged by the memory of the frustration he had suffered and the ignominy that had been put upon him. The same is true of Vasari's statement, which does not differ substantially from Condivi's, except that it is slightly exaggerated. In the same way later biographers and historians have contrived, however unwittingly, to confuse the issue still further.

The story begins in 1515, when by an instrument of May 18th the Florentine Republic acquired from the Commune of Seravezza the sole rights for the quarrying of the marbles to be found in the region of Mte. Altissimo and Mte. Ceresola, both in Tuscan territory (*Milanesi, p. 643*). At this period the work on the Florentine Duomo, Santa Maria del Fiore, was still incomplete and extensive supplies of marble were needed by the Commissioners, the *Operai del Duomo*. As representatives of the wealthy Guild of Wool Merchants, the *Arte della Lana*, whose patronage of the Cathedral had been confirmed by a bull of Pope Martin V in 1427 (*Staley, p. 521*), they assumed responsibility for opening the quarries and constructing the necessary roads for the transport of the marbles to be excavated. Prior to this date the Marquisate of Carrara had enjoyed a virtual monopoly in the quarrying of marble for use throughout Italy and elsewhere in Europe and it was not to be expected that the Carrarese would look with favour on the Tuscan venture, yet even so it is probable that they would have viewed it with less animosity had not Michelangelo, the foremost sculptor in Christendom and a Florentine to boot, inevitably become involved, albeit much against his will.

Now there is no doubt that from the outset Michelangelo himself was exceedingly apprehensive about the whole affair. He had first gone to Carrara as a youth in 1498 to quarry the marble for the *Madonna della Febbre* and had ever since remained on excellent terms both with the local quarry masters and with the Marquis, Alberigo Malaspina himself, and had therefore no wish either to disrupt these good relations or to seek his marbles elsewhere. But that he feared that some pressure to support the Florentine enterprise might be brought to bear upon him is evident in the first references to the matter in his letters from Rome in the summer of 1515. Thus, in his letter of June 2nd to Buonarroto *(No. 96)* he enclosed a letter to be sent to Carrara 'secretly' and without the knowledge of anyone at the *Opera*, and again on July 7th *(No. 99)* he wrote saying, 'Although it is no use depending on Michele for anything, I thought he at least knew the answer to my question, that is, whether I'm going to get marbles from Pietra Santa this summer; because here Domenico Buoninsegni told me that he heard that the road was nearly finished.' Then on August 4th *(No. 102)* he made a further enquiry about the progress of the road and asked for a prompt reply, because he was 'uneasy'. The same note of apprehension persists and not without reason, since on his return to Carrara at the beginning of September 1516 he encountered 'some unpleasantness' *(No. 112)* from the Carrarese, owing to their suspicions that he was lending his support to the new project. How little they were warranted in this assumption transpires from the correspondence of the following year.

Having been summoned to Rome in December 1516 and having come to a verbal agreement with the Pope, Leo X, about the projected façade of San Lorenzo, Michelangelo returned to Carrara at the beginning of January, having spent a few days in Florence *en route*. Various *ricordi* referring to his movements at this time have been preserved in the British Museum, the Florentine State Archives and the Casa Buonarroti, but there are certain discrepancies which make it impossible to be precise in regard to the actual dates. These discrepancies are unimportant, but when he left for Pietra Santa on January 7th to survey the *monti* and to report on the quality of the marbles, he cannot have taken his departure from Florence, as stated in one *ricordo (Milanesi, p. 567)*, but must have proceeded direct from Carrara. The entry was not made on the day in question and the mention of Florence must be due to a lapse of memory. This is confirmed by a letter from Bernardo Niccolini, *Camerlingo* to the Archbishop, addressed to Michelangelo in Carrara on January 7th, in which he wrote, 'It is said that you have gone to Rome; you ought to be in Pietra Santa' *(Frey, Briefe, p. 55)*. This, then, is the significant date as far as Michelangelo's participation in the development of the Florentine quarries is concerned, and that there was a good deal of speculation as to what his reactions would be is shown by a singularly interesting reference to the matter made in a letter from Buonarroto to his brother, dated January 13th, to which, after informing him that Jacopo Salviati had left that morning for Pietra Santa (whither he was going at the Pope's request to report on the situation), he added a postscript saying, '. . . Michele tells me that it is said here that you will stand by that lord there *[i.e. by the Marquis of Carrara]* and that it is owing to you that they are not quarrying at Pietra Santa' *(Frey, Briefe, p. 57)* – a statement which shows that Michelangelo had made no secret of his unwillingness to draw his marbles elsewhere than from Carrara.

Although his report has not survived, we know from Condivi that Michelangelo wrote to the Pope saying that the marbles at Pietra Santa were unsuitable and would be difficult and expensive to quarry (as proved to be the case) owing to the fact that roads would have to be built over intractable terrain. Similarly, we know from the peremptory letter he received from Cardinal Giulio de' Medici in reply that this report was ill looked upon by the Pope, who was determined to assert his independence of Carrara at all costs. The letter in question reads as follows:

> *Spectabilis mio carissimo* – We have received your letters and shown them to Our Lord, and considering that all your proceedings are in favour of Carrara, you have caused His Holiness and ourselves no little surprise, because they do not correspond with what we learn from Jacopo Salviati, who has been to the site of the marble quarries, together with many intelligent masters, and reports that quantities of the most beautiful marbles are to be found there and that they are easy to transport. This being the case, we have our suspicions that for some reason of your own you seek to favour the marbles of Carrara overmuch and to denigrate those of Pietra Santa. This you should certainly not have done, in view of the trust we have always placed in you. We therefore inform you that His Holiness, Our Lord, putting aside every other consideration, wishes the marbles for the work to be undertaken at St. Peter's, at Santa Reparata *[i.e. the Duomo]* and for the façade of San Lorenzo, to be drawn from Pietra Santa and from nowhere else, both for the reasons given above, and also because it is understood that they will be less expensive than those from Carrara. But in any event, even if they were more expensive, His Holiness wishes this to be done, in order to inaugurate and to begin this enterprise at Pietra Santa for the public good of the City.
>
> Therefore see that you carry out the orders we have given you and fail not to do so, because if you do otherwise, against the will of His Holiness and ourselves, we shall have great cause of complaint against you, and our Domenico *[Buoninsegni]* will be writing you to the same effect. Answer him as to how much you need, and quickly, banishing all obduracy from your mind. *Et bene valete.* The 2nd day of February 1517.
>
> (Daelli, 12)

It will be noted that the letter, as transcribed by Daelli, is dated in full, but for some reason best known to himself the date was omitted by Gotti *(I, p. 109)*, who published the original text, as well as by Symonds *(I, p. 332)* and by Thode *(I, p. 280)*, both of whom published translations of the letter based, apparently, on Gotti. The omission of the date has naturally led to speculation among scholars as to whether the Cardinal's letter should be assigned to 1517, following the verbal agreement about the façade, or to 1518, following the formal contract. When considered in relation to the letters quoted above, it is obvious that it belongs to the 1517 sequence of events; when considered only in relation to the fact that Michelangelo continued at Carrara during the greater part of 1517 and only began operations at Pietra Santa in March 1518, it is understandable that Venturi, Frey and Thode should have assigned it to 1518, supposing the date, February 2nd 1517, to be *ab Incarnatione*, which it manifestly is not. Had it been so, it must necessarily have been stated in the letter, which being written in Rome was naturally dated according to Roman usage.

Notwithstanding these imperative commands, Michelangelo, as *archimaestro sculptore della Sedia Apostolica*, entered into further contracts with the Carrarese during the early months of 1517 *(Milanesi, pp. 660, 662, 664)*. It is true that the one negotiated on February 12th, in which he contracted for all the marbles needed for the façade of San Lorenzo, was replaced by another on March 14th, in which he contracted for a limited amount only. Yet even so it would be difficult to account for such a proceeding, in face of the Cardinal's letter, and in the absence of any documents to justify it, were it not for a letter of Domenico Buoninsegni's written, not at this time, but on November 3rd 1516, during the preliminary negotiation for the work *(Frey, Briefe, p. 39)*. In this letter to Michelangelo he had referred to the question of the quarries in these words – 'The Cardinal *[Giulio de' Medici]* tells me that he does not think the Pope will listen to this talk of obtaining the marbles from Carrara, because his heart is set upon Pietra Santa.' Then, having gone on to mention the further five hundred ducats which the Pope was contributing towards the cost of the road (making one thousand ducats in all), Buoninsegni had concluded by saying, somewhat opprobriously one may think, 'the Cardinal is of the opinion that you may amuse yourself by quarrying a few marbles at Carrara *until the road is finished*; afterwards you will have what you need from Pietra Santa'. In other words, the contracts drawn up early in 1517 would appear to have been allowed as an interim measure, intended perhaps as a sop to Michelangelo, who may have been obliged to cancel the contract of February 12th by order of the Cardinal. We cannot be certain about this, however, because the phrase used by Michelangelo *(No. 114)* with reference to the cancellation – *per buon rispetto* – is the convenient phrase which he frequently uses to justify his actions, concealing as it does, much more than it reveals.

We might, accordingly, be warranted in supposing that Michelangelo was in fact compelled by the Pope to seek his marbles at Pietra Santa, but there are other aspects of the affair which must give us pause, since they imply that in betaking himself to the Tuscan quarries he acted as a free agent. The first and most important indication that this may have been so is provided by the terms of the actual contract for the work, which was drawn up on January 19th 1518 *(Milanesi, p. 671)*, in which it is specifically stated that the façade was to be made of fine white marbles from Pietra Santa *or* Carrara, whichever were the more suitable. The second indication that he may not have been acting under compulsion is provided by his final summary of the whole affair *(No. 144)*. In this account he stated categorically that having accepted the commission he went to Carrara, but 'as they had not fulfilled the contracts and previous orders for the marbles for the said work, and as the Carrarese were bent upon balking me, I went to have the said marbles quarried at Seravezza'.

We are therefore left in considerable uncertainty as to the true facts of the case, but two further points in regard to it may be noted. In the first place, there is no doubt at all that once Michelangelo had committed himself to Pietra Santa, he was not at liberty to place any more orders with the Carrarese without the express permission of the Pope, as is plainly shown by the letter he received from Jacopo Salviati in January 1519, by which he is granted such permission, but for the supplying of two or three columns only, as 'the Pope does not wish the marble to be supplied except from Pietra Santa' *(Frey, Briefe, p. 134)*. In the second place, there is equally no doubt that Michelangelo's contemporary biographers were under the impression that in abandoning Carrara he acted under duress.

We cannot say precisely what were Michelangelo's intentions as to Pietra Santa when he returned to Florence at the end of August 1517 to prepare the final model for the façade of San Lorenzo. We only know for certain that from the inception of the Florentine project he had been regarded with suspicion by the Carrarese, who, though, on the one hand, they might implore him to return 'as they would implore Christ' *(No. 123)*, did not hesitate, on the other, to do everything in their power to balk him in the matter of the shipment of the quarried marbles from Avenza *(No. 120)*. Nor was he left in any doubt as to the position, for the Carrarese notary, Lionardo Lombardello, who was well disposed towards him, wrote on October 30th 1517, telling him of the Marquis's growing animosity *(Frey, Briefe, p. 81)*. Indeed, so great was the hostility he encountered, to which he refers in his letter to Buoninsegni in the spring of 1518 *(No. 119)*, that he was eventually forced to abandon Carrara and to proceed to Pietra Santa, as he himself stated plainly in his final account of the whole affair as quoted above. The precise position in regard to this particular aspect of the matter remains, however, to some extent obscure and, in all likelihood, will never be more certainly ascertained. All that we know beyond any doubt is that the mental and physical strain it involved for Michelangelo personally was out of all proportion to anything that was either lost or gained.

By the terms of the concession granted to him by the Commissioners of the *Arte della Lana* on April 22nd 1518, three things are made clear which are not specifically stated elsewhere. It is evident, firstly, that up to this time no progress had been made at Pietra Santa, beyond the construction of some sections of the road; secondly, that the Commissioners, who may not have found and certainly had not appointed anyone capable of opening up the quarries, were only too glad to enlist Michelangelo's services immediately the opportunity offered – he being deemed, in the words of the aforesaid instrument, *più apto* than anyone else to undertake the task; and thirdly, that he agreed to do so in return for the right, granted to himself and to his heirs in perpetuity, to quarry marbles for their own use in the region of Mte. Altissimo *(Milanesi, p. 679)*. That he set great store by the granting of this concession is confirmed in his letter to Buonarroto, written four days earlier *(No. 123)*, which does not suggest that he was under any compulsion to draw his marbles from the Florentine quarries, but was at liberty, if he wished, to return to Carrara.

Once having accepted the contract for the façade, having obtained the concession, having undertaken the work at Pietra Santa, and having, at his own request, assumed responsibility for the supervision of the road, he did everything in his power to make the enterprise a success. On April 27th he appointed Donato Benti as his agent at Pietra Santa for the quarrying, blocking out and transport of the marbles for the façade, and he continued to engage local *scarpellini* and *scarpellini* from Settignano to work at the quarries. But the difficulties he had originally anticipated were as nothing in comparison with those he eventually encountered. From the very beginning, and even before the concession was actually granted, he was continually beset by vexations and worries of every kind, as witness the postscript to his letter to Buonarroto mentioned above, in which he wrote – 'Oh cursed a thousand times be the day I left Carrara! It's the cause of my undoing.' He could rely on no-one; even Benti failed him at one point *(see No. 139)* while the *scarpellini* he engaged proved, for the most part, to be wholly ignorant of the work they were required to undertake, and unteachable and intractable into the bargain, so that in the end he had to remain there altogether *(No. 137)* and was driven into the anomalous position of engaging Carrarese labour to work at the rival quarries *(Milanesi, p. 689)*. And then in the end all this to no purpose whatsoever, since with the cancellation of the contract for the façade of San Lorenzo in March 1520 his activities at Pietra Santa came to an end. But although Donato Benti continued as his agent at Pietra Santa *(Tolnay, III, p. 227 et seq.)*, when he undertook the work at the New Sacristy a year later, it was for most part from Carrara that he drew his marbles.

In conclusion it may be worth while to consider some of the statements that have been made by Michelangelo's biographers about the enterprise at Pietra Santa, particularly those relating to the circumstances in which he went there and the time he lost in the process, and to note the general consensus of opinion as to where the blame lay for the ultimate failure of the undertaking.

Condivi, whose account is, as we have seen, slightly distorted by reason of its brevity, is at pains to emphasize the business of the road and the hostility of the Marquis, saying, 'The Pope . . . *ordered* him to make the road', and 'the Marquis of Carrara thinking that Michelangelo, as a citizen of Florence, might have been the originator of the quarrying at Pietra Santa . . . would not allow him to return to Carrara afterwards' *(Condivi, xxxix)*. Vasari, who devotes one short paragraph to the incident, informs us that 'Michelangelo *was forced to go to Seravezza*' and that 'he spent *many years* in fulfilling the Pope's wish' *(Vasari, VII, p. 190)*.

Grimm, whose narrative abounds in mis-statements and *non sequiturs*, puts forward an entirely different view, maintaining that *Michelangelo instituted* investigations in 1517 as to the nature of the stone and had convinced himself of its availability, and that *he* began the road and the stone quarries at Seravezza *as his own affair (Grimm, I, p. 414)*. Gotti's version is much more detailed and in the main more accurate, but in referring to the cancellation on April 7th 1517 of a contract for marbles made in 1516 with the Carrarese quarry-master, Francesco da Pellicaia *(Milanesi, p. 652)*, 'in order to demonstrate his resolve to obey *[the Pope's wishes in regard to Seravezza]*' *(Gotti, I, p. 110)*, he omits to mention that he entered into an agreement with other Carrarese quarrymen ten days later. Heath Wilson, while likewise dealing with the subject in considerable detail, devotes more attention to the personal aspect of the affair, and writes at some length of what he regards as the enormity of the Pope's conduct towards Michelangelo in giving him orders 'to proceed to the defiles and bare mountain slopes above Seravezza in search of marbles in quarries long abandoned and from which there were no roads . . . and should thus have constituted him engineer and roadmaker, in fine, quarryman', so that, as he goes on to say, 'it may be doubted whether in the history of art there may be found a comparable instance of so cruel a disregard of the claims of genius, or so pitiless an indignity as *the unworthy labour forced upon* Michelangelo *by the despotic will of Leo X*'. This period of 'compulsory labour', as he calls it elsewhere, he estimates as having lasted 'four years' *(Wilson, pp. 226, 249)*. Justi, on the other hand, sought to exonerate the Medici and to blame the failure of the whole project upon Michelangelo, a view with which Thode, who is more objective in his approach, entirely disagrees, alleging that, as fate had decreed that the execution of the façade should depend upon the opening of the quarries at Seravezza, it was rather the Pope's impatience, the pressure brought to bear upon Michelangelo and Malaspina's intrigues that brought the enterprise to an end *(Thode, I, p. 289)*.

As always, Symonds provides one of the most reliable accounts of what took place, but in assigning the Cardinal de' Medici's letter to 1518 instead of to 1517, he supposes that Michelangelo acted under duress when he finally left Carrara for Pietra Santa in the March of 1518. The time wasted on the façade he also estimates as four years. Not so Holroyd, however, who writes as follows: 'The friendly relations of Michelangelo with the natives of Carrara continued *until the Pope obliged him to leave their quarries and open up those of Pietra Santa* in Tuscan territory, by which act Michelangelo lost much time. He had *positively* to make roads down the mountains and over the marshes before he could get a single block of marble to the river. The Marquis of Carrara became his enemy and the contracts with the people of Carrara caused him much annoyance and great loss. The orders from Rome were peremptory and had to be obeyed. *Ten years* of the best of Michelangelo's working life were wasted . . .' *(Holroyd, p. 156 et seq.)*. Schiavo, a more recent authority, makes no such startling allegation, being content to dismiss the whole episode, without comment, in some twelve lines, in which he repeats the usual statement that Leo X, having decided upon the opening of the quarries, *ordered* Michelangelo to Pietra Santa *(Schiavo, Vita, p. 30)*.

It will be seen at a glance that while most of the views expressed above have certain features in common, the extent to which they differ from one another in other respects is less remarkable than the extent to which they differ from the known facts which, as established from contemporary sources, may be recapitulated as follows:

The time wasted over the façade of San Lorenzo and in obtaining the necessary marbles amounted, in all, to three years, as Michelangelo himself states in his summing up of the whole matter *(No. 144)*, that is to say, from the beginning of 1517 to the end of 1519, a period which by no stretch of imagination can be extended to even four years, much less to ten, however indignant one may feel on Michelangelo's behalf.

As to the Carrarese, we have ample proof from Michelangelo's letters alone that they adopted a hostile and obstructive attitude towards him, but how far the Marquis, Alberigo Malaspina, was personally to blame for this we have no means of judging. That he became less friendly we know from Lionardo Lombardello's phrase, 'I cannot candidly write to you of the goodwill of the Marquis himself towards you' *(Frey, Briefe, p. 81)*, yet even so it is probable that Malaspina was less responsible for the delays which ensued over the delivery of the marbles than was generally supposed at the time. He certainly repudiated the suggestion and expressed himself as being 'stupefied' by the terms of the papal brief issued in connection with the matter in October 1518 *(Frey, Briefe, p. 123)*. However this may be, there is no foundation for Condivi's categorical statement, based perhaps on a misinterpretation of something Michelangelo said years later, that the Marquis would not allow him to return to Carrara afterwards, even for the marble he had already quarried. It is certain, in any case, that Michelangelo subsequently drew his marbles both from Pietra Santa and from Carrara, but from the latter in the main.

Finally, the question remains as to how far Leo X was to blame for the way in which Michelangelo's powers were wasted at the new quarries. Although it may be true that he ordered him 'to proceed to the defiles . . . above Seravezza in search of marbles', it cannot honestly be said that he 'ordered him to make the road', since it was at his own request, as shown by his letter to Buonarroto in April 1518 *(No. 120)*, that Michelangelo undertook its supervision. In justice to the Pope and to the Cardinal it must also be allowed that if, in fact, they compelled him to leave Carrara in order to open up the quarries at Pietra Santa, they could have had no notion what this would involve, nor could they have supposed that it would be necessary for him to superintend so much of the work himself. Indeed, it is fair to say that it would never have entered their minds to impose upon him tasks as manifestly unworthy of him as those he ultimately found himself obliged to perform, or to misapply his genius as it was eventually misapplied. So that if in the end these things befell, they befell not by the will of the Medici, but by the force of circumstances, over which they had as little control as Michelangelo had himself. But while Leo may be absolved in respect of the beginning of the enterprise, he cannot be exonerated in respect of the manner of its termination.

Appendix 14

Michelangelo and the Machinations of the Papal Entourage

Part I

The Façade of San Lorenzo: the contract and its cancellation

A CONCISE account of the commission for the façade of San Lorenzo (the contract for which was signed in January 1518) and of its subsequent cancellation is given by Michelangelo in the statement he prepared as a basis for the draft of a brief for the Pope's signature, confirming that he had been released from the contract and had fully discharged his obligations. Milanesi's conjecture that the statement was addressed to Sebastiano del Piombo, who in any case did not hold the office of *Piombatore* at this time, is manifestly unacceptable, since he was in no way concerned with Michelangelo's professional concerns at this time. In view of the fact that the artist had been advised to have such a document drawn up, it is reasonable to assume that the recipient was a notary – perhaps Ser Bonaventura di Leonardo, who had drawn up other documents connected with the enterprise.

In this statement (*No. 144*) the circumstances in which the project was undertaken are clearly, though briefly, set forth, but those in which it was abandoned are less clearly recounted, mainly because Michelangelo himself was not fully informed as to the position, owing to the disgraceful nature of the plots and counterplots of which he became the victim.

Although we know from his own *ricordo (Milanesi, p. 581)* that the commission was finally cancelled on March 10th 1520, the imprecision of the phrase *dipoi in questo tempo medesimo* makes it difficult to determine when he was actually informed that he was to cease work on the façade. At first sight the phrase in question would appear to refer to a time shortly after March 1519, but this is certainly not the case, since throughout the greater part of that year he continued to supervise the quarrying at Seravezza.

It is asserted by Venturi *(IX, pt. I, p. 656)* that on September 12th Michelangelo was still being encouraged in the work on the façade by the Cardinal de' Medici, who had been resident in Florence since the death of Lorenzo, Duke of Urbino, on May 4th 1519. In his letter of September 17th *(No. 143)* to his assistant Pietro Urbano, who had been ill, Michelangelo wrote saying, 'I would have come to Pistoia to see you, but I'm so busy I cannot leave', from which we may conclude that he had as yet received no intimation that by the Pope's orders the work on the façade was to be discontinued, that the quarries at Pietra Santa and Seravezza, which he had opened up, were to be handed over to the Commissioners of Santa Maria del Fiore and that the marbles he had excavated at such cost to himself were to be diverted to the paving of the Duomo. As we know from his own account of what happened *(No. 144)* that it was the Cardinal who had the invidious task of informing him of the Pope's decision, it cannot but be that he received the announcement some time between September 17th and September 27th at the latest, since the Cardinal, who was about to leave Florence, arrived in Rome at the beginning of October *(Sanuto, xxviii, 14)*. The phrase quoted above in the original can therefore only be taken to mean 'later on in that same year'. In any case, from Michelangelo's letter to Pietro Urbano *(No. 142)*, it appears that the visit of inspection to the quarries made by certain *scarpellini*, presumably on behalf of the Commissioners, took place in September, shortly after Michelangelo's return to Florence, when he left Pietro ill at Seravezza. It is true that Pietro was paying out money at Seravezza on Michelangelo's behalf (and once in his presence) as late as March 1520 *(Milanesi, p. 580)*, but this can only have been a final settling of the accounts, prior to the formal cancellation of the contract on March 10th, the last payment in respect of the façade having been made two days previously.

As a sequel to the foregoing it may be noted, incidentally, that there is an entry in Lapini's *Diario Fiorentino (p. 94)* on February 28th 1524 to the effect that the paving of the choir of the Duomo in white, red and black marble was completed on that day. More correctly the entry should have read, 'On February 28th 1524 the Commissioners completed the paving of the choir of the Duomo with the white, red and black marble, which Michelangelo had quarried for the façade of San Lorenzo.' But if, as Cardinal, Giulio de' Medici had no alternative but to acquaint Michelangelo with the Pope's decision, without vouchsafing him any explanation as to why the work on the façade was being discontinued (perhaps the most intolerable aspect of the whole affair), as Pope Clement VII, he afterwards did everything in his power to compensate him for the ignominious treatment he had received.

(The circumstances in which Michelangelo undertook the Façade of San Lorenzo have been fully discussed in Appendix 11.)

Part II

The Façade of San Lorenzo: the reasons for the cancellation of the contract

The difficulties and frustrations by which Michelangelo was continually beset from 1518 onwards are explicable only in terms of the graft, jealousies and intrigues which characterized the Renaissance in general and the art politics of the period in particular, more especially where the patronage of the Pope was concerned. Being above corruption himself, Michelangelo was entirely unsuited to the world of duplicity and subterfuge in which he found himself, for by rejecting certain proposals made to him and by refusing to become party to illicit practices, he inevitably incurred the hostility which he himself bitterly described, in another context, as the reward of all honest men.

Thus, the incidents referred to in his letter to Giovan Francesco Fattucci of October 1525 *(No. 174)* had their origin in his opposition to the machinations of the Commissioners, the 'arch-notaries and sub-purveyors' mentioned in his letter to Domenico Buoninsegni of March 1518 *(No. 119)*, though whether at this time he wrote in ignorance of Buoninsegni's own intentions, or in an attempt to forewarn him, one cannot say. In either case, it appears to be Domenico Buoninsegni to whom the source of many of Michelangelo's subsequent troubles may be traced, if we may accept Vasari's account of what occurred.

Because this account is not given in his life of Michelangelo (possibly in deference to Michelangelo's own wish), but in that of his inveterate enemy, Baccio Bandinelli, the most plausible explanation for the cancellation of the contract for the San Lorenzo façade and for what happened afterwards has generally been overlooked.

According to Vasari, 'Domenico Buoninsegni endeavoured to obtain Michelangelo's secret co-operation to make a profit out of the façade of San Lorenzo, but Michelangelo refused, as he did not wish his genius to be used for the purpose of defrauding the Pope. Domenico was so enraged that he employed every means to humiliate and injure Michelangelo, though he acted covertly'. And, as Vasari goes on to say, 'he contrived that the façade should be abandoned' *(Vasari, VI, p. 148 et seq.)*.

This explanation of what occurred gives point to several statements made in the letters. Since Buoninsegni 'acted covertly', it will readily be understood why it was that Michelangelo said that he did not know why he had been so shamefully treated, and why he never received an official explanation. His remark in the letter of April 1518 to Buonarroto *(No. 120)*, that Jacopo Salviati would never find himself cheated over anything he entrusted to him, likewise becomes more significant.

But if Domenico Buoninsegni was corrupt in his dealings, Bernardo Niccolini, whom Lodovico regarded as a man not to be trusted *(Frey, Briefe, p. 76)*, was no less so. His evident desire to discredit Michelangelo publicly is shown in the episode in the haberdasher's shop, to which Michelangelo so bitterly objected *(No. 137)*, while he, perhaps even more than Buoninsegni, was to blame for the endless troubles which Michelangelo encountered later when he was engaged on the work on the Tombs in the New Sacristy. This is confirmed by contemporary correspondence. In a letter from Rome dated January 28th 1525, Fattucci wrote to him saying, 'Domenico Buoninsegni and Bernardo Niccolini are the ones who are prolonging the work and delaying the marbles in order to provoke you', and, indeed, such was their animosity that two months later Jacopo Salviati was obliged to remove control of Michelangelo's affairs from their hands, and to place it in those of Giovanni Spina; so that on April 12th of the same year Fattucci was at last able to declare that he thought that 'by now you are out of the hands of Bernardo Niccolini, which seems to me no small advantage. No longer will he be able to make you toil and sweat either over the marbles or over anything else, thank God' *(Frey, Briefe, pp. 246, 251)*.

But while for Michelangelo there was no compensation for the loss of what might have been three of the most creative years of his life, let us not think of the unadorned façade of San Lorenzo in wholly negative terms. Let us rather say to ourselves in face of it, 'This façade remains as a witness not to Michelangelo's genius as an artist, but to his probity as a man.'

Part III

The 'Hercules Slaying Cacus': the project and the intrigues connected with it

A further instance of Domenico Buoninsegni's duplicity is also related by Vasari. 'In the time of Leo X,' he writes, 'a piece of marble . . . had been quarried at Carrara with the marble for the façade of San Lorenzo at Florence. In this piece Michelangelo proposed to make a *Hercules slaying Cacus*, to put on the piazza beside the colossal *David*. He made several models and designs and had sought the favour of Cardinal Giulio de' Medici and Pope Leo . . . but on the death of Leo both the façade and the statue were abandoned.' But Buoninsegni, not satisfied with the other injuries he had done Michelangelo, 'persuaded the Pope *[Clement VII]* to give the marble for the giant to Baccio *[Bandinelli]* . . . saying that these two great men would stimulate each other by competition. The Pope thought the advice good and followed it. . . . . . Baccio boasted that he would surpass Michelangelo's *David*, while Buoninsegni declared that Michelangelo wanted everything for himself' *(Vasari, VI, p. 149)*.

It is clear from a letter, dated October 30th 1525, addressed to Michelangelo by Jacopo Salviati in reply to one of his, that it is to this episode that Michelangelo also refers in the letter to Fattucci of October 24th of the same year *(No. 174)*. In his letter Salviati, who had a great respect and affection for Michelangelo, did his best to comfort him and to urge him on, by saying, 'For my part, I do not see, nor can I understand, how in any respect Baccio can be compared to you . . . . .' *(Frey, Briefe, p. 264)*.

The marble block in question suffered many vicissitudes. On the way from Carrara it fell into the Arno and was only retrieved with great difficulty. According to a wit of the period, 'after being destined for the genius of Michelangelo, *[it]* had learned that it was to be mauled by Baccio, and in despair had cast itself into the river'.

From No. 175 it is evident that the Republic was still anxious that Michelangelo should execute the *Hercules slaying Cacus*, while in a document of 1527 *(Gaye, II, p. 98)* the partially blocked out marble was allocated to him 'notwithstanding the fact that it had been in the past allocated to others'. Although he abandoned the idea of the *Hercules*, and purposed to do a *Samson slaying two Philistines* instead, Michelangelo was prevented by political events from carrying out the work, and Bandinelli eventually completed the group, which to-day disfigures the Piazza della Signoria in Florence.

Appendix 15

The Implications of Michelangelo's Letter to Cardinal Bernardo Dovizi da Bibbiena (No. 145)

As a letter of recommendation, that which Michelangelo sent to Cardinal Bernardo Dovizi da Bibbiena at the request of his friend Sebastiano Luciani (later known as Sebastiano del Piombo), must surely be unique. But in order to savour it to the full one needs to be acquainted with the circumstances in which it was written and with the personality of the man to whom it was addressed.

On April 12th 1520 Sebastiano had written to Michelangelo to tell him of Raphael's death, which had occurred five days previously, and to ask him to use his influence with Cardinal Dovizi, Raphael's patron, to obtain for him some share in the work of decorating the Vatican apartments upon which Raphael had been engaged at the time of his death (*Milanesi, Corr., p. 6*).

From Michelangelo's point of view this request could hardly have been more untimely. When the letter reached him he was still smarting under the insult, both personal and professional, that had been put upon him by the cancellation of the contract for the façade of San Lorenzo and had, in all probability as a result of the shock he had undoubtedly sustained, been thrown into a fever from which he seems not to have recovered for several weeks. Although Sebastiano was apparently unaware of it, this information had already reached Rome, since in his letter of April 11th to Antonio di Marsilio in Venice, announcing the death of Raphael and of Agostino Chigi, Marcantonio Michiel concluded by saying that Michelangelo was ill in Florence (*Bottari, I, p. 574*).

Had he not been ill Michelangelo would certainly have complied with Sebastiano's request earlier than he did. For although his letter to the Cardinal is undated, it was probably not written before the end of May or the beginning of June, if we may judge from Sebastiano's acknowledgment, dated July 3rd, in which he says that it is some time – *molti zorni* – since he received Michelangelo's letter, enclosing the one addressed to the Cardinal. Unfortunately for Sebastiano, the work at the Palace had already been allocated to Raphael's followers by the time these letters reached Rome, as Dovizi informed him when he went to present the letter. During the interview the Cardinal asked him whether he had read it, to which he replied that he had not. Thereupon, as Sebastiano went on to say in his reply to Michelangelo, 'he laughed heartily, as if it were a great joke, and with friendly words I left. Afterwards I learnt from Baccio *[Bandinelli]* . . . that the Cardinal had shown him your letter and had also shown it to the Pope and that it is almost the only topic of conversation and makes everyone laugh' (*Milanesi, Corr., p. 6 et seq.*).

As addressed to a Cardinal and without reference to the character of the man to whom they were written, the terms of this letter might seem a trifle bizarre and somewhat out of place. But when considered in relation to Dovizi, whom Michelangelo had probably known since the days of Lorenzo the Magnificent, his first patron, they take on a different complexion.

The young Bernardo Dovizi (1470–1520) had been introduced into the Medici household through the influence of his brother, Piero, Lorenzo's secretary, and having been appointed private secretary to the youthful Cardinal, Giovanni de' Medici, had followed him into exile and had finally been instrumental in securing his election to the Papacy as Leo X. Although Leo immediately raised him to the cardinalate, Dovizi was in no sense a churchman, the bent of his mind being perhaps more nearly indicated by his comedy, *Calandria*, a vivid and entertaining work, albeit in somewhat doubtful taste. A skilful and dependable negotiator, he was essentially a man of the world, gifted, pleasure-loving and amusing, who seldom took himself seriously, as witness his portrait by Raphael and his correspondence with Isabella d'Este, in which he habitually referred to and signed himself *il Moccicone* – the Sniveller.

In regard to Michelangelo's letter it should not be forgotten, moreover, that he had not supposed it would be beneath Dovizi's dignity to accept a 'rake-off' of one hundred ducats when Dovizi secured the payment of the two thousand ducats due to him on the completion of the Sistine vault. And in the event, Michelangelo's supposition had not proved to be wrong *(No. 157)*. If, therefore, in vulgar parlance, Michelangelo may be said to have 'known his onions', may it not also be said that he knew his Cardinal?

Appendix 16

The New Sacristy and the Medici Tombs in San Lorenzo

THE task of completing the New Sacristy of San Lorenzo was undertaken by Michelangelo towards the end of 1520. By this time the building (which was on a Quattrocento foundation) was well advanced, having been under construction since the March of that year. Although always described as a sacristy, it was essentially as a burial chamber and chantry chapel for the Medici family that it was conceived, and by November 1520 Michelangelo was already in communication with Cardinal Giulio de' Medici about the designs for the tombs.

After a considerable correspondence *(Tolnay, III, pp. 33 et seq.)* it was decided to erect four tombs of which, however, only two were eventually executed, namely that of Lorenzo, Duke of Urbino, who died in 1519, on the west wall of the Chapel, and that of Giuliano, Duke of Nemours, who died in 1516, on the east. A double tomb with two sarcophagi, one for Lorenzo the Magnificent, who died in 1492, and the other for his brother Giuliano, who was murdered in the Pazzi conspiracy in 1478, was designed for the south wall facing the altar, but owing to events wholly beyond Michelangelo's control this was never carried out. In 1527 the city was thrown into a state of commotion by the advance of the Imperial troops and by the subsequent sack of Rome; in the same year and again in 1528, the work was further interrupted by an outbreak of plague, to which Buonarroto, Michelangelo's favourite brother, succumbed during the second epidemic; while in 1529 the work had to be abandoned altogether when Michelangelo was appointed Procurator-General for the fortifications in anticipation of the Pope's attack on the city.

Having been resumed in the autumn of 1530, the work was continued without undue interruption for the next four years, but when Michelangelo left Florence for good in September 1534, only the two ideal figures representing the Dukes (referred to by Michelangelo as the *Capitani*) had been completed and set in place. Of the other figures mentioned in the letter to Fattucci *(No. 177)* the *Madonna and Child*, intended for the niche above the double tomb 'at the top end' of the Chapel, and the four symbolical figures for the sarcophagi, that is to say, *Day* and *Night*, *Dawn* and *Twilight*, were in varying stages of completion, but the four *River Gods*, designed to support the symbolical figures, were not even begun. Two large-scale models for these had been made, however, and are mentioned by Doni *(pt. iii, p. 24)* as being in the Chapel in the mid-sixteenth century, but only the one now preserved in the Accademia in Florence has survived. The two less important figures to which Michelangelo also refers in his letter, namely the patron saints of the Medici family, *SS. Cosmas and Damian*, which were begun under his supervision, were afterwards completed by the sculptors to whom he had assigned them, the *S. Cosmas* being executed by Fra Giovanni Montorsoli (1507–1563) and the *S. Damian* by Raffaello da Montelupo (c. 1505–1566).

28. *The New Sacristy, San Lorenzo, Florence*

(a) *The Madonna and Child.* *Michelangelo*

(b) *The Madonna and Child with SS. Cosmas and Damian, as at present grouped.* *Michelangelo, Montorsoli and Montelupo*

(c) *Sketch for the Double Tomb.* *Michelangelo.* British Museum, London

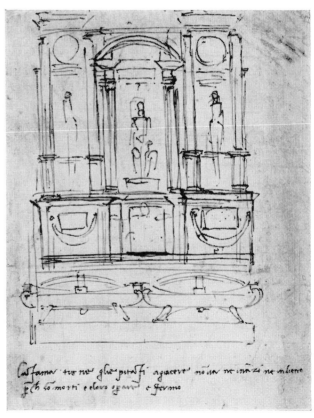

Although by the summer of 1526 the stage had been reached at which the painting of the cupola could be undertaken, it was not until 1532, two years after the raising of the siege, that Giovanni da Udine (1494–1564), whose style was eminently suited to harmonize with the existing sculptural ornament of the *quadro*, was sent by Pope Clement 'to decorate the tribune of the new sacristy of San Lorenzo'. Here, as Vasari relates, 'he did some beautiful foliage, bosses and other ornaments of stucco and gold'. No trace of this stucco ornament now remains, while the paintings, which were afterwards said to be too pale and not to 'tell' from the ground, were whitewashed over, regrettable though it may seem, by Vasari's orders, in 1556. As to the decoration of the rest of the Chapel, we have no certain means of knowing what Michelangelo intended, though various conjectures have been hazarded *(Tolnay, III, p. 48)*. But it is safe to assume that neither the lunette zone nor the recess behind the altar, both of which appear to have been designed for fresco, would have been left without their appropriate decoration, had the work been carried to completion.

But if, in the absence of the required colour which necessarily renders the sacristy colder and more austere in effect than it should be, we can form no conception of the finished scheme as Michelangelo envisaged it, how much less can we do so in the absence of the double tomb of the *Magnifici* 'at the top end' of the Chapel. Without this *sepultura di testa* the Chapel loses its meaning and the beholder remains unaware of its correct orientation. For, as Tolnay has shown *(III, pp. 31 et seq.)*, 'The Altar has the form of a *mensa*, and the celebrating priest stood behind it, facing into the Chapel, according to the early Christian tradition.' By this arrangement the celebrant, like the *Capitani* and *SS. Cosmas* and *Damian* (on either side of her) would look towards the *Madonna and Child* in the central niche of the double-tomb on the south wall. Shown as she is to-day, however, and as she has been for the past four hundred years, at too low a level, lacking the proper isolation, and without the necessary emphasis of a niche, *Nostra Donna*, as Michelangelo conceived her, is inevitably diminished in glory and the chapel as a whole is deprived of its dramatic significance.

But while the missing frescoes cannot now be supplied nor the lost decorations restored, the *sepultura di testa* could still be erected, without presumption, in accordance with the style of the lateral tombs and on the basis of the rough but impressive sketch which Dr. Wilde regards as the most authoritative of those preserved in the British Museum *(Wilde, 28 recto)*. The sculpture already exists; all that is wanting to complete the Chapel as it was designed is the architectural frame with its two sarcophagi. Is such a project, one wonders, beyond the possibility of realization? Or might its undertaking be thought to provide a not unfitting form of commemoration on the occasion of the fourth centenary of Michelangelo's death –

Michel più che mortale Angel divino.

Appendix 17

The Attempted Purchase of a Site in the Borg' Ognissanti

O N the basis of the undated letter *(No. 148)* to the Cardinal de' Medici, which Milanesi tentatively assigned to September 1518, Tolnay, who accepted this date, assumed that Michelangelo acquired the site in front of Ognissanti for the workshop he wanted. 'The third workshop', he says, 'was on *[sic]* the Piazza Ognissanti, and is mentioned for the first time in December 1518; it was built for the execution of the sculptures for the façade of San Lorenzo' *(Tolnay, III, p. 14)*.

For a number of reasons, both the assumed date of the letter and the assumption that Michelangelo had a workshop in the Borg' Ognissanti are unacceptable.

In the first place, the letter must have been written earlier in the season than September, since the weather, which is mentioned by Michelangelo, broke early in the mountains, for which reason it cannot have been written later than midsummer, so that June would seem a more likely month than September. In the second, the year 1518 seems on the face of it improbable, since, as we know from Michelangelo's letter to the Cardinal, dated July 15th 1518 *(No. 125)*, he had bought a site in the Via Mozza the day before, a site for which he had been negotiating for two months, and for which the contract was drawn on November 24th 1518, as is noted in the *Ricordi (Milanesi, p. 575)*. It therefore seems highly unlikely that at one and the same time he was negotiating for another site in a different part of Florence. It is significant, moreover, that there is no reference whatsoever to any such workshop in the *Ricordi*, whereas the one in the Via Mozza is constantly mentioned. In addition, the order for marble placed with the Carrarese, to which Michelangelo refers, cannot belong to 1518, since he did not again return to Carrara for marble until the spring of 1519. Finally, the request for a thousand ducats 'in two months time' does not correspond with the known facts about payments for the façade.

To what year, then, if not to 1518, may this letter be assigned? Without doubt to the late spring or early summer of 1521.

In April 1521 Michelangelo received two hundred ducats on account for the purchase of the marble he required for the project on which he was then engaged – the completion of the New Sacristy and the execution of the Medici Tombs. This was at a time when he was still receiving marble from Pietra Santa and Seravezza, for the supplying of which Donato Benti was made overseer in July 1521 *(Tolnay, III, p. 227)*.

Now for this project, with its full-scale models, it may well be that Michelangelo felt he needed another workshop, for which the site in the Borg' Ognissanti was evidently proposed – a site nearer San Lorenzo being unobtainable. Though plausible, such an argument would be inconclusive, were it not for further evidence provided in a letter addressed to Giovan

Francesco Fattucci in the spring of 1523 *(No. 152)*. In this letter, after outlining the methods he had proposed for the execution of the Medici Tombs, he went on to say 'That was when we wanted to buy the Caccini garden', adding (significantly), 'Nothing came of it, as you know'. But while this statement is in itself indicative, it becomes even more so when it is established that, like the piazza in front of Ognissanti, the Caccini gardens likewise belonged to the *Umiliati (Staley, p. 148)*, with whom, on Michelangelo's behalf, the Syndic, Matteo Bartoli, who belonged to that Quarter, was in negotiation.

Still further confirmation that the time at which this attempt to buy a site in the Borg' Ognissanti took place was in 1521 is supplied by other information given in the letter to Fattucci, already mentioned. After the reference to the Caccini garden, Michelangelo continues, 'Then, as soon as I heard that the Cardinal was going to Lombardy, I went to see him.' What, then, was the purpose of the Cardinal's visit to Lombardy, and when did it take place? The answer to both questions is conclusive.

At the behest of Leo X, the Cardinal left Florence in all haste on September 29th 1521, to avert the growing breach between the leaders of the Imperial forces, the *condottiere*, Prospero Colonna, and the Marquis of Pescara, who were encamped near Parma in preparation for an attack on the French army in Lombardy, under the command of Maréchal Lautrec. The Cardinal effected a reconciliation between the rival commanders and, to the immense satisfaction of Leo, Milan fell to the Papal and Imperial forces in the following November.

But whether it was owing to the Cardinal's preoccupation with other matters or to the pressure of political events, or for some other reason of which we are ignorant, it is certain, on Michelangelo's own telling, that nothing came of the negotiations to purchase a site in the Borg' Ognissanti. Had he acquired what Tolnay is pleased to refer to as a 'third workshop' (though this is not strictly correct, as the house that was rented for him near San Lorenzo was not, in fact, a workshop) he would scarcely have had the models for the Tombs made amid the chaos and clamour which prevailed in the New Sacristy while the cupola was being plastered, as we know from the *Ricordi* that he did.

In this letter, as in others of the period, Michelangelo was at pains to emphasize his willingness to serve the Cardinal. Hitherto he had worked mainly in the service of the Pope, and it was, presumably, in order to correct a general impression that he 'had no mind to serve the Cardinal', and not from any sycophantic motive, as it might seem, that he reiterates his desire to devote himself to his service.

Appendix 18

Michelangelo's Salary and the House near San Lorenzo

WHEN the Cardinal de' Medici became Pope as Clement VII in November 1523 one of the first matters to which he turned his attention was that of making Michelangelo some adequate provision. This may be attributed partly to Clement's anxiety to establish an exclusive right to his services, partly to the affectionate regard in which he held him, and partly to a desire to compensate him for the shameful way in which he had been treated over the façade of San Lorenzo.

Shortly after Clement's election Michelangelo went on a short visit to Rome, presumably to pay his respects. Immediately on his return he received a letter dated December 30th from Giovan Francesco Fattucci, who was acting as an intermediary and was then in Rome, in which the subject of a stipend or benefice was introduced. This letter was followed by another dated January 2nd 1524, in which it was suggested that Michelangelo should renounce marriage and enter minor orders, to enable him to enjoy the income from a benefice. This offer (which he did not apparently receive very kindly) Michelangelo declined. A monthly salary was then proposed, and he was invited to suggest an amount. He did so, estimating the worth of his services at fifteen ducats at month, a sum which Fattucci, in his letter of January 13th, summarily rejected as ridiculous. After chiding Michelangelo for his want of spirit and saying that Piero Gondi's suggestion of twenty-five ducats a month was no nearer the mark, Fattucci went on to say that Jacopo Salviati, acting for the Pope, had given orders to Giovanni Spina, his agent in the Salviati bank in Florence, to pay him fifty ducats a month and the expenses for the work at San Lorenzo in addition. In concluding his letter, Fattucci asked Michelangelo to pretend to have heard the news from Spina and to write to Salviati to acknowledge this provision. In his letter in reply to Michelangelo's, Salviati, who always recognized his quality, wrote saying his thanks were superfluous, as his virtues merited much more than had so far been done for him. In a further letter, dated January 18th, Fattucci wrote saying that Salviati wished above all to content him, adding that he should take a house near San Lorenzo and get Spina to pay the rent together with the other expenses.

Michelangelo was, however, distracted with worry at this time, being under an obligation to the heirs of Julius II to complete the Tomb, on the one hand, and to Clement VII to complete the New Sacristy and the Medici monuments, on the other. He was therefore loath to seem to the heirs of Julius to be wholly committed to the service of Clement and in consequence, although he had accepted the salary in principle, he declined either to draw it or to take up residence in the house – the Casa di Macciagnini – that had been provided for him. This proceeding is made clear in a letter addressed to him on March 5th by Fattucci, who urged him strongly to take the house. Again, on March 24th, his friend Lionardo, the saddler, wrote from Rome saying that his obduracy in the matter both of the salary and of the house was a folly amounting almost to madness. It is clear, however, from another letter of Fattucci's, dated April 3rd, that Michelangelo was anxious to wait for the settlement of the Julius affair, which Fattucci was negotiating on his behalf in Rome, before availing himself of the facilities open to him. Hence, despite all persuasions, he remained adamant, not only because he was unwilling to commit himself at this stage, but also because, being too distracted to devote his attention wholeheartedly to the work at San Lorenzo, he did not feel himself entitled either to the salary or to the house.

This state of affairs continued until the end of August, when, for the reasons set out in his letter of the 29th to Giovanni Spina *(No. 166)*, he changed his mind and asked to be allowed to take possession of the house, and to be paid the arrears of his salary. After two months' negotiation with Rome, matters were finally arranged in October 1524, and on the 19th he received the accumulated salary for eight months, amounting to four hundred ducats, while on the 26th Spina wrote saying that he had received authority from Jacopo Salviati to rent the Casa di Macciagnini and had paid the rent for a year in advance.

Over this episode in Michelangelo's career there has been a certain amount of misunderstanding. From Gotti to Tolnay, his biographers have all assumed that he took possession of this house, abandoned it in a fit of depression over the Julius Tomb, and subsequently returned to it. Tolnay, moreover, has added to the confusion by supposing that the house in question was the one allowed him by the terms of the contract for the façade of San Lorenzo in January 1518 – the house which, as we know, he never managed to find.

Now the question of the house was first mooted in Fattucci's letter of January 18th and since, on an analogy, it took nearly two months to arrange matters in respect both of the salary and of the house, when Michelangelo finally decided to accept both in August 1524, it can hardly be supposed that the original arrangements for the same house were made much more quickly. So that, by the end of February, there would scarcely have been time for him to have moved in and then 'in an attack of pessimism' to have moved out. Nor do the terms of Fattucci's letter of March 5th suggest such an interpretation. On the contrary, they make it clear that Michelangelo, who had written to him about the matter on February 28th, had refused to take possession of the Casa Macciagnini, for which a tenancy had been arranged. After expressing his surprise about Michelangelo's decision, he assured him that he was entitled to the house and advised him to give it a trial.

Although there has been a good deal of loose thinking about this (Gotti, for instance, supposing that Michelangelo's change of mind on August 29th was determined by his friend Lionardo's letter of March 24th), part of the difficulty has understandably arisen over the interpretation of two words which occur in the correspondence. One is the verb *licenziare*, which has been assumed to mean 'give up the tenancy of a house already occupied', whereas in the context and under the circumstances occupancy cannot by any means be assumed. The other is the verb *tornare*, which in this connection has hitherto been translated by the verb 'to return'. It is noteworthy, however, that this verb is used by Michelangelo with reference to a *temporary* residence. Thus, in No. 3, where he speaks of Buonarroto 'lodging' at the inn, the verb used is *tornare*. Again in No. 124, where he speaks of Signorelli 'lodging' at a shoemaker's, the verb used is likewise *tornare*. So that when he asks to be allowed to '*tornare nella casa*' that had been taken for him, it does not follow that he had lived in the house before. Indeed, the phrase *tornare nella casa* strictly means, not to return, but to go to live in for the first time, *a casa* being different from *in casa*, as various lexicographers have pointed out. With his usual optimism, Michelangelo certainly underestimated the time the work at the New Sacristy would take, and having property of his own in Florence, as well as a house in Rome, he would not have regarded the Casa Macciagnini as being anything but a temporary residence.

Yet even if there were not discrepancies between the statements made by Michelangelo's biographers and the evidence afforded by the letters of his correspondents sufficient to discredit the view that, having taken up residence in the Casa Macciagnini, he suddenly left it in March 1524, there are still grounds for rebutting the charge that he acted in 'a capricious manner'. Scrupulous, proud and over-sensitive, and feeling, as he himself said that he had become an impostor against his will, he not unnaturally lived in an agony of suspense and indecision during the whole of the time pending the settlement of the Julius affair. And just as when working on the Sistine ceiling in 1509 he had written to his father saying 'it is now a year since I had a *grosso* from this Pope, and I do not ask for anything as my work does not seem to me to go ahead in a way to merit it', so, even when he had at last agreed to accept the eight months' arrears of his salary and had moved into the house near San Lorenzo, he still failed, in spite of Spina's persuasions, to draw anything during the following year, owing to the preoccupations which prevented him from working as he wished to, as he explained in the letter to Fattucci of October 24th *(No. 174)*. Judging by a letter addressed to him by Spina on November 1st of the same year and from subsequent references in his own letters, he was apparently prevailed upon to take what was owing and thereafter continued to do so regularly until the time of the threatened disasters, which culminated in the sack of Rome, when he wrote two characteristic letters, one to Fattucci and one to Spina *(Nos. 178 and 180)* in both of which he expressed his willingness to forgo his salary in view of the times, but to continue to work for the Pope, notwithstanding.

It is not certain at what date the payment of his salary was temporarily discontinued, but it may be presumed to have been in April/May 1527. In March 1528, three months after his flight to Orvieto, the Pope enquired of the Florentine envoy, Lionardo Niccolini, whether Michelangelo was working, and was told that he was weighed down with the expenses, whereupon Clement ordered five hundred ducats to be remitted forthwith, and provision to be made thereafter.

Such payments as may have been made between this date and October 1529, when Florence was invested, are not recorded. During the siege Michelangelo's salary was naturally discontinued, but in November 1530, following the capitulation in August, the Pope expressed pleasure in Michelangelo's willingness to continue the work at San Lorenzo, and sent strict orders to the sub-prior, Figiovanni, that 'above all Michelangelo is to be cajoled'. Clement was not anxious, however, to precipitate matters in regard to the salary, and was annoyed about the payment of a hundred ducats made in November, as he desired 'to coerce him into being more diligent in the matter of the building'. But following Cardinal Cibo's visit of inspection to San Lorenzo on behalf of the Pope in the middle of November, the payment of the monthly salary of fifty ducats was finally confirmed on December 11th 1530 *(Gaye, II, pp. 222 et seq.).*

(All the letters to Michelangelo quoted in this Appendix may be found in Frey, 'Sammlung ausgewählter Briefe an Michelangiolo Buonarroti', pp. 201–294 – always supposing that Frey, 'Sammlung ausgewählter Briefe', may be found.)

29. *Pope Clement VII*
(after the sack of Rome)

Sebastiano del Piombo
Museo Nazionale, Naples

The Historical Situation during the Pontificates of Adrian VI : 1522-1523 and Clement VII : 1523-1534

On January 9th 1522, the Flemish Pope, Adrian VI, ascended the Papal throne in succession to Leo X, who had died at the beginning of the previous December. Unlike his two immediate predecessors, the new Pope was set upon a policy of pacification and reform which was scarcely less unpopular than his determination to put an end to the corruption of the Court in the midst of which he found himself. As between the Pope and the Curia the disapproval was mutual. Rome, being accustomed to Popes who were off with the rochet and on with the hunting boots on the slightest pretext, was, not surprisingly, 'consumed with unutterable disgust'; and it is small wonder that, after a pontificate which lasted less than two years, his reign was brought to an abrupt end by means of poison on September 14th 1523.

Two months later, on November 19th, Cardinal Giulio de' Medici assumed the tiara and took the name of Clement VII. His election was received with universal acclamation, as may be seen from numerous contemporary references, including that by Michelangelo in his letter of November 25th 1523 *(No. 156)*. But the struggle between France and the Empire for possession of Milan and for domination in Italy was soon renewed, the Pope inclining first to one side and then to the other, as seemed the more politic or as best suited his ambitions, less perhaps as the Vicar of Christ than as sovereign of the Papal States and a Medici to boot.

At first he was favourable to France, being anxious to provide some measure of security against the excessive power of Charles V, but following the defeat of the French at the Battle of Pavia in February 1525, when Francis I was taken prisoner, he quickly changed sides, but to little purpose. As usual, alliance followed alliance in bewildering succession. But following the formation of the so-called Holy League against him, the Emperor Charles determined to punish Clement for his duplicity and in September 1526 incited the powerful Colonna family, who were Spanish in sympathy, to attack the Vatican. Clement was forced to take refuge in the Castel Sant' Angelo and even the sacristy of St. Peter's was pillaged. On regaining his liberty, Clement lost no time in revenging himself upon the Colonna, notwithstanding an undertaking not to do so, which had been one of the conditions of his release imposed by Charles. Well might Michelangelo in writing to Rome at this time refer apprehensively to 'the times in which we are living'.

In the meantime the Emperor was in process of mustering a formidable army of Spaniards under Lannoy and of 'Lutheran' landsknechts – the most terrible of all troops – under Freunsberg and Bourbon, the renegade Constable of France, with which to punish Clement and to attack the Papal States. By March 1527, this fierce and terrifying force, intent upon pillage, bloodshed and rape, and by this time almost beyond control, was encamped near Bologna, and Florence was seriously threatened. But by putting herself into a state of defence, the city averted the danger – or, as Cambi afterwards expressed it, 'the divine mercy, moved by the prayers of certain pious persons . . . sent that destroying host to sack and plunder Rome and all its clergy' instead. On the fateful morning of May 6th the Imperial army reached its objective and by the evening the Eternal City had fallen. The terrible sack of Rome ensued. Terror-stricken, the Pope fled with his entourage through the covered passage to the fortified Castel Sant' Angelo, where he remained a prisoner during the seven months in which Rome, occupied by the soldiery, witnessed scenes of such wickedness, profanation and horror that even at this distance of time they are scarcely to be contemplated. Indeed, such was the devastation that when, on the final withdrawal of the rabble, a return to Rome became possible, the Mantuan Ambassador, writing to Federigo Gonzaga, Marquis of Mantua, on October 12th 1528 *(Pastor, X, p. 489)* described himself as being completely stupefied amid the ruins and the desolation. The Pope, who from the Castel Sant' Angelo fled first to Orvieto in December and thence to Viterbo, did not himself return to Rome until October of the following year.

From Clement's point of view the defection of Florence and the expulsion of his representative, Silvio Passerini, Cardinal of Cortona, and of the Medici family in the persons of Ippolito and Alessandro de' Medici in May 1527, following the fall of Rome, could only be considered perfidious. This act of defiance and the re-establishment of the Florentine Republic is said to have been more intolerable to Clement than all his other misfortunes. It was not, however, an act of defiance that he was prepared to suffer, and later, after his reconciliation with the Emperor, they entered into an alliance by which it was agreed that the Republic should be crushed and Alessandro, the Pope's illegitimate son – or should one say nephew? – created hereditary Duke of Florence and given the Emperor's illegitimate daughter Margaret in marriage.

The siege of Florence ensued *(see Appendix 21)*. After ten months the city was finally forced to capitulate and on August 12th 1530 opened its gates to the besiegers. But, by the express orders of the Pope, Florence was spared the horrors of a sack. The first Duke, Alessandro, took up his residence in July 1531, though he was not formally declared Duke until April 1532, and the Signoria never entered into office again.

Except for threats of a General Council, the remainder of Clement's reign was relatively peaceful. He went twice to Bologna – for the coronation of Charles V in 1530 and again in 1532 for a conference with him – and once to Marseilles, where he met Francis I on the occasion of the marriage of his niece, Catherine de' Medici to the King's son, the Duke of Orleans, afterwards Henry II – a method of biting his thumb at the Emperor which, with his sense of humour, Clement may well have relished. He did not, however, long survive this triumph. After four months' illness he died in the following year on September 25th 1534. His pontificate of eleven years was regarded as so disastrous that on his death he was ignominiously described as *In*Clemens Pontifex Minimus – an epitaph which in many respects he did not deserve.

Appendix 20

Piero Buonaccorsi

I N certain folios from the official account books for the New Sacristy and the Library at San Lorenzo, which were discovered in the Strozzi Archives and later published by Georg Gronau in 1911, the name of Piero Buonaccorsi twice appears *(Gronau, pp. 77, 80)*. Both payments, for the same amount in each case, namely, 105 *lire* (which in terms of gold currency was equivalent to 15 ducats) were made in the spring of 1526. The same payments were presumably continued until November, when, in his letter of November 10th *(No. 179)*, Michelangelo informed Giovanni Spina that there was no longer any need to retain him, but as the sheets from the Strozzi archives terminate with the May accounts, this can only be surmised. From an economic point of view it is noteworthy that Buonaccorsi was in receipt, not only of a monthly salary, as opposed to a weekly wage, but also of one that was relatively high. In any event, it was thought to be worth saving at a time when Michelangelo had been asked to reduce expenditure.

In the first entry Buonaccorsi is described as *Provveditore alla fabrica*, a description which is difficult to interpret in the absence of any further particulars. It would appear, however, that he was a man of some account who had been commissioned for a special purpose and for a relatively short period, and who, though answerable not to Michelangelo but to Giovanni Spina, the Pope's agent in Florence, was in a position to make his own arrangements and might well complain if he were not given adequate notice, a contingency that Michelangelo was clearly anxious to avoid.

In view of all this, some speculation naturally arises as to whether the said Piero Buonaccorsi may be identified with Piero di Giovanni Buonaccorsi, who, having been taken to Rome in early life by his master, Fiorenza il Vaga, became better known there as Perino del Vaga (1501–1547).

According to Vasari, when he was first taken to Rome, Perino devoted himself to design, to the study of the antique and to learning the methods of stucco, to such purpose that, while still a youth, he was employed by Raphael, in association with Giovanni da Udine, 'a unique master of the craft', to do arabesques, figures and scenes for the Vatican loggias, which he executed with consummate lightness and grace. During a virulent outbreak of plague in Rome in 1523, Buonaccorsi had been persuaded by his friend Piloto, the goldsmith, to seek refuge in his native Florence, where he resided for some time with another friend of his, Ser Raffaello di Sandro del Zoppa, a chaplain at San Lorenzo, so that he became, in consequence, a familiar figure in what might be described as 'San Lorenzo circles', and therefore knew something of the work being executed at the New Sacristy. With the election of the Medici

Pope, Clement VII, at the end of the year, he returned to Rome where 'he did many things', being finally entrusted with the painting of a chapel belonging to the Company of the Crucifix at San Marcello. But the work proceeded unsatisfactorily, being interrupted by many misfortunes, the men of the Company leaving him, so it was said, short of money, and the matter dragged on until the sack of Rome. In these circumstances Buonaccorsi may therefore perhaps have sought to employ himself elsewhere during unremunerative intervals and may well have returned to Florence for a short period again returning to Rome at the end of 1526 to continue his work at San Marcello, since we know he was there in 1527, as he was taken captive during the sack and was forced to pay a ransom sufficient, according to Vasari, 'to unseat his reason'. There is therefore nothing by which the less, as they say in Latin, the Piero Buonaccorsi in question should not have been employed at San Lorenzo during the relevant period, but as to the task on which he, or some other man of the same name, was engaged at this time, this is largely a matter of speculation.

As we know from Michelangelo's letter to Giovanni Spina of June 1526, he was then ready for the painting of the vault of the New Sacristy, which, at the Pope's wish, was to be undertaken by Giovanni da Udine, who specialized in stucco relief and in the execution of 'animals, arabesques, festoons and friezes'. After some correspondence Maestro Giovanni undertook to come, without fail, in September, but in September, not having completed the work on which he was engaged at the Pope's *vigna*, he informed Michelangelo, through Fattucci, that he would not be able to come that winter, but would come, again without fail, in the new year *(Frey, Briefe, p. 288)*. It was not, however, until 1532 that he eventually arrived, the sack of Rome and the siege of Florence having rendered it impossible for him to do so during the intervening period.

If one may hazard a guess, Piero Buonaccorsi, or Perino del Vaga, as he should perhaps be called in this context, may have been concerned, on behalf of Giovanni da Udine, with whom he was closely associated, in the supervision of the plastering of the vault, for which payments are shown in the same sections of the accounts. The question of the lime to be used was still under discussion in July, the Pope being anxious that *calcina di trevertino* should, if possible be used *(ibid., p. 286)*, while in September when he finally announced that he could not leave Rome until the spring, Giovanni had a consultation with Fattucci about the problem of the lime, a matter, we may suppose, of some importance where the use of stucco ornament was involved *(ibid., p. 288)*.

It is possible, alternatively, that Perino had been engaged, on his own account, to furnish detailed designs and drawings for the festoons, urns, grotesques and so forth, the pseudo-classical motifs which decorate the attics of the Tombs, the recesses above the pediments and those below the tabernacles, which are certainly more consonant with 'the light and graceful style' for which he was famous, than with Michelangelo's more virile and robust handling of ornament. It is established, moreover, by Vasari that he thoroughly understood the requirements of relief ornament and of architectural settings as a whole, as is borne out by the decorations he later undertook in Genoa, where, for Prince Doria, he did designs and models for 'a Doric doorway in marble . . . . with pedestals, bosses, shafts, capitals, architraves, friezes and cornices . . . . a work that was carved by Maestro Giovanni da Fiesole' *(Vasari, V, p. 612).*

If Pietro Buonaccorsi, *Provveditore alla fabrica,* may in fact be identified with Perino del Vaga, then it is difficult to imagine any other capacity in which he could have been employed; but if he cannot be so identified, then it seems unlikely that he can be identified at all, and the work on which he was engaged at 15 ducats a month remains an insoluble problem.

Appendix 21

Michelangelo and the Siege of Florence

O N May 16th 1527, ten days after the sack of Rome and the virtual imprisonment of the Pope in his own Castel Sant' Angelo, the Florentines, taking advantage of his misfortunes, hastened to cast off the Medici yoke and to restore the ancient Republican constitution. From that moment the city inevitably became an object of the Pope's vengeance and following his reconciliation with the Emperor, he lost no time in compassing his designs. By the Peace of Barcelona, signed on June 29th 1529, it was agreed that the Imperial army, under Philibert, Prince of Orange, should lay siege to Florence and that when she had been reduced and the popular government overthrown, a Medici dukedom should be set up, under the Pope's illegitimate son Alessandro, to whom the Emperor promised the hand of his illegitimate daughter, Margaret, in marriage.

The besieging army appeared before the walls of Florence and encamped in the valley of the Arno on October 10th 1529.

From the time of the Pope's escape to Orvieto in December 1527 the Florentines had been under no misapprehension as to the peril in which the city stood; they immediately enrolled a militia and at once began to take measures to put the city into a state of defence.

In this extremity, despite the invidious position in which he stood, personally, *vis-à-vis* the Pope, Michelangelo was not slow to offer his services, devoting himself 'diligently, gratis and of his own free will' to the common cause. On January 10th 1529 he became a member of the Council of Nine for the Militia *(Nove della Milizia)* and by an instrument dated April 6th, prefaced by a preamble extolling his unsurpassed virtues and accomplishments, he was appointed 'Superintendent and Procurator General over the constructions and fortifications of the city walls, as well as over every defensive operation'. On his appointment, which was for one year, he received a salary of one gold florin a day *(Gotti, II, p. 62)*.

From the outset, the chief task to which he devoted his attention, in spite of some initial opposition from certain quarters, was the fortification of the hill of San Miniato, the most strategic position overlooking the city, south of the Arno. From a letter addressed to him on October 3rd 1528 on behalf of the Signoria, we know that by the time of his official appointment he had already been engaged in the enterprise of erecting bastions and other defensive works for some considerable time. So that when, at the end of July 1529, he departed with letters of the highest recommendation on a visit to Ferrara to inspect the fortifications, for which that city was famous, and to acquire information of which he was in need, the work at San Miniato was already advanced, but not entirely to his satisfaction. On the occasion of this visit to Ferrara, he was gladly received by the Duke, Alfonso d'Este, the most eminent authority of the age in such matters, who 'riding with him in person . . . shewed him everything, even more than was needful'.

Now it was while he was engaged on the bastions outside the gate of San Niccolò in the following September that the episode took place, which he relates in his letter to Battista della Palla *(No. 184)*, in which, while giving an account of his actual departure, he understandably says nothing as to the real cause which led up to it. This information is happily provided by two accounts, substantially the same, both of which are based on Michelangelo's own narrative at a later date. One is given by Condivi in his life of Michelangelo, and the other in one of Giovanbattista Busini's letters to the historian, Benedetto Varchi, who used it as the basis of his own account. There is also Vasari's version of what occurred.

Having become aware, both from what he had heard, and had himself observed, of suspected treachery on the part of Malatesta Baglioni, the *condottiere* who had been engaged as general of the Florentine forces, Michelangelo immediately 'betook himself to the Signoria and discovered to them what he had seen and heard, but instead of thanking him, they abused and reproached him with being a timid man and too suspicious'. Therefore 'when Michelangelo perceived how little his word was considered', as Condivi goes on to say, 'and how the ruin of the city was certain, by the authority he had, he caused one of the gates to be opened and went out with two of his people' *(Condivi, xlii)*.

The main discrepancy in the accounts in question is that concerning his companions. Condivi mentions 'two of his people', whom Vasari is correct in identifying with his friend Piloto, the goldsmith, and with Antonio Mini, his assistant; whereas Busini mentions Rinaldo Corsini who went with him and one other, 'that man of his who was always with him', that is, Antonio Mini. These slight differences are not, however, difficult to reconcile, since Michelangelo and 'two of his people' may well take no account of Rinaldo Corsini, who accompanied them part of the way. Again 'and one other' may, equally, take no account of Piloto, who was not in Michelangelo's service. But in either case, in recalling an incident at a distance of time, small omissions of this kind are unimportant. But that Michelangelo left Florence for Venice accompanied by Corsini, Piloto and Mini is proved by a list of expenses incurred on this journey, written in Michelangelo's own hand *(Milanesi, p. 601)*, in which all three are mentioned.

There is, however, one feature in this connection which has involved historians in endless speculation and debate. The list of expenses is jotted down on a sheet of paper headed by the opening lines of a discarded letter dated 'this tenth day of September in Venice', whereas on Michelangelo's own telling he did not leave Florence till September 21st; whence it has been argued that he went twice to Venice. In the absence of any other evidence of such a visit, the mission has conveniently been supposed to have been a 'secret' one. He cannot, however, have been in Venice on September 10th, since, from another entry in the *Ricordi (Milanesi, p. 602)* it is known that he was paying wages in Florence on September 14th. It is nevertheless categorically stated by Heath Wilson, following Gotti, that he went twice to Venice, on the first occasion with the companions mentioned, and the second time alone – a possibility so remote as to be discounted. Furthermore, the fact that the names of both Michelangelo and Corsini appear in the list of those who had been placed under a ban for leaving Florence without permission makes it highly improbable that Corsini would also have been with Michelangelo on the presumed first visit.

How then is this difficulty to be resolved? Symonds has without doubt provided the most plausible, and indeed the only feasible, explanation. Thus in his *Life of Michelangelo (I, p. 424)* he writes as follows: 'I have examined the original document in the Archivio Buonarroti. The date is certainly correctly given by Gotti. The unfinished letter runs thus, *Ho^{do} mio maggiore – in Venegia oggi questo di dieci secte* . . . The date may possibly have contained the error of *September* when Michelangelo wished to write *October* and for this reason the word *secte* may not have been finished. That the letter was begun and flung aside for some reason seems certain. Perhaps he preferred to rewrite the proper date *October 10th.*' With regard to this last observation of Symonds', it is noteworthy that if he made a slip Michelangelo generally preferred to correct it by saying *ovvero*, 'or rather', instead of crossing out. In a formal letter of the kind in question he could hardly have done either. It is amusing to reflect on the astonishment that would have been his had he been informed at the time that whether he listed the expenses on the partially used sheet or on a fresh piece of paper would prove to be a matter of moment and would later involve historians in considerable difficulty.

As has already been stated, Michelangelo, together with twelve others, was declared an outlaw on September 30th. All were threatened with severe penalties if they did not return within a week, but although Michelangelo, unlike Corsini, was not among those who turned back, his property was not confiscated like that of some of the others, though by October 19th his old friend Granacci had taken what steps he could to conserve it *(Milanesi, p. 602).*

In the meantime Florence was agog with speculation as to the motives for Michelangelo's flight and his friends, intent only upon inducing him to return, were in a ferment of agitation. On October 24th Battista della Palla, who had already written, wrote again, enclosing no less than ten letters from other friends in Florence *(Gotti, I, p. 195).* Before October 13th, however, Michelangelo had already made up his mind to return, precisely for what reason is not known. In any case, he wrote (perhaps on *October* 10th) to Galeotto Giugni, the Florentine envoy in Ferrara, requesting him to make his submission to the Signoria and asking for a safe-conduct. This was granted on October 20th *(Gaye, II, pp. 209, 210).* When the *scarpellino*, Sebastiano di Francesco Balena, who had been despatched with the safe-conduct and the letters, reached Venice is not known. In any case, it was not until November 9th that Michelangelo reached Ferrara, when it was stated by the Florentine envoy that his journey would be delayed, as he was travelling in company with Antonfrancesco degli Albizzi, his wife and two children who were ill, and could not abandon them *(Gaye, II, p. 212).* Battista della Palla went to meet him at Pisa or Lucca (both on the only route still open to Florence, which had already been invested by the besieging army), but as Michelangelo had not arrived by the 19th, he was obliged to return to Florence. Michelangelo must, however, have arrived immediately after this, as on November 23rd the sentence of outlawry was commuted and the penalty of exclusion from the Great Council for a period of three years (though with the right of an annual appeal) imposed instead, for there is no doubt that the Signoria was far more anxious to have him back and to retain his services than to punish him.

Upon his return, at which, according to Varchi, there was general rejoicing, except in certain envious quarters, he threw himself into the task of repairing and improving the already damaged defences at San Miniato. Indeed, as Gotti writes, 'his fearless conduct during the siege warrants us in not attaching too much blame to his unauthorized and precipitate flight'.

There is, however, more to be said in extenuation of the course he took. In the first place he was, as previously stated, in a singularly invidious position. Until the beginning of the siege he had been in the service of the Pope, and had previously served other members of the Medici family. Then, in spite of the confidence apparently reposed in him by the newly restored Republic, and when he had, for all he knew, jeopardized all chances of further Papal employment (even supposing that, in the event of the city's capitulation, he survived Clement's wrath), he did not receive the support and co-operation of the Council essential to the success of his enterprises. Thus Giovanbattista Busini, in a letter to Benedetto Varchi dated January 1549, wrote as follows: 'Whatever the reason may have been, Niccolò Capponi while he was Gonfalonier did not wish the hill of San Miniato to be fortified and Michelangelo, who is a man of absolute veracity, tells me that he had great trouble in convincing the other leaders, but that he could never convince Niccolò. However he began the work. . . . But Niccolò made him abandon it . . . and when he was elected to the Nine they despatched him twice and thrice outside the city. Each time, on his return, he found the hill dismantled, whereupon he complained, feeling this a blot upon his reputation and an insult to his magistracy' *(Gotti, I, p. 186)*. When, therefore, to insults, which he could not brook, threats of assassination were added, of which he was warned by his informant at the San Niccolò gate, who shall blame him for a flight even more precipitate than that from Rome, under somewhat comparable circumstances, twenty-three years earlier? The reasons for his going (of which fear of facing the horrors of a siege was not one) are therefore obvious, just as it is evident that, on reflection, he was in doubt as to the wisdom of the course he had been prompted to take. As to the motives of his informant two possibilities exist. Either Baglioni, who is said to have been kept informed of everything that was going on in the city, became aware of Michelangelo's communications to the Council, and was bent upon his destruction; in which case the man who came was a well-wisher; or else, perhaps not daring to compass such a deed, Baglioni was determined, nevertheless, to be rid of him; in which case the man sent was a decoy. The latter would appear, on the whole, to be the more probable conjecture.

At the beginning of August 1530 Florence capitulated, having been betrayed into the hands of the enemy by the arch-traitor, Malatesta Baglioni, as Michelangelo had anticipated. In view of the prominent part he had taken in the heroic defence of the city under the Republic, Michelangelo, who had moreover returned to Florence, after having left it, stood in real danger from Clement's wrath. The Pope's first intention to have him seized was foiled, however, as, on the entry of the enemy, he had gone into hiding and could not be found; nor did he emerge until Clement's fury had abated and it had been made known that the Pope would allow him to remain at liberty, if he would undertake to continue the work on the Medici Tombs. Orders were given, moreover, that when found he was to be treated with courtesy.

Thus, after an assault lasting ten months the siege of Florence was brought to an end. With the fall of the city her civil liberties were lost to her for ever and as a Republic she ceased to exist – a calamity which Michelangelo continued to lament for years to come. But if it was a defeat for the city, it was little more than a Pyrrhic victory for Clement. The siege had cost him some seven hundred thousand ducats and he never set foot in Florence again.

Appendix 22

The Death of Lodovico Buonarroti

THE death of Lodovico Buonarroti, Michelangelo's father, which is unfortunately not re-corded in the *Libri de' Morti*, is generally supposed to have taken place either at the end of 1533 or in June 1534. This conjecture is founded on the declaration of Michelangelo's pro-perty, the *Denunzia de' Beni*, returned in 1534 *(see Appendix 6)* in which his father's property at Settignano is seen to have passed into his possession. There is, however, an entry for the year 1532, under the later addenda to the Buonarroti *Denunzia* for 1498, which should give us pause. It is the last entry, and the only one in which Michelangelo is mentioned. It reads as follows: 'In *[respect of]* Michelangelo di Lodovico, Ward of the Waggon *[gonfalone di carro,* i.e. the ward of which Santa Croce was the principal church] by *[transfer from]* the *Monte* number 341, florins 18. 1. 3' *(Frey, Denunzia)*. From the amount of the assessment, which varied like all assessments from year to year, the eighteen florins, as against twenty-two for 1534, was evidently the tax paid by Michelangelo in respect of the farm at Settignano, from which it would appear that he had already inherited the property.

But before drawing any hasty conclusions from this addendum, we should perhaps ex-amine the statements made about Lodovico's death by some of Michelangelo's biographers. The event is not mentioned by either Vasari or Condivi, but Gotti makes this statement: 'At the end of 1533 or the beginning of 1534 Lodovico Buonarroti, having returned from Pisa to his villa at Settignano, died at the age of about ninety years' *(Gotti, I, p. 228)*. This reference to the return from Pisa, where, with his grandson, Lionardo, he had been sent for safety when the city was invested, is based on a document in the Buonarroti Archives. But what precisely it has to do with the matter, if Lodovico died as late as 1533/4 is not made clear, since shortly after the termination of the siege in August 1530 the old man was already agitating about his return home. Passing over this difficulty as though it did not exist, Gotti continues with suit-able reflections on Michelangelo's filial piety and on the nobility of Lodovico's character – he being dead. Heath Wilson omits the reference to Pisa, but otherwise follows much the same line. Symonds, on the other hand, is more critical, but accepts 1534, perhaps June, as the probable date, on the ground that in the *Capitolo*, which Michelangelo wrote on his father's death, he speaks of him as being ninety years of age. Tolnay, while referring to Professor Wilde's contention that Lodovico died, not in 1534, but in 1531, nevertheless accepts the former as being approximately correct, though without giving his reasons for doing so.

Now from an entry in a *Libro delle Età* in the Florentine Archives, it has been established that Lodovico was born on June 11th 1444, so that in June 1534 he would have been exactly ninety years of age. But when, on the one hand, the age of a very old man is involved (always a somewhat apocryphal affair) and where, on the other, poetic licence is permissible, there is no reason to suppose that Michelangelo, in speaking of Lodovico's 'ninety years', was in any way concerned with precise statements of fact, even supposing that he were certain of the year of his father's birth. Of this he might well have been ignorant, seeing that in the Buonarroti *Denunzia de' Beni* of both 1470 and 1480, Lodovico is incorrectly given as being two years younger than he actually was, by which reckoning he would not have been ninety until 1536. Michelangelo's poetic reference to the age of his father could not, in any case, be accepted as providing incontrovertible proof that he died at the age of ninety, since in the lines –

> *Novanta volte el sol suo chiara face*
> *Prim' ha nell' ociean bagniata e molle,*
> *Che tu sie giunto alla divina pace. . . .*
> *(Guasti, p. 300)*

it would have been prosaic, to say the least of it, to have attempted, however cunningly, to work in *ottanta sette* or *ottanta cinque*. Yet, even so, there would be less occasion to question its truth, if the only other data available for the determination of the year of Lodovico's death were not at variance with the supposition that he died in 1534.

The only document which bears any relation to the event is a copy of a *ricordo*, made by a later hand, giving the expenses which Michelangelo incurred on his father's behalf. It is the document, already mentioned, which was published by Gotti *(II, p. 81)* and reads as follows:

Ten ducats I sent to my father in Pisa, by Giovanni Quaratesi.
Ten ducats I sent by Bernardino Basso the day he returned from Pisa.
About twelve ducats I sent him at the villa on several occasions, by Bernardo Basso or by Bastiano Balena.
Four ducats for chickens, capons and sweetmeats *[probably funeral provisions]*.
Twenty-five ducats for bringing down his body *[i.e. from Settignano to Florence]* for the obsequies and the interment *[at Santa Croce]*.
Three ducats to Bernardo, mason, and twelve to Cremona as a present.
Six ducats to Cremona for Pazzolatica.
Fourteen ducats to the farmer at Pazzolatica for an ox.
Five ducats and a half to Mona Margarita *[Lodovico's servant]* on my father's account.
One ducat for canes *[and]* tips.
Eight *lire [to]* Antonio Mini for the cloak.
Twenty-four *[to]* Antonio *[for his]* salary.
Twenty ducats in a place where he *[Lodovico?]* was no longer obliged to live. *[Perhaps for the lodgings at Pisa.]*
Four *lire* for the making of a jerkin for Nardo.

What, then, is the significance of these entries, and to what year do they belong? The earliest date possible for the first entry is 1530/31, while Lodovico was still in Pisa, immediately following the siege, and the latest date possible for the last entry but two is November 1531, when Antonio Mini left Michelangelo's service and departed to France. This being so, the only interpretation that can be put upon the document is that Lodovico died at Settignano not later than September or October 1531. At the time of his father's death Giovansimone was ill and in the autumn of 1531 Gismondo too appears to have been indisposed, judging from his letter to Michelangelo of October 15th, while Michelangelo himself, though not actually ill, is known from the letter of Giovanbattista Mini, Antonio's uncle, to Baccio Valori, the Pope's representative in Florence *(Gaye, II, p. 228)*, to have been very run down at this time. It may therefore be presumed that they were all suffering in varying degrees from the privations and from the aftermath of the siege, which makes it all the less probable that a man of Lodovico's temperament and advanced age should have survived. There is one further point which must not be overlooked. In the letters of 1532/33 to Giovansimone (in which there is no mention of Lodovico) his father's servant, Mona Margareta, appears to have been in Michelangelo's own service, which would not have been the case had his father been still alive.

All things considered, it may therefore be accepted as being beyond all reasonable doubt that Lodovico Buonarroti died in 1531, and most probably in the spring or early summer of that year.

Appendix 23

Tommaso de' Cavalieri

Tommaso de' Cavalieri, the young nobleman whom Michelangelo met in the late autumn or early winter of 1532, during his first prolonged visit to Rome after the siege of Florence, was a man of singular charm and great personal distinction. In legal documents of the period he is described as *Patritius Romanus di regione Sancti Eustachii*, but his un-Roman baptismal name, Tommaso, he probably owed to the Florentine banker, Tommaso Baccelli, who is believed to have been his maternal grandfather, and from whom he is thought to have inherited the property in Florence which formed part of his estate. He was known to everybody in his circle as 'Messer Tommao'.

Considering the nobility of his descent and the part he played in the public life of sixteenth century Rome, the want of documentation respecting his personal history seems curious, since the names of his parents, the date of his birth, the date of his marriage, the name of his wife and the date of her death appear to be unknown. It is therefore only by a process of deduction that we can hope with some plausibility to supply at least a few of the missing facts.

As regards the approximate date of Cavalieri's birth, it may be assumed with some degree of confidence that he was virtually the same age as his life-long friend and colleague, Prospero Boccapaduli, of whom it is recorded that he married his first wife as 'a *very* young man' in 1525. Assuming that at the time Boccapaduli was sixteen or seventeen years of age, we may assign the date of his birth to the end of the first decade of the sixteenth century – a conjecture which is supported by the fact that he did not enter public life until 1530. If Messer Tommao was indeed born at about the same time as his friend, he would have been about twenty-three when he met Michelangelo in 1532. He can scarcely have been more, since in his reply to Michelangelo's first letter, written at the end of the December of that year, he describes himself as *appena nato* – a 'mere babe and as ignorant as can be', as he may well have felt himself to be in comparison with Michelangelo.

During the sack of Rome both Boccapaduli and Cavalieri, together with members of their families, took refuge in the palace of Cardinal Andrea della Valle, into whose family Cavalieri evidently married, as his executor, Valerio della Valle, is described as his brother-in-law. Only a very tentative guess can be made, however, as to the date of the marriage, which may possibly have taken place at about the same time as Boccapaduli's second marriage, which was solemnized in 1538. All that can be said with certainty is that Cavalieri's elder son, Mario, who predeceased him, married Vittoria Vellia in 1562, and may therefore be presumed to have been born about 1540. The second son, Emilio, was not born until 1550, but whether there were any other children of the marriage is problematical. At all events, only his son Emilio, his daughter-in-law Vittoria, and her children by Mario are mentioned in Cavalieri's will, which was drawn on February 27th 1580. There are several codicils to this will, the last being dated June 30th 1587, the day of his death, which took place two years after that of his friend Boccapaduli. They were both buried, each in his family chapel, in Santa Maria in Aracoeli, a church near Cavalieri's house on the Capitoline hill *(Steinmann-Pogatscher, Rep. xxix, pp. 496 et seq.).*

In his will Cavalieri expressed the wish to be buried by night, without ceremony, dressed in the black habit of a member of the Confraternity of the Crucifix of San Marcello. In this connection it is interesting to observe that during the last two decades of the sixteenth century the Oratory of San Marcello, where the Confraternity held their services, was an important centre of musical activity. This is the more significant in view of the fact that Emilio Cavalieri (1550–1603) was himself a musician and a composer of eminence. He became a leading member of the Florentine *Camerata* and a prominent musical figure at the ducal court of Ferdinand I, though it was in Rome, at the Oratory of Santa Maria in Vallicella that Agostino Manni's drama, *Rappresentazione di anima e di corpo*, which was set to music by Emilio Cavalieri, was first performed in 1600. It is, moreover, largely to him that we owe the development of monody and of the *stilo recitativo*.

An interest in music may therefore well have been yet another bond between Michelangelo and Tommaso Cavalieri, both of whom, by their wide cultural interests and essential humanity, were pre-eminently men of the Renaissance. Though less active in public life than the versatile Boccapaduli, Cavalieri held several public offices and, as one of the *Conservatori*, was responsible, in association with Boccapaduli, for the direction of the architectural and decorative work at the Capitol, which was carried out in accordance with Michelangelo's designs, but was not completed until some years after his death *(Pecchiai, pp. 346 et seq.).* Cavalieri, who was himself versed in the arts and a considerable connoisseur, possessed a collection of antique sculpture typical of his period, as well as a number of valuable drawings, including that of himself in classical attire with a medal in his hand – one of the rare portraits executed by Michelangelo. All the drawings in Cavalieri's possession were later acquired by Cardinal Alessandro Farnese some of which eventually passed into the Royal collection at Windsor Castle.

From the early days of their friendship until the day of Michelangelo's death, his Messer Tommao remained entirely devoted to him. According to a letter from Bartolomeo Angiolini in Rome to Michelangelo in Florence, written on September 6th 1533, Cavalieri had expressed to Angiolini his gratitude for having formed so great a friendship with a man as supremely gifted as Michelangelo. Again, when, as an old man, Michelangelo had taken umbrage at some imagined offence, Cavalieri wrote protesting his innocence, averring that Michelangelo knew he had never had a better friend than himself, and saying, 'I promise you, if you don't want me for a friend, you can say so, but you will never prevent me from being a friend of yours or from seeking to serve you.' And when Michelangelo was dying, his friend, Diomede Leoni writing to his nephew, Lionardo Buonarroti, to inform him of his uncle's illness, added, 'You may feel at ease when you remember that Messer Tommaso de' Cavalieri, Messer Daniele *[da Volterra]* and I are here to render every possible assistance.'

Appendix 24

The Recipient of Letter No. 195—A Possible Identification

THE Niccolò to whom Michelangelo addressed this undated letter *(No. 195)* was presumed by Milanesi to be Niccolò Quaratesi, but on what grounds he does not say. He likewise assigns the letter tentatively to the year 1518, but again without giving his reasons. In the absence of any information to support these conjectures, they may as well be abandoned, since Quaratesi would seem a most improbable recipient and 1518 a most unlikely date.

As no Niccolò Quaratesi has ever been mentioned in connection with Michelangelo and nowhere else appears, the presumption would seem in the highest degree arbitrary, while in 1518 Michelangelo, being constantly on the road between Florence and the quarries at Pietra Santa and Seravezza, would have had no difficulty in making this an excuse for refusing the request asked of him.

A much more probable identification of the Niccolò in question is Niccolò di Raffaello de' Pericoli (1500–1550) who, because he was continually in trouble as a child, became known as il Tribolo. As a youth he was apprenticed to Jacopo Sansovino and afterwards worked on the façade of S. Petronio at Bologna and later on the Chapel of the Madonna – *la Santa Casa* – at Loreto, first in 1526 and again from 1530 to 1533, when with other sculptors employed there by Clement VII, he was sent to Florence some time after July 1533 to help Michelangelo with the completion of the work on the Medici Tombs and the Laurentian Library *(Milanesi, Corr., pp. 104, 108)*. In speaking of this commission in his life of Tribolo Vasari writes as follows: 'Michelangelo wanted Tribolo to do two nude statues to go on either side of his own Duke Giuliano, one representing *Earth* . . . and the other *Heaven*. . . . But when Tribolo was about to begin the *Earth* he fell sick of the ague, through change of air, his delicate constitution, or some excesses, and he remained prostrate for many months, tormented by the grief of having lost the work, while the frate *[Montorsoli]* and Raffaello *[da Montelupo]* were engaged upon it. But in order not to be distanced by his rivals . . . sick as he was he made a large clay model of the *Earth* and then began it in marble. But the death of Clement, when least expected, removed the animating spirit. . . . This quite discouraged Tribolo, who was still sick'.

As Niccolò is not one of the more common names, it seems reasonable to associate the Niccolò in question with someone of that name with whom Michelangelo is known to have been in contact and someone, moreover, to whom he stood in a professional relationship. Assuming, therefore, for argument's sake, that the identification with Tribolo is correct, then the meeting at the Canto de' Bischeri almost certainly took place shortly after the arrival of the sculptors from Loreto, in which case the father of the boy, whose charms were not to be resisted, may well have been someone whom Tribolo had met on the road to Florence, since the terms of Michelangelo's letter suggest that the man was an acquaintance rather than a friend of Tribolo's. The letter must, accordingly, have been written either in August or in September 1533, before Tribolo was taken ill, and in any event before the end of October when Michelangelo returned to Rome. It is unlikely that the encounter took place after his return (possibly in June of the following year, the precise date being unknown), since Tribolo was ill for many months and was still ill when the Pope died on September 25th 1534.

There is a further consideration relevant to the problem as to the date of the letter, and that is Michelangelo's unspecified reason for refusing to take the lad into his service. If, however, we are right in assigning it to August/September 1533, then the real reason may be discovered in the fragmentary draft of a letter to his intimate friend Bartolomeo Angiolini, written on July 28th 1533 *(Draft No. 6)*, in which he stresses the state of uncertainty in which he found himself at this time, knowing, as he says, neither what the Pope wanted him to do nor where he wished him to be. Under these circumstances, is it not obvious that he would be both unwilling and indeed unable to commit himself to the engagement of any apprentice, much less a foreigner?

But while the foregoing arguments may be thought to be plausible and even perhaps convincing, it must be emphasized that both the identity of the recipient and the date of the letter in question still remain, and seem likely to remain, unconfirmed.

Appendix 25

Michelangelo's Final Departure from Florence

THE date of Michelangelo's final departure from Florence has long been a matter of dispute. It is known from one of his letters written in 1557 (No. 434) that he left for Rome some time in September 1534 and arrived there two days before the death of Clement VII on September 25th. It has generally been assumed, however, that he returned to Florence shortly afterwards, prior to leaving finally in December of the same year.

This assumption is based on his correspondence with a young friend of his, Febo di Poggio, to whom he wrote a farewell letter on the eve of his departure, saying that he would never return (No. 198). To this letter Febo's of January 14th 1535 has always been accepted as a reply. On closer examination, however, it becomes clear that Febo's letter (Symonds, II, p. 403) is not an answer to the letter Michelangelo wrote on leaving Florence for good, but to a subsequent letter, written in Rome, in which some reference to the subject of the previous letter appears to have been made. In his letter Febo begins by saying that Michelangelo's communication had been given to him by a friend of his at the bank, which indicates from the outset that it came from a distance (i.e. from Rome), since a letter written in Florence to a recipient in Florence would not have been sent through a bank. He then said that he was glad to hear that Michelangelo was well, and continued with various comments which have no meaning in relation to Michelangelo's extant draft (No. 198). The conclusion to be drawn from the two surviving letters of the correspondence is therefore as follows:

The day before his departure Michelangelo wrote to Febo, saying he was leaving; Febo received it and called the next day, but found that Michelangelo had already left. Finding him gone, and being, as would appear from his existing letter, a selfish and self-seeking young man wholly unworthy of Michelangelo's fatherly interest and affection, he did nothing further about it until he received a second letter, to which he replied on his return from a visit to his father in Pisa. In this reply Febo, having commented on Michelangelo's second letter, excused himself for not having called in time and protested that he was not offended with Michelangelo, who had always treated him like a son, and then proceeded to take advantage of Michelangelo's generosity by pressing him for money, more it would seem from greed than of necessity.

Thus, whereas the date of Febo's letter – January 1535 – has hitherto been held to show that Michelangelo left Florence in December rather than in September 1534 – since it is unlikely that four months could have elapsed between Michelangelo's farewell letter and Febo's reply – it is as much by reason of its date as of its contents that it affords evidence precisely to the contrary.

But Febo di Poggio apart, it is obvious, on Condivi's evidence, that once Pope Clement was dead, Michelangelo would not have dared to set foot in Florence again, owing to the hostile attitude adopted towards him by Alessandro de' Medici, 'a young man, as everyone knows, very fierce and vindictive', who had been created hereditary Duke of Florence in May 1532. For, as Condivi goes on to say, 'There is no doubt that had it not been for fear of the Pope, he [*Michelangelo*] would have been put away long ago; the more so as this Duke of Florence when erecting those fortresses of his, sent for Michelangelo by Signor Alessandro Vitelli, to ride out with him and indicate where they could most usefully be placed, and he would not, replying that he had no such commission from Pope Clement. The Duke was much angered, so that for this reason, as well as for the old ill-will he bore him, and on account of the nature of the Duke, Michelangelo had good reason to fear him, so that it was truly a blessing of God that Michelangelo was not in Florence at the time of the death of Clement.' Thus, far from returning to Florence after the death of the Pope, Michelangelo may rather be supposed, if anything, to have hastened his departure, once the death of Clement, who had been seriously ill for four months and had received Extreme Unction on August 24th, appeared to be imminent. Similarly, it seems more reasonable, in this connection, to suppose that Cardinal Cesis, whom Michelangelo accompanied to Rome, was likewise on his way thither in September, in anticipation of the Pope's death and of the coming conclave, at which he is known to have been present, than to suppose that he left for Pescia after the election of the new Pope, Paul III, on October 13th, and returned to Rome shortly afterwards.

It is known from Michelangelo's draft letter to Bartolomeo Angiolini of July 1533 (*Draft No. 6*), and from letters to him from Sebastiano del Piombo during the same period, that his movements at this time were very uncertain. A great effort was being made to hasten the work at San Lorenzo, the Pope, with this end in view, having ordered a number of the sculptors working for him at Loreto to proceed to Florence to assist Michelangelo in his task. It is likewise established from the correspondence of Roderigo Nino, the Imperial Ambassador in Venice (*Pastor, X, p. 363*), that by February 1534 the Pope had prevailed upon Michelangelo to undertake the painting of the altar wall of the Sistine Chapel. When, therefore, Michelangelo returned to Florence in the spring or early summer of the same year, it was presumably with a view to clearing up his affairs in Florence before beginning work on the new project in Rome where, for personal reasons, he desired to reside permanently. Various motives may have actuated Clement in deciding to recall Michelangelo to Rome, in Condivi's words 'before he had quite finished the Tombs at San Lorenzo'. He may have wished to spare Michelangelo the apprehension he undoubtedly felt in Florence owing to the enmity of Duke Alessandro; he may have realized that under the circumstances Michelangelo was unlikely to contribute very much more to the work on the Library and the New Sacristy; he may have desired to employ him in Rome, partly in order to complete the Sistine, and partly for the pleasure of having him near him, for, as Condivi has emphasized, 'Clement respected this man like one sacred and talked with him familiarly, on subjects both grave and gay, as he would have done with his equals'.

Thus, even without Michelangelo's confirmation of the fact that he did not return to

Florence after Clement's death *(No. 434),* every presumption would be against it. It is therefore virtually certain that it was in September 1534, perhaps about the 14th, allowing for the diversion to Pescia and Pisa, that Michelangelo left Florence for the last time and took his departure for Rome which he reached on September 23rd, two days before the death of the Pope.

Index of Correspondents

Index

The Index relates to the Introduction, the Letters and the Appendixes only. The folios shown in Roman numerals refer to the Introduction; the folios shown in Arabic numerals refer to the text and footnotes of the Letters, and, where preceded by an asterisk, to the Appendixes.

Errata

p. 255	*For* 'Girolamo Staccioli, protonotary of', *read* 'Girolamo Staccoli, notary to'
p. 256	*For* 'Girolamo Staccioli', *read* 'Girolamo Staccoli'
p. 257	*For* 'Girolamo Staccioli', *read* 'Girolamo Staccoli'